RAY TRACING CREATIONS

Generate Photorealistic Images on the PC

Drew Wells and Chris Young

WAITE GROUP PRESS™
Corte Madera, CA

Staff

Publisher: Mitchell Waite
Editorial Director: Scott Calamar
Managing Editor: Joel Fugazzotto
Content Editor: Harry Henderson
Technical Editor: Alexander Enzmann
Production Director: Julianne Ososke
Cover Design: Michael Rogondino
Illustrations: Pamela Drury Wattenmaker
Production and Design: Side By Side Studios

Library of Congress Cataloging-in-Publication Data
Wells, Drew.
    Ray tracing creations generate 3D photo-realistic images on the PC/Drew Wells, Chris Young.
       p. cm.
    Includes index.
    ISBN 1-878739-27-1: $39.95
    1. Computer graphics. 2. POV-Ray. I. Young, Chris, 1955-
II. Title.
T385. W465 1993
006.6'869—dc20

93-18355
CIP

*With love to my mother, Magaret Wells,
who believes in me even when she's not so sure about me.*

Drew Wells

For my friend Pamela who convinced me I could write.

Chris Young

Acknowledgments

It would take a good size ballroom to hold a celebration for all that contributed in some way to making this book and the program, POV-Ray, a reality. No ballroom was available at press time, though, so a short list will have to suffice. To all those who deserve thanks but wouldn't fit on this short list, a 3D virtual glass of bubbly is raised in your honor.

First off, the biggest thanks go to the other Persistence of Vision team members, David Buck, Aaron Collins, Alexander Enzmann, Dan Farmer, and my co-author, Chris Young. These five people are incredibly dedicated and talented. I feel privileged to be able to work with them. They have put uncountable hours into creating, supporting, debugging, and enhancing the POV-Ray program. These hours were in addition to their jobs, family, and normal lives. Somehow they've managed to maintain a sense of humor and a little bit of sanity. Big thanks to each of them.

Readers of Fractal Creations and Image Lab have already heard of Larry Wood and the CompuServe Graphics Forums. Larry is a big supporter of group projects like POV-Ray and Fractint. I can't show enough appreciation to Larry for providing a home and headquarters for POV-Ray development and support. Thanks also to Matt Drury, David Shaver, and the other graphics forum staff members who keep things running so smoothly. The GRAPHDEV forum on CompuServe is the place to be for computer graphics fanatics.

Sincere thanks to Tim Wegner, best-selling author and skillful programmer, for providing a great example and helping me into this project.

The Intel Code Builder compiler was chosen to compile POV-Ray after testing many different compilers. Thanks to Bob Montgomery for great technical support and Intel Software for a great product.

An application like POV-Ray wouldn't seem nearly as exciting without the stunning artwork produced by Truman Brown and Mike Miller. Their radically different styles show off the best of POV-Ray's capabilities. We're all indebted to them for making POV-Ray shine and making our jaws drop at their talent.

The cast and crew at the Waite Group Press are a remarkable ensemble who create the finest computer books in the industry. Thanks to Scott Calamar and Joel Fugazzotto for their good humor and capable direction. I'm grateful to the magic of Julianne Ososke for making this book so visually appealing. Thunderous applause to Harry Henderson for the great content editing. And especially, finally, I can't thank Mitch Waite enough for his vision and support of this book.

Biographies

DREW WELLS

The POV-Ray project grew out Drew's dissatisfaction with the graphic tools available at the time. Encouraged by other members of CompuServe like Mike Schoenborn, Tom Price, and Bill Pulver, Drew started a group effort to create a new ray tracer. David Buck heard of this effort and proposed that his fine ray tracer DKBTrace be used as the foundation of this effort. Drew gladly accepted and launched the group effort to create the new package. He works on all facets of the POV-Ray package and is looking forward to creating even better new versions.

Drew primarily works as a computer consultant and software developer. He currently works as a software developer at a Southern California theme park and occasionally does outside projects.

CHRIS YOUNG

Chris Young has a B.S. in Computer Sciences from Indiana University - Purdue University at Indianapolis (I.U.P.U.I.). He has held several sysop positions on CompuServe since 1985 and has been part of the "Go Graphics" Forums staff since 1990. He joined the POV-Ray team soon after it formed and specializes in improvements and additions to the POV-Ray Scene Description Language.

Chris was born with a congenital neuromuscular disease similar to muscular dystrophy. He is confined to a motorized wheelchair and has never walked. Having limited use of his right hand, he types by poking the keys with a stick.

Presently Chris lives in Indianapolis, Indiana near the Speedway, where he operates his one-man software consulting firm, Cyborg Software Systems, Inc. He does programming, consulting, and free-lance technical and feature writing. He is also active in the local Catholic Church and many of his consulting clients are churches.

DAN FARMER

Dan Farmer got started in ray tracing in 1989 when he downloaded a copy of the DBW Render ray tracer. It wasn't long before he had discovered QRT, another ray tracer that had found its way over to the PC from the Amiga world. Just about the time he was getting comfortable with QRT, David Buck and Aaron Collins unleashed DKB Trace for the PC and Dan was forever hopelessly lost amid checkerboard plains and mirrored spheres.

Dan plays a major part in the POV-Ray development by being the self-proclaimed "squeaky wheel" when things don't seem to work just right. He has provided a number of supporting utilities for POV-Ray, including TCE, Lissajous, Anibatch, Suds, and others, and manages the POV-Ray scene and utilities libraries.

Dan, author of Chapter 6, currently lives in Bloomington, Minnesota. His background includes oil field truck driving, press photography, and computer programming.

Introduction

Ray Tracing Creations is about creating high-quality, three-dimensional, photo-realistic images using your personal computer. This is a hands-on book that comes bundled with the Persistence of Vision Raytracer, POV-Ray, the top ray tracing program in its class. All the images on the color plates were generated using only this remarkable application. With this book and your PC, you can create fantastic computer images just by giving POV-Ray a description of the image you want to create. It takes your description and mathematically simulates the scene in memory complete with camera angle and lighting. Then it creates an extraordinary picture of the scene with perfect shading, true color, correct perspective, and realistic reflections. It doesn't take any special skills or knowledge to create these scenes. A complete beginner can create images of startling beauty and quality. An expert will find the power of the program exhilarating. Many professional graphic designers are already using POV-Ray to create images previously only possible with very expensive computer systems. Almost any scene imaginable can be created using this book and a PC.

The Ray Tracing Creations suite includes bundled disk and book. On the bundled disk you'll find the complete POV-Ray application, handy accessories and POV utilities, the example scenes, and all the utilities necessary to render, convert, and view images on your PC. The book contains software installation instructions, seven chapters, and a color plate section.

Chapter 1 begins the book with a primer on ray tracing that describes what ray tracing is and how it works. Those who are interested in creating images right away can skip ahead to Chapter 2 where the hands-on tutorial starts. Be sure to come back and read it later, though, it contains a lot of interesting information that will help you to understand and master ray tracing.

Chapter 2 shows how to install the software, create a simple scene, and

begin rendering images. Any scene on the disk can be rendered and viewed using the steps outlined in this chapter.

Chapters 3 through 5 describe the many features of POV-Ray and teach how to use them to create scenes. All aspects of scene design are covered.

Chapter 6 is a tutorial on creating ray traced animations. It demonstrates how to render the frames of an animation, compile those frames into a viewable file, and how to view the animation on VGA or SVGA displays.

The final chapter, 7, is a reference section with detailed descriptions and example scenes for every POV-Ray concept and keyword. Each entry also includes a corresponding image in the color plate section.

ABOUT THE SOFTWARE

The POV-Ray program is copyrighted freeware which you can use for non-commercial purposes without charge. Some of the included utilities are shareware. The on-disk documentation indicates which programs are shareware. Shareware distribution allows you to try out the software to determine if it meets your needs. The shareware software is included with this book as a convenience for the reader. It should be registered with the authors if it is used beyond the evaluation period. Some of the authors provide enhanced versions upon registration. More information on registration is included in the on-disk documentation with each program.

Support for POV-Ray and most of the utilities is provided through the CompuServe on-line service in the Graphics Developers forum (GO GRAPHDEV). The authors of the program are on-line in Graphdev as well as many computer artists and part-time POV-Ray experts. The authors can also be contacted at the addresses listed in the software documentation on the program disk.

Support and contact information for the other programs is described in each program's on-disk documentation.

SYSTEM REQUIREMENTS

The version of POV-Ray included with this book requires an IBM-PC compatible computer with a 386 CPU, a hard drive, and at least 2 megabytes of RAM to run. The program can generate images without any special display, but a VGA or SVGA display is highly recommended for viewing. This program will run under DOS, Windows, and OS/2.

Animations may be created without any special display, but a VGA or SVGA display is required to view the animations.

Quick Start

We're sure that you're anxious to get started with ray tracing. Just follow these few easy steps and you'll soon be looking at beautiful ray traced images.

BACK UP YOUR PROGRAM DISK

Before you do anything else, make a backup copy of your bundled software disk. To do this, first make sure you are at a DOS prompt. (If you are in Windows, exit Windows or click on a DOS prompt icon to bring up a DOS window.)

Put your bundled software disk in a 3.5" disk drive. Find a second 3.5" disk that is either blank or that contains data that you no longer need. (The disk need not be formatted.)

Now type `diskcopy` followed by the letter of the drive that contains your bundled software disk. Follow this letter with a colon (:) and repeat it twice. For example, if the drive is drive B, your command will look like this:

```
C:\>diskcopy b: b:
```

(If you are using drive A instead, you will have `a: a:` instead of `b: b:`)

Press `ENTER`. DOS will prompt you as follows:

```
Insert SOURCE diskette in drive B:
Press any key to continue . . .
```

Your "source diskette" is the bundled software disk. Since you've already put this disk in the drive, simply press any key on the keyboard. DOS will begin copying the disk:

```
Copying 80 tracks
18 sectors per track, 2 side(s)
```

After a few moments, DOS will prompt you to put your second (blank) disk in the drive. (DOS calls this the "target diskette.")

```
Insert TARGET diskette in drive B:
Press any key to continue . . .
```

After a few more moments, DOS will again ask you to put your source diskette in the drive. Simply remove the blank disk and replace it with the bundled software disk. When DOS again prompts you for the "target diskette," remove the bundled software disk and replace it with the blank disk. Continue swapping disks in this way until DOS says:

```
Volume Serial Number is 12EE-1852
Copy another diskette (Y/N)?
```

Type n (unless you're the cautious sort and want to make another copy). Put the original bundled software disk away in a safe place. You will use your copy to install the bundled software.

INSTALL THE BUNDLED SOFTWARE

The next step is to install the bundled software on your hard disk. Make sure your copy of the bundled sotware disk is in a floppy drive. Now look at your DOS prompt. The prompt should begin with the letter C, meaning that DOS has directed its attention to your hard drive. For example:

```
C:\>
```

(If your prompt begins with another letter, such as A:\>, type C: followed by (ENTER) to set DOS to your hard drive. If you want to install the software to a different hard drive, such as D:, type that letter instead.)

Now type the letter of the drive that has your software disk, followed by a colon and the word install, and press (ENTER). For example, if your software disk is in your B drive, type:

```
C:\>b:\install
```

and press (ENTER). The install program will begin running and show you the following screen:

```
LHA's SFX 2.13L (c) Yoshi, 1991

+--------------------------------------------------------------+
| The Waite Group's Ray Tracing Creations by Drew Wells & Chris Young
|
+---------------------------------------------------------+
This program will install the Persistence of Vision
```

Raytracer (POV-Ray) and all of its accociated programs as
well as all sample files needed for this book on your current
drive.

It also creates the directory \POVRAY and several subdirectories
of \POVRAY. It requires about 4 megabytes of free hard disk to
install this program.

If you do not want to install POV-Ray to the current hard drive
the type N at the prompt below.

Do you wish to continue installing POV-Ray to this drive? [Y/N]

Press ⓨ (or any key except ⓝ to continue the installation. The install program will automatically "unpack" a large number of files and copy them to a directory called \POVRAY on your hard disk. This process will take a few minutes. Each file will be listed as it is copied, but you don't need to read the list. The install program will display a message to tell you that it is finished.

Set Up Your Environment for POV-Ray

The next step is to specify settings that will tell POV-Ray how to run, and that will help DOS find the POV files automatically. DOS calls these setting "environmental variables." You will specify these in your AUTOEXEC.BAT file so that they will take effect automatically when you start your PC.

Each user's AUTOEXEC.BAT file looks a bit different, depending on the programs that are usually in use. Here's a typical example:

```
PATH=C:\DOS;C:\WP;C:\BATCH; C:\UTILS
LOADHIGH C:\DOS\SMARTDRV.EXE C
LOADHIGH C:\MOUSE.MOUSE.COM
@ECHO OFF
PROMPT $P$G
SET COMSPEC=C:\DOS\COMMAND.COM
```

To set things up for ray tracing, you need to add two items to your AUTOEXEC.BAT file. The easiest way to do this is to use a text editor such as the EDIT program that comes with DOS 5.0 and later versions, or the Notepad program that comes with Windows. Alternatively, you can use a word processor.

First, look for the line in your AUTOEXEC.BAT that begins with the word PATH. To the end of this line, add a semicolon (;) followed by \POVRAY. This tells DOS to look in your POVRAY directory for programs, and lets you run the POV-Ray program (or its utilities) from anywhere on your hard disk. When you have added the \POVRAY directory to your PATH, the PATH line in your AUTOEXEC.BAT will look something like this:

```
PATH=C:\DOS;C:\WP;C:\BATCH;C:\UTILS;C:\POVRAY
```

Next, add the following line to your AUTOEXEC.BAT file. (You can put it anywhere, but you might want to put it with any existing SET commands):

```
SET POVRAYOPT=+W120 +H90 +X +V +LC:\POVRAY\INCLUDE
```

For now, don't worry about what these commands mean. Basically, they make it easy for you to get started creating quick ray traced images.

Now save your edited AUTOEXEC.BAT file. If you used a word processor, be sure to save it as an "ASCII text" or "DOS text" file without any special formatting.

NOW, CREATE YOUR FIRST RAY TRACED IMAGE

You're just about ready to see the results of your labor. First, reboot your PC (by pressing (CTRL)-(ALT)-(DEL)), so your new AUTOEXEC.BAT settings will take effect. On your hard drive, change to the CHAPTER2 subdirectory of your \POVRAY directory:

```
C:\>cd \povray\chapter2
C:\POVRAY\CHAPTER2>
```

Now type the following command, and press (ENTER):

```
C:\POVRAY\CHAPTER2>pov first
```

This command runs a batch file (POV.BAT) that runs POV-Ray, renders the ray traced image specified in the file FIRST.POV, converts the resulting image into a GIF file, and displays it on your screen. Depending on how fast your PC is, this whole process will take somewhere between a few seconds and a couple of minutes. Enjoy the realistic lighting and shadows of a ray traced image.

Did something go wrong? If you got the BAD COMMAND OR FILE message from DOS, check to make sure you are in the \POVRAY\CHAPTER2 directory. Also check to make sure you added the \POVRAY directory to your PATH in your AUTOEXEC.BAT file, as discussed earlier.

FIND OUT MORE ABOUT RAY TRACING
AND POV-RAY

We hope that you were excited and intrigued by what you saw. Turn to Chapter 2 to read more details about how POV-Ray works and ways in which you can improve its performance on your system. (Since you've already installed POV-Ray, you can skip over the installation sections in Chapter 2).

Dear Reader:

I guess I misunderstood when Tim Wegner, author of our book *Image Lab*, told me to take some time off and soak in some rays. Then he explained. He was suggesting that we do a chapter on a ray tracing program called POV-Ray. I had heard about ray tracing, and I doubted people would be willing to wait hours to ray trace a scene. Furthermore, describing these scenes using a scripting language was a step backwards —these days people demand GUI interfaces. And they want a modeling program that can manipulate the objects.

Tim told me to first ray trace a single sphere with POV-Ray before I slammed the door. I downloaded the most recent version of POV-Ray at that time (0.5) and figured out how to describe a simple sphere, set up a light source, and trace it. To my surprise, it took about 10 seconds instead of hours to trace the sphere. Unfortunately, it came out gray and lifeless. After reviewing the POV-Ray docs, I discovered a library of fantastic surfaces to use. I learned how to apply a surface (easy), and suddenly I had a beautiful blue marble sphere!

Next I stretched a sphere into an ellipse and made it look like a pedestal base. I learned to make a cone, duplicated a few more shapes, and soon I had my first computer art. . . a beautiful jade-green marble pawn on an onyx and alabaster chessboard. I put the camera fairly low to create an image of the pawn towering above the viewer. I must admit a feeling of exhilaration and power at my ability to create such beauty without a single brush stroke. I was mesmerized. Originally I was afraid I'd have to spend too much time ray tracing, but after using POV-Ray, I was worried I couldn't get enough.

The only problem was that POV-Ray was so incredibly rich and powerful that it needed a book to help make it shine. *Ray Tracing Creations* documents the powerful POV-Ray 1.0 in all its glory; syntax, CSG, animation, surfaces, and much more. You'll find everything you need to immediately take advantage of this program.

After working with POV-Ray, you might like to take the next logical step and learn to make animated ray-traced movies. For guidance and inspiration on that subject, check out our book, *Making Movies on the PC.*

We hope you enjoy the book. If you have any questions or suggestions please fill out the Reader Report Card at the back of the book and send it in. We'll send you a catalog in return. You can reach me on CIS as 75146,3515, MCI mail as mwaite, and usenet as mitch@well.sf.ca.us.

Sincerely,

Mitchell Waite

Mitchell Waite
Publisher

Overview of Contents

Table of Contents

Let there be light

—Genesis 1:3

1

Ray Tracing Primer

This book is about creating realistic 3D images using mathematical principles, an understanding of light, and the power of a desktop computer. We'll be creating computerized models of scenes including objects, light sources, and an observer. The process is called *ray tracing* because the computer traces the path that rays of light in the real world take between light sources, objects, and an observer.

When you ray trace a scene you are creating your own imaginary universe. You describe all of the objects in the scene, pick a location and direction from which to view this world, and "let there be light." The computer performs a simulation of light rays reflecting from the objects you described and produces a stunningly realistic image from this "imaginary" universe.

WHY RAY TRACING?

Modeling a universe and re-creating the laws of physics concerning light probably seems like the hard way to create an image. You could use a variety of methods to create images using a computer. Let's look at a few.

ALTERNATIVES TO RAY TRACING

You can use a computer mouse, trackball, or other pointing device with a painting program to draw images. Such software enables production of some automatic special effects that only a computer can provide. Solid areas can be filled automatically. Color palettes can be changed. Sections can be duplicated, rotated, or resized at will. A great deal of artistic skill is required, however, to create realistic images with painting programs.

You can use computer-aided design (CAD) software such as AutoCAD by Autodesk to create three-dimensional (3D) models of objects by dividing the shapes into collections of polygons. Renderman by Pixar is another popular tool for 3D rendering. Such programs use a rendering technique called *z-buffering* to project the polygons onto the two-dimensional (2D) screen to produce an image with accurate perspective. With Autodesk 3D Studio, you can apply colors or textures to the 3D shapes.

RAY TRACING'S STRENGTHS

While z-buffered rendering packages can create realistic images, there are serious limits to what they can do. With them, reflections from shiny surfaces, refraction through transparent objects, and accurate shadows are difficult or impossible to create. Ray tracing not only performs as well in creating accurate 3D perspective and applying realistic textures, it easily creates accurate reflection, refraction, and shadows with dramatic realism.

Figure 1-1, for example, shows a computer-generated image with three simple geometric solid shapes. A moderately skilled computer user could create such an image with a mouse and painting software or with a 3D rendering software that can perform simple shading. Now look at Figure 1-2, which was created with ray tracing software. The block on the left has a realistic wood grain pattern. The cylinder on the right has a realistic marble texture with a shiny highlight. Shadows have been added. While z-buffered rendering software can produce such effects, the reflecting metallic sphere in the center is difficult to create without ray tracing. Complex multiple reflections and refractions are easily made with ray tracing but are impossible to render accurately with other techniques.

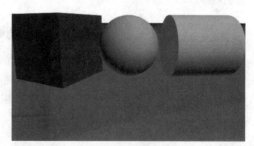

Figure 1-1 An Ordinary Computer Image of Simple Shapes

Figure 1-2   A Ray Traced Image of Simple Shapes

These software packages and others like them are often quite expensive, costing hundreds or even thousands of dollars. You might think that ray tracing software, because it can produce more accurate, realistic effects, would be even more expensive. You would be wrong! Figure 1-2 and all of the other ray traced images in this book were created with the Persistence of Vision Raytracer (POV-Ray), a copy of which is included for free on the disk bundled with this book.

THEORY OR PRACTICE?

You don't need to know exactly how a ray tracing program works in order to use one. Chapters 2 through 5 teach you how to use the basic features of POV-Ray. Chapter 6 discusses ways to combine POV-Ray images into animated scenes. Chapter 7 provides a complete reference to the POV-Ray program. You can jump right in with Chapter 2 if you'd like to begin creating images.

If you are curious about the theory behind ray tracing and wonder how POV-Ray works, relax, put your feet up, and read on.

IMAGE AND LIGHT

Philosophers debate whether falling trees produce a sound when there is no one there to hear them. Fortunately for us, the distinction between *light* as a real physical phenomena and *image*, which is an observation of that phenomena, is not as debatable. The process of creating an image involves reproducing the way that light stimulates the human visual system.

It is not necessary to build a simulation of a human brain, but we do have to create a stimulus that the brain can interpret as an image. Computers are powerful simulation tools, but it is necessary to have an understanding of both light and image before the process of creating images can be computerized. Artists concern themselves with creating images. Scientists study light as a physical phenomena. Both art and science provide important insights to solving the problem of creating realistic images with ray tracing.

THE ART OF IMAGES

Artists spend considerable time and effort thinking about light and the way it affects their images. Understanding the importance of light, they manipulate it to create a particular mood or to make a statement. The task of simulating the real world in an image is not a simple process. Much of the history of visual art has dealt with humanity's struggle to understand and reproduce the effect of light entering our eyes so that our brain can interpret it as an image.

The earliest forms of art were scratchings on the walls of caves. These primitive images treated objects in their simplest forms: circles for heads, ovals

Figure 1-3 Primitive Cave Drawings Using Simple Shapes

Figure 1-4 Pre-Renaissance Art with a Lack of Perspective

Figure 1-5 Renaissance Art Showing Perspective

for bodies, straight lines for arms and legs (see Figure 1-3). To work with computer models of objects, it is also necessary to consider such primitive aspects of form.

The artistic skill to create more realistic images evolved slowly over the centuries. Although greater attention was given to details such as shape and color, images remained flat, lifeless, and two dimensional. Figure 1-4 shows a sample of pre-Renaissance art that is more detailed than the cave drawings but lacks depth or three-dimensional *perspective.*

It wasn't until the Renaissance, with the birth of scientific inquiry and advances in applied mathematics, that the concept of perspective began to be understood. Figure 1-5 is an example of Renaissance-era art that demonstrates an understanding of the geometry of perspective. In some cases, science was driven by the needs of artists to understand the world they were trying to reproduce, and artists in turn were the beneficiaries of scientific and mathematical discoveries. This partnership between art and science was personified in Leonardo da Vinci, who was a master of both.

Today, we follow these historical steps in learning to draw. In kindergarten we begin with stick-figure people, houses made of boxes, and trees resembling lollipops. Everything is flat. This builds a foundation for our understanding that complex objects are actually variations or combinations of simple shapes. Later in childhood we learn to add detail and concentrate on form and proportion, but many of us find that the complexities of perspective, shading, and the effect of illumination on color are beyond our ability. Only the person with artistic talent seems able to master the delicate processes that lead to realism. Still, limited by the media in which they work, even accomplished artists avoid scenes with complex reflection, refraction, and detailed shadows. Ray tracing is one medium that enables us to create the complex shadows, reflections, and refractions that most artists wouldn't normally attempt. However ray tracing has its own peculiar limitations which will create new struggles for us.

As you learn to create ray traced images, you will start with simple shapes, then add colors and textures, and eventually graduate to more complex topics. From cave dweller to da Vinci, from kindergarten to art school, from Chapter 2 through Chapter 7 of this book, the artist's struggle continues.

THE SCIENCE OF LIGHT

Artists generally deal with light, color, shadow, reflection, and perspective from an abstract point of view. The process of ray tracing requires something more because it is a simulation of light as a real, physical phenomena that obeys the laws of physics.

Light is undoubtedly one of the most important phenomena that scientists study. The linear nature of light and the way that light reflects off mirrors was understood in ancient times. It wasn't until the thirteenth century, however, that science studied *refraction*, the way light bends when passing through dense, transparent objects such as lenses. Roger Bacon, considered by many to be the world's first true scientist, described how lenses could be used to correct vision problems. In the early 1600s Dutch spectacles makers invented the telescope, and in 1610 Galileo used it to discover Jupiter's moons and Saturn's rings. While scientists realized that the amount of refraction varies with the color of the light, it wasn't until the 1700s that Sir Isaac Newton used this color-dependent nature of refraction to illustrate that white light comprises all of the colors of the spectrum. He used a prism to break the light into its component colors.

Modern physics tells us that light consists of tiny particles of energy that are called *photons*, yet these particles have wavelike properties. Today the dual nature of light as both wave and particle remains a paradox that is only partially understood.

This paradox creates a problem for us. How can you create a model of light that is both particle and wave? Even if we limit the model to consider only the particle nature of a photon, there are problems to be overcome. An uncountable number of photons are emitted by light sources like the light bulb you may be using to help you see this page. How can we expect to deal with such a vast number of particles reflecting around the room? We need to simplify the problem some way.

Illustrating Lines and Rays

An infinite object like a ray is difficult to depict in a simple illustration. When you draw a line between two points you are technically drawing a *line segment*, not a line. Mathematically, a line is infinite in both directions. Standard notation for depicting a line is to draw a line segment with an arrow on each end which emphasizes that the line extends infinitely in both directions. A ray on the other hand, has a starting point and extends in one direction for infinity. A ray is depicted as a line segment with an arrow on one end only. Figure 1-6 illustrates lines, line segments, and rays.

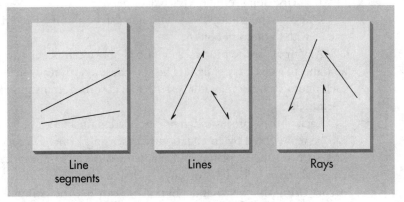

Line segments   Lines   Rays

Figure 1-6   Illustrations of Line Segments, Lines, and Rays

A RAY OF HOPE

Fortunately, we don't have to deal with light at the subatomic level of individual photons or resolve the dual nature of light as particles and waves in order to understand light well enough to create images. Long before we understood photons, waves, and other complexities about the true nature of light, we understood that light travels in *rays*. A ray is a straight line that has a fixed starting point and continues from that point in one direction for infinity. The path of a photon has a starting point and it continues in a straight line for infinity unless it strikes an object. For our purposes, we can simplify our concept of light by considering rays of light as a whole rather than struggling with individual photons.

When you turn on a light switch, rays of light travel all over the room and strike objects. When a ray of light strikes a surface, a number of things can happen. The light can be *reflected*. As rays strike the surface they bounce off in different directions. Some of the rays happen to reflect in our direction and enter our eyes. The light is interpreted by our brain and we "see the object." We do not actually see the object, however. What we see is the reflected light. Later we'll see why this distinction is important.

The light can be *absorbed*. Its energy is usually converted to heat and that's the end of the story. Objects that look black do precisely that. Light striking a black surface is absorbed, so we see little or no light reflecting back to our eyes.

The light can be *transmitted* through transparent objects, which means that light can pass through. We already have learned that light passing into or out of a dense object can be refracted, or bent.

One other possibility exists. The light can be absorbed and *re-emitted*. This occurs with fluorescent objects.

Any or all of the processes described above can occur at once in varying amounts to a given ray of light. This is because a ray is really many photons and each photon may or may not be reflected, absorbed, transmitted, refracted, or re-emitted.

Each of these processes can be described mathematically. For example, rays can be represented by an equation representing a line. Objects struck by the rays, such as spheres, planes, and geometric surfaces, can be described in mathematical terms. The laws of physics describe how reflection and refraction occur. Using this math and physics, we can tell the computer where light sources are, where objects are, where our eyes are, and then let the computer do all the dirty work of tracing rays of light from the source to objects and onwards to our eyes.

It sounds relatively simple, but in practice it is virtually impossible because as an individual ray leaves a light source it may end up doing any or all of the above processes many, many times. This is compounded if you consider the collection of rays emitted by the light source.

A further simplification of the problem can come when we realize that the only rays which contribute to the scene are those rays whose ultimate destination is our eyes. We could easily spend a great deal of time working on rays that contribute nothing to the image. In fact, most of the rays that come from a light source do not contribute to the image at all. For example, as I type this manuscript, a lamp on the desk is sending light rays onto the keyboard. Some rays strike the keys and are partially absorbed and partially reflected. A few reflected rays make it to my eyes so that I can see well enough to hunt and peck at the keys. But adjacent to those rays are countless other rays that sneak between the cracks of the keys, bounce around inside the keyboard, and are absorbed. Other rays come from the lamp, pass by me out my window, and fly into space.

We cannot eliminate these seemingly useless rays from our calculations because there is no way to predict where they will end without following them to their ultimate destinations. The idea of creating a computer model that duplicates how light really works is a great idea that remains a practical impossibility.

We need a new strategy if we wish to pursue creating images with the computer.

THINKING BACKWARDS

When scientists or mathematicians face a problem that cannot be solved directly, they use a number of strategies to transform the problem into one that can be solved. We already used the strategy of making a simplifying assumption when we decided to treat light as rays. Another strategy is to start with the solution and work backwards. After tracing thousands of rays that do not contribute to the image, we might wonder how we can see anything at all. Yet some rays of light obviously do reach our eyes. By starting at the end and tracing the path of these relatively few rays backwards from our eyes outward towards objects and from there farther to light sources, we can simplify the problem sufficiently to create realistic images with a mathematical model that is backwards from the way light works in the real world. This approach means only rays reaching our eyes are examined. All others are ignored.

The ray tracing method described in the following section is this type of backwards solution; it is the heart of the POV-Ray.

THE RAY TRACING METHOD

We have decided that the next simplifying assumption we will make is to turn the problem inside out and to trace rays from viewer to objects to light sources. This can lead to some rather awkward language—"the ray in the direction from which the light comes" and other confusing phrases. So let's agree not to do that. Instead let's turn the rays around. Figure 1-7a shows the way light really travels. We have a light ray leaving a source and striking the object. It reflects off the object and enters our eye along the path of another ray called a *reflected ray*. This approach is called forward ray tracing. However, our solution uses backwards ray tracing as shown in Figure 1-7b. Here we have a *viewing ray* leav-

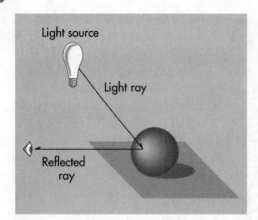

Figure 1-7a   Forward Ray Tracing

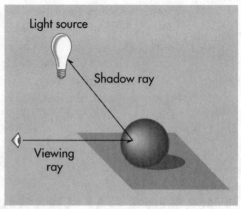

Figure 1-7b   Backwards Ray Tracing

ing the eye and striking a surface. In order to determine if that point is illuminated or is in shadow a *shadow ray* is sent back to the light source.

This is opposite of the way light really travels but that does not mean the backwards solution will not work. Although this method will rarely adversely affect the accuracy of the model, we'll discuss the limits of the backwards ray tracing model in the final section of this chapter, and we will show ways that backwards tracing fails.

ELEMENTS OF A RAY TRACER

The ray tracing method has three key elements: light sources, objects, and an observer. For our purposes we will assume the observer is a simple camera that is going to take a photograph of the scene. This avoids the complications of the stereo effects of binocular vision caused by our having two eyes.

The Camera

A ray tracing program can be thought of as an imaginary camera that photographs imaginary objects illuminated by imaginary light sources. The simplest kind of real camera is called a pin-hole camera. Figure 1-8 shows such a camera. It consists of a simple closed box with a tiny pin hole in one face. Light rays enter the box through the pin hole and strike the film placed on the inside of the opposite surface. The pin hole ensures that only rays from one direction strike any given point on the film. As you can see, the image produced is inverted. The path of the light rays between the pin hole and the film forms a four-sided pyramid of light which projects the image onto the film.

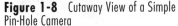

Figure 1-8 Cutaway View of a Simple Pin-Hole Camera

Figure 1-9 A Typical Ray Tracing Camera

Most ray tracing programs use this pin-hole model or a model that is functionally equivalent. A typical ray tracing camera model is shown in Figure 1-9. Essentially the pyramid of rays has been turned inside out. In place of the pin hole, which lets light rays into the box, is a *view point* that sends out a pyramid of viewing rays. The viewing rays radiate forward through an imaginary *viewing window.*

This window is the "film" of the ray tracer's imaginary camera. It is helpful to think of this window as if it were a piece of transparent graph paper with a grid etched on it. Each tiny square on the window corresponds to a single pixel of the final image. The ray tracer sends one viewing ray out of the viewing point through a square on the view window. It attempts to figure out what color to paint that pixel.

The ray tracer proceeds left to right, row by row, top to bottom, sending rays outwards to determine what color each pixel should be. When all of the pixels are filled in, the image is complete!

The Objects

A scene without objects is going to be pretty boring. The light would not bounce off anything and there would be nothing to see. For depiction, the objects will have to be represented in the computer's memory in some mathematical, geometric form. This imposes some limits on the types of objects that can be created. Fortunately many everyday objects can be represented by combinations of geometric shapes.

Arms and legs are really just cylinders. Heads are really elongated spheres. You might doubt that primitive shapes such as spheres, boxes, cones, disks,

Figure 1-10   A Dürer Woodcut Shows a Window Grid Used to Study Perspective

Renaissance Ray Tracing

The idea of looking through a transparent grid to create images is not new with computerized ray tracing. As noted earlier, the investigation of perspective dates back to the Renaissance. It began in fifteenth-century Florence and spread throughout Europe. Among the early pioneers of perspective was the German artist Albrecht Dürer. He envisioned his canvas as a window through which he observed his scene. In fact the word *perspective* comes from the Latin *perspicere* which means "to look through."

Figure 1-10 shows a device Dürer used to study perspective. It resembles the ray tracing camera we are using. The artist looked through a small hole near the top of an upright pole at the front of the device. This served to fix the view point at a single location. Some distance away was a frame holding a glass plate which was the viewing window. A grid of lines was ruled on the glass. The artist's paper was also ruled with a similar grid. The artist would look at the squares one at a time and would sketch the contents of each "pixel" onto the appropriate square of the paper.

rings, and planes can be used to create anything but the most trivial object, but consider the complex objects shown in Figures 1-11 and 1-12. Although these images look like photographs they are not! They are ray tracings created by artist Mike Miller using POV-Ray and employing only primitive, geometric shapes in various combinations.

For more complex or irregular shapes, sophisticated computer modeling software such as 3D CAD programs can create arbitrary shapes of any kind by approximating the shape with hundreds or thousands of small triangles. If these triangles are cleverly shaded, the sharp seams between them can be eliminated

Figure 1-11 Camera by Mike Miller

Figure 1-12 Teapot by Mike Miller

and the results look as though a smooth shape has been created. In Chapter 5 you'll learn how triangle-based models created by Autodesk 3D Studio can be converted for use with POV-Ray.

In addition to "shape," objects also differ in the materials from which they are made. A crystal ball, a bowling ball, a beach ball, and a steel ball bearing are all spheres but they look quite different because they are made of different materials that react to light in different ways. The properties of that material include its color or pattern of colors, transparency, reflectivity, roughness, shine, dullness, and smoothness. Ray tracing program designers have come up with a variety of ways to model these material features mathematically. When all else fails, a two-dimensional image that looks like the surface can be wrapped around a three-dimensional object to create almost any material you can imagine.

The Light Sources

Real light can come from a variety of sources. Light bulbs, flames, electric arcs, sunlight, and the glowing phosphors of a television screen are just a few examples. Light sources have a number of important properties: color, intensity, location, size, and shape.

The physical principles of how light radiates from a source are very complex. This is another area where some simplifying assumptions will cut the problem down to size. One typical assumption used in ray tracing is that the light from any given source is of a single color. Recall that Newton discovered that white light is actually composed of a whole spectrum of colors. Modern physics tells us that each photon has just one color and light rays usually consist of photons of many different colors combined. Our model of light must treat the light as if it were one color such as white, orange, pink, cyan, or magenta, even though real light, which looks to be of these colors, is actually composed of a wide range of colors mixed together.

Look briefly at a low-wattage light bulb. (Don't stare! You'll damage your eyes.) The bulb is about 2 inches in diameter and has an oblong shape. Light is emitted in varying amounts from various parts of the bulb. Place a small object near the light and notice the shadow it creates. The shadow has fuzzy edges because not all of the light from the bulb is blocked (see Figure 1-13). The center of the shadow is dark because light from all parts of the bulb is blocked. This dark area is called the *umbra*. The fuzzy shaded area is only partially blocked; some rays from parts of the bulb get through. This area is called the *penumbra*.

When tracing rays to determine where shadows fall, remember that the light does not come from a single point, which might make accurate ray tracing impractical. Therefore another common simplification is the assumption that light comes from individual point sources. With a point source, the rays cannot sneak around the edges to form a soft penumbra. This results in ray traced

images with hard-edged shadows. See Figure 1-14.

TYPES OF RAYS

Let's get down to the business of tracing rays. The viewing ray that comes from the camera is only the first of many types of rays used. Shadow rays, transmitted rays, and reflected rays also are needed.

VIEWING RAYS

The camera sends out one ray for each rectangle of the grid of the viewing window and that ray is used to compute the color of the corresponding pixel in the final image. The program has an internal list of all of the objects defined in the scene. Every object in the list is tested to see if it is hit by the viewing ray. This process, called a *ray-object intersection test*, involves solving a set of equations. Many highly accurate, time-consuming floating-point calculations are required.

Recall that a ray extends out an infinite distance from its starting point. Therefore, it is necessary to determine which object the ray intersects first. The closest object is the one the camera actually "sees." Because the order in which objects are tested cannot be determined, the process cannot stop with the first successful intersection test found. There may be closer objects that block the

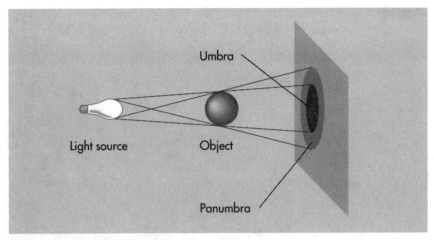

Figure 1-13 How Soft Shadows Are Created

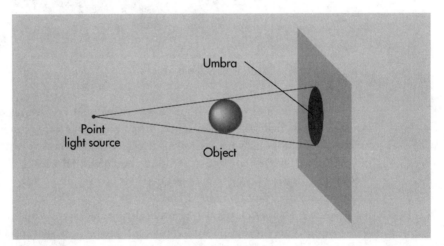

Figure 1-14 How Point Light Sources Create Hard Shadows

view, so the ray must be tested against every object in the scene. The location of every ray-object intersection point is stored and after all objects have been tested the closest one is chosen (see Figure 1-15). The ray is found to intersect the first object in the list, which is the box, but there are other objects to be tested. The cylinder is tested but the ray doesn't intersect it. Then the sphere is tested and found to be closer. That is the object that the camera sees.

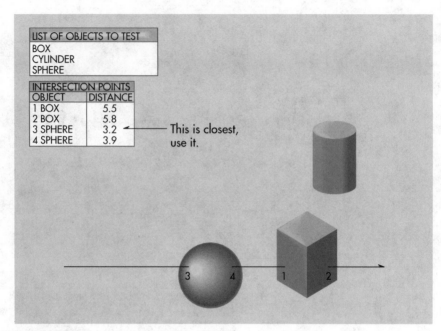

Figure 1-15 How a Ray Intersects Several Objects

The information stored with each object includes everything we need to know about its material. The most important piece of information is the color of the particular point where the ray intersected. However, knowing the color at that point isn't enough to determine the color that the pixel should be because the *apparent color* of an object depends on how much light is illuminating that particular point on the surface.

Figure 1-16 shows a viewing ray intersecting an object. When the apparent color of the object at that point is computed, the color of that pixel is filled in and the program moves on to the next pixel.

When light from a light source strikes an object, the light is scattered in all directions unless the object has a mirrored surface. (Mirrored surfaces are discussed later.) Because the light spreads outward in all directions this light is called *diffuse illumination*. Obviously, not every light source illuminates every point of every object. Some points are in shadowed areas because another object blocks the light from reaching that point. If a light source is on the far side of the object, light is blocked by the object itself. Using the earlier example of the light shining on a keyboard, the areas deep inside the keyboard might be

Figure 1-16 A Viewing Ray Intersects an Object

brightly colored but if no light reaches them then a viewing ray which sneaks between the keys should result in a black pixel.

To determine how much diffuse illumination is at the intersection point we must first determine which, if any, light sources have a clear path to that point. This requires a new set of rays called *shadow rays*.

SHADOW RAYS

Once the viewing ray is known to intersect a point on an object, a shadow ray is sent out for every light source defined in the scene. Each shadow ray begins at the viewing ray-object intersection point and passes through the location point of a light source. The ray-object intersection tests start from scratch and the shadow ray is tested against every object in the scene. If we ignore the special case of transparent objects for now, finding just one object hit by the shadow ray tells us that this light source does not contribute to illuminating that particular point. However, there is always the chance that the last object in the list might be the only one causing a shadow so this process can be lengthy.

If the shadow ray is blocked, we simply quit and go on to another shadow ray until we have traced one ray to each light source. If there are no objects blocking light from a particular source, we must determine how much light is contributed by that source.

Figure 1-17 shows a scene with two objects and two light sources. The viewing ray travels from V and intersects the sphere at point P. From there we send a shadow ray to each light source. The shadow ray from P to A is blocked by the box so we know that no light from source A reaches that point on the sphere. Another shadow ray is sent towards light source B and is unobstructed. Thus light source B contributes to the illumination at P. Note that at point Q on the sphere both light sources are unobstructed and there is no shadow. The apparent color of point Q will be brighter than P even though the sphere is of a uniformly colored material.

The color of the light is very important in determining the apparent color of the point. Suppose we are looking at a plain white surface in the open with no other objects causing shadows. If we shine a red light on the white surface, then the surface will look red. If we shine a red light on a green surface, then the surface will look black. This is because the green pigment on the surface absorbs all colors of light except for green light. That is why white light (composed of all colors) shining on a surface with green pigment looks green: The surface reflects the green light and absorbs all others.

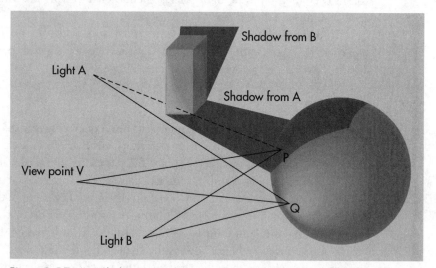

Figure 1-17 How Shadow Rays Work

This is why it is important to realize that we don't see objects, we see the light that is reflected from an object. The amount and color of light makes a big difference in what is seen.

Once we have determined the amount and color of light contributed by various light sources we can begin to figure out the apparent color of the object. A number of other factors are involved: The angle that light strikes a surface affects the amount of illumination (steep angles give more illumination); shiny objects have highlights created by bright light reflecting off microscopic bumps in the surface; and florescent surfaces glow. A number of methods are available for simulating these effects.

We now turn our attention to reflection and transmission.

REFLECTED RAYS

There are two kinds of reflection. *Diffuse reflection* occurs when light reflects off a dull surface and scatters in all directions. This accounts for the light we see from most everyday objects and its contribution to their apparent color was handled by the shadow ray calculations. *Specular reflection* is the reflection from smooth surfaces such as mirrors, chrome-plated metal, and squeaky clean dishes (remember the TV commercials?). This light is reflected not just from light sources but from all surrounding objects including faces, walls, and furniture.

When light reflects off a mirror or other smooth surface, it is not scattered in every direction. Figure 1-18 shows that for such surfaces the angle of reflection is equal to the angle of incidence. Because we can compute the angle which a viewing ray strikes a surface, we can compute the direction of an

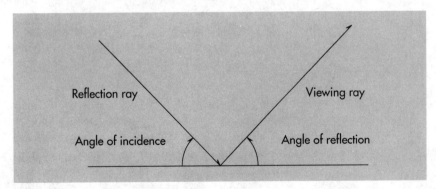

Figure 1-18 How Rays Reflect Off a Surface

incoming ray which will reflect back at us. The incoming ray is reversed and it is called a *reflection ray*. It starts at the reflection point and extends outwards along the angle of incidence. Recall that the purpose of a viewing ray was to figure out what light was reaching our camera. Similarly, the reflection ray is used to compute the light that reaches the reflection point.

This ray might reflect again and again with many recursive levels of calculations. Generally, ray tracing software limits the levels of reflection to be computed. When the amount and color of light from specular reflection have been determined, they are added to the accumulated light from other calculations. Figure 1-19 shows a viewing ray striking a mirror. The reflection ray then strikes an object and a shadow ray is sent to the light source.

There is one more item that contributes to the apparent color of the viewing ray intersection point and that is the light that comes through the object.

TRANSMITTED RAYS

Transparent or partially transparent objects permit light to come through them in the form of *transmitted rays*. Because light may be filtered if the glass is tinted or bent from refraction effects, it makes things easier to start tracing a new ray and see where it goes.

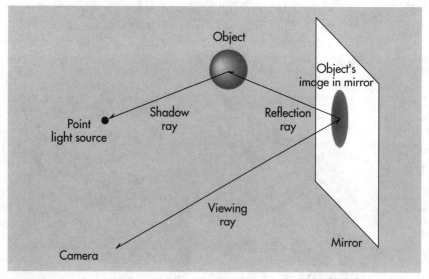

Figure 1-19 Tracing Reflection Rays

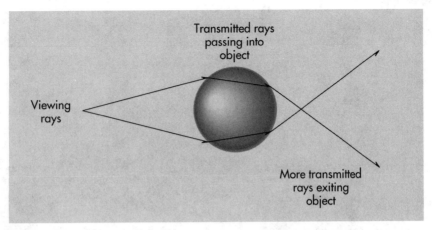

Figure 1-20 How Rays Are Refracted

The physics of refracted light is beyond the scope of this book. For our purposes, we need only say that the angle of the ray with respect to the surface is important and the difference in the density of the substances on either side of the surface is important. The shallower the angle between the ray and the surface, the more the ray bends, but rays striking perpendicular to the surface do not bend at all. The greater the difference in density between two substances, the more the ray bends when passing through the surface between them.

Most transmitted rays will pass into and back out of a transparent object. When the transmitted ray exits a solid object, it refracts yet again and changes its direction. Therefore it is necessary to stop tracing that ray and create yet another transmitted ray. Figure 1-20 shows rays striking a transparent sphere. Notice that rays near the top of the sphere are refracted downward and rays near the bottom are refracted upward. The rays eventually cross, which is why things look upside down when looking through a transparent, refracting sphere, as seen in Figure 1-21.

Scenes with many transparent and reflective surfaces can create a large number of reflective, transmitted, and shadow rays from a single viewing ray. In a typical 640x480 pixel image there are 302,700 viewing rays, perhaps 4 to 6 or more shadow rays per viewing ray, and up to 10 times more reflected or transmitted rays on top of that!

A highly complex image rendered at such resolution can take 30 or more hours to complete on fast 33-50–MHz 486 computers. Most ray trace artists create their images at low resolution with simple, nonreflective, nontransparent

Figure 1-21   Looking Through a Refracting Sphere

materials, and make test renderings that take from 5 to 30 minutes each. Then they set up higher resolution versions with full details for processing overnight. Many images take several overnight sessions to complete, but the results are truly worth waiting for! Ray tracing creates fantastic images that look like they are real photographs. POV-Ray provides the hobbyist and professional alike with a powerful tool that can create near perfect images.

THE LIMITS OF RAY TRACING

Did we say "near perfect"?

Along the way a number of simplifying assumptions were made in order to make ray tracing feasible. The main assumption was that the problem could be solved backwards without hurting the accuracy of the image much. This section provides a brief overview of how these simplifications hurt accuracy a little. In addition to explaining the limitations inherent in ray traced rendering in general, we note how POV-Ray works around some—but not all—of these limits. Also noted are problems with ray tracing that are not necessarily impossible to overcome, but are of such difficulty that the POV-Ray does not yet support the necessary solutions.

LIMITS OF PIXEL-BASED IMAGES

Images created by computers are made up of rows and columns of pixels. Ray traced images are created by tracing one viewing ray per pixel in order to determine the color of the pixel. This creates a number of problems because every possible ray is not traced. Theoretically, an infinite number of rays can fit in a finite space by bunching them closer together. Therefore it is necessary to take a *sample* of rays based on the fixed geometric grid of our viewing window. Higher resolution used with more rays and with more pixels provides a better sample, but it is still just a sample. Errors, noise, or distortion created by sampling data are called *aliasing* because the data looks like something that it is not. Techniques for limiting aliasing are called *antialiasing*.

Jagged Lines

The most common type of aliasing, shown in Figure 1-22a, is affectionately called the "Jaggies." A straight line that is nearly vertical or nearly horizontal has a jagged, stair-step look when represented by pixel-based graphics. The line looks jagged when it really is not. Ray-object intersection tests are a hit-or-miss operation; a ray cannot partially hit an object. Figure 1-16 used a very low resolution grid on the viewing window to make the pixels visible. In addition to the stair-step look of the sphere's edges, you'll note that the eyes of the face are of slightly different sizes. This occurred because the pixel grid lined up slightly dif-

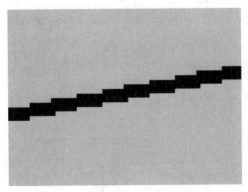

Figure 1-22a A Jagged Line Showing Aliasing

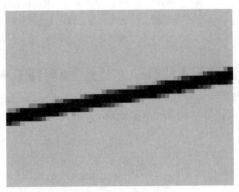

Figure 1-22b An Antialiased Jagged Line

ferent for one eye than the other. At normal resolutions the effect is minimal but it does create an imperfection in the image.

By subdividing pixels into smaller areas we can send multiple rays for each pixel and average the results, giving the pixel a color that is an average of those rays which hit the object and those that miss. Figure 1-22b shows the results achieved using this process that is called *supersampling*.

Typically, nine rays in a 3x3 pattern within the area of the pixel are used in supersampling. That means 9 times as many viewing rays are traced per pixel and perhaps 90 times as many total rays. This also means it will take 90 times longer to trace an image. Some ray tracers use *adaptive* techniques for antialiasing, only supersampling when adjacent pixels have colors that differ by more than some threshold amount. This saves time because supersampling is only performed on those pixels that need it. By slightly wiggling the supersample rays, some of the adverse effects of a fixed grid of pixels can be overcome. This is called *jittering* a ray. POV-Ray optionally uses an adaptive jittered supersample antialiasing technique.

Missed Small Objects

Tiny objects such as raindrops or thin objects such as wire or string can be missed completely when ray tracing at low resolution. The entire object might exist in the space between adjacent pixels and the viewing rays of these pixels might *both* miss the objects! Adaptive supersampling doesn't help in this situation because it doesn't take effect unless the first viewing ray of a pixel notices a transition from one color to another. Higher resolution might help but there is still the possibility that tiny details will be missed.

Graphics programmers have developed alternatives to ray tracing that allow them to create and animate *particle systems* such as raindrops, dust storms, or flocks of birds. These are beyond our scope because they are not ray tracing methods and are not supported in POV-Ray.

LIMITS OF THE LIGHT MODEL

In developing ray tracing techniques, several simplifying assumptions have been made about light:

- Light consists of rays of one color rather than streams of photons of many colors.
- Light does not exhibit wave properties such as interference or diffraction effects.
- Light comes from infinitely small point sources.

- A surface is illuminated only by light that comes directly from light sources.

These assumptions create problems that cause inaccurate images or prohibit us from reproducing certain real phenomena.

Rainbow Problems

Ray tracing easily calculates the way that light bends when passing through transparent objects such as lenses, prisms, diamonds, and raindrops. All of the light does not bend by the same amount, however. Photons of different colors bend by different amounts, resulting in an effect called *chromatic aberration*. Therefore when white light, which is made of all colors combined, refracts through transparent objects, it splits into a rainbow of colors. Because ray tracing treats light as a single colored ray, refractive objects such as prisms cannot be used to split white light into a rainbow of colors. It is possible to accurately model the way refraction occurs when looking through transparent objects, but this rainbow effect is beyond our capability and POV-Ray makes no attempt to overcome the problem.

There is one rather creative alternative that can produce a limited chromatic effect. It is possible to render multiple versions of the same scene, each with different colored light sources and a slightly different index of refraction. Then you add the images together in a program such as Piclab, producing a limited chromatic effect.

In addition to refraction, a spectrum of colors is also visible when light reflects off surfaces with finely etched lines. This is called *diffraction* and is caused by light of different wavelengths interfering and canceling out or adding together. You can see the effect by looking at the underside of an audio compact disc (CD). However ray tracing depends on the single colored light model, which ignores the wave properties of light and so does not generate diffraction effects.

Soft Shadow Problems

Real light sources are not infinitely small points. They are 3D objects with size and shape that can significantly affect the way shadows are cast. Light rays from different parts of the light source will strike at different angles, creating soft edged shadows in areas where only part of the light is blocked. The calculations used in ray tracing depend on using point sources of light. You can define multiple point sources close to each other to simulate larger light sources but this means that more shadow rays must be traced and more time-consuming calculations made to determine the illumination contributed by the sources.

Some ray tracing software provides adaptive extended light sources in which the extra shadow rays for multipoint sources are computed only near the edges of objects. This is similar to the adaptive antialiasing techniques described earlier. Jittering of multiple shadow rays by small random amounts can also soften shadows. In the current version, POV-Ray does not implement soft shadow methods, but adaptive extended light sources with jittered shadow rays are under development.

Specular Illumination Problems

If you look closely at a flashlight or the headlights of a car, you'll notice that behind the light bulb is a curved reflector. This reflector makes use of the light radiated from the back and sides of the bulb by reflecting it forwards where it will add to the useful illumination. Similarly, if you point a flashlight into a mirror, the light bounces off and illuminates an area elsewhere.

If we were tracing rays of light forward it would be simple to trace a ray from the source to the mirrored surface and then onward at easily calculated angles. When tracing backwards, however, the calculations become prohibitively difficult or impossible. It is easy to trace a viewing ray to the object and then trace a shadow ray directly to the light source but it is not easy to compute what point on the mirror (if any) would reflect a ray from the light source.

For flat mirrors, some calculations would solve the problem by treating the mirror as though it were a window into a room that is identical except that everything is reversed. This is a complex process and doesn't work for curved mirrors. Like most ray tracing programs, POV-Ray makes no attempt to solve this class of problems. The bottom line is that in ray tracing, illumination does not bounce off reflective surfaces. Therefore placing a reflector behind a light source does not redirect the light. Lamps can be seen in a mirror but the light coming from a lamp does not reflect in a mirror.

Ambient Illumination Problems

The problem described above deals with specular reflection of illumination off shiny or mirrored surfaces. However illumination also reflects off dull finishes by diffuse reflection. If you turn on a single light in a dark room you will still be able to see objects in the shadows. This is because light is reflecting off such objects as the walls or ceiling and illuminating shadowed areas. Photographers often exploit this effect by aiming their flash equipment at the ceiling to create a "bounce flash." This softens shadows because the entire ceiling becomes one huge light source.

Most ray tracing software, including POV-Ray, uses a trick called *ambient lighting*, a uniformly distributed light that comes equally from all directions. It simulates the reflected diffuse illumination from other objects in the scene so that shadowed areas are not totally black, but it is *only* an approximation.

The illumination from diffuse reflection not only brightens shadows, it also affects an object's apparent color. If you place a white sofa in your living room with blue walls, blue carpet, and blue curtains, the sofa will look like it is tinted blue even with white light bulbs in the room. This is because some of the light which illuminates the sofa has reflected off the blue furnishings. Ambient lighting cannot reproduce this effect.

Although a solution, called *radiosity*, is available, ray tracing in general and POV-Ray in particular do not utilize it. Image software which uses a radiosity model divides objects into small colored patches and treats each patch as a light source. It computes the apparent color of a surface irrespective of the camera location. Radiosity takes longer to compute than ray tracing but you can move the camera without recalculating everything. Radiosity creates more accurate diffuse reflection but does not handle specular reflection at all. Some software uses combinations of ray tracing and radiosity to reap the benefits and to overcome the weaknesses of each but such software is very, very slow.

Refractive Illumination Problems

We noted earlier that you can look in a ray traced mirror and see an accurate image but illumination does not reflect off mirrors. A similar problem exists with refraction. You can look through a ray traced lens and see an accurate image, but a lens cannot be used to focus the light from a light source. For instance, you cannot focus ray traced sunlight on an imaginary piece of paper to burn a hole. Similarly, the bright and dark spots on the bottom of a pool caused by light refracting through surface ripples cannot be accurately reproduced. These effects are called *caustics*. In general, ray tracing cannot reproduce caustics.

Some ray tracing software attempts to simulate caustics by brightening or darkening parts of the shadows cast by transparent objects based on the angles that shadow rays enter or leave an object. POV-Ray does not attempt this method, which is not very accurate.

Highlight Problems

Smooth, shiny objects, especially curved surfaces, have bright spots where a bright light source reflects off the surface, creating a *highlight*. Highlights are a combination of diffuse and specular reflection. In very shiny objects a highlight is a near-perfect specular reflection in which the light source appears as in a mirror. On rougher objects, the reflection diffuses more from bouncing off tiny surface imperfections.

In theory, highlights could be reproduced by directly simulating tiny surface flaws and computing perfect specular reflection. This would be difficult, impractical, and unnecessary. There are mathematical models that describe how highlights look without actually calculating reflections at microscopic levels. The *Phong highlight* is a popular, accurate model. Another method, called *specular highlight*, is based more closely on actual specular reflection and produces more realistic highlights, especially when light reflects at shallow angles near the edge of an object. POV-Ray supports both Phong and specular highlights.

The highlights on a surface give us important visual clues about its shape. Ripples on a pond are more visible when sunlight makes sparkling highlights on them. Ray tracing can exploit this by creating false highlights and reflections that simulate bumps, dents, ripples, or waves. Such effects are quite realistic and are more efficient than directly creating a 3D model of a bumpy surface. To the extent that these methods are not 100-percent accurate models of the way highlights occur in nature, the effects created may be inaccurate. Generally, though, the shortcuts used in simulating highlights do not cause noticeable errors.

Now that you understand how ray tracing works and have looked at some of the tradeoffs involved, it's time to put POV-Ray to work. Chapter 2 shows you everything you need to get started making your own ray tracing creations.

SUMMARY

The process of creating an image simulates the way light enters our eyes for our brain to interpret.

Computer models of light sources, objects, and observers can be created. The laws of physics can be used to determine the paths that light travels from light sources to objects to observers. Because most such paths do not end with light reaching the observer, this method is impractical and cannot be used to create images in a reasonable amount of time.

By tracing viewing rays, shadow rays, transmitted rays, and reflected rays, we can trace the path of light backwards from observer to objects to light sources and can create realistic images in an acceptable amount of time.

Many of the simplifying assumptions made in creating the ray tracing method create inherent limitations. In some of these cases, there are ways to minimize the limitations. POV-Ray utilizes most of them.

It is here in mathematics that the artist has the fullest scope of his imagination.

—Havelock Ellis

2

Using POV-Ray

avelock Ellis could easily have been describing ray tracing when he made the statement on the preceding page. If you've read through the discussion in Chapter 1, you know that ray tracing is a method for generating photo-realistic, 3D images of objects that exist only as descriptions in computer files and visions in the creator's mind. The ray tracer creates these images by mathematically simulating the effect of light rays on objects in a scene. Imagine any scene and it can be visualized with a ray tracer.

Ray tracing an image requires thousands or even millions of calculations. Ray tracing was thus not practical before the advent of high-speed computers. Even after high-speed computers were invented, this method of creating images was only available to scientists and mathematicians who understood the equations and algorithms used in ray tracing. The mathematics were very complicated, and ray tracing required very expensive and fast computers like the multimillion-dollar Cray supercomputer. Ray tracing was off limits to the average artist and computer user.

The Persistence of Vision Ray Tracer (POV-Ray) bundled with this book is a sophisticated software package that allows you to create amazing images using ray tracing on a personal computer. The scene description language you use to create images is easy to understand, so you won't have to be a mathematician to make ray traced pictures.

As you will soon see, you can use POV-Ray to create just about any picture you can conceive. Drawing and painting skills aren't needed because the program automatically generates realistic 3D images from a file you've created describing your scene. Using this software, you can create images that have chrome spheres, glass mountains, rippling water, stormy clouds, jade panthers, and much more.

This chapter introduces POV-Ray, teaches you how to create a scene file, and explains the language used to create the scene file. Next, you'll see how to generate a ray traced image from the scene file and view the image on your screen. This book assumes that you've never used ray tracing software or POV-Ray before, but even if you have, you should find plenty of useful information here.

UP AND RUNNING

This section describes what computer hardware you need to run POV-Ray, how to install the bundled POV-Ray software on your hard disk, and how to configure it to work with your computer.

Table 2-1 is a list of the required and recommended computer hardware required for POV-Ray.

CPU

You'll need an IBM-PC compatible computer with a 386sx CPU or better to run the POV-Ray software. An IBM-PC compatible computer with a 486 or higher CPU is recommended for best performance. The software will not run on 286 or IBM-XT class computers.

Table 2-1 POV-Ray Hardware Requirements		
Hardware	**Minimum Required**	**Recommended**
Computer	IBM-PC compatible with 386sx CPU	IBM-PC compatible with 386/387 or 486 CPU
Math Coprocessor	Not mandatory	Highly recommended
Display	No special display required	VGA or Super VGA
Hard Disk Space	5 megabytes of free disk space	10 megabytes or more of free disk space
RAM Memory	2 megabytes	4 megabytes or more

MATH COPROCESSOR

A math coprocessor is an extra chip for your computer that does floating-point math calculations much faster than the main CPU can. The ray tracing software doesn't require a math coprocessor, but it will run several times faster if your system has one, so it is recommended. The ideal IBM-PC compatible system for ray tracing has a CPU with a built-in math coprocessor, like the 486. (Note that a 486sx does not have a built-in coprocessor, although you can buy an add-on chip that provides one. A built-in math coprocessor will run even faster than a standard one.) The faster your computer performs floating-point math calculations, the sooner your images will be completed, because ray tracing is math intensive.

DISPLAY HARDWARE

No graphics display is required to create images with POV-Ray, but you will need a graphic display device to view the completed images. You can view the images on any EGA, CGA, or even monochrome display system, but you won't get the full impact that way. Ray traced pictures have subtle and realistic coloring, so a Super VGA display card and monitor are highly recommended for enjoying the realistic qualities of ray traced images. POV-Ray can generate a preview of an image while it is running, but the preview will not show you the full range of colors in the output file. Use of the preview-image option requires VGA or Super VGA; for details, see the "Command-Line Switch Reference" section in Chapter 7 on the +D switch. This text assumes you have at least a VGA display card and color monitor.

Because ray traced images have such realistic and subtle coloring, the ultimate display hardware for viewing these images is a 16- or 24-bit true color display card. These are graphics cards, like Truevision's Targa series, that can display up to 16.7 million colors onscreen at once. They are called 16- and 24-bit cards because they use 16 or 24 bits of display memory to store the color of each pixel. A standard VGA card uses 8 bits of display memory for each pixel, so it can only display a maximum of 256 colors at once. True color cards and monitors used to be very expensive, but they are now very affordable ($99) and are included as standard equipment on many new computers.

You may not need to buy a special card to see the images in true color. Many Super VGA cards now use special chips like the Sierra High Color chip to be able to display 16- and 24-bit true color. Check your display card's manual to see if the card supports this option.

DISK SPACE

POV-Ray creates image files that can be quite large. An image 640 pixels high by 480 pixels wide created for a Super VGA display consumes almost 1 megabyte (MB) of disk space. You'll want to have at least 5MB of hard disk space available before you install POV-Ray. The more space you can free up, the better. A good starting point is 10MB of available hard disk space. Ray tracing is addictive, and you'll be using up all of your free disk space before you know it!

MEMORY

You will need a minimum of 2MB of RAM to run POV-Ray and to create the example scenes. POV-Ray has a virtual memory manager built in which will use your hard disk as virtual memory: Virtual memory disk swapping can slow down processing, however, so more RAM is highly recommended. Some of the sample scenes bundled with this book require more than 4MB of RAM. Memory has become one of the least expensive components of a computer system, so you should try to have as much as possible. POV-Ray does not require a memory manager but it is compatible with most popular memory managers.

OPERATING ENVIRONMENT

The version of POV-Ray bundled with this book is a protected mode DOS application and is intended to be run from the MS-DOS prompt. You may run POV-Ray in a DOS box under Windows, but there are restrictions on using preview displays. Several programmers have written Windows applications that configure and launch POV-Ray in a DOS box. You can find this on CompuServe. POV-Ray can run as a DOS application under OS/2. POV-Ray will not run under Desqview or Desqview/X. Check the GRAPHDEV forum on CompuServe for possible new versions of POV-Ray; new versions and features are constantly being developed.

INSTALLING POV-RAY

This section describes the steps required to install the bundled POV-Ray software on your hard disk. It assumes you understand the basic DOS commands, the names of your disk drives, and how to edit a DOS batch file.

Table 2-2 Directories Created by the Install Program

Directory	Contains
\POVRAY	Executable files for POV-Ray and all utilities needed for this book.
\POVRAY\INCLUDE	Standard POV-Ray include files.
\POVRAY\CHAPTER2	Sample scenes used in Chapter 2.
\POVRAY\CHAPTER3	Sample scenes used in Chapter 3.
\POVRAY\CHAPTER4	Sample scenes used in Chapter 4.
\POVRAY\CHAPTER5	Sample scenes used in Chapter 5.
\POVRAY\CHAPTER6	Sample scenes used in Chapter 6.
\POVRAY\CHAPTER7	Sample scenes used in Chapter 7.
\POVRAY\SAMPLES	Sample scene files that are normally distributed with POV-Ray.
\POVRAY\DOCS	Documentation files that are normally distributed with POV-Ray.
\POVRAY\UTIL	Several directories of support files for the utilities bundled with this book.

The installation process for POV-Ray is quite simple. The files on the bundled disk have been compressed using a special program called LHA so that more information would fit on the disk. The installation procedure will decompress those files and copy them onto your hard drive. The Install program will also create directories on your disk to store these files. Table 2-2 lists the directories created by the POV-Ray installation program and their contents after the installation. Before starting to install, you should make a copy of the bundled disk and use the copy for installation. Store the original in a safe place in case something happens to the backup.

To begin the installation, put the included disk in drive A or B. (If you are running Windows, you'll need to go into a DOS session to execute these commands.) Type the following at the DOS prompt:

```
C:\>A:\INSTALL (ENTER)
```

```
LHA's SFX 2.13L (c) Yoshi, 1991

─────────────────────────────────────────────────────────────
The Waite Group's Ray Tracing Creations By Drew Wells and Chris Young

This program will automatically install the Persistence of Vision
Raytracer (POV-Ray) and all of its associated programs
to the current drive.
It also creates the directory \POVRAY and several
subdirectories of \POVRAY.
It requires 5 megabytes of free hard disk storage.

If you do not want POV-Ray installed on the current hard drive,
type N at the prompt below.
─────────────────────────────────────────────────────────────
Do you wish to continue installing POV-Ray? [Y/N] Y
/POVRAY/POVRAY.EXE ...............
/POVRAY/POVRAY.DEF .
/POVRAY/PICEM.EXE ....
/POVRAY/INCLUDE/COLORS.INC .
/POVRAY/INCLUDE/SHAPES.INC .
/POVRAY/INCLUDE/SHAPES2.INC .
/POVRAY/INCLUDE/SHAPESQ.INC .
/POVRAY/INCLUDE/TEXTURES.INC
```

Figure 2-1   POV-Ray Install in Progress

Or if you put the bundled disk in drive B then you should type

`C:\>B:\INSTALL`(ENTER)

instead of A:\INSTALL.

If you wish to install to a hard disk other than C, then you should change
to that drive before typing the Install command.

The Install program displays a block of text telling you that it plans to
install the software and how much disk space it will take. At the bottom of the
text is a line that says:

`Do you wish to continue installing POV-Ray? [Y/N]`

If you've made a mistake and want to install the software to another disk
drive or you would like to quit and free up some disk space, you can abort the
installation before it begins transferring files. If you need to, quit the Install
program by pressing ⓝ. If everything looks fine and you want to proced with
the installation, answer ⓨ and let the Install program decompress and copy
the files to your hard drive. Your screen will look similar to Figure 2-1 while the
software is being installed. When it finishes, the program will display a message
saying the installation is completed.

CONFIGURING YOUR SYSTEM

Once the Install program has transferred the files to your hard disk, you'll need to configure your system to work with POV-Ray. You'll add the directory \POVRAY to your DOS path so you can run the program from any directory on your hard disk. Then you'll use a DOS environment variable to set special global options for the ray tracer.

ADDING POV-RAY TO YOUR DOS PATH

The scene files we'll be using with POV-Ray are stored in a different directory than the program, so you'll need to add the directory \POVRAY to your DOS PATH environment variable. \POVRAY is where the POV-Ray executable programs are stored. As you probably know, the DOS PATH variable is a list of directories where DOS will look for executable programs it can't find in the current directory. Once you've set your path correctly, you'll be able to create images in any directory.

You should already have a PATH statement in your AUTOEXEC.BAT file. Load your AUTOEXEC.BAT file into a text editor and look for a line something like this:

```
PATH=C:\;C:\DOS;C:\WP51
```

(No doubt your path will list different directories than ours.) Once you've found the line, add the directory \POVRAY to the end of the PATH so it looks something like this:

```
PATH=C:\;C:\DOS;C:\WP51;C:\POVRAY
```

If you don't see a PATH line in your AUTOEXEC.BAT, add the following line. If you installed POV-Ray to a hard disk other than C, substitute that drive letter.

```
PATH=C:\POVRAY
```

Make sure you've got the spelling correct, save the file, and exit the editor. The changes to the PATH won't take effect until your computer is rebooted.

SETTING THE POVRAYOPT
ENVIRONMENT VARIABLE

POV-Ray includes many options that affect how it runs on your system. You
can specify these options on the command line when you run the program, but
to reduce your typing you can add the options you use frequently to the
POVRAYOPT environment variable. (See "Command-Line Switches" in
Chapter 7 for details on specifying switches.) POV-Ray will read the options in
the environment variable no matter what directory you're in on the hard disk,
so it's a good place to store global settings. If you wish to use different options
later, any that you set directly on the command line will override the global
POVRAYOPT options.

Add the POVRAYOPT environment variable to your AUTOEXEC.BAT
now so it's set every time you turn on your computer.

We'll set the global options for:

- Setting the default image size
- Allowing you to interrupt with a keypress while POV-Ray is creating an
  image
- Showing the line numbers being worked on during the image's creation
- Specifying the POV-Ray library path where the ray tracer looks for extra
  files

Load AUTOEXEC.BAT into a text editor and add this line at the top of
the file:

```
SET POVRAYOPT=+W120 +H90 +X +V +LC:\POVRAY\INCLUDE
```

(Note that we show the command switches in POVRAYOPT in uppercase
for clarity, but you can type them in lowercase if you wish.)

Examine the SET POVRAYOPT command. The first two options,
+W120 and +H90, establish the default image width and height in pixels. An
image traced with these options in effect will be 120 pixels wide by 90 pixels
high. This is a small image and a good setting for quick image tests. You can
create your final image at any width and height as long as you have enough
memory. The 120x90 size is also useful because it has the same width-to-height
ratio as a Super VGA screen. It will have the same proportions when created at
larger sizes like 640x480 and 800x600.

The +X option tells the program to watch for a keypress and if any key is
pressed, to stop creating the image and quit to DOS. This is useful if you

decide that you don't want to complete an image. The +V option causes the program to display the number of the line being worked on while creating the image. This will give you an idea of how far along POV-Ray is in the process of rendering an image.

The last option you need to set is +L, the library path. The +L option is very much like the DOS Path statement. It lets POV-Ray know where to look for Include files it can't find in the current directory. Include files (they have the suffix .INC) are written in the scene description language and contain predefined scene elements. These free you from having to create all the elements in a scene from scratch. The directory \POVRAY\INCLUDE contains several standard Include files. You won't use these to create your first image, but they'll become a large part of every image you create after that. (See Appendix A for an overview of the Include files and a complete listing of their contents.)

When POVRAYOPT is set correctly, save the file, exit to DOS, and reboot your computer so the new settings will take affect.

READY TO RUN!

You've installed and configured the software. Now you're ready to do some ray tracing. The next section describes how to create and view your first ray traced image.

HOW TO USE POV-RAY

Creating images in any medium can get confusing if you don't know what to expect. Ray tracing is no exception. Figure 2-2 shows the steps you follow to create and view a ray traced picture.

CREATING A SCENE FILE

Now let's walk through the steps from idea to finished image, following the diagram in Figure 2-2.

Imagine

Picture a shiny red ball sitting on a green floor. This is a good image to start with. It's easy enough to comprehend, but interesting enough to demonstrate how powerful ray tracing is. Now you need to describe the scene in a way that POV-Ray can understand.

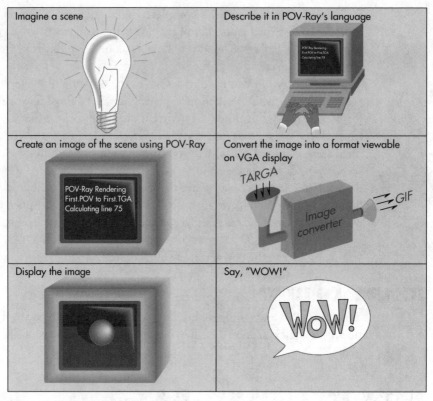

Figure 2-2   Ray Traced Image: Concept to Creation

What Is a Scene File?

A scene file contains the description of a 3D area and all of the objects located in the area. Simple or complex, POV-Ray reads the scene file and creates a 2D picture from the 3D information you provide. It's like a computer snapshot of a scene from your imagination.

The scene file describes the location and properties of each element in the scene and POV-Ray uses this information to create an image with realistic coloring, shading, and perspective. These images are called *photo-realistic* because they are so realistic that people often mistake them for photographs.

A scene file can contain a description of just about any place or object. For instance, the room you're in right now could be described in a scene file. The chair you're sitting in, the book you're reading, the walls around you, and the light from the lamp are all elements of this scene. In the scene file, you describe the material these objects are made of so POV-Ray can create an accurate picture of them. The lighting in the room is also an element of the scene, and you describe that aspect, also. You enter information on where the light is located and what color it is radiating, and the program is able to simulate that light in the scene. Every element is precisely described in a scene file so that the ray tracer can accurately portray them.

The scene file is made up of three types of elements: objects, lights, and a camera. Every scene must have at least one of each type of element. A scene file may have multiple objects and lights, but only one camera. Let's go over these element types.

What Is a Camera?

All scene files must include a camera to view the scene. (POV-Ray does provide a default camera if you don't specify one in the scene file.) The camera is not an actual camera, but a handy analogy that the program uses to make ray tracing easier to understand. You describe the location of the camera and where it's pointing so the program knows how to "look" at the scene.

This camera is not a visible part of the scene because it is "taking a picture" of the scene. When POV-Ray creates an image of a scene, it's as if the image were a snapshot taken from the camera described in the scene file. Without the camera description, POV-Ray wouldn't know how to create the image.

What Is an Object?

Objects are anything you can see, like a ball or a pencil. They can be any size, shape, or material as long as you can describe that size, shape, or material to POV-Ray. When you describe an object in a scene file you tell the program the object's shape and material. For example, a marble sphere, a green cone, and a glass box are all valid objects.

Every object must have a shape and material. An object's shape can look like almost anything. It can be as simple as a ball or as complicated as a steam train. An object's material can be just as diverse. It can range from a shiny, transparent jade to a black, rusty iron.

One scene can have thousands of objects visible to the camera. The first scene you create, however, will have only two visible objects: a shiny red sphere and a green floor.

What Is a Light?

Lights are a special type of object and an exception to the rules. Lights don't have a shape or material, and they aren't visible in a scene, though their effects certainly are. As their name implies, lights illuminate the objects in the scene.

You describe light by location and color. The light casts shadows just like a light in the physical world. And it will create highlights on shiny objects just like in the physical world. A light can be any color or brightness and there can be many lights in a scene. For simplicity, your first scene will have one white light.

DESCRIBING THE SCENE

You know what a scene file is now, but how do you create one? You need to describe the scene in POV-Ray's scene description language.

Scene files are not difficult to create; they are standard ASCII text files that can be read and edited by any word processor or text editor. After you save the file and exit the editor, you start POV-Ray with an option telling it to create an image using your scene file.

Because POV-Ray does not have a built-in scene file editor, you need to have an ASCII text editor to create and edit scene files. The editor that comes with DOS 5.0 or higher, EDIT.EXE, works very well, or if you have Microsoft Windows you can use the Notepad application to create and modify your scene files. You can also use your word processor. Almost all word processors can load and save ASCII text files. Check your word processor's manual to find out what commands you need to use to save and load ASCII text format files.

Now, you can create the scene file. Listing 2-1, FIRST.POV, is a simple and complete scene file. It describes an image of one shiny red ball on a green floor lit by one white light. Notice that the descriptions of the elements in the scene file are in English with some special punctuation—nothing too tricky here.

There are no restrictions on spacing or indentation of scene file text. You can bunch the statements together or spread them out. It is a good idea to use the one-statement-per-line indented style used in this book so that your files can be easily understood.

The scene files in our examples are included on the disk in the directories for each chapter. FIRST.POV can be found in \POVRAY\CHAPTER2. You can save time and effort by using these files instead of typing in the listings by hand. If you choose to type the listings in, though, make sure you've got the spelling and punctuation correct. If you type `lite_source` instead of `light_source` the program won't know you mean a lamp and not a place to buy low-cal food. Also, note that POV-Ray is case sensitive. Typing "Object" or "OBJECT" instead of "object" will generate an error.

Even if you don't type the listing in, load FIRST.POV into your editor to make sure the file was copied onto your hard disk correctly. Loading it into your editor ensures that you'll be ready to use your editor for the later examples.

If you typed the scene in, save it now in the directory \POVRAY\CHAPTER2 as file name FIRST.POV. Quit from your editor now and go to the DOS prompt.

The scene file should now be complete, in the correct directory, and ready to be used by POV-Ray. You can create an image with it!

Listing 2-1 FIRST.POV

```
// First POV-Ray scene - A shiny red ball on a green floor.
camera {
  location <0 1 -2>
  look_at <0 1 2>
}
object {
  sphere { <0 1 2> 1 }
  texture { color red 1 phong 1}
}
object {
  plane { <0 1 0> 0  }
  texture { color green 1 }
 }
object {
  light_source { <3 3 -3> color red 1 green 1 blue 1 }
}
```

RENDERING THE SCENE FILE

As shown in Figure 2-2, the next step is to *render* the scene file. Creating an image with a ray tracer is referred to as rendering the image. You are now going to render the scene file FIRST.POV using the POV-Ray software.

Running POV-Ray

To make sure you're in the POV-Ray examples directory, at the DOS prompt, type

`C:\>CD \POVRAY\CHAPTER2` ENTER

You're now in the directory where FIRST.POV is stored. Before you start to render the file, make sure the environment variable POVRAYOPT is set correctly. At the DOS prompt, type

`C:\POVRAY\CHAPTER2>SET ENTER`

Several lines should be listed. One of them should look like this:

`POVRAYOPT=+W120 +H90 +X +V +LC:\POVRAY\INCLUDE`

(The switch letters, like +W and +H, will be in lowercase if you typed them that way; that's okay.) If you don't see this line, then you should go back to the section on setting the POVRAYOPT environment variable and make sure you went through all the steps correctly. You need to have this variable set for the examples to work correctly.

Now run POV-Ray to begin rendering the scene file. Type at the DOS prompt

`C:\POVRAY\chapter 2>POVRAY +IFIRST.POV +OFIRST.TGA E`

The +I and +O Options

The command-line option +I<filename>.POV tells the program which scene file to use as input—in this case, FIRST.POV. The command-line option

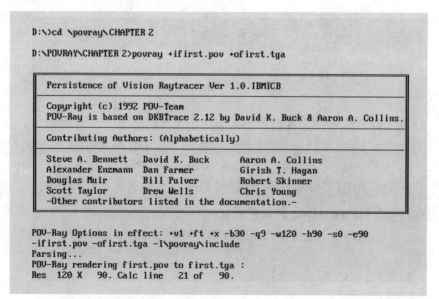

```
D:\>cd \povray\CHAPTER 2

D:\POVRAY\CHAPTER 2>povray +ifirst.pov +ofirst.tga

    ┌─────────────────────────────────────────────────────────────┐
    │ Persistence of Vision Raytracer Ver 1.0.IBMICB                │
    │                                                               │
    │ Copyright (c) 1992 POV-Team                                   │
    │ POV-Ray is based on DKBTrace 2.12 by David K. Buck & Aaron A. Collins. │
    │                                                               │
    │ Contributing Authors: (Alphabetically)                        │
    │                                                               │
    │ Steve A. Bennett    David K. Buck      Aaron A. Collins       │
    │ Alexander Enzmann   Dan Farmer         Girish T. Hagan        │
    │ Douglas Muir        Bill Pulver        Robert Skinner         │
    │ Scott Taylor        Drew Wells         Chris Young            │
    │ -Other contributors listed in the documentation.-             │
    └─────────────────────────────────────────────────────────────┘

POV-Ray Options in effect: +v1 +ft +x -b30 -q9 -w120 -h90 -s0 -e90
-ifirst.pov -ofirst.tga -l\povray\include
Parsing...
POV-Ray rendering first.pov to first.tga :
Res 120 X  90. Calc line   21 of   90.
```

Figure 2-3 POV-Ray Title Screen and Rendering in Progress

+O<filename>.TGA tells the program to output the newly created image to the file <filename>.TGA—in this case FIRST.TGA. (Again, you can enter the I and O in lowercase if you wish.)

After you press (ENTER) POV-Ray goes to work and begins to create an image from your first scene file. Your screen should look like Figure 2-3. Notice that the "Options in effect" line on the opening screen includes the options from the POVRAYOPT environment variable you set earlier. The image should take a few seconds to render.

Errors

Murphy's Law says, "Anything that can go wrong, will go wrong." So if you get an error message when you first try to render the file, don't let it worry you. You've probably made some small spelling mistake either in typing FIRST.POV or on the command line when you tried to run POV-Ray. Examine the error message to find out where you went wrong. If you made a spelling mistake in the scene file, POV-Ray will tell you which line it didn't understand and you can check it against Listing 2-1. You might have entered one of the options incorrectly when you set POVRAYOPT, or you might have neglected to put the \POVRAY directory in your path. (In the latter case, DOS will give you the "Bad Command or File Name" error message.) If you can't figure out what the problem is from the error message, carefully go back over the steps of installing POV-Ray and creating FIRST.POV to make sure you did everything correctly.

RENDERING IN PROGRESS

What is POV-Ray doing during the rendering process? First, it reads your scene file, FIRST.POV, and translates your description into a numeric format so it's easier for the computer to work with. While you're waiting for the file to finish rendering, the program is performing many floating-point math calculations on the converted scene file information and outputting the image line-by-line to a file called FIRST.TGA. The program also displays the line number it's calculating as it works.

This picture won't take long to render because this is a small version of a very simple scene. If you have a fast computer, it will be finished in just a few seconds! If you press a key while the program is rendering, it will stop the rendering and quit to DOS. If this happens, just start the program rendering again and let it finish correctly. You'll need a completed image file in the next section.

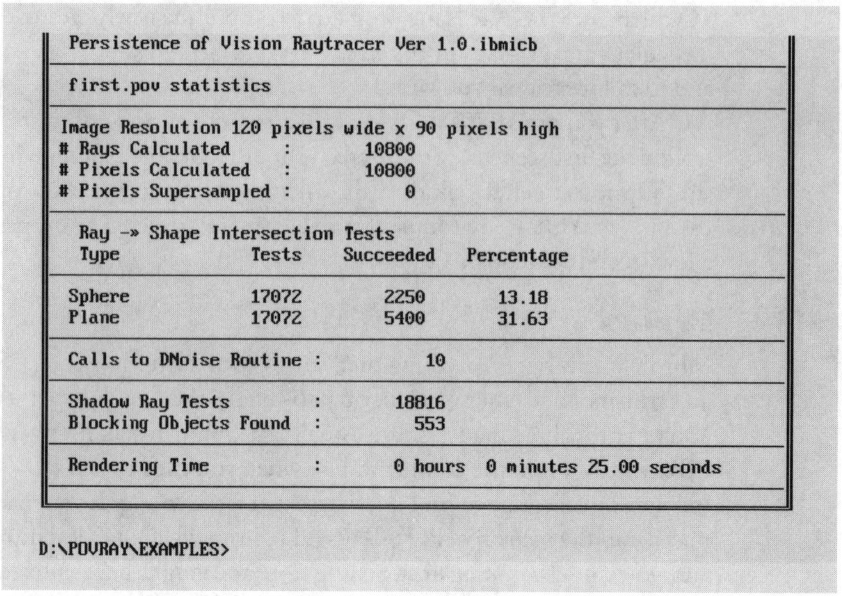

```
 ┌─────────────────────────────────────────────────────────────┐
 │  Persistence of Vision Raytracer Ver 1.0.ibmicb              │
 ├─────────────────────────────────────────────────────────────┤
 │  first.pov statistics                                        │
 ├─────────────────────────────────────────────────────────────┤
 │  Image Resolution 120 pixels wide x 90 pixels high           │
 │  # Rays Calculated    :        10800                         │
 │  # Pixels Calculated  :        10800                         │
 │  # Pixels Supersampled :          0                          │
 ├─────────────────────────────────────────────────────────────┤
 │   Ray -» Shape Intersection Tests                            │
 │   Type            Tests      Succeeded    Percentage         │
 ├─────────────────────────────────────────────────────────────┤
 │   Sphere          17072        2250         13.18            │
 │   Plane           17072        5400         31.63            │
 ├─────────────────────────────────────────────────────────────┤
 │   Calls to DNoise Routine :         10                       │
 ├─────────────────────────────────────────────────────────────┤
 │   Shadow Ray Tests        :       18816                      │
 │   Blocking Objects Found  :         553                      │
 ├─────────────────────────────────────────────────────────────┤
 │   Rendering Time          :     0 hours  0 minutes 25.00 seconds │
 └─────────────────────────────────────────────────────────────┘

  D:\POVRAY\EXAMPLES>
```

Figure 2-4 POV-Ray Statistics Screen

When the program has rendered the image, it displays a list of statistics and exits to DOS. Figure 2-4 shows the screen when POV-Ray has completed rendering FIRST.POV.

The statistics displayed after POV-Ray is done rendering are a breakdown of the work it did to create an image from your scene file. Each statistic represents many sets of calculations. The more complicated the picture, the higher the numbers will be in the statistics. When you are adept at creating scene files, you can use these numbers to help you make changes in your scene file that will speed up the calculation of your scenes.

CONVERTING TARGA TO GIF

The image you just created is stored in a file called FIRST.TGA. This file is in a special image format called Targa, which was originally created by Truevision for use with its 24-bit Targa display cards. It is now commonly used for storing pictures with realistic and accurate coloring like scanned and ray traced images. Most image file formats like PCX and GIF can use a maximum of only 256

Why doesn't POV-Ray output GIF files?
Why does POV-Ray go to the trouble of outputting Targa files that can use up to 16.7 million colors when most users have to convert the image to a 256-color GIF to view it?

When POV-Ray is rendering an image it does very accurate floating-point calculations to determine the color and shading of each object in a scene. These color values can be stored without special conversion directly in a Targa file. When the image is finished rendering, specialized programs like TGA2GIF can analyze the entire image and pick the best 256 colors to display the image on a VGA screen. It is impossible to determine the best 256 colors for an image without first having the entire image. POV-Ray outputs the image as it's working on it, so there's no way for it to ascertain the best 256 colors while it is rendering. POV-Ray leaves that job up to post-processing programs such as TGA2GIF that are specifically designed to do that.

---

colors, but that's not enough for the subtle colors and shading in a ray traced image. A Targa file can have as many as 16.7 million colors! Of course, not every Targa file uses all 16.7 million colors; that's the maximum you can use in an image. If you have a monitor and display card capable of displaying Targa files, you can enjoy the image files in all their glory. If you've got a VGA display, take heart, you can still view these amazing images.

Because the files that POV-Ray creates have so many colors, they can't be directly viewed on a VGA display. VGA can only display 256 colors out of a palette of 262,000 colors. That works great for GIF and PCX files, but it's not enough to view all the colors in a Targa file. Therefore, you'll have to convert the 16.7 million-color Targa file to a 256-color GIF file to view it on a VGA display. You'll want to be sure to pick the best 256 colors to use, so the GIF image looks as much like the Targa image as possible. But how do you do this?

Fortunately, the program TGA2GIF bundled with your book does a fantastic job of automatically picking the best 256 colors to use in the GIF and converting the file to GIF format.

Simply type TGA2GIF followed by the file name with no extension like this:

`C:\POVRAY\CHAPTER2> TGA2GIF FIRST` (ENTER)

Figure 2-5 Your First Ray Traced Scene

The program looks for the file FIRST.TGA and creates the file FIRST.GIF. A number of command-line options are available with TGA2GIF. For complete details see the file \POVRAY\UTIL\TGA2GIF\TGA2GIF.DOC on your disk. You may also use any other utilities you might have for Targa to GIF conversion.

VIEWING A GIF FILE

It's time to view your first creation. You imagined a scene, created a description of it in POV-RAY's scene language, rendered it with POV-Ray, converted it from a 16.7 million-color Targa file to a 256-color GIF file using TGA2GIF, and now you finally get to see it!

The GIF viewer program Picem was transferred onto your hard drive when you installed POV-Ray. (If you have a favorite GIF file viewer, you can use it instead of Picem.) To use Picem, type at the DOS prompt

`C:\POVRAY\CHAPTER2>PICEM FIRST.GIF` (ENTER)

Picem automatically detects what type of VGA display you have, clears the screen to black, and displays FIRST.GIF. In the middle of your screen should be a small image. It should look like Figure 2-5, an accurately shaded, shiny red ball on a green floor. You can press ⒯⒜⒝ to make the image fill the entire screen.

Congratulations, you've just rendered, converted, and viewed your first POV-Ray scene! Notice how smooth and realistic the shading is and notice the highlight on the sphere. This is the simplest scene you can create with POV-Ray and it makes most other computer graphics look like doodling. The shadow of the ball is mathematically correct and you didn't even have to describe it! The ray tracer created it automatically by simulating the effects of light in the scene.

Because rendering, converting, and viewing files will be done dozens and dozens of times in this book, a handy batch file, POV.BAT, has been included in the \POVRAY directory. It renders a file, reroutes the rendering statistics to a text file, converts the Targa output to GIF, and views it with Picem. See Listing 2-2 for the commands it uses.

With this batch file you can accomplish all of the steps we went through by hand by simply typing

```
C:\POVRAY\CHAPTER2> POV FIRST ⒺⓃⓉⒺⓇ
```

The file FIRST.POV is rendered and the statistics are sent to a plain text file FIRST.LOG for you to look at later. POVRAY outputs FIRST.TGA which is converted to FIRST.GIF by TGA2GIF. The GIF is then displayed with Picem. You may wish to modify this batch to add custom command-line options or to delete the TGA file once it has been converted to GIF.

Other POVRAY command-line options may follow the file name. For example to render the same file at higher resolution try

```
C:\POVRAY\CHAPTER2> POV FIRST +W320 +H200 ⒺⓃⓉⒺⓇ
```

Now let's look at the FIRST.POV scene file in more detail. In the next section, you'll learn exactly what all the words and punctuation mean, and how they determine what the image will look like.

Listing 2-2 POV.BAT

```
POVRAY +I%1.POV +O%1.TGA %2 %3 %4 %5 %6 %7 > %1.LOG
TGA2GIF %1
PICEM %1.GIF
```

UNDERSTANDING FIRST.POV

The language used to create the scene file FIRST.POV is not difficult to understand. You'll find a complete description of the POV-Ray language in Chapter 7, including an explanation of the syntax notation used in this book.

COMMENTS

The first line in FIRST.POV is

```
// First POV-Ray scene - A shiny red ball on a green floor.
```

This line is a comment and is ignored by the ray tracer. The double slashes (//) introduce a comment and everything that follows them on the same line is ignored by the program. A comment can be on a line by itself or following scene information on the same line.

Comments are extra information for anyone reading the file. They usually identify a section of the scene or explain something to the reader. You should use comments liberally because good comments make scene files much easier to read.

THE CAMERA

The next part of the scene is the camera:

```
camera {
  location <0 1 -2>
  look_at <0 1 2>
}
```

Though the camera is not a visible object, every scene must have a camera description. The camera information allows the program to simulate a virtual camera that POV-Ray uses to "take a snapshot" of the scene.

The camera, like many other POV-Ray language statements, starts with an open curly brace ({) and ends with a closing brace (}). The information between the two braces is called the *body* of the statement, or in this case, the camera body. The camera body tells POV-Ray where to put the camera (location), and where to point the camera (look_at).

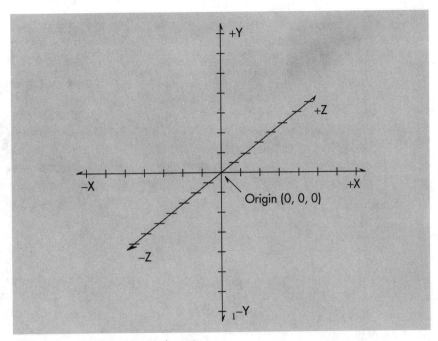

Figure 2-6 The X, Y, and Z Coordinate Axes

Specifying Location

The camera body starts with the line:

```
location <0 1 -2>
```

Location describes the position of the virtual camera. Its syntax is

```
location <point>
```

The three numbers enclosed in the brackets constitute a *vector*. This partic-ular vector is used to specify the *x, y,* and *z coordinates* of the camera's location. They describe the exact point where the camera is in relation to the *x, y,* and *z coordinate axes.*

X, Y, and Z Coordinates

If you've ever had a geometry class, you'll remember describing a point using *x, y,* and *z* coordinates and the *x, y,* and *z* coordinate axes. Figure 2-6 is a picture of

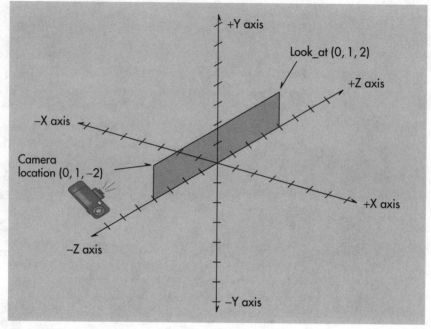

Figure 2-7 Camera Location and the Look_At Point

the coordinate axes. The axes aren't objects in a scene. They are an abstract concept used to make working in three dimensions easier.

The point where the axes meet is called the *origin*, which has the coordinates <0 0 0>. The location of a point in a scene is described by specifying how far the point is from the origin on each of the three axes. The first number, the *x* coordinate, tells POV-Ray how far to the right or to the left of the origin the point is on the *x* axis. Positive *x* values are to the right of the origin and negative *x* values are to the left of it.

The second number, the *y* coordinate, tells the program how far up or down from the origin the point is on the *y* axis. Positive *y* values are above the origin and negative *y* values are below it.

The third number, the *z* coordinate, describes how far in front of or behind the origin the point is on the *z* axis. Positive *z* values extend into the screen in the same way that the numbered page of a book extend away from you in increasing numbers. The negative *z* values extend toward you, away from the origin.

The location of the camera in this scene is $x=0$, right in the middle of the x axis; $y=1$, 1 unit above the origin on the y axis; and $z=-2$, 2 units toward you from the origin on the z axis. Figure 2-7 shows the camera in relation to the axes.

The units used in the program do not directly correspond to any measurement in the real world. They can represent any unit of length or size you prefer as long as you are consistent in your usage. Units can range in value from approximately 0.05 to 10,000,000. (Note: Internally, POV-Ray uses many values that are as small as 0.0000000001 but for technical reasons 0.05 is the lower limit for the location and size of objects.)

If it helps you to visualize the scene, think of a unit as being equal to 1 meter. This analogy would put the camera 1 meter above the origin and 2 meters behind it (toward you).

POINTING THE CAMERA WITH LOOK_AT

Look_at tells POV-Ray what point the camera is looking at. Its syntax is

```
look_at < point >
```

In FIRST.POV, the look_at statement is

```
look_at <0 1 2>
```

The camera is aimed straight ahead at a point 1 unit above the origin and 2 units in front of it. Figure 2-7 illustrates the camera and the look_at point where the camera is aimed.

CONSTRUCTING OBJECTS

Basic objects in POV-Ray are made up of a shape and a material. A shape is the form of an object. An object could be cubical, cylindrical, or cone shaped, for example. A material is what the shape is made out of, and it determines how the surface of the shape appears. A shape could be shiny, reflective, purple, marble colored, or transparent, for example. Materials are called *textures* in the scene language and shapes are referred to by their names. The syntax for a basic object is

```
object {
  shape { ... }
  texture { ... }
}
```

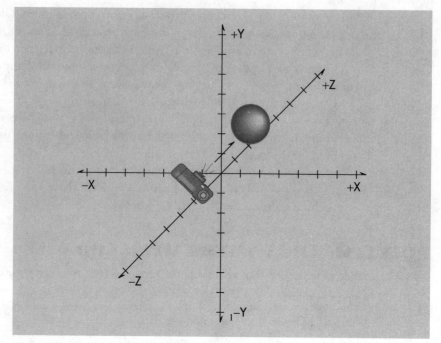

Figure 2-8 Sphere with Camera and Coordinate Axes

As with the camera, the information between the braces after the word *object* is called the *object body*. This scene has two basic objects: a sphere and a plane.

The Sphere

Baseballs, globes, jawbreakers, and oranges are all spheres. The sphere is probably the most common shape in the world and so in ray tracing as well. Because spheres are so common in ray tracing, they have been highly optimized to render quickly. You only have to specify a center point and a radius to describe a sphere. The sphere shape is used in the first object:

```
object {
  sphere { <0 1 2> 1 }
  texture { color red 1 phong 1}
  }
```

The syntax for a sphere is

```
sphere { <center_point> radius }
```

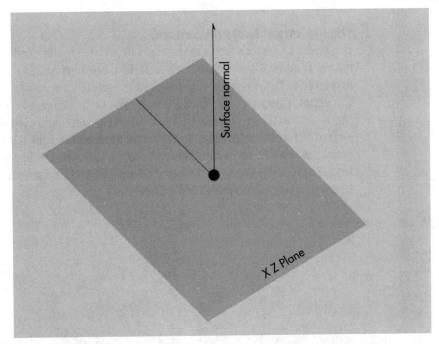

Figure 2-9 Plane Surface Normal

The radius of a sphere is half of its width, so the sphere in FIRST.POV is actually 2 units wide. Figure 2-8 shows the sphere in relation to the coordinate axes and the camera.

Notice that the center of the sphere's *y* coordinate is set to the same value as its radius, so the bottom of the sphere rests at *y*=0, which is where the floor will be. The next part of the object body is the texture.

The Plane

The "floor" in the scene is actually a plane. A plane is completely flat and it is infinitely wide and long. The second object in FIRST.POV is a plane:

```
object {
  plane { <0 1 0> 0 }
  texture { color green 1 }
}
```

Although it looks similar, the method of describing a plane is very different from that of the camera and sphere. The syntax for a plane is

```
plane { <surface_normal> location }
```

What Is Normal About the Surface?

The phrase *surface normal* is confusing. Contrary to regular English usage, the word "normal" is the noun and "surface" is the adjective. The "normal" is the vector that describes the slope of the surface at a particular point. This vector is simply a line that is perpendicular to the surface at that point. The surface normal is important to ray tracing because light reflects off a surface differently depending on the angle between the light ray and the normal as well as the angle between the normal and the line of sight between the viewer and the surface. For more on surface normals see the Chapter 7 entry on *NORMAL_PATTERNS*.

Cuts straight through center of the sphere

Figure 2-10a   Plane at Y=1

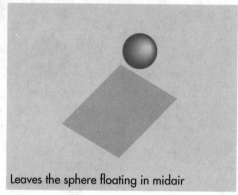

Leaves the sphere floating in midair

Figure 2-10b   Plane at Y=−1

Instead of a location, the vector describes something called a *surface normal*, which is like a short line that's perpendicular to the surface of a plane. It starts at the origin <0 0 0> and goes up to <0 1 0>. Picture the green floor from FIRST.POV with a nail poking straight up through it, its point aimed at the sky. That nail is oriented like the plane's surface normal. The picture labeled XZ Plane in Figure 2-9 illustrates the surface normal of this plane. It's called the XZ Plane because it stretches out infinitely left, right, backwards, and forwards parallel to the *x* and *z* axes.

If it were defined as <0 0 −1>, the surface normal would start at <0 0 0> and go towards the camera to <0 0 −1> and it would be on the *z* axis. The plane would stretch up and down on the *y* axis and left and right on the *x* axis, and it would look like a wall instead of a floor. The imaginary nail would be pointed at the camera instead of the sky. This is called an *xy* plane.

The location of the plane specifies where the plane is located on its perpendicular axes. The perpendicular axis of the *xz* plane in FIRST.POV is the *y* axis. The plane is located on the center of the *y* axis at *y*=0. If the plane's location were changed to 1.0, it would rise up to *y*=1 and pass straight through the center of the sphere and the camera. Figure 2-10a illustrates this example. If the plane's location were dropped to −1, it would lie 1 unit below the sphere, leaving it floating in mid-air. Figure 2-10b illustrates the latter example.

SPECIFYING TEXTURE

Closely following the sphere shape is the texture of the sphere:

```
texture { color red 1 phong 1}
```

The texture is described in the body of an object (or occasionally in the body of a shape). Textures describe the surface properties of an object and they can be very complex. Color, roughness, reflectiveness, transparency, and bumpiness are just a few of the properties that can be manipulated in a texture. This object's texture is simple: red and shiny. The solid red color was created using the keyword `color`. And the keyword `phong` makes the object shiny.

Color and Its Components

Creating colors in POV-Ray is a lot like mixing paint, but instead of paint, you mix colored light. Instead of a white canvas and a palette full of colors, you start with a black screen and are given only three colors of light to add. These three primary colors of light are red, greeen and blue. If you look at a color TV screen or computer monitor with a magnifying glass, you'll notice the screen is made of tiny clusters of red, green, and blue dots. Almost any color can be created at each cluster point on the screen by specifying the brightness of red, green, and blue light. The screen adds these three primary colors together to create the entire range of colors. This is called additive or RGB color and it's modeled after the way light works in the physical world. You may be familiar with color design using paints, inks, or stained glass which use subtractive color. Subtractive color starts with white and uses a different set of primary colors: red, yellow, and blue. POV-Ray uses the additive method of creating colors.

The syntax for color in POV-Ray is

```
color  red amount    green amount  blue amount
```

The *amount* is any number from 0.0 to 1.0, where 1.0 means that 100 percent of the light is of this color. For instance, sky blue is made up of 20 percent red, 60 percent green and 80 percent blue. You write that in a scene file as

```
color red .2 green .6 blue .8
```

If the amount of the red, green, or blue component is to be zero you don't need to specify that color component. For example, the sphere's color in FIRST.POV is 100 percent red with no green or blue color. It is described as

```
color red 1
```

The red ball in FIRST.POV was not completely red, though. It had a white highlight that made the ball look shiny. The highlight was added to the texture by using the word `phong`.

Phong Highlights

A highlight is created by light in a scene reflecting off shiny surfaces oriented towards the viewer. It's a difficult task for a traditional artist to create accurate highlights on all the objects in a scene. The shape, color, smoothness, and position of the highlighted object have to be considered, as well as the color and position of the light or lights creating the highlights. So many factors have to be considered that many capable artists just ignore highlights altogether.

Accurate highlights greatly enhance the realism of an image, though, if they can be done correctly. POV-Ray can render accurate highlights automatically just by using the name of the scientist who created the method for calculating them. Bui Tuong Phong created the original highlighting procedure in 1973. POV-Ray uses a variant of it that is invoked by using the keyword `phong`. The syntax for adding a phong highlight to an object's texture is

```
texture {
  ...
  phong amount
}
```

The phong statement must be in the texture body, though it can appear before or after other texture components like color. The *amount* is a number from 0.0 to 1.0 that represents the *saturation* of the highlight by the light creating it. A value of 0.5 means the highlight will have half of the object's color and half of the coloring of the light creating it. A value of 1.0 means the highlight will be completely saturated by the color of the light creating it. It will be made up of 100 percent of the creating light's color.

SPECIFYING THE LIGHT SOURCE

The last object in FIRST.POV is the exception to the earlier rules about objects. This object doesn't have a shape or texture and it isn't visible in the scene. It contains a light source:

```
object {
    light_source { <3 3 –3> color red 1 green 1 blue 1 }
}
```

The light source syntax is similar to the sphere syntax:

```
light_source { <location> color red amount  green amount blue
amount }
```

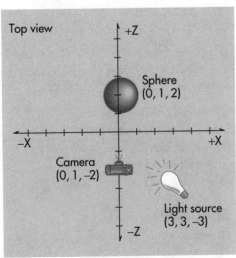
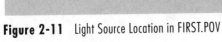
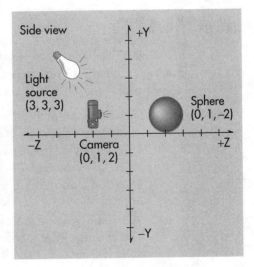

Figure 2-11 Light Source Location in FIRST.POV

The *<location>* is the point where all of the light in this scene originates. This light's location is at the point <3 3 –3>. It is 3 units to the right on the *x* axis, 3 units up on the *y* axis, and 3 units back on the *z* axis. Figure 2-11 illustrates the light source's position relative to the other objects in FIRST.POV.

Earlier, this object was described as an exception to the rules. Don't call the ray tracing police just yet, this object isn't actually breaking the rules, just interpreting them differently for your convenience.

POV-Ray treats light sources as if they were shapes. You can even give the light source a texture if you wish, but that won't have any affect on the light. The light source is stored as a point—it has no size, shape, or material, and it is not visible in a scene even if it's directly in front of the camera. All of the light rays coming from a light source originate from an invisible point. Lights are calculated as points to save time. A true light source shape would cast so many light rays for the program to calculate that you'd be waiting days for it to finish one image. By treating lights as shapes, POV-Ray enables you to add them to special objects made out of multiple shapes. Using this technique, you can create objects like desk lamps, car headlights, or track lighting.

SUMMARY

Through this chapter, you installed and configured the POV-Ray software package, created your first scene file, rendered a ray traced image, and learned some basics about the POV-Ray scene language.

- These are some of the options for the POV-Ray program:
  +W#### sets the width of the ray traced image in pixels.
  +H#### sets the height of the image in pixels.
  +V turns on the work-in-progress text messages.
  +X tells the ray tracer to allow an abort with a keypress during rendering.
  +L tells POV where to look for additional Include files.
  +I<filename>.POV specifies the input scene file name.
  +O<filename>.TGA specifies the output image file name.

- A scene file is a description of the objects in a scene, the light sources illuminating those objects, and the camera with which to view the scene.
- You create a scene file using a standard ASCII text editor.
- Ray tracing simulates the effect of light in a scene to create a photo-realistic image with accurate shading, colors, shadows, and highlights.
- A basic object is made up of a shape and a texture. A texture is the material from which an object or shape is made.
- A sphere is the most common shape in ray tracing and is highly optimized to render quickly.
- Phong highlights are named after Bui Tuong Phong, who originally wrote the procedure to create them in 1973.
- Light sources are not really shapes, but are treated as shapes by the ray tracer in order to make them easier to use.

And as the imagination bodies forth the forms of things unknown, the poet's pen turns them to shapes.

—*A Midsummer-Night's Dream,*
William Shakespeare

3

Basic Shapes

WHAT IS A SHAPE?

A shape is the outline or form of an object. A basketball's basic shape is a sphere. The basic shape of a pen is a cylinder. A megaphone is essentially a cone. Every object you see has some basic shape. Figure 3-1 illustrates a few objects and their basic shapes.

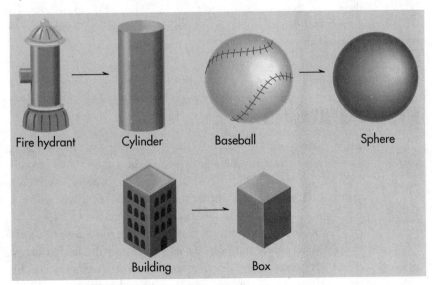

Figure 3-1   Some Objects and Their Basic Shapes

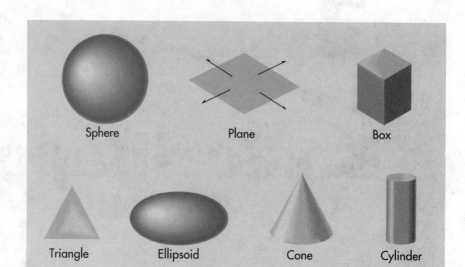

Figure 3-2 Some POV-Ray Basic Shapes

Shapes are the foundation of objects in ray tracing. Each object in a scene file is made up of a shape and a texture. The first step in building a scene is to describe the shapes that make up each object. The basic shapes in POV-Ray are the sphere, box, ellipsoid, cone, and cylinder. Figure 3-2 illustrates some of these basic shapes. Many objects are made out of more than one basic shape, of course, but before you start to combine shapes, you need to be able to handle the basic shapes.

THE SPHERE

You've already used the sphere (the red ball) in your first scene, FIRST.POV. The sphere is the simplest and most basic shape: it's a shape which often appears in nature. The planets and stars are spheres (well, approximately), many fruits are spherical, and astronomers used to call the universe the "Heavenly Sphere." Figure 3-3 shows a variety of ray traced spheres.

To create a sphere with the ray tracer, use the keyword `sphere` and then give the location of the point at its center and the length of its radius. The radius of a sphere is the distance from its center to its surface. Figure 3-4 is a graphic depiction of a sphere's radius. Notice that the radius is half the diameter

Figure 3-3 Spheres

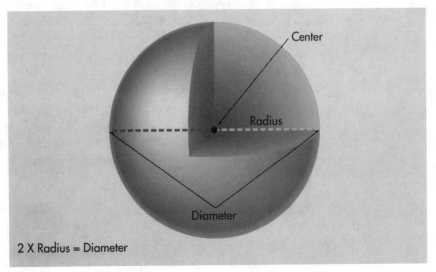

Figure 3-4 Sphere's Radius and Diameter

or width of the sphere. When you create a sphere of radius 1.0, you're telling the ray tracer to make a 2-unit-wide sphere.

THE FASTEST SHAPE

Spheres are the most basic geometric shape and are attractive and easy to create. They are very popular in ray traced pictures and have been widely used since the first ray tracer was created. Because of their simplicity and popularity, the calculations used to render a sphere are highly optimized, making them very fast and efficient. Spheres render faster than any other shape in POV-Ray. Just tell the program where to put the sphere and how big it is and the ray tracer does the rest for you. The syntax for a sphere is

```
sphere { <X Y Z> radius }
```

where *<X Y Z>* is the location of the center of the sphere on the *x, y,* and *z* coordinate axes and *radius* is half the diameter of the sphere. You can locate the sphere at any point and it can be any size you wish: from tiny to gargantuan. This is true of all shapes in ray tracing: you can position and size them any way you like.

REUSING SCENES

Let's create a scene with spheres and use it to demonstrate some points about ray tracing. The foundation of the new scene will be the scene from Chapter 2, FIRST.POV. You'll save a lot of time and effort by reusing elements of scenes and even reusing complete scenes when ray tracing. This is one of the big advantages of computer art over traditional art.

A painter can't reuse a background after she has painted it. If she paints a similar scene, she must duplicate her efforts from the first painting. If she creates a ray traced scene, she can just copy the original scene and reuse it, only modifying the parts that must differ. She could even render the scene from a completely different point of view by moving the camera. You'll do just that in this new scene.

The SPHERE.POV file in the\POVRAY\CHAPTER3 directory is a copy of FIRST.POV with a couple of changes. Two spheres have been added and the floor's color has changed from green to yellow by combining equal parts red and green. Listing 3-1 is the text of SPHERE1.POV. Notice that the scene file has been heavily commented. You could probably understand the scene without them, but with the comments you can tell at a glance how the file works. Later, when the scene file gets more complex, these comments become even

more valuable. It's always a good idea to liberally comment a scene file as you create it.

Listing 3-1 SPHERE1.POV

```
// SPHERE1.POV
// Listing 3-1

// Point straight ahead at the red sphere's center
camera {
  location <0 1 -2>
  look_at <0 1 2>
}
// Original red sphere from FIRST.POV
object {
  sphere { <0 1 2> 1 }
  texture { color red 1 phong 1}
}
// Two new spheres the same size as the red sphere
// A green sphere on the right of the red sphere
object {
  sphere { <3 1 2> 1 }
  texture { color green 1 phong 1}
}
// A blue sphere on the left of the red sphere
object {
  sphere { <-3 1 2> 1 }
  texture { color blue 1 phong 1}
}
// The yellow floor
object {
  plane { <0 1 0> 0  }
    texture { color red 1 green 1 }
}
// A white light behind the camera to the right and above
// Think of it as being behind and above your right shoulder
// as you view the scene
object {
  light_source { <3 5 -3> color red 1 green 1 blue 1 }
}
```

Now render, convert, and view the scene file and we'll go over the changes.

The basic commands are the same for rendering, converting, and viewing any scene file, so after this example, we'll just tell you to render and view the scene file instead of outlining the exact steps. If an example requires different steps, we'll detail them for you as we have done here.

The scene files for this chapter are in the \POVRAY\CHAPTER3 directory. To change to the proper directory and render the file type:

Figure 3-5 Three Spheres with Two Cut Off

```
C:\POVRAY\CHAPTER2> CD \POVRAY\CHAPTER3 (ENTER)
C:\POVRAY\CHAPTER3> POV SPHERE1
```

The POV.BAT file will render, convert and display the file. You should see a picture of three spheres of different colors sitting next to each other with the blue and green spheres on the left and right halfway out of the scene. Figure 3-5 illustrates this.

THE VISIBILITY OF OBJECTS

The blue and green spheres demonstrate that an object doesn't have to be completely visible to the camera to be a part of the scene. And just because an object is in a scene file does not mean that it's visible to the camera. You can describe objects in the scene as being located at any point, but they won't appear in the scene unless they are in front of the camera and within its field of view. You can cut the heads off your subjects with a ray tracing camera just as easily as with your old Instamatic. Fortunately, you can easily correct your ray traced images, unlike the pictures from your camera.

REPOSITIONING THE CAMERA

Since the new objects don't completely fit in the image, you've got to move the camera back so it can view the entire scene. The current camera location is $x=0$, $y=1$, $z=-2$. To move backwards, the camera should be shifted on the z axis in the negative direction. Moving 4 units back should probably correct the image. This gives a new camera location of $x=0$, $y=1$, $z=-6$. Figure 3-6 shows an overhead view of the old and new camera locations. Now you can change the z value of the camera's location (move it 4 units backwards) and save the new file as SPHERE2.POV:

```
camera {
  location <0 1 -2>
  look_at <0 1 2>
}
```

to:

```
camera {
  location <0 1 -6>
  look_at <0 1 2>
}
```

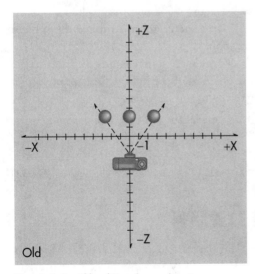
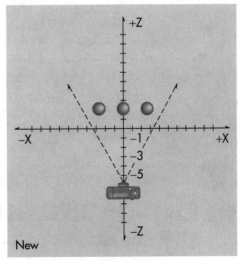

Figure 3-6 Old and New Camera Locations

Figure 3-7 Moving the Camera Back

Render and view SPHERE2.POV. Figure 3-7 shows the result.

Now that the camera is farther back, there's room to move the spheres around in order to demonstrate a few points.

Since the camera has moved back, the light source is now in front of the camera, so the comments about the position of the light source are no longer true. Change the comments above the light_source to read:

```
// A white light in front of the camera to the right and above
// Think of it as being in front of and above your right shoulder
// as you view the scene
```

OVERLAPPING OBJECTS

What happens when two objects are overlapping in a scene? Will the ray tracer generate an error? Let's modify SPHERE2.POV so some objects are overlapping to see how the ray tracer deals with it.

Move the green sphere down 1 unit so only its upper half is above the floor.

The lower half will overlap the floor for the experiment. "Down" is on the *y* axis in the negative direction. Change the sphere's center *y* value from 1 to 0.

```
sphere { <3 1 2> 1 }
```

becomes

```
sphere { <3 0 2> 1 }
```

Move the blue sphere up 1 unit and 2 units to the right so that it perches on the red sphere. "Up" is on the *y* axis in the positive direction. Change the sphere's center *y* value from 1 to 2. "Right" is on the *x* axis in the positive direction, so change the *x* value from –3 to –1.

```
sphere { <-3 1 2> 1 }
```

becomes

```
sphere { <-1 2 2> 1 }
```

We'll leave the red sphere alone. Now save the new scene file as SPHERE3.POV. Listing 3-2 is a complete listing of SPHERE3.POV. Render and view this file. Figure 3-8 shows the resulting image.

Figure 3-8 Overlapping Objects

Listing 3-2 SPHERE3.POV

```
// SPHERE3.POV
// Listing 3-2

// Point straight ahead at the red sphere's center
camera {
  location <0 1 -6>
  look_at <0 1 2>
}
// Original red sphere from FIRST.POV
object {
  sphere { <0 1 2> 1 }
  texture { color red 1 phong 1}
}
// Two new spheres the same size as the red sphere
// A green sphere on the right of the red sphere sinking into the floor
object {
  sphere { <3 0 2> 1 }
  texture { color green 1 phong 1}
}
// A blue sphere on the left of the red sphere overlapping it on top
object {
  sphere { <-1 2 2> 1 }
  texture { color blue 1 phong 1}
}
// The yellow floor
object {
  plane { <0 1 0> 0 }
  texture { color red 1 green 1 }
}

// A white light in front of the camera to the right and above
// Think of it as being in front of and above your right shoulder
// as you view the scene
object {
  light_source { <3 5 -3> color red 1 green 1 blue 1 }
}
```

Obviously, the ray tracer didn't generate an error. It rendered the scene file exactly the way it was described. The blue sphere is overlapping the red sphere. It looks like one object made out of two shapes. It seems a bit like a child's toy falling over. The green sphere is overlapping the floor and looks as if it's sinking into the floor.

POV-Ray enables you to place objects anywhere in a scene. One object can overlap another object or even be enclosed in another object. It's possible to place objects so they appear to be floating. The ray tracer assumes you know exactly what you are doing when you place objects, and it doesn't report an

74

error if an object isn't in the scene, is overlapping another object, or inside another object. You're given the power to create any object you can conjure up, but the program won't protect you from your own mistakes.

A MATTER OF PERSPECTIVE

We stated earlier that a ray tracer creates images with perfect perspective, meaning the apparent size of the objects in the image is relative to their distance from the viewer. Objects close to the viewer look relatively large and objects farther from the viewer look relatively small. In ray tracing, you are the viewer, looking through the ray tracing camera. You saw the effects of perspective in SPHERE2.POV when the camera was moved back. When the camera was close to the objects, they appeared large and when the camera was moved away, the objects appeared to be smaller. The objects did not change size, only their position relative to the camera changed. Change the actual position of the objects now so you can see a vivid demonstration of perspective.

Using SPHERE2.POV (not SPHERE3) as the starting point for this new scene, make the following changes and then save the result as SPHERE4.POV. Listing 3-3 shows the modified scene file.

Move the camera back 6 units so it can view a larger area. Change its location from <0 1 –6> to <0 1 –12>. Move the blue sphere back toward the camera, along the z axis, by 7 units. Change its center from <–3 1 2> to <–3 1 –5>. Move the green sphere forward, away from the camera, on the z axis, by 7 units as well. Change its center from <3 1 2> to <3 1 9>. Now the camera is farther back, the blue sphere is 7 units in front of the red sphere, and the green sphere is 7 units behind the red sphere. Nothing has moved up or down or to the right or left. Render and view SPHERE4.POV. Figure 3-9 shows what has happened.

Listing 3-3 SPHERE4.POV

```
// SPHERE4.POV
// Listing 3-3

// Point straight ahead at the red sphere's center
camera {
  location <0 1 -12>
  look_at <0 1 2>
}
// Original red sphere from FIRST.POV
```

```
object {
  sphere { <0 1 2> 1 }
  texture { color red 1 phong 1}
}
// Two new spheres the same size as the red sphere
// A green sphere on the right of the red sphere
// and seven units behind the red sphere
object {
  sphere { <3 1 9> 1 }
  texture { color green 1 phong 1}
}
// A blue sphere on the left of the red sphere
// and seven units in front of the red sphere
object {
  sphere { <-3 1 -5> 1 }
  texture { color blue 1 phong 1}
}
// The yellow floor
object {
  plane { <0 1 0> 0  }
  texture { color red 1 green 1 }
}

// A white light in front of the camera to the right and above
// Think of it as being in front of and above your right shoulder
// as you view the scene
object {
  light_source { <3 5 -3> color red 1 green 1 blue 1 }
}
```

This image shows strong perspective. The spheres are all the exact same size, but they appear to be three different sizes. The blue sphere is closest to the camera, so it seems the largest. The green sphere is far away and looks very small. The spheres also appear to be different distances to the right and left of the red sphere. The blue sphere looks much farther to the side of the red sphere than the green sphere does, but the scene file shows their positions as exactly the same distance to each side. Did the ray tracer miscalculate or did you make an error?

Neither, actually. The spheres are still the same distance to each side as they were and POV-Ray is correctly showing what they would look like from that viewpoint. If you are skeptical, you can verify this by placing three round objects on a table and placing them close to each other like the three spheres in this scene. Then lower your eye level so you are looking straight across the table at the center of the middle sphere. Close one eye, move the left sphere straight towards you, and notice how it appears to grow larger and the distance between it and the middle sphere also appears to grow larger. Move the right sphere

Figure 3-9 Perspective in POV-Ray

straight back and notice how it appears to grow smaller and the distance between it and the middle sphere also seems to be getting smaller.

The point of this demonstration is that perspective in ray tracing is realistic, but it won't always look like you would expect. Before you blame the program, be sure to check your scene file carefully. One effective way to check your scene layout is to change the position of your camera and render the scene from a different viewpoint. Let's try that with SPHERE4.POV. Move the camera up 30 units and forward by 12 units to give you an overhead view of the scene. Keep the look_at point the same so that the camera is still pointing at the red sphere.

Change the current camera location in SPHERE4.POV to a comment by putting two slashes in front of the line so the ray tracer will ignore it. Now add a new camera location just below the old one:

```
// location <0 1 -12>
   location <0 31 0>
```

The comment acts as a kind of place holder allowing you to switch easily between camera locations by commenting-out one line or the other. If you want to compare the straight-on view with the overhead view, save this scene to

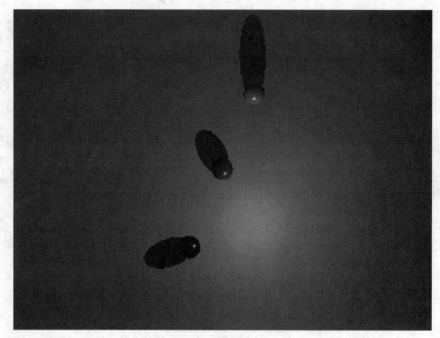

Figure 3-10 Rendered Overhead View of SPHERE4

a new file name like SPHERE4A.POV and render under that name so you don't overwrite the original SPHERE4 files. Render and view the overhead view of this scene. Figure 3-10 shows the rendered overhead view of SPHERE4.POV.

It's easier to see from this viewpoint that the spheres are still the same size and are located where you wanted them to be. The overhead view is handy for this type of checking, but you must take care not to put the camera directly above the look_at point. From that placement, you'll get nothing but a black image because of the way the ray tracer calculates the view angle. You can put it just 1 or 2 units behind the look_at point on the z axis and you'll get a very effective overhead view. Figure 3-11 shows the overhead view in Figure 3-10 diagrammed with coordinates.

What you've learned about spheres in these four scenes applies to all shapes and scenes in POV-Ray, including the next shape, the box.

THE BOX

A box shape is just what it sounds like: six rectangular sides put together to make a box. You create a box by following the keyword box with the positions of two opposite corners on the box. The syntax for a box is

```
box { <corner1> <corner2> }
```

Where *corner1* is the *x, y, z* location of one of the box's corners and *corner2* is the *x, y, z* location of the corner opposite *corner1*. Each of the *x, y, z* values of *corner1* must be smaller than the corresponding *x, y, z* values of *corner2* or the box will not render in the scene. For example, if you have a box with one of its corners at <0, 0, 0> and the opposite corner at <1, 1, 1>, you must describe the box as

```
box { <0 0 0> <1 1 1> }
```

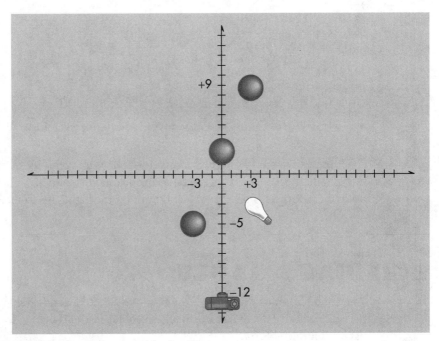

Figure 3-11 Arrangement of Overhead View

If you were to reverse the corners so that it looked like this:

```
box { <1 1 1> <0 0 0> }
```

the box would not appear in the scene. Listing 3-4 shows a box shape in a scene. Render BOX1.POV and view it.

Listing 3-4 BOX1.POV

```
// BOX1.POV
// Listing 3-4
// A camera to the right of the box and pointed at its center
camera {
  location <3 3 -3>
  look_at <0 1 0>
}

// A red box 2 units wide, 2 units long and 2 units high
// with its center 1 unit above the origin.
object {
  box { <-1 0 -1> <1 2 1> }
  texture { color red 1 phong 1}
}
// The yellow floor
object {
  plane { <0 1 0> 0  }
  texture { color red 1 green 1 }
}

// A white light to the right of, above and behind the camera
object {
  light_source { <10 15 -20> color red 1 green 1 blue 1 }
}
```

Notice that the Phong highlights don't show up as nicely on the box as they did on the spheres. That's because the box has perfectly flat sides and perfectly sharp corners. There aren't any bumps for the highlights to reflect from.

BUILDING A TABLE

You can build many things with the box. We'll build a simple table using five box shapes: four tall, skinny boxes for the table's legs and one wide, long, and flat box for the table top.

In the previous scenes, it didn't really matter exactly where the spheres were placed because you were just moving them around to admire some features of

the ray tracer. When building something like a table, though, the exact position and size of each shape really matters. The table would look pretty strange with four different sized legs arranged haphazardly. To ensure accuracy when placing the legs, use graph paper and sketch the positions of the shapes. This table will be about 4 units high and 5 units wide and long. The four legs of the table will be one-half unit, or 0.5 unit square along their length and 4 units tall. The table top will be exactly 5 units square and only 0.2 unit tall. Figure 3-12 is a "sketch" of this table. A side view is shown so all coordinates can be seen. Each square of the graph paper represents 0.5 unit. Notice that we're not trying to create a perfect image of the table with the graph paper. We use it to help visualize the layout and proportions of the shapes. Sketches on graph paper only have to look good enough that the positions of the shapes can be discerned.

Sometimes it is helpful to sketch an overhead view, too. Figure 3-13 shows an overhead view of our table on graph paper.

Notice that we used a few fractional numbers here. To this point we've used whole numbers or integers in the examples to make them easier to read, but POV-Ray converts these internally to floating-point numbers.

A floating-point number, also known as a *float,* is a number with a fractional component, like 1.23, 0.5, 3.1415681247399, 6.0, or –3.0. If the fractional portion is zero, it can be left off, so 6.0 and –3.0 become 6 and –3. Floating-point numbers allow much greater precision than whole numbers. Floating-point numbers can be 0.000000001 or even smaller. That's one one-millionth of a unit. (Note that objects smaller than 0.05 unit may not always render properly.) Using integers, you can only specify coordinates in measurements of whole units, so the most precise placement of an object is just the closest whole number.

Floating-point calculations are taxing on the average computer, which is why a floating-point math coprocessor is recommended for ray tracing. This chip helps the main CPU calculate floating-point math and makes your calculations faster and more precise. You use floating-point numbers to describe any location or size and for most other values in POV-Ray. From now on, we'll use floating-point numbers in almost all scenes.

FIRST LEG UP

TABLE1.POV is the start of the table scene. It has one leg of the table built and the camera positioned to look at it. Listing 3-5 is TABLE1.POV. Render TABLE1.POV and view it.

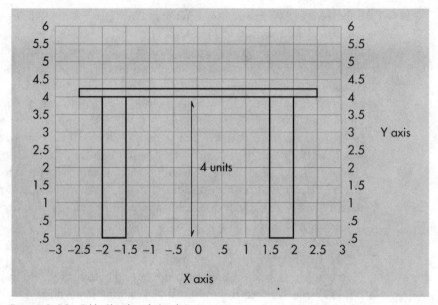

Figure 3-12 Table Sketch with Graph Paper

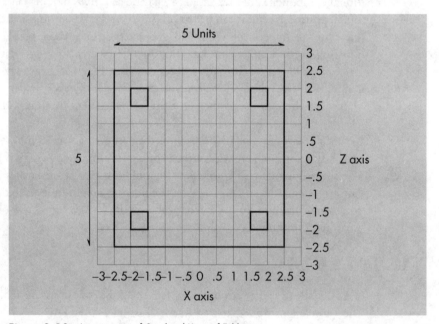

Figure 3-13 Arrangement of Overhead View of Table

Listing 3-5 TABLE1.POV

```
// TABLE1.POV
// Listing 3-5
camera {
  location <5 6 -8>
  look_at <0 5 0>
}

// Several box shapes making a table
// Back left leg
object {
  box { <-2 0 1.5> <-1.5 4 2> }
  texture { color red 1}
}

// The yellow floor
object {
  plane { <0 1 0> 0  }
    texture { color red 1 green 1 }
}

// A white light to the right of, above and behind the camera
object {
  light_source { <10 15 -20> color red 1 green 1 blue 1 }
}
```

Figure 3-14 shows the first leg. You should see a thin red box standing alone on a yellow floor. The first table leg is defined as

```
box { <-2 0 1.5> <-1.5 4 2> }
```

This gives a tall, skinny box 0.5-unit wide and long and 4 units tall. The first corner is on the floor at –2,0,1.5 and the opposite corner is up in the air at –1.5, 4,2. Notice that all values for `corner1` are less than the values for `corner2`. It's a good idea to build scenes piece-by-piece this way. If a problem turns up, you know that the last change you made is probably what caused it.

ADDING MORE LEGS

That one leg looks correct, so now we add three more legs. Color each one differently so they are distinguishable from one another. When all the shapes are positioned correctly, we'll change the color to something that looks more like a normal table. Listing 3-6 includes three new table legs.

Listing 3-6 TABLE2.POV

```
// TABLE2.POV
// Listing 3-6
```

```
camera {
  location <5 6 -8>
  look_at <0 4 0>
}

// Several boxes making a table
// Back left leg
object {
  box { <-2 0 1.5> <-1.5 4 2> }
  texture { color red 1}
}
// Front left leg
object {
  box { <-2 0 -2> <-1.5 4 -1.5> }
  texture { color blue 1}
}
// Back right leg
object {
  box {  <1.5 0 1.5> <2 4 2>}
  texture { color green 1}
}
// Front right leg
object {
  box { <1.5 0 -2> <2 4 -1.5> }
  texture { color red 1 blue .5 }
}

// The yellow floor
object {
  plane { <0 1 0> 0  }
   texture { color red 1 green 1 }
}

// A white light to the right of, above and behind the camera
object {
  light_source { <10 15 -20> color red 1 green 1 blue 1 }
}
```

Notice the color used for the front right leg, color red 1 blue 0.5. This description means the front leg will be colored with 100 percent of the maximum amount of red and 50 percent of the maximum amount of blue. The resulting hue is a reddish-purple. You can specify any amount between 0 and 1 for red, green, or blue in any color description. You can create a color with any shade or hue using this method.

Figure 3-14 The First Leg

Render and view TABLE2.POV. Figure 3-15 shows the table legs all in place.

You should see four different colored boxes arranged in a rectangle. Because the camera is positioned to the right of the table, the rectangle looks a bit like a diamond. The table legs are positioned correctly, so now we add the table top.

THE TABLE TOP

The table top is a long, wide, flat box positioned on top of the table legs. Add this description right *after* the closing brace for the front right leg description in TABLE2.POV:

```
//Table Top
object {
  box { <-2.5 4 -2.5> <2.5 4.2 2.5> }
  texture { color red .7 green .7 blue .7}
}
```

Figure 3-15 Four Table Legs

Be sure to insert this object after the closing brace. If you accidentally put the description in the wrong place, the ray tracer will generate an error like "} expected, but object found instead." This means POV-Ray was reading in some object or element and hadn't finished reading it when it found the errant object description. When you've added the table top correctly, save this file as TABLE3.POV. Render TABLE3.POV and view it. Figure 3-16 shows the table with its top.

The box shapes actually look like a table now! All the box shapes are properly positioned and sized. Now the only thing that isn't quite right is the color of the table. This coloring would be good for Romper Room, but we could make the table look more suitable for entertaining adult guests. You could experiment with different values for the colors until you found the one color that looked just right, but that could take quite awhile. Instead, you can take advantage of a special file that already has a slew of colors defined and ready to use. They're even named already so you can choose them as though you were picking paint cans off the shelf at the hardware store. The colors are stored in an include file.

Figure 3-16 Adding the Table Top

INCLUDE FILES

An include file in POV-Ray is an ASCII text file that contains predefined scene elements. It uses the same language as a scene file, but is not a scene in itself. It is meant to be "included" in a scene file and can be reused. By convention, these files have an .INC extension. Your disk came with several standard include files of shapes, colors, and textures. You installed them to the hard disk in the directory \POVRAY\INCLUDE.

In this scene, we'll use the file that defines colors: COLORS.INC. Use the keyword #include to tell the ray tracer to include a file. The syntax is

```
#include "filename.inc"
```

When the program sees this line in a file, it will read in FILENAME.INC as if it were inserted in the scene file at this line. If it doesn't find FILENAME.INC in the current directory, it will search through the directories listed in the library path for the file. In the installation, we set the library path to C:\POVRAY\INCLUDE using the +L option in the POVRAYOPT environment variable. Because this option is set, you don't have to specify the path name when you use the standard include files.

87

The include file can be of any length and can contain any number of definitions or elements. The standard include files contain only definitions of elements to use in a scene. These elements won't actually be part of the scene until you use them.

Before you include COLORS.INC in the table scene file, use the text editor to view the COLORS.INC file from the \POVRAY\INCLUDE directory. Listing 3-7 is an excerpt from COLORS.INC.

Listing 3-7 COLORS.INC

```
...
#declare White = color red 1.0 green 1.0 blue 1.0
#declare Red = color red 1.0
#declare Green = color green 1.0
#declare Blue = color blue 1.0
#declare Yellow = color red 1.0 green 1.0
#declare Cyan = color blue 1.0 green 1.0
#declare Magenta = color red 1.0 blue 1.0
#declare Black = color red 0.0 green 0.0 blue 0.0
#declare Aquamarine = color red 0.439216 green 0.858824 blue 0.576471
#declare BlueViolet = color red 0.62352 green 0.372549 blue 0.623529
#declare Brown = color red 0.647059 green 0.164706 blue 0.164706
#declare CadetBlue = color red 0.372549 green 0.623529 blue 0.623529
#declare Coral = color red 1.0 green 0.498039 blue 0.0
#declare CornflowerBlue = color red 0.258824 green 0.258824 blue
0.435294
...
```

DEFINING COLORS WITH DECLARE

Each line in Listing 3-7 is a definition of a different color. Use the keyword `#declare` to define these colors. Having these colors defined makes scene files using them easier to read and saves typing time. The word Aquamarine is much easier to understand and type than the actual element, color red 0.439216 green 0.858824 blue 0.576471. The syntax for `#declare` is

```
#declare identifier = scene_element
```

The identifier should be a word that describes the element, like a nickname. When POV-Ray sees the identifier used later, it remembers the declared scene element and inserts it at that point in the scene file.

The identifier name may be up to 40 characters long, must start with a letter or underscore, and can contain any combination of upper- and lowercase letters, numbers, and the underscore. Floyd_The_Barber911 is a valid identifier name, for example, while Floyd The Barber is not valid because it contains spaces and 911Floyd is not valid because it doesn't have a letter as the first character. Generally, identifier names are capitalized to distinguish them from the built-in keywords in the POV-Ray scene language.

The scene element after the equal sign is required and must be a full description of a scene element. Leaving it out or not completing it will cause the program to generate an error.

Not only colors but most other scene element types can be defined using the #declare keyword. In this section, we'll describe how a color is defined and used. Declared elements don't become part of a scene's image when they are declared; they must be used in the scene file. How do you use a declared color?

The syntax for using a declared color is

```
color identifier
```

and you can use it anywhere you would normally put a full color description. For example:

```
object {
  sphere { <0 1 0> 1 }
  color Aquamarine
}
```

is identical to typing

```
object {
  sphere { <0 1 0> 1 }
  color red 0.439216 green 0.858824 blue 0.576471
}
```

and it is much easier to understand.

Add the COLORS.INC include file to TABLE3.POV. The #include instruction should go near the top of the file, right after the opening comments:

```
// TABLE3.POV
// Chapter 3

#include "COLORS.INC"

camera {
  location <5 6 -8>
  look_at <0 4 0>
}
...
```

Save this file as TABLE4A.POV. Render TABLE4A.POV and view it. It should look exactly like Figure 3-16. The declarations in COLORS.INC are being read as if they were in TABLE4A.POV, but they won't affect the scene until they are used. Change all five boxes in TABLE4A.POV to use the defined color Tan.

```
texture { color Tan }
```

The color Tan is defined in COLORS.INC, so when the ray tracer works on the image, it will see their texture as

```
texture { color red 0.858824 green 0.576471 blue 0.439216 }
```

Save the modified file as TABLE4.POV, render, and view it.

Now that you know how to use the colors in COLORS.INC, you can go in and change the floor from color red 1 green 1 to color Yellow. You could also change the light from color red 1 green 1 blue 1 to color White. Experiment with the scene and try using different colors from COLORS.INC for the table, the floor, and even the light. Save your changes in a different file name, though, because you'll be using TABLE4.POV in the next section.

PREDEFINED BASIC SHAPES

Besides making colors easier to handle, the POV-Ray include files also make it easy to use a variety of predesigned shapes in your scenes.

QUADRIC SHAPES

A quadric shape is actually more than one type of shape. The basic quadric shapes are the ellipsoid, the cylinder, and the cone.

There is a standard include file for shapes called SHAPES.INC and it is the standard method for using quadrics. Users need not actually define the quadric shapes' parameters.

The Ellipsoid

An unmodified ellipsoid is a sphere, but unlike a sphere, an ellipsoid can be sized unevenly to create interesting new shapes. An ellipsoid looks sort of like a ball of clay that's been squashed. An ellipsoid can have any length, width, or height that you choose. Figure 3-17 shows some ellipsoids.

Figure 3-17 Ellipsoids

Figure 3-18 A Default Ellipsoid

Let's use an ellipsoid in a scene. The syntax is

```
quadric { Quadric_Name }
```

The quadric name is the identifier of a predefined quadric. For this example, we'll use the identifier Ellipsoid.

Reuse SPHERE2.POV to create this new scene. Add the following lines to the beginning of the file:

```
#include "colors.inc"
#include "shapes.inc"
```

Delete the three spheres from SPHERE2.POV now, and add this object after the camera definition:

```
//Purple Ellipsoid
object {
  quadric { Ellipsoid }
  texture { color SpicyPink phong 1 }
}
```

Save the modified file as ELLPSD1.POV. Render and view ELLPSD1.POV. Figure 3-18 shows the result.

You should see a purple sphere sinking into a yellow floor. Why is the ellipsoid down there? Notice that quadric definitions do not have a specified location or size; all predefined quadrics in the include files are created at the origin, 0 ,0, 0. This is why the ellipsoid seems to be sinking into the floor. The predefined quadrics are also defined with their size as 1 unit. When you used the Ellipsoid, it's as if you created a sphere of radius 1 with the center at 0, 0, 0. The ellipsoid isn't stuck there though; you can move it by doing what is called a *transformation*.

TRANSFORMATIONS

A transformation is a change or modification to a scene element. In POV-Ray there are three kinds of transformations: translate, scale, and rotate. You use *translate* to change the location of a scene element, *scale* to change the size of an element, and *rotate* to turn an object to a new orientation or location.

TRANSLATION

The `translate` keyword changes the position of an element relative to its current position. The syntax is

```
translate <X-amount Y-amount Z-amount>
```

where X, Y, and Z are the number of units you wish to move the element in the direction of the *x*, *y*, and *z* axes. Like all transformations, `translate` can be used with all scene elements, but we'll focus on shapes and objects in this section.

The syntax for using `translate` with a shape is

```
shape { (shape info) ... translate <X-units Y-units Z-units> }
```

The translation information is enclosed in the shape description after the shape-specific information. Use `translate` in ELLPSD1.POV to move the Ellipsoid out of the floor plane so that it appears to be resting on the floor.

The ellipsoid in this scene is listed as

```
//Purple Ellipsoid
object {
  quadric { Ellipsoid }
  texture { color SpicyPink phong 1 }
}
```

All of the quadrics defined in SHAPES.INC have their centers at 0, 0, 0. We want to move the ellipsoid up 1 unit on the *y* axis so its center is at 0, 1, 0, instead of its original 0, 0, 0:

```
//Purple Ellipsoid
object {
  quadric { Ellipsoid translate <0 1 0> }
  texture { color SpicyPink phong 1 }
}
```

When you've made this change, save the file as ELLPSD2.POV. Like all transformations, `translate` is relative to the previous location; it does not move the item to an absolute location. In this example, the shape was originally at the origin so although it might seem as though you were moving the shape to coordinates 0, 1, 0, you were actually moving it 0 units on the *x* axis, 1 unit up on the *y* axis, and 0 units on the *z* axis. If the position of the shape had originally been 1, 2, 3, when `translate <0 1 0>` was read by the program, it would have moved to 1, 3, 3, not 0, 1, 0. Render and view ELLPSD2.POV. Figure 3-19 shows the result of the translation.

The ellipsoid is now resting on the plane with its center 1 unit up on the *y* axis. You can use multiple `translate` commands with the same element. Make another change to the ellipsoid in ELLPSD2.POV:

```
quadric { Ellipsoid translate <0 1 0> translate <1 0 -2> }
```

Save this file as ELLPSD2A.POV. Render and view ELLPSD2A.POV. Figure 3-20 shows the result.

Figure 3-19 Raising the Ellipsoid

Figure 3-20 Multiple Translations

The second `translate` command in the shape clearly demonstrates that transformations are relative, not absolute. The ellipsoid is created by the Ellipsoid identifier at 0, 0, 0, and the first `translate` command moves it 1 unit up on the *y* axis. The second `translate` moves the ellipsoid 1 unit on the *x* axis, 0 units on the *y* axis, and –2 units on the *z* axis. The ellipsoid ends up at 1, 1, –2. If transformations were absolute, the second `translate` would have overridden the first. Instead, it added on to the first.

Translating an object is basically the same as for a shape. The syntax is

```
object {
  shape { ... }
  texture { ... }
  translate <X-units Y-units Z-units>
}
```

The `translate` comes after the shape and texture descriptions and affects the entire object, shape, and texture. In this chapter, textures are solid colors and a `translate` will not visibly affect them. In later chapters, you'll learn how transformations are used with textures too. Note that a transformation on an object affects the entire object and not just the shape.

CHANGING THE SCALE

The `scale` command changes the size of a scene element relative to its current size. The syntax for `scale` is

```
scale <X-amount Y-amount Z-amount>
```

where X, Y, and Z are the amount to scale the element in each direction. The syntax for using `scale` with a shape is

```
shape { (shape info) ... scale <X Y Z> }
```

The scale information is enclosed in the shape description after the shape-specific information. Notice that this is the same syntax as `translate`; the syntax is identical for all transformations, though, of course, their effects are different. Use `scale` to make objects larger or smaller.

Use `scale` with the ellipsoid in ELLPSD2.POV to scale it to 6 units wide, and 2 units long and tall. The ellipsoid has a radius of 1, so it's currently 2 units wide, 2 units long, and 2 units tall. To scale it up to 6 units wide, change its description to

```
//Purple Ellipsoid
```

```
object {
  quadric { Ellipsoid translate <0 1 0> scale <3 1 1>}
  texture { color SpicyPink phong 1 }
}
```

This change tells POV-Ray to scale the ellipsoid 3 times on the *x* axis, that is, make the ellipsoid three times wider. The Y and Z components are set to 1 which tells the program to scale them by 1, that is, to leave them the same size. Notice that scale *multiplies* the size of the element by the scale parameters, so this ellipsoid with a size of X=2, Y=2, Z=2 becomes $2 \cdot 3$, $1 \cdot 1$, $1 \cdot 1$, or X=6, Y=2, Z=2. Save the modified file as ELLPSD3.POV. Render and view ELLPSD3.POV to see the effect of these changes. Figure 3-21 shows the scaled ellipsoid.

The ellipsoid is much wider now: triple the width of the original. You can make it taller by raising the Y scale value. You can make it longer by raising the Z value.

It's also possible to use scale to make an element smaller. Scale parameters set to 1 leave that part of the element the same size. Scale parameters set larger than 1 will make that component of the element larger. Scale parameters

Figure 3-21 Scaling the Ellipsoid

between 0 and 1 will make the component smaller. For example:

```
scale <1 1 1> // No change to the element
scale <1 2 4> // Double the Y component,
              // Make the Z component 4 times larger
scale <.5 .5 .5> // Make X, Y, and Z components half size
```

Use scale values between 0 and 1 to make the ellipsoid in ELLPSD3.POV shorter. Change the Y component of the scale from 1 to 0.25 so the ellipsoid will be 25 percent of its original size:

```
//Purple Ellipsoid
object {
  quadric { Ellipsoid translate <0 1 0> scale <3 .25 1>}
  texture { color SpicyPink phong 1 }
}
```

Save this file as ELLPSD4.POV. Render and view it. Figure 3-22 shows the rather odd-looking result.

The ellipsoid is now wide and flat, as if a steamroller hit it. Notice that the shape no longer sits at location 0, 1, 0. The center of the ellipsoid was translated from 0, 0, 0 to 0, 1, 0, but the scale was done after the translation and

Figure 3-22 Shrinking and Stretching

changed the Y value of the height from 1 to 0.25 because all scaling is relative to origin.

Suppose you have a piece of paper with a word written in the corner. If this page is copied on a machine that can reduce or enlarge an image, you could scale the size of the text. However, the distance between the word and the center of the page would change as well as the size of the text. That is what has happened in our example. Scaling the shape has caused it to move as well.

The *x* and *z* position coordinates weren't changed because they were 0. Any value multiplied by 0 is, of course, 0.

To avoid this side effect of changed position, move the `scale` in front of the `translate`:

```
//Purple Ellipsoid
object {
  quadric { Ellipsoid scale <3 .25 1> translate <0 1 0>}
  texture { color SpicyPink phong 1 }
}
```

Render and view the scene again. The ellipsoid is now floating above the plane instead of resting on it. These two scenes demonstrate that each transformation changes the element and the succeeding transformations will be made to the changed element, not to the original element. The order of transformations is very important because of this. One more thing about scale, the program will generate a warning message if you try to scale an element by 0 in *x, y,* or *z* directions. Scaling by 0 would make the object nonexistent and impossible for the program to render. Note that a sphere is the only shape that cannot be unevenly scaled. Because of its optimizations, it can only be shaped like a perfect sphere. Attempts to scale a sphere unevenly will generate an error.

ROTATING AN OBJECT

The `rotate` transformation turns a scene element around the coordinate axes. To effect a rotation, you specify the number of degrees to turn the element around each of the *x, y,* and *z* axes. The syntax for `rotate` is

```
rotate < X-degrees Y-degrees Z-degrees >
```

The degrees should be between –360 and 360 and represent the angle of rotation. Figure 3-23 illustrates how degrees are measured: 90 degrees is a quarter turn, 180 degrees is a half turn, 270 degrees is a three-quarter turn, and 360 degrees is one full turn.

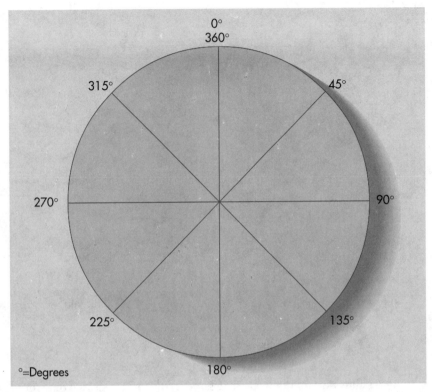

Figure 3-23 Degrees

Left-Handed Axes

Using negative degrees will turn the element in the opposite direction. Which direction is positive and which is negative? Figure 3-24 shows a mnemonic device for remembering how the axes work in POV-Ray.

Hold your left hand up with the thumb pointing to your right, your middle finger pointing forward, your index finger pointing up, and the other fingers curled. It should be in the same position as the hand in the center of the axes in Figure 3-24. Notice that your thumb points in the positive x direction, your middle finger points in the positive z direction, and your index finger points in the positive y direction. This is why the default coordinate system in POV-Ray is called "left-handed."

Now, hold your left hand in a fist with the thumb pointing out to the right in the direction of the positive x axis. Your fingers are curled in the positive degrees direction for the x axis. The opposite direction is the negative degrees

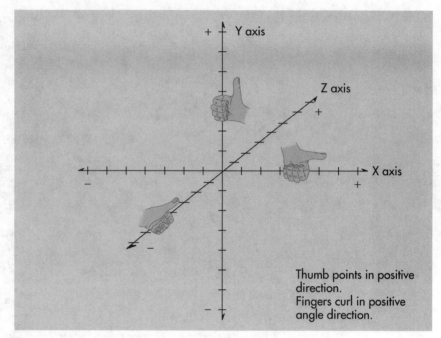

Figure 3-24 Left-Handed Coordinate System

direction for the *x* axis. The same is true for the *y* axes. Point your left thumb in the direction of the positive *y* axis and curl your fingers. Your fingers are now curled in the positive degrees direction for the *y* axis. The opposite direction is the negative degrees direction for the *y* axis. You've probably guessed how to determine the positive degrees direction for the *z* axis. Point your left thumb in the direction of the positive *z* axes and curl your fingers. Your fingers are curled in the positive degrees direction for the *z* axis. The opposite direction is the negative degrees direction for the *z* axis.

Rotating the Ellipsoid

Armed with this knowledge, turn the ellipsoid in ELLPSD3.POV 45 degrees on the *z* axis. Also, move `scale` before the `translate` and `rotate`. Here's a listing of the changes:

```
//Purple Ellipsoid
object {
  quadric { Ellipsoid scale <3 1 1> rotate <0 0 45> translate
<0 1 0> }
  texture { color SpicyPink phong 1 }
}
```

Save this scene as ELLPSD5.POV. Render and view it. Figure 3-25 shows the result.

The ellipsoid is now tilted with the right end up in the air and the left end overlapping the plane. Notice that we used the `rotate` to turn the object on the *z* axis only. Rotations should be done one axis at a time. Be careful of the order used; each rotation turns the element and following rotations will turn the "turned" element. For example, hold a pen or pencil in front of you horizontally like the ellipsoid in ELLPSD4.GIF. Rotate it 45 degrees on the *z* axis. It should be oriented like the ellipsoid, right end up, left end down. Now, make a 90-degree turn on the *y* axis by turning the right end so it points toward you without changing its angle. The end pointing towards you should be tilting up and the end away from you should be tilting down. Hold the pen horizontal again and do the rotations in a different order. First, rotate the pen 90 degrees on the *y* axis. It should be level with the floor with the end pointing towards you. Rotate it 45 degrees on the *z* axis. (Remember, the *z* axis hasn't moved; the pen is now aligned with it and rotating it won't change its position.) Now after the two rotations, the pen should still be pointing at you, but the end is level

Figure 3-25 Rotating the Ellipsoid

now instead of tilting up. You can see why you must be aware of the order of your transformations!

Transformation Order

You moved the `scale` transformation in front of the `rotate` and `translate` in ELLPSD5.POV so it wouldn't affect them. Remember that transformations affect a scene element in the order they are specified. Giving them in the incorrect order produces unexpected results.

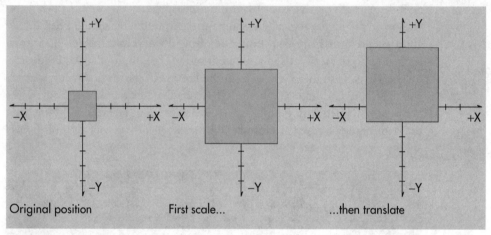

Figure 3-26a   Scaling Before Translating

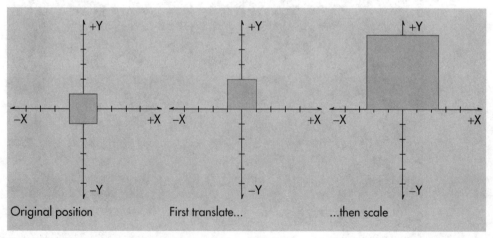

Figure 3-26b   Translating Before Scaling

In general, it is best to scale or rotate before you translate. This is because scaling and rotation are centered about the origin. Usually you want to begin with the shape at the origin. By scaling before you translate you avoid scaling the distance between the shape and the origin.

Figure 3-26a demonstrates a `scale` before a `translate` and Figure 3-26b shows a `translate` before a `scale`.

Using `rotate` after `translate` can also produce unexpected results. `Rotate` always uses the origin, 0, 0, 0, as the center point around which it rotates. When the element is centered on the origin, the `rotate` command will behave as expected, turning the object around but not changing its basic position. If the element has been translated prior to a `rotate`, it still rotates around 0, 0, 0, but its center is no longer at that point. The element is essentially "in orbit" around the origin. Rotating it will not only change its angle, but also its position. Figure 3-27a and 3-27b demonstrate the effect of order on a `rotate` and a `translate`.

Take special notice that each transformation affects the element in order. The transformation order can be changed for special effects, but while learning the basics you should stick to the scale, rotate, translate order of transformations.

THE CYLINDER

A cylinder is a quadric shape that looks like a tube or a pipe. It is circular along its length and can be scaled unevenly along its width or height. Unlike a tube or a pipe though, a quadric cylinder's length is infinite like that of a plane: scaling doesn't affect the length.

There are three cylinders in SHAPES.INC: Cylinder_X, Cylinder_Y, and Cylinder_Z. By default, each has a radius of 1, so they are infinitely long and 2 units wide and high. Cylinder_X runs with its length parallel to the *x* axis, its center at Y=0, Z=0. Cylinder_Y runs with its length parallel to the *y* axis, its center at X=0, Z=0. Cylinder_Z runs with its length parallel to the *z* axis, its center at Y=0, X=0.

The syntax for using one of the quadric cylinders is the same as with other quadrics:

```
quadric { Quadric_Name }
```

For example:

```
quadric { Cylinder_X }
quadric { Cylinder_Z }
```

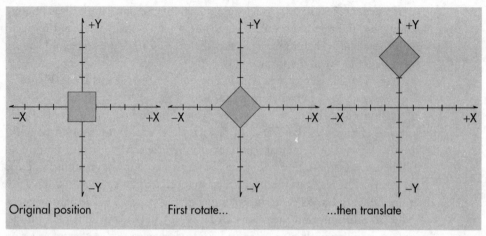

Original position   First rotate...   ...then translate

Figure 3-27a   Rotating Before Translating

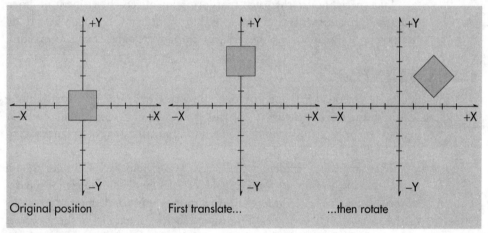

Original position   First translate...   ...then rotate

Figure 3-27b   Translating Before Rotating

Modify ELLPSD2.POV to display a Cylinder_Y instead of an ellipsoid. Change the object from

```
//Purple Ellipsoid
object {
  quadric { Ellipsoid translate <0 1 0> }
  texture { color SpicyPink phong 1 }
}
```

to

```
//Purple Cylinder
object {
  quadric { Cylinder_Y translate <0 1 0> }
  texture { color SpicyPink phong 1 }
}
```

Save the modified file as CYLINDER.POV. Render and view it. Figure 3-28 shows the resulting cylinder.

The quadric cylinder is a basic shape, but its infinite length makes it impractical for use by itself. A special technique is used to define a cylinder with limited length. This new shape based on the quadric cylinder is called a disk and is very useful as a shape by itself. Like the cylinder, there are three defined Disks: Disk_X, Disk_Y, and Disk_Z. These disks are 2 units in length and have a radius of 1. They are about the same size as the Ellipsoid.

The technique used to create the disks is called *intersection*, an advanced shape creation method explained fully in Chapter 5. In this chapter, though, we'll take advantage of the intersection shapes in SHAPE.INC without explaining how they work so you can use an advanced shape type as a basic shape. The syntax for using an intersection shape is

Figure 3-28 A Cylinder

```
intersection { Intersection_Identifier }
```

Intersections are like any other shape. They may be scaled, rotated, and transformed. They may be used with any texture. And they can be used anywhere in a scene file where a shape is appropriate. Change CYLINDER.POV to use a Disk_Y intersection:

```
//Purple Cylinder
object {
  quadric { Cylinder_Y translate <0 1 0> }
  texture { color SpicyPink phong 1 }
}
```

to

```
//Purple Disk
object {
  intersection { Disk_Y translate <0 1 0> }
  texture { color SpicyPink phong 1 }
}
```

Save this file as DISK1.POV. Notice that the translate statement is left in. The standard quadric and intersection shapes have their center at the origin, 0, 0, 0. If we want to have them "resting" on the plane, then we have to translate them so their centers are above the plane by the amount of half their height. If we hadn't translated the disk, half of it would be inside of the plane. Render and view DISK1.POV. You can see the top of the purple disk. It has finite length and is much more useful as a basic shape than a cylinder. You can change the shape, orientation, and position of a disk just like you would with quadrics. Before going on to the next section, try scaling and rotating the disk. Substitute Disk_X and Disk_Z for Disk_Y. Experiment a bit with the values. Render the files and look at the results of your changes. This is the best way to become proficient with new features.

THE CONE

A cone is a shape like a megaphone or a dunce cap. It has a circular base and a point at its top. Figure 3-29 shows some cones.

The basic quadric cone looks like two cones with infinite length placed point-to-point and is very rarely used. Three intersection shapes based on the quadric cone are included in SHAPES.INC. They are Cone_X, Cone_Y, and Cone_Z. They have a base of radius 1 and are 2 units long. They point in the positive direction. Like disks and cylinders, their length is parallel to the coordinate axes of the same name: Cone_X is parallel to the x axis, Cone_Y is paral-

Figure 3-29 Cones

lel to the *y* axis, and Cone_Z is parallel to the *z* axis. Unmodified, like the other predefined quadrics and intersections, their centers are at the origin, 0, 0, 0. They may be transformed like any other shape.

The syntax for using a cone is the same as for a disk, just substitute the word *cone* for *disk*. Modify DISK1.POV to use a cone. Change it from

```
//Purple Disk
object {
  intersection { Disk_Y translate <0 1 0> }
  texture { color SpicyPink phong 1 }
}
```

to

```
//Purple Cone
object {
  intersection { Cone_Y translate <0 1 0> }
  texture { color SpicyPink phong 1 }
}
```

Save this file as CONE1.POV. Render and view it. The purple cone should be sitting on the plane where the disk was in DISK1.POV.

SETTING THE TABLE

You now know how to use several basic shapes. Let's use that knowledge and put some of these shapes together to make a couple of items for the table created earlier. We'll use the ellipsoid, disk, and cone to make a plate, a wine goblet, and an egg on the plate.

THE PLATE

A simple plate can be made easily with a Disk_Y shape. The basic disk is 2 units wide and 2 units high, but a plate should be smaller and thinner. The width or diameter should be about 1.5 units, and the height about 0.1 unit. To scale a disk 2 units wide by 2 units high down to 1.5 units in diameter and 0.1 unit in height, use this scale command with a Disk_Y:

```
intersection { Disk_Y scale <.75 .05 .75> }
```

The diameter of a Disk_Y is set by the X and Z values. 1.5 is 75 percent of 2, so we scale X and Z by 0.75. The height of a Disk_Y is set by the Y value. Scaling it by 0.05 reduces the 2-unit high plate to 1/20th of its original size, 0.1 unit.

To place the disk on the table, we must account for both the height of the table and the height of the object. The center of the disk must be translated up on the *y* axis to the table height plus one-half of the disk's height. The table top is 4.2 units high and the plate is 0.1 unit high. Make the disk rest on top of the table by translating the plate to table height, 4.2, plus 50 percent of the height of the disk, 0.05, which comes to 4.25.

Add this object to TABLE4.POV after the table top

```
// Blue plate special
object {
  intersection { Disk_Y scale <.75 .05 .75>
  translate <0 4.25 0> }
  texture { color Blue }
}
```

Also, let's change the camera position so it's closer to the table. The old location was

```
camera {
  location <5 6 -8>
  look_at <0 4 0>
}
```

Change it to

```
camera {
  location <5 6 -4>
  look_at <0 4 0>
}
```

Save the modified file as TABLE5.POV. Render it and view it. Figure 3-30 shows the plate on the table.

The blue plate should be sitting in the middle of the table top. That's not the way a table is set, though. Move the plate to the edge of the table. The table's right edge is at X=2.5 and the plate has a radius of 0.75. To move the edge of the plate near the right edge of the table, change the X value of the translate to 1.5:

Figure 3-30 Table with Plate

```
// Blue plate special
object {
  intersection { Disk_Y scale <.75 .05 .75>
  translate <1.5 4.25 0> }
  texture { color Blue }
}
```

Save the modified file as TABLE6.POV. Render and view it. Remember that you're viewing the table from the right side. The plate should be near the edge of the table closest to the camera. Now, let's add the goblet.

THE GOBLET

The goblet is more complex than the plate. You'll use three shapes to create it: a disk and two cones. The disk will be the stem of the goblet and the cones will be the base and cup of the goblet.

Scale the disk so it's long and thin: 0.1 unit wide by 1 unit tall. Add the disk to TABLE6.POV *after* the plate:

```
// Goblet Stem
object {
  intersection { Disk_Y scale <.05 .5 .05>
  translate <0 4.7 0> }
  texture { color Orchid }
}
```

Remember, the disk is 2 units wide and 2 units tall, so we have to scale the width by 0.05 to make it 0.1 and the height by 0.5 to make it 1. Save this file as TABLE7.POV. Render and view it. There should be a small stem sitting in the center of the table. Now it needs two cones for a base and a cup.

The standard cone is 2 units high and its base is 2 units in diameter, which is far too big for the base of the goblet. It should be scaled down so it's shorter and narrower. Let's make it 0.6 unit wide and 0.2 unit tall. Add this object to TABLE7.POV after the stem:

```
// Goblet Base
object {
  intersection { Disk_Y scale <.3 .1 .3> translate <0 4.3 0> }
  texture { color Orchid }
}
```

Save the new file as TABLE8.POV. Before you render it, add the cup to the top of the goblet. The cup will be similar to the base, but larger and rotated so its point is facing down. It will also have to be positioned higher up. Make a new object after the base for the goblet cup:

```
// Goblet Cup
object {
  intersection { Disk_Y }
  texture { color Orchid }
}
```

Scale this cone so it's 1.2 units in diameter and 0.4 unit high :

```
intersection { Disk_Y scale <.6 .2 .6> }
```

Rotate it 180 degrees on the *z* axis to turn it over so its point faces down:

```
intersection { Disk_Y scale <.6 .2 .6> rotate <0 0 180>}
```

Now translate up on the *y* axis so it's sitting on the stem. The stem is 1 unit tall sitting on the table top up 4.2 units. That puts the top of the stem at 5.2. The top cone should overlap the stem, so put the center of the cone at the top of the stem:

```
intersection {
  Disk_Y scale <.6.2 .6> rotate <0 0 180> translate <0 5.2 0>
}
```

Save TABLE8.POV. Render and view it. Figure 3-31 shows the result.

The goblet should be in the center of the table in front of the plate. Now we add the egg.

Figure 3-31 Adding the Goblet

THE EGG

The egg is a very simple addition to this scene. Take an ellipsoid and scale it down so it's small and a bit longer than it is tall or wide. Add this object *after* the goblet cup in TABLE8.POV:

```
// Egg
object {
  quadric { Ellipsoid scale <.14 .14 .2>
  translate <1.5 4.39 0> }
  texture { color White }
}
```

Move the goblet 1 unit forward on the *z* axis so it will be in the correct spot for a right-handed diner: Change all three goblet `translate` statements from `translate <number, number, 0>` to `translate <number, number, 1>`:

```
// Goblet Stem
...
  intersection { Disk_Y scale <.05 .5 .05> translate <0 4.7 1>
}
...
// Goblet Base
...
  intersection { Cone_Y scale <.3 .1 .3> translate <0 4.3 1> }
...
// Goblet Cup
...
  intersection {
    Cone_Y scale <.6 .2 .6> rotate <0 0 180> translate <0 5.2 1>
  }
...
```

Save this file as TABLE9.POV. The eggy ellipsoid's length is parallel to the *z* axis and it has been translated to be sitting right on top of the center of the plate. Render and view this scene. Figure 3-32 shows the egg in place.

The table is now fully prepared! Now that the scene's basic layout is complete, you can play with the colors, modify the shapes, and position them to your liking. The steps you used to create simple shapes and objects in a scene are the same steps you should use for more complex scenes.

Visualize the scene and make rough sketches. Graph paper is always helpful for getting the measurements right. Create the scene one piece at a time, and render small versions as you go so you can check your progress. Number each version of your scene so you can go back to it if you make a

Figure 3-32 Finally, the Egg!

mistake. Reuse scenes and scene elements when you can as this technique is a huge time saver. When the basic layout of the scene is complete, fine-tune it.

This scene looks good enough and complete enough that you should do a higher-resolution render of it. Try rendering TABLE9.POV at 640x480 resolution. If your system doesn't have a high-res display, or if it's particularly slow, use the 320x200-high resolution. Use the +W640 +H480 or +W320 +H200 as options and render a high-quality version of this scene. One small warning—this scene will probably take from 1 to 3 hours to render at high resolution on your system so you may want to set it to render while you sleep.

SUMMARY

In this chapter, you learned how to use POV-Ray's basic shapes, you created some interesting objects, and you learned about some features like transformations and include files. You learned that:

- Each object in a scene file is made up of one shape and one texture (material).

113

- The syntax for a sphere is
  ```
  sphere { <center> radius }
  ex: sphere { <-7 3 1> 4 }
  ```
  The sphere renders faster than any other shape in POV-Ray. Spheres cannot be scaled unevenly.
- The ray tracer doesn't place restrictions on location or size of a shape. Any shape can have any position or size.
- An object must be positioned in the camera's field of view to be visible in the scene.
- Overlapping objects are allowed.
- The syntax for a box shape is
  ```
  box { <corner1> <corner2> }
  Ex: box { <0 0 0> <1 1 1> }
  ```
  Corner1 must be smaller than corner2.
- Sketching objects and scenes on graph paper aids greatly in positioning and sizing objects.
- Include files are ASCII text files that contain predefined scene elements. The syntax for using an include file is
  ```
  #include "filename.inc"
  Example: #include "shapes.inc"
  ```
  Include files should be listed in a scene file before the regular scene data begins.
- The `#declare` keyword is used to predefined scene elements for use in other scenes. Most scene elements can be `#declared`.
- Positioning the camera directly over the look_at point will generate an error.
- The syntax for using a predefined quadric is
  ```
  quadric { Quadric_Name }
  ```
- The syntax for using the predefined quadric Ellipsoid is
  ```
  quadric { Ellipsoid [transformations] }
  Ex: quadric { Ellipsoid translate <0 1 0> }
  ```
  Ellipsoids, like all shapes other than the sphere, can be scaled unevenly.
- A transformation is a change to a scene element. There are three types of transformations in POV-Ray: `scale`, `rotate`, and `translate`. Transformations are relative and affect each other in the order they are specified. Transformations should usually be done in the order of scale, rotate, and translate.
- The syntax for scale is
  ```
  scale <X-amount Y-amount Z-amount>
  Ex: scale <10 1 .5>
  ```

Using `scale` multiplies the components of the element. Scaling by a value larger than 1 will make the component larger. Scaling by 1 will leave the component the same size. Scaling by less than 1 will shrink the element. Scaling along any axis by 0 will generate an error. Any transformations done to an element before a scale in the same element will be multiplied by it.

- The syntax for `rotate` is

  `rotate <X-degrees Y-degrees Z-degrees>`
  `Ex: rotate <20 0 0> rotate <0 -34 0>`

  The X, Y, and Z degrees should be between –360 and 360. A rotation of 45 degrees is a 1/8 turn, 90 degrees is a 1/4 turn, 180 degrees is a 1/2 turn, and 360 degrees is a complete turn. Rotation should be done separately for each axis.

- The syntax for `translate` is

  `translate <X-units Y-units Z-units>`
  `Ex: translate <0 .005 -98>`

  The `translate` changes the position of a scene element relative to its current position. The `translate` command specifies a number of units to move, not a point to move to.

Now that you have a repertoire of useful shapes, it's time to look at the variety of textures that you can use to create them. The rich world of texture will be the subject of Chapter 4.

I'm living in a material world. —Madonna

4

Basic Textures

Shapes are the foundation of any scene created in POV-Ray, but shapes only describe the form of an object. Textures are needed to give color, substance, and life to these forms. Textures describe the material from which shapes are made.

To realize the importance of texture, examine an object in front of you. What color or colors is it? What patterns do the colors make? Is it reflective or dull? Is it bumpy or smooth? Is it transparent? The texture answers all of these questions.

Textures in POV-Ray range from lead glass to golden metal to rosewood to polished jade. There are many options available to describe textures and using appropriate textures and a bit of imagination you can create almost any material.

This chapter explains what a texture is, how to create one, and how to use the standard textures. We'll also add new textures to the table scene and improve its realism.

WHAT IS A TEXTURE?

A texture is the description of the material from which a shape is made. An oak ball has a wooden texture. A brass ball has a metallic texture. The texture only affects the surface appearance of an object or shape and never its actual form. A

117

Figure 4-1 Three Identical Spheres with Three Different Textures

brass ball and a wooden ball both have the same underlying form—a sphere—only their material is different. Figure 4-1 shows three spheres with three very different textures.

These three shapes look very different, but they are all just basic spheres with different textures applied to them. Texture can affect many facets of a shape's appearance, including its color, color pattern, reflectivity, bumpiness, and transparency. All of these features are easily accessed by adding words and numbers to the texture definition.

A texture is described in much the same way an object is. After the word `texture` there is a description of the texture between two curly braces ({ }). The texture description can appear in the body of a shape:

```
object {
  box { <0 0 0> <1 1 1> texture { color red .5  green 1 reflection .4 } }
```

Or the texture can be placed in the body of the object:

```
object {
  box { <0 0 0> <1 1 1> }
  texture { color red .5  green 1 reflection .4 }
}
```

In this example, it doesn't matter where the texture is placed. It will affect the shape in the same way in either position. Later, when you are creating objects using multiple shapes, it will make a difference that you are able to apply the texture to either the object or the shape. Objects using multiple shapes can apply different textures to each shape.

A texture can be as simple as this

```
texture { color red 1}
```

or very complex, like this example:

```
texture {
  granite
  color_map {
    [0.0 0.9 color DustyRose alpha 1 color DustyRose alpha 0.5 ]
    [0.9 1.0  color DarkSlateGray color DarkSlateGray ]
  }
  ambient 0.25
  turbulence 0.25
  specular 1.0   roughness 0.0001
  phong 0.25     phong_size 75
  brilliance 4
  rotate <0 0 33>
  scale <2 2 2>
}
```

Both are complete descriptions of materials. The first is solid, dull red and the second is a subtly colored shiny stone. Let's create a texture that's somewhere in between the two in terms of complexity.

CREATING TEXTURES

Creating a texture is not difficult; you've already done it in your earlier scenes. Let's start with one of those scenes and embellish its simple texture to create something more interesting. The file TEX1.POV is a slightly modified copy of FIRST.POV. (Don't forget to change to the \POVRAY\CHAPTER4 directory.) It's a simple scene with one sphere and a plane acting as a floor.

The sphere already has a texture description:

```
texture {
  color red 1
  phong 1
  }
```

The order of the different parts of the texture description doesn't matter. This texture would be identical if it were in this order:

```
texture {
  phong 1
  color red 1
  }
```

But the specific components of each part do need to be in proper order, for instance, "1 phong" is not the same as "phong 1" and "1 red color" instead of "color red 1" would cause the scene file to generate an error when parsed by the renderer. And, of course, all texture-related keywords must appear between the curly braces after the keyword `texture`. Texture modifiers outside of the braces will generate an error when parsing.

The syntax of each texture modifier used in this chapter will be listed when it is introduced. You can find the syntax for the entire set of texture modifiers listed in Chapter 7.

The two modifiers `color` and `phong` have already been discussed. The syntax of `color` is

`color red` *amount* `green` *amount* `blue` *amount*

where *amount* is a number from 0.0 through 1.0 or

`color` *color_identifier*

When used by itself `color` sets the basic hue of the shape. It must be followed by the amount of red, green, and blue in the color or by the name of a previously defined color.

The syntax for `phong` is

`phong` *amount*

Here, *amount* is a value from 0.0 through 1.0. `phong` turns Phong highlighting on, making the shape look shiny by causing reflection of the light shining on it. The number following `phong` is the amount of light color in the highlight. `phong 1` tells the ray tracer to create a highlight that is 100 percent the same color of the light that is creating it. `phong .5` creates a highlight that is 50 percent of the light shining on it and 50 percent of the shape's color. Lower values cause the object to look less shiny.

Let's modify the sphere's texture so it has a *color pattern* instead of just one solid color.

COLOR PATTERNS

A color pattern is two or more colors used in a specific format to create a pattern or design. Color patterns range from alternating square blocks of solid color to vertical color bands to swirling mixes of colors. The simplest color pattern is `checker`.

Checker

The `checker` keyword does just what its name implies: it creates alternating rectangular blocks of two colors. The syntax for `checker` is

```
checker COLOR1 COLOR2
```

Both colors must be specified and either may be a color identifier. This is a valid checker for example:

```
checker color red 1 green .5 color Aquamarine
```

Now change the sphere texture in TEX1.POV so that it uses a checker of blue and white instead of the solid red color. Your changes should look like this:

```
object {
  sphere {<0 1 2> 1}
  texture {
    checker color blue 1 color red 1 green 1 blue 1
    phong 1
  }
}
```

An easier way to do this is is to include COLORS.INC at the top of the file and then use the declared colors Blue and White like this:

```
#include "colors.inc" // this line at top of file, after comments
  ...
object {
  sphere {<0 1 2> 1}
  texture {
    checker color Blue color White
    phong 1
  }
}
```

Save the new file as TEX2.POV, render, and view it. Figure 4-2 shows the result.

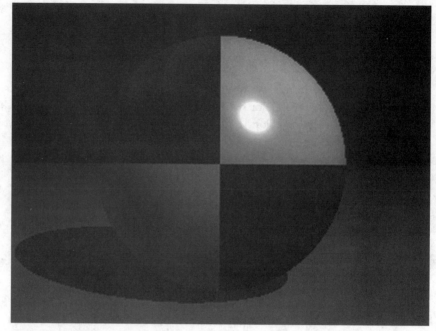

Figure 4-2 Sphere with Checker Pattern

Looks a bit like a big beach ball doesn't it? What if you wanted a smaller checker pattern? Textures can be scaled just like objects can. To make the pattern smaller, scale by a number smaller than 1. Add a scale to the sphere's texture so it looks like this:

```
object {
  sphere {<0 1 2> 1}
  texture {
    checker color Blue color White
    phong 1
    scale <.5 .5 .5>
  }
}
```

Save the new file as TEX3.POV, render, and view it. Figure 4-3 shows what happens.

In addition to scaling, textures can be rotated and translated just like shapes and objects can. This capability allows textures to be precisely sized and positioned.

The checker pattern is commonly used on the floor of a scene to enhance the sense of perspective. Modify the scene so the checker pattern is on the floor instead of the sphere. Change

```
object {
  plane { <0 1 0> 0 }
  texture {
    color green 1
  }
}
```

to

```
object {
  plane { <0 1 0> 0 }
  texture {
    checker color Blue color White
  }
}
```

Now change the sphere so it's solid red again, but use the identifier Red and change the phong to 0.3:

```
object {
  sphere {<0 1 2> 1}
```

Figure 4-3 Checker Pattern Scaled Down

```
texture {
  color Red
  phong .3
 }
}
```

Save this file as TEX4.POV, render, and view it. Figure 4-4 shows the checker pattern on the floor—something like linoleum.

Notice the highlight on the sphere is now much less pronounced. It makes the sphere look like it's made of a "softer" material. The checker on the plane makes the scene look more dramatic. It's easier to see that the plane recedes far into the distance when the visual cue of the checkers is added.

The checker pattern was one of the first used in 3D computer graphics and it is still used today so widely that it has become something of a cliche. Don't let that stop you from using it in your scenes, though. It has been used often because it looks good and is very useful. If `checker` isn't scaled, each square is exactly 1 unit wide and 1 unit long. You can use this to help visualize the unit size of elements in your scene and to help position them, using the checker pattern as a grid.

Now let's add a more sophisticated texture—like marble—to the sphere.

Figure 4-4   Checker Pattern on the Floor

Marble

Alter the sphere's texture so that it uses the marble color pattern instead of the solid color red. Change it from

```
object {
  sphere {<0 1 2> 1}
  texture {
    color Red
    phong .3
  }
}
```

to

```
object {
  sphere {<0 1 2> 1}
  texture {
    marble
    phong .3
  }
}
```

Figure 4-5   Marble Color Pattern

Save this file as TEX5.POV, render, and view it. Figure 4-5 shows the resulting pattern. The marble pattern is made of smoothly changing vertical bands of different colors.

This pattern is interesting, but it doesn't look much like marble. Most POV-Ray color patterns are just starting points. You must modify them to resemble real-world materials. Unmodified, the marble pattern is just straight bands of color. To make it look more like a type of stone, it needs to be mixed up with a technique called *turbulence*.

TURBULENCE

The `turbulence` keyword uses a special formula to redistribute the colors in a color pattern. The syntax for turbulence is

```
turbulence amount
```

The number following `turbulence` may be any floating-point number, positive or negative. Turbulence 0 is legal, but will produce no effect on the pattern. Larger numbers will mix up the pattern more. Add turbulence 1 to the sphere texture:

```
object {
  sphere {<0 1 2> 1}
  texture {
    marble
    turbulence 1
    phong .3
  }
}
```

Save this file as TEX6.POV, render, and view it. Figure 4-6 shows the result of adding turbulence.

That's more like it! Turbulence mixed up the bands of colors so that the sphere now looks like an exotic stone. Different turbulence values will make the marble pattern look very different. Experiment with some different values like 0.1, 0.3, or 10. Turbulence can be used on most patterns to stir them up. Because turbulence is semirandom, it will act differently for different textures and positions, but it will create the same pattern each time you render the picture. The effect of turbulence is based on the position of the texture. If the texture is not moved, the pattern produced by turbulence will not change.

Figure 4-6 Turbulence 1 Added to Marble Pattern

PATTERNS AND THE COLOR MAP

To use the marble pattern all you did was insert the word marble into the texture. You didn't have to specify the colors used in the pattern as checker required. When using a pattern such as marble, POV-Ray will often have a default set of colors. What if you wanted different colors with the marble pattern? To do this, you need to specify a *color map* for the pattern. The color map is where POV-Ray gets the colors for all color patterns other than checker.

Each pattern is a mathematical function that converts the *x, y, z* coordinates of each point on the surface into a floating-point value in the range 0.0 through 1.0. A color map is a table of colors which specifies how the color of the surface blends and changes from point to point depending on the value computed by the pattern function.

The syntax for a color map is

```
color_map {
   [ low high COLOR1 COLOR2 ]
   [ low high COLOR1 COLOR2 ]
```

127

```
    [ low high COLOR1 COLOR2 ]
    ...
    [ low high COLOR1 COLOR2 ]
}
```

Each entry in a color map is enclosed in square brackets. There may be any number of color map entries, but the *low* value of the first entry should be 0 and the *high* value of the last entry should be 1. The values between define what colors are found between 0 and 1. POV-Ray computes the pattern value and searches the entries until it finds the proper low-to-high range. If *COLOR1* and *COLOR2* are different, the program will smoothly change from *COLOR1* to *COLOR2* across the low and high values specified. For example:

```
color_map {
    [0.0 0.3 color Red color White]    // 0-.3    smoothly change from Red
                                       //         to White
    [0.3 0.6 color White color Blue]   // .3-.6   smoothly change from
                                       //         White to Blue
    [0.6 0.75 color Yellow color Red]  // .6-.75  smoothly change from
                                       //         Yellow to Red
    [0.75 0.8 color Red color Green]   // .75-.8  smoothly change from
                                       //         Red to Green
    [0.8 1.0 color Orange color Grey]  // .8-1    smoothly change from
                                       //         Orange to Grey
}
```

or

```
color_map {
  [0.0  0.3 color Blue color Blue ]   // 0-.3    use the color Blue
  [0.3  1.0 color Blue color White ]  // .3-1    smoothly change from
                                      //         Blue to White
}
```

or even

```
color_map {
  [0.0  1.0   color Black color White ]  // 0-1 smoothly change
                                         //     from Black to White
}
```

If any range of values between 0 and 1 is left undefined, an error is generated. There may be up to 20 entries in the color map.

Each of the color patterns uses the color map differently. The marble pattern uses it to create parallel stripes of color; the colors blend from the color map values 0 through 1 and then backwards from 1 to 0 over and over. Other patterns such as the gradient pattern blend from 0 to 1 and then start over again at 0. See Chapter 7 for details on how the patterns work.

Now add a new color map to the `marble` sphere texture and comment-out the turbulence so you can clearly see the stripes of color. Change it to look like this:

```
object {
  sphere {<0 1 2> 1}
  texture {
    marble
    color_map {
      [0 .4  color Red color Yellow]    //   0-.4    change smoothly from
                                        //           Red to Yellow
      [.4 .6 color Yellow color Yellow] // .4-.6     use solid Yellow
      [.6  1 color Yellow color Green]  // .6-1      change smoothly from
                                        //           Yellow to Green
    }
    //turbulence 1
    phong .3
  }
}
```

Save this file as TEX7.POV, render, and view it. You can clearly see the stripes of color going from red to yellow to green and then back again from green to yellow to red. The center of the sphere is at 0; notice that the complete pattern runs from the center of the sphere to its edge at X=1. Most built-in color patterns are 1 unit wide and are repeated over and over through other values. For example, unmodified, `marble` is the same from X=6 to X=7 as it is from X=0 to X=1. Turbulence changes the pattern so that it isn't regular. Using turbulence causes the pattern to be different at all values.

Uncomment the turbulence in the pattern and render it again. This texture looks a great deal like the rare Guinea Fulig stone. You can use any colors you like and differ the values of turbulence to greatly alter your patterns. We've used primary colors to accentuate the appearance of the pattern, but if you want to create more realistic looking textures, try using darker, more subtle colors.

You can also make dramatic changes in a texture just by changing its color pattern without changing its color map or its other properties. Change `marble` in TEX7.POV to the word `granite`. Save this file as TEX8.POV, render, and view it. Figure 4-7 shows the new appearance.

Notice the difference in the appearance of the texture that was caused just by changing one word! Here's a list of some color pattern types you can try:

- agate
- bozo
- granite

Figure 4-7 Granite Pattern on the Sphere

- leopard
- onion
- spotted
- wood

Remember, unmodified, these textures don't look much like their names. They are meant as starting points, foundations for building your textures. You don't have to be an expert at building textures to use expert textures, though. POV-Ray includes files that define dozens of outstanding textures you can use right away.

TEXTURES ARE THREE DIMENSIONAL

Textures in POV-Ray are like giant blocks of stone from which the shapes are carved. For example, the veins in marble aren't like paint or wallpaper; they are three dimensional and can be scaled, rotated, and translated just like a shape. When turbulence is used to "stir up" a color pattern, it mixes it up across all three dimensions, not just the surface. Figure 4-8 illustrates how a texture is three dimensional.

It's important to be able to visualize this when you are creating textures. Think of yourself as a sculptor and textures as the bulk material from which you carve your objets d'art. Because they are 3D, you can change the texture in the same ways you change a shape. You can scale, rotate, and translate them to make very different looking effects than the original.

USING STANDARD TEXTURES

You've had some experience now using POV-Ray shapes and colors with the SHAPES.INC and COLORS.INC files. Textures can also be defined in the same manner as shapes and colors. The TEXTURES.INC and STONES.INC files contain definitions for many textures that you can use just by including the file and using the texture names.

For example, to use the texture Blue_Sky2 from TEXTURES.INC, you would create a texture like this:

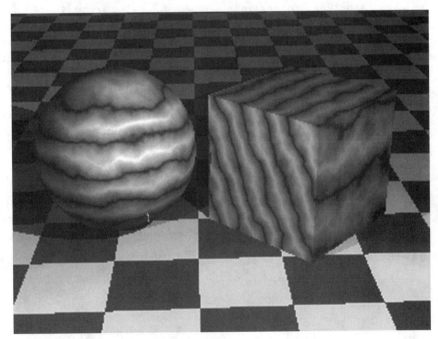

Figure 4-8   Textures Are Three Dimensional

```
object {
  sphere {<0 1 2> 1}
  texture {
    Blue_Sky2
  }
}
```

That's all there is to it. You may want to scale or rotate the texture to adapt it to the shape you're using, but many textures will look wonderful without any modification.

TEXTURES.INC

TEXTURES.INC contains over 60 general-purpose textures that you can use on any shape or object. You can use the TEXTTEST.POV file to try out these textures. Just include TEXTURES.INC and change the sphere and/or floor's texture to one of the textures described below and render the image. TEXTURES.INC uses some of the colors from COLORS.INC, so you must include it before TEXTURES.INC. To include TEXTURES.INC in your scene file, add these two lines near the top *before* any scene information:

```
#include "colors.inc"
#include "textures.inc"
```

Here is a brief survey of some of the textures from TEXTURES.INC and suggestions on using them.

Jade

Jade is a swirled green texture based on the `marble` color pattern. See Figure 4-9 (these black and white illustrations can't do justice to the colors in these textures, but they will give you an idea of the shading and pattern).

White_Marble

White_marble is a soft-edged black and white `marble` pattern. Try it out on the floor. Also try using it on a sphere in a space scene as a moon texture. Be sure to scale it to the same size as the sphere. Figure 4-10 shows White_Marble on a sphere.

Blood_Marble

Blood_Marble is a blue and black marble with veins of blood red. Its pattern is similar to Jade.

Figure 4-9   Jade Texture on a Sphere

Figure 4-10   White_Marble on a Sphere

RAY TRACING

Sapphire_Agate

Sapphire_Agate is a beautiful deep blue, swirling texture that almost glows. This one looks good on almost any shape in almost any setting. Try it with White_Marble as a background.

Brown_Agate

Brown_Agate is a soft-edged brown and white pattern that evokes a feeling of stone and earth.

PinkAlabaster

PinkAlabaster is a masterpiece of subtle shading and delicate colors. This pink and gray texture looks best at high resolutions so all of its features can be appreciated.

Blue_Sky

Blue_Sky is just that, a basic blue sky with white, fluffy clouds. Also available are Blue_Sky2, Blue_Sky3, and Bright_Blue_Sky. These are all designed to look good on a large sphere used as a sky background. For example, you can add a "sky" to almost any scene with this line:

```
object {
  sphere { <0 0 0> 10000}
  texture { Blue_Sky scale <10000 10000 1000> }
}
```

This large sphere will encompass the scene and create a "sky" on which you can apply an appropriate sky texture. Figure 4-11 shows an example of Blue_Sky2.

Blood_Sky

A foreboding, red and yellow sky. Use it on scenes that are a bit surrealistic. The pattern is similar to Blue_Sky, but the coloring is much different.

Apocalypse

Apocalypse is a black background on which red-purple clouds look like they're glowing in a nuclear aftermath. This texture is obviously the product of a troubled mind. Use it as a sky on scenes that stray far from the path of realism. The pattern is similar to Blue_Sky, but the coloring is much different.

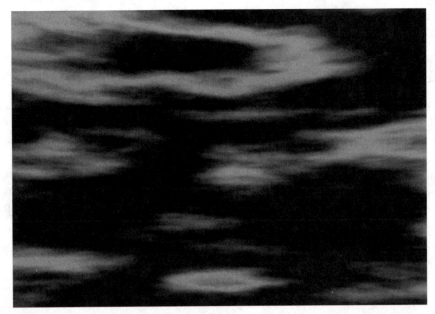

Figure 4-11   Blue_Sky2 with Fluffy White Clouds

Clouds

Clouds is a texture with fluffy white clouds on a transparent background. This texture can be used to create interesting special effects. Try adding it to the sphere in TEXTEST.POV like this:

```
object {
  sphere {<0 1 2> 1}
  texture {
    Clouds
    scale <.4 .2 .4>
  }
}
```

Glass

Glass is just what it sounds like. This texture makes a shape look like it's made of shiny, slightly reflective glass. This is a very impressive texture when used well. Ray tracers are noted for their realistic glass textures.

Be sure to have an interesting background when using glass. Glass against a solid colored background doesn't give any visual clues to help the viewer recognize it as glass. TEXTURES.INC also includes Green_Glass and Glass3, which look like bottle glass and lead glass, respectively.

These transparent, refracting textures take much longer to render than the simpler, color pattern textures do because the ray tracer has to do extra calculations to simulate glass. Figure 4-12 shows a sphere made of glass.

Mirror

Mirrored textures are also a strength of ray tracers and can be used to create some mind-bending scenes. The texture Mirror in TEXTURES.INC is a perfectly reflecting mirror. Try creating several Mirror balls floating in the air near each other over a checkered plane. Be sure to have a sky sphere encompassing the scene, also. A black sky doesn't look very interesting reflected in a sphere. See the section below on modifying standard textures to learn how to use reflection with other textures.

Note that these reflective textures take much longer to render than the simpler, color pattern textures do because the ray tracer has to do extra calculations.

Figure 4-12 A Glass Sphere

Figure 4-13   A Cube Textured with DMFWood4

DMFWood4

DMFWood4 is an excellent, general-purpose wood texture. Figure 4-13 shows DMFWood4 on a cube. Notice the rings of the wood face the viewer and this texture is oriented horizontally on the *x-z* plane. If the shape you are applying wood to has a more vertical orientation, rotate the wood texture about 90 or –90 degrees on the *x* axis:

```
texture { DMFWood4 rotate <90 0 0> }
```

This will place the rings of the wood facing upward and downward.

Often a wooden plank does not exactly follow the grain of the wood. If you rotate by slightly more or less than 90 degrees you can create a more realistic look.

Some other outstanding woods in TEXTURES.INC are Yellow_Pine, Rosewood, and Sandalwood.

Silver_Metal

Silver_Metal is a bright, reflective texture that looks best when it is near something it can reflect. Other metals are Gold_Metal, Brass_Metal, and Chrome_Metal. Note again that these reflective textures take much longer to render than the simpler, color pattern textures do because the ray tracer has to do extra calculations to simulate the reflections.

Metal

Metal is a texture that adds metallic properties to any color texture. Use Metal before the other texture elements:

```
texture { Metal color_texture }
```

For example:

```
texture { Metal color red 1 }
```

or

```
texture { Metal color Purple }
```

or

```
texture {
   Metal
   marble
   color_map {
      [0 .9 color Grey30 color Gray80]
      [.9 1 color Gray80 color Gray90]
   }
}
```

Two texture identifiers in one texture won't work, however, so the following won't make a Jade Metal:

```
texture { // This won't work as expected
   Metal
   Jade   // The second texture overrides the first
}
```

The second texture identifier overrides the first, so this texture is just Jade, not Jade Metal. To make a Jade Metal, copy the actual contents of the Jade declaration into the texture after the Metal identifier:

```
texture { // This gives you a "jade metal"
   Metal
   // following is from "Jade" definition in TEXTURES.INC
   marble
   turbulence 1.8
```

```
colour_map {
    [0.0 0.8   colour red 0.1 green 0.6 blue 0.1
    colour red 0.0 green 0.3 blue 0.0]
    [0.8 1 colour red 0.1 green 0.6 blue 0.1
    colour red 0.0 green 0.2 blue 0.0]
  }
}
```

(Note that the include files use the British spelling, "colour." POV-Ray understands both British and American spellings.)

You could make Metal Agate or Metal Clouds this way. Let your imagination run wild!

Candy_Cane

The red and white Candy_Cane texture makes the shape look like it's wrapped and ready for the holidays. Try this one on a few tall Disk_Ys.

Peel

Peel is the same basic texture as Candy_Cane, but it's transparent where Candy_Cane is white and orange where Candy_Cane is red. This texture makes the shape look like a portion of it was "peeled" away, leaving nothing underneath. It's a great way to give your scene that M.C. Escher feel. The "striped" sphere we saw in Figure 4-1 had the peel texture.

STONES.INC

The STONES.INC file contains over 80 stunning, specialized stone textures that you can use on any shape or object. Use the STONETST.POV file to try out these textures. Just change the sphere or floor's texture to one of the textures below and render the image. STONES.INC uses some of the colors from COLORS.INC, so you must include it before STONES.INC. To include STONES.INC in your scene file, add these two lines near the top *before* any scene information:

```
#include "colors.inc"
#include "stones.inc"
```

The file TEXTURES.DOC contains descriptions of the individual textures in STONES.INC. You can experiment with them just by knowing the naming convention used in the file. STONES.INC contains three types of texture names: Grnt#, Grnt#a, and Stone#.

Grnt0 – Grnt29

These are stone textures created with the granite color map pattern. They are numbered 0–29. Here's an example of the use of one:

```
texture { Grnt13 }
```

Grnt0a – Grnt24a

These stone textures are also created with the granite color map pattern, but they contain some partially transparent colors. Here's an example of the use of one:

```
texture { Grnt8a }
```

Stone1 – Stone24

These sophisticated stone textures are created by combining textures from the Grnt and Grnta list. Use them in the same manner as the Grnts:

```
texture { Stone20 }
```

MODIFYING STANDARD TEXTURES

You can modify the standard textures included with POV-Ray without disturbing the original textures in the include file. For example, any texture can be made shiny by adding `phong 1` to it. To make a Brown_Agate shiny, for instance, the syntax is

```
texture {
   Brown_Agate
   phong 1
}
```

The modifiers listed after the texture name will override any values set previously. Be careful not to override all the features of the defined texture, though. For instance, if you entered

```
object {
   sphere { <0 1 2> 1 }
   texture {
      Brown_Agate
      color Red
   }
}
```

the sphere would be solid red, not Brown_Agate, because the color Red statement overrides the color pattern in Brown_Agate.

Here are two modifiers that you can use to adjust the standard textures to your liking.

PHONG AND PHONG_SIZE

You already have experience creating highlights using phong. phong_size allows you to control the relative size of the highlight on the shape. The syntax for phong_size is

```
phong_size tightness_value
```

For example:

```
phong_size 300 // A very small, tight highlight
phong_size 40  // A moderately soft highlight
phong_size 5   // A large, very soft highlight
```

Note that the higher the number, the smaller and tighter the highlight. Figure 4-14 shows three spheres with different phong_size values. The sphere at top left is phong_size 5, the one at top right is phong_size 40 (the default), and the bottom center sphere is phong_size 5.

REFLECTION

Reflection is one of the flashiest features of ray tracing. Scenes with a lot of reflection have a high-tech, glossy look. Accurate reflections on metal and glass objects make them look very realistic. The syntax for reflection is

```
reflection reflection_amount
```

For example,

```
reflection 1   // reflect 100% of the scene around this texture
reflection .5  // reflect  50% of the scene around this texture
reflection .21 // reflect  21% of the scene around this texture
```

Be sure to have objects and textures near the reflective object so it has something to reflect. Use TEXTEST.POV to try adding 25 percent or 50 percent reflection to a White_Marble floor with a sphere made of Blood_Sky sitting on it.

BUMPS

You can make any texture look bumpy by using the bumps keyword. Its syntax is

Figure 4-14 Three Different Phong_size Values

`bumps` *amount*

The `bump` amount may be any number from 0–1. Zero calls for no bumps and 1 gives a very bumpy appearance. For example,

```
object {
  sphere { <0 1 2> 1 }
    texture {
      color red 1
      phong 1
      bumps .6
      scale <.5 .2 .5>
    }
}
```

This creates a red sphere with small bumps all over its surface. The bumps will be wider than they are tall because the texture is scaled more on the x and z axes than on the y axis. This texture does not change the shape of the sphere. The sphere is still perfectly round; the change in the shading of the sphere simulates a bumpy surface. The sphere reflects light as if it were actually bumpy. To verify this, look at the edges of the sphere, which are still perfectly curved. If the sphere were actually bumpy, the edges would also be bumpy.

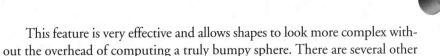

This feature is very effective and allows shapes to look more complex without the overhead of computing a truly bumpy sphere. There are several other bumpy texture modifiers, including

```
dents dent_amount
ripple ripple_amount
wrinkle wrinkle_amount
```

The range of these amounts is 0–1, with 0 giving no bumpiness and 1 causing a very bumpy appearance. These textures look best when they have a Phong highlight and light shining on them from one side. Only one of these may be used on a specific texture; they may not be combined.

SPEED CONSIDERATIONS

As you have seen, creating even a simple image using ray tracing involves many thousands of sophisticated calculations and these calculations take time. A complex scene can bring even the fastest PC to its knees. The ray tracer spends the largest amount of time working on the shapes to see if a particular ray intersects a given shape. Simple textures like a solid color or a standard marble don't add much time at all to the render, but some textures can add considerably to the trace time.

Reflection and transparency require more calculations than any other features. A complex scene with glass and metal traced at high resolution might take days to render. If this is the case with a scene you are working on, here are a few things to ease the way. These tips apply to any scene that's taking a long time to render.

- *Don't use the fancy textures for test renders.* Reflection and transparency look fantastic, but you don't need to use them when you are designing shapes or placing objects. Use solid color textures that will render more quickly when you are testing the placement of objects.
- *Run the ray tracer in the background.* If you're really getting into ray tracing, then you probably have at least a fast 386 CPU. CPUs like the 386 and 486 have special memory-management features that allow more than one program to run at once if your operating system supports that feature. If your image is taking hours to render, you don't need to tie up the computer with just that task. Windows and OS/2 allow you to run

the ray tracer as a background process so that you can do other things with your computer at the same time. (If you aren't sure whether POV-Ray can run under your multitasking environment, see the "Operating Environment" section in Chapter 2. Also check in the GRAPHDEV forum on CompuServe to see if new versions of POV-Ray are available that can take advantage of your multitasking environments.)

- *Use only one light source for test renders*. Each light source has to be checked against each object for shading, shadows, and highlights. The rendering time increases substantially with each added light source. For test renders, then, try using just one bright light rather than several dim lights. Several lights will look better in the final version, but for a test they just slow things down unnecessarily.

ADDING NEW TEXTURES TO THE TABLE SCENE

The table scene you created in Chapter 3 is made of interesting shapes, but the textures are plain and unrealistic. Very few scenes in the real world have that much solid color. Use the textures in TEXTURES.INC to make this scene more realistic. TABLE10.POV is a slightly modified version of TABLE9.POV. The camera has been moved a bit and a sky sphere has been added. We'll use this scene to demonstrate how you can greatly improve a scene by adding standard textures. You can render the scene at any point during the instructions to see how the changes affect the scene, or you can make all the changes and then render the complete scene only once. You'll probably want to render along the way if you have a faster computer. If your computer is slower, just follow along with the text and render the final version.

A WOODEN TABLE

The table should be made of wood, of course. DMFWood4 is a good wood texture that will look great on this table. DMFWood4 is sized for a unit object, but the table is approximately twice the size of a unit object. We'll make the texture even a little larger than that, so it can be seen well even at lower resolutions. The texture should be scaled by 3 on all axes to make it fit well with the table. Change all of the table textures from

```
texture { color Tan }
```

to

```
texture { DMFWood4 scale <3 3 3>}
```

(Don't forget to change the texture in each object where it appears. If your editor has a global search and replace feature, use it to speed this operation.) Save this file. (Render it too, if you wish.)

The table top looks good, but the legs may look strange because they are oriented vertically while the table top is oriented horizontally. Rotate the texture on the legs to fix this.

Change the texture on the four table legs from

```
texture { DMFWood4 scale <3 3 3>}
```

to

```
texture { DMFWood4 scale <3 3 3> rotate <-87 0 0> }
```

This turns the wood textures on the legs 87 degrees away from you. The grain of the wood will be parallel with the legs and should make them look more realistic.

A MARBLE EGG

This is an easy modification. Change the egg's texture from

```
texture { color Red }
```

to

```
texture { Red_Marble scale <.1 .1 .1> }
```

The egg has already been scaled down, so the Red_Marble is scaled down to ten times smaller to fit the egg.

A FINE CHINA PLATE

Change the "Blue Plate Special" from

```
texture { color Blue }
```

to

```
texture { PinkAlabaster scale <.35 .35 .35> }
```

The PinkAlabaster texture is set up for a unit object, and the plate is scaled

145

to be 75 percent of a unit object so it should be scaled down to fit the plate. In this case, the texture is scaled to half the size of the object so it will look more detailed. Don't take the default size of textures and objects as gospel. They are meant to be modified to whatever state looks best in your scene.

A GOLDEN MARTINI GLASS

Transform the orchid-colored goblet into a golden metal martini glass by changing the textures of all its components from

```
texture { color Orchid }
```

to

```
texture { Gold_Metal }
```

This gives a shiny, gold metal with a bit of reflection. The reflection will add to the rendering time, but it's worth it.

THE NEW SCENE

Save the changes to the file as TABLE11.POV, render, and view it. You should render a high-resolution version to fully appreciate all the details of the textures in it. Ideally, you should do it at 640x480, but if your computer is just too slow, try 320x240. Figure 4-15 shows the enhanced table.

You've enhanced this scene considerably with just a minimum of effort. The standard textures can be used quickly and easily to make even simple scenes look like a professional production.

Before you go on to the next chapter, experiment with TABLE11.POV and TEXTURES.INC. Try out different textures on the objects in the scene (don't forget the sky and floor).

Also, try reflection and Phong to modify the textures. For example, here's a highly polished wood texture:

```
texture { DMFWood4 phong 1 reflection .4 }
```

That effect is created by adding just a couple of words. Be daring and create your own textures for the scene. As with the other things you've learned, the best way to really grasp these concepts is to play with them creatively.

SUMMARY

- A texture is the material of which an object or shape is made.
- The texture description controls all facets of the surface appearance, including color, color pattern, shine, reflection, transparency, and more.
- The texture only modifies the color and shading on a shape, not the actual form of the shape.
- A texture may be placed in the body of the shape or the object. If it's placed in the shape body, it will only affect that shape. If it's placed in the object body, it will affect all shapes that make up that object.
- Some textures, like shapes and colors, are already defined in the TEXTURES.INC and STONES.INC files. These may be modified at the time of use without disturbing the original descriptions.
- The coloring of a texture may be solid or a pattern. Color patterns use two or more colors in some type of regular pattern generated mathe-

Figure 4-15 The Enhanced Table

147

matically. Patterns may be made more natural looking by adding turbulence.

- The checker color pattern creates a texture made up of alternating blocks of color. Its syntax is

```
checker COLOR1  COLOR2
```

- Texture patterns are three dimensional. You can think of applying a texture to an object as sculpting the object out of stone made from this texture material.

- Turbulence *amount_value* added to a texture using a color pattern will randomly "stir up" the texture across three dimensions. You can use any value for turbulence amount. Small values like 0.04 will only "stir" the texture slightly. Large values like 1 or 12 will "stir" the texture quite a bit.

- Color maps are used with color patterns like `marble`, `bozo`, and `agate` to provide them with a palette from which to choose colors for the pattern. There may be up to 20 entries in a color map. The syntax for color map is

```
color_map {
  [ low high COLOR1 COLOR2 ]
  [ low high COLOR1 COLOR2 ]
  [ low high COLOR1 COLOR2 ]
  ...
  [ low high COLOR1 COLOR2 ]
}
```

- Like shapes or objects, textures may be scaled, rotated, and translated.

- Phong_size *tightness_value* controls the size or tightness of the Phong highlight in a texture. Larger values make a smaller, tighter highlight, and smaller values make a larger, softer highlight. Values range from 1 (very, very small) to 1000 (very large).

- Reflection *value* controls the amount of reflection in a texture. Values range from 0 (no reflection) to 1 (100-percent reflective). Adding reflection to a texture adds greatly to the rendering time.

- Textures with transparency and/or reflection will take much longer to render than simple colored textures. Use simple textures for test renderings to save time.

- Wood textures are created from co-centric cylindrical bands of color centered on the *z* axis and may need to be rotated to look correct. For example, if you use wood on a vertically (*y*-axis) oriented object, rotate the wood texture by about 90 degrees on the *x* axis, like this:

```
texture { DMFWood4 rotate <89 0 0> }
```

- Any texture can be made to appear bumpy by using bumps, ripples, dents, or wrinkles. Shapes using one of these in their texture will appear to be bumpy even though the actual form of the shape is unchanged. Only the way the shape reflects light has been changed. Phong highlights look very good on bumpy shapes.

Enjoy your newfound mastery of shapes and textures. In Chapter 5 we'll explore some of the advanced features of POV-Ray and their use with shapes and textures.

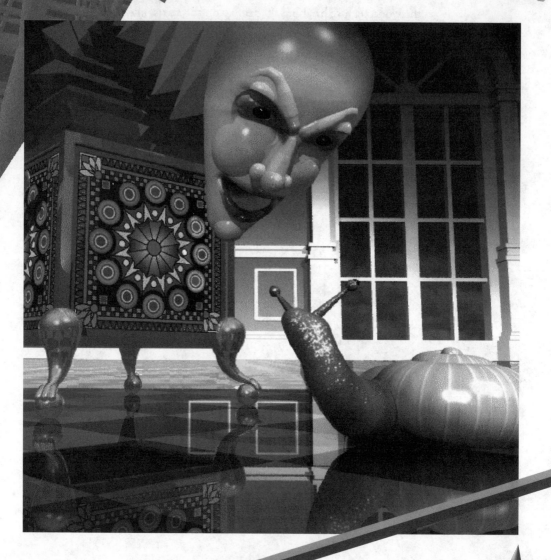

"A little learning is a dangerous thing."

—Alexander Pope

5

Advanced Shapes and Textures

Fortunately, that old warning isn't true when you're exploring the frontiers of computer art with your new ray tracer. You have now learned enough about POV-Ray and its features to create many interesting ray traced images. The variety of shapes you have already encountered can be combined in a truly infinite number of ways. The textures surveyed in Chapter 4 add another dimension: changing the texture imparts a new "feel" to the object. This chapter introduces some of the most useful advanced shapes and textures. We'll cover the two types of advanced shapes: compound shapes and complex primitives.

A compound shape is a single shape made of two or more shapes. CSG and composite are the two basic methods for making compound shapes. CSG techniques use logical operations to create the shape, and the composite technique joins two or more objects to create one object.

The complex primitives are built-in shapes that are more difficult to describe, but seeing them in images will give you some ideas for their use. These shapes include Height-Fields, quartics, and blobs.

Finally, we'll look at some advanced textures and techniques for changing the appearance of objects. You will learn how to control the transparency of objects and how to determine degree of refraction. You will also learn about layering textures one upon another to create subtle effects.

COMPOUND (CSG) SHAPES

Constructive Solid Geometry shapes, or more commonly, CSG shapes, are two or more shapes that are combined logically to create one shape. The basic idea behind them is to add and/or subtract several basic shapes to and from each other to create a single more complex shape. For instance, you can create a cane by adding a cylinder to a sphere or fashion a bowling ball by subtracting three small cylinders from a sphere.

Why not just have a basic shape for every object instead of going to all the trouble of creating the object from many parts? POV-Ray has to solve complex equations to render a basic shape. Relatively few objects have a shape that can be represented easily with a mathematical formula for the renderer to solve. It might somehow be possible to find an equation to describe a complex shape like an eagle or a sports car, but it would be highly specialized and very, very slow. It would be impossible to create the wide variety of shapes needed for a really terrific image.

CSG shapes can be made of any material and they can be scaled, rotated, and translated as you would the basic shapes they comprise. The only major difference between a CSG shape and a basic shape is that you can't specifically assign a material to a CSG shape. You must assign the material (or materials) to the individual shapes or to the parent object.

Shape creation with constructive solid geometry is a powerful tool. Let's take a look at how it works.

INSIDE AND OUTSIDE

Shapes must have a clear, definable inside and outside to be used effectively in a CSG shape. Figure 5-1 illustrates the concept of inside and outside as it is used in ray tracing.

The circle encloses an area of space with its surface. Any point within that area between its center and its surface is *inside* the circle. Any point not inside the circle is *outside* the circle. Points A and D are outside the circle. Points B and C are inside the circle. This simple concept is true for every shape that has a clear inside and outside.

When one shape is used alone in an object, the knowledge of which points are inside and which outside is not very useful. When more than one shape is

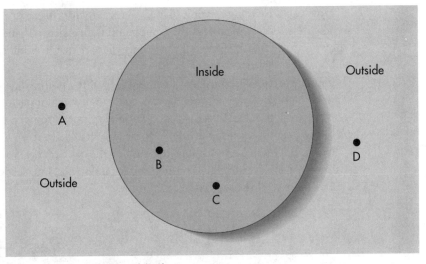

Figure 5-1 Inside and Outside a Shape

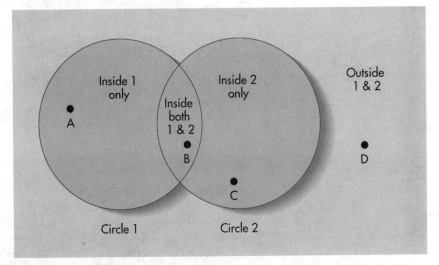

Figure 5-2 Overlapping Circles

used, however, this information can be used to create more interesting shapes. Figure 5-2 shows two circles overlapping each other. Notice that what is inside and what is outside is not as simply defined now. Point A is inside circle 1 and outside circle 2. Point B is inside both circles. Point C is inside circle 2 and outside circle 1. Point D is outside both circles.

How can a more interesting shape be created with this information? You can now describe a shape that is the combination of these two shapes. Figure 5-3 shows a shape that includes all the points that are inside either shape. This combination is called a *union*.

Figure 5-4 illustrates a shape that contains all the points that are in both shapes. If a point is only in one shape or the other, it is not part of the combined shape. This CSG shape is called an intersection. (You can identify the area of intersection because the lines become cross hatched there.)

Using unions and intersections to combine the basic shapes, you can create almost any object imaginable. Let's describe union and intersection in more detail using example POV-Ray scenes.

Figure 5-3   Union of Two Circles

Figure 5-4   Intersection of Two Circles

UNIONS

SPECIFYING A UNION

The CSG union of shapes is not hard to understand. Everything inside the shapes listed in the union are part of the shape. The syntax for union is easy, also:

```
object {
   union {
     shape_1
     shape_2
     shape_3...
   }
}
```

For example,

```
object {
   union {
      sphere { <0 0 0> 1 }
      sphere { <0 1 0> 1 }
   }
   texture { color red 1 }
}
```

Use the union keyword to start the shape block, and then list all the shapes that are part of the union shape. This union has only two shapes, but there is no limit to the number of shapes that could be in the union. This is also a valid union:

```
object {
   union {
      sphere { < 0 1 0> 1 }
      sphere { < 0 2 0> 1 }
      sphere { < 1 1 0> 1 }
      sphere { <-1 1 0> 1 }
      sphere { < 0 0 0> 1 }
      rotate <0 30 0>
   }
   texture { color red 1 green .3 phong .4 }
}
```

Notice the line where rotate is used. The set of spheres will be rotated by this line. So we see that CSG shapes like union can be transformed like any basic shape.

Any type of shape may be used in a union, for example:

```
object {
   union {
     sphere { <0 0 0> 1 }
     box {
       <1 0 1> <2 2 2>
       texture { color green 1 }
     }
   }
   texture { color red 1 }
}
```

The file UNION.POV shown in Listing 5-1 is a union of two shapes. (Don't forget to change to the \POVRAY\CHAPTER5 directory.) Render and view the file. Figure 5-5 shows the results.

Listing 5-1 UNION.POV

```
// Ray Tracing Creations
// Chapter 5
// This scene file demonstrates CSG shape techniques
//

#include "colors.inc"
#include "textures.inc"

camera {
   location     <5     10    -20>
   direction    <0     0     2>
   up           <0     1     0>
   right        <1.33  0     0>
   look_at      <0     0     0>
}
// Light source
object {   light_source { <25 25 -30> color red 1.5 green 1.5 blue 1.5 }
}

// This object uses CSG techniques
#declare BoxSize = 4
#declare SphereSize = 3.5
object {
   union {
     box {
       <-BoxSize -BoxSize -2> <BoxSize BoxSize BoxSize>
       texture { color Red }
     }
```

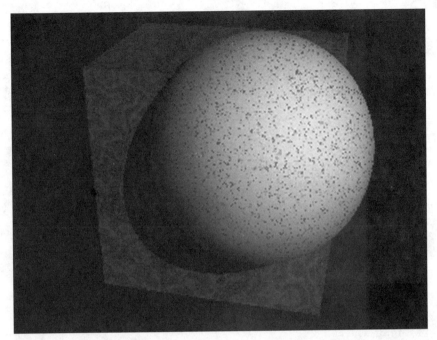

Figure 5-5 A Union Shape

```
    sphere { <1.8 1.8 -1.8> SphereSize
    }
  }
  texture {
    Cork
    scale <1.5 1 1>
  }
}
```

Though this appears to be two shapes, the program treats this as one shape. All the points in both spheres are unioned to make one shape. Note that a union does not imply that the shapes must be touching, the shape components could be a thousand units apart and still be one shape, and it can be textured as a complete shape.

TRANSFORMING A UNION

A union may be scaled, rotated, and translated like any other shape. When the union is transformed, all components of the union are affected. This is true of any CSG shape. The components of the CSG shape may also be transformed individually. Let's see how a union is transformed.

First, we'll modify UNION.POV so that the entire shape is scaled by <1 .5 1> to make it half its original height. Before it can be scaled unevenly, the sphere in this union must be replaced by a quadric ellipsoid because spheres cannot be scaled unevenly. Listing 5-2 shows UNION2.POV with these modifications.

Listing 5-2 UNION2.POV

```
// Ray Tracing Creations
// Chapter 5
// This scene file demonstrates CSG shape techniques
//

#include "colors.inc"
#include "textures.inc"
#include "shapes.inc"

camera {
   location    <5     10    -20>
   direction   <0     0     2>
   up          <0     1     0>
   right       <1.33  0     0>
   look_at     <0     0     0>
}
// Light source
object {   light_source { <25 25 -30> color red 1.5 green 1.5 blue 1.5 }
}

// This object uses CSG techniques
#declare BoxSize = 4
#declare SphereSize = 3.5
object {
   union {
     box {
        <-BoxSize -BoxSize -2> <BoxSize BoxSize BoxSize>
        texture { Jade }
     }
     quadric {
        Ellipsoid
        scale <SphereSize SphereSize SphereSize>
        translate <1.8 1.8 -1.8>
     }
     scale <1 .5 1> // Scale entire union
   }
   texture {
     Cork
     scale <1.5 1 1>
   }

}
```

The scale will not affect the texture because it was placed inside the union block. If we wanted to scale the texture also, we would place the scale line after the shape and the texture. Render and view UNION2.POV. Figure 5-6 shows what it looks like.

The entire shape, scaled as one, is now half its original height.

The individual parts of CSG shapes can also be transformed separately. Notice that the quadric ellipsoid in UNION2.POV was translated separately from the rest of the union. Listing 5-3 shows UNION3.POV, which scales the quadric ellipsoid and rotates the box. These examples emphasize the ability to transform CSG components independently.

Listing 5-3 UNION3.POV

```
// Ray Tracing Creations
// Chapter 5
// This scene file demonstrates CSG shape techniques
//

#include "colors.inc"
#include "textures.inc"
#include "shapes.inc"

camera {
    location      <5    10   -20>
    direction     <0    0    2>
    up            <0    1    0>
    right         <1.33 0    0>
    look_at       <0    0    0>
}
// Light source
object {   light_source { <25 25 -30> color red 1.5 green 1.5 blue 1.5 }
}
// This object uses CSG techniques
#declare BoxSize = 4
#declare SphereSize = 3.5
object {
    union {
        box {
            <-BoxSize -BoxSize -2> <BoxSize BoxSize BoxSize>
            texture { Jade }
            rotate <-30 0 0>
        }
        quadric {
            Ellipsoid
            scale <SphereSize SphereSize SphereSize>
            scale <.5 1 .5>
            translate <1.8 1.8 -1.8>
```

```
        }
    }
    texture {
        Cork
        scale <1.5 1 1>
    }

}
```

Render and view UNION3.POV. It should look like Figure 5-7.

The union keyword is usually used to combine shapes into one so the resulting shape can be transformed as one. Otherwise, each shape would have to be transformed individually. For example, in Chapter 3 we created a table using several different objects. If we wanted to rotate, scale, or translate that table we would have to place identical transformations in each object block making up the table, keeping everything "in synch." This wouldn't be easy, so instead, let's take that table and change it into a union so it can be transformed more easily. To do this, the shapes making up the table must be placed together

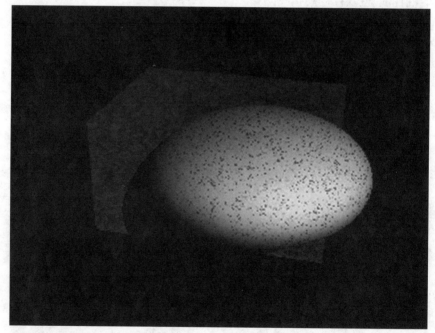

Figure 5-6   Scaling with a Union

into a union block. Listing 5-4 shows UNTABLE.POV, in which the table has been converted to a union shape.

Listing 5-4 UNTABLE.POV

```
// Ray Tracing Creations
// Chapter 5
// This scene file demonstrates CSG shape techniques
//

#include "colors.inc"
#include "textures.inc"

camera {
  location <5 6 -8>
  direction <0 0 1.5>
  look_at <0 2 0>
}

// Several boxes making a table combined in a union
object {
  union {
    box { <-2 0 1.5> <-1.5 4 2> }         // Back left leg
    box { <-2 0 -2> <-1.5 4 -1.5> }       // Front left leg
    box { <1.5 0 1.5> <2 4 2>}            // Back right leg
    box { <1.5 0 -2> <2 4 -1.5> }         // Front right leg
    box { <-2.5 4 -2.5> <2.5 4.2 2.5> } } // Table Top
  }
  texture {
    DMFWood4
  }
}
// The yellow floor
object {
  plane { <0 1 0> 0  }
    texture { checker color Blue color White scale <5 5 5> }
}


// A white light to the right of, above and behind the camera
object {
  light_source { <10 15 -20> color White }
}
```

The table is not only easier to transform this way, but the use of a union also makes the code easier to read. Notice that we are able to use just one tex-ture statement to apply the DMFWood4 texture to all the shapes in the

Figure 5-7   Independent Transformation in a Union

unioned table. A blue and white `checker` is applied to the floor to enhance the sense of perspective. Render and view UNTABLE.POV. Figure 5-8 shows the enhanced scene.

The table should appear just like it did before it was a union. `union` does not modify the shapes in any way, nor does it change the speed with which the shapes are rendered. Now that the table is conveniently packaged into a union, let's try transforming the union. Add a line to rotate the table by –30 degrees on the z axis. The `rotate` directive should be placed after the `union` and the `texture` so the texture will be rotated along with the union. Listing 5-5 demonstrates where and how you should place the `rotate` line in the scene file. Save the new file as UNTABLE2.POV.

Listing 5-5 Excerpt from UNTABLE2.POV

```
...
// Several boxes making a table combined in a union
object {
  union {
    box { <-2 0 1.5> <-1.5 4 2> }          // Back left leg
```

```
    box { <-2 0 -2> <-1.5 4 -1.5> }        // Front left leg
    box { <1.5 0 1.5> <2 4 2>}             // Back right leg
    box { <1.5 0 -2> <2 4 -1.5> }          // Front right leg
    box { <-2.5 4 -2.5> <2.5 4.2 2.5> } // Table Top
  }
  texture {
    DMFWood4
  }
  rotate <0 0 -30>
}
// The yellow floor
...
```

Render and view UNTABLE2.POV. Figure 5-9 shows the result of UN-TABLE2.GIF. The entire table is now "falling over."

The table can be transformed as one object any way you like. This is much simpler than trying to keep track of many objects and all their associated transforms. The union is often used to create objects to be animated. Scale a union to create a shrinking table, rotate a union to create a spinning table, or translate a union to "fly" the table through space. (Chapter 6 introduces some other

Figure 5-8 The Table as a Union

Figure 5-9 Tipped Table

Since the example programs are starting to get longer, we will sometimes provide only partial listings, focusing on the parts of interest for our discussion.
The complete files are, of course, on the provided disk and should have been
installed in your \POVRAY\CHAPTER5 subdirectory.

techniques useful for animation.) Use union anytime you need to treat a group
of shapes as one shape.

TEXTURING A UNION

Unions can be made of any material or even of multiple materials, but the
textures are not applied in the same manner as with the basic shapes. The
texture can't be applied directly to the union itself in the union block. To get
around this and texture the union, you can apply the texture to each

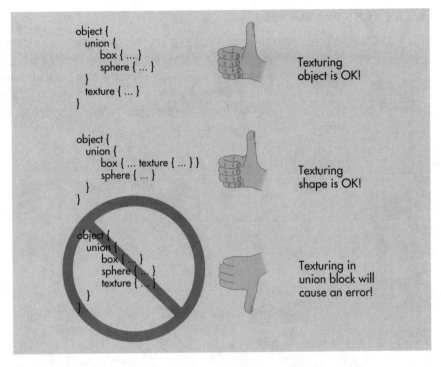

Figure 5-10 Texturing a Union

individual shape in the union or to the entire object the union belongs to. Texturing each component allows for more control over the exact scaling and positioning on each piece. Texturing the entire object will give the object the "carved from one piece" look. Figure 5-10 illustrates how a union can be textured.

A union without any textures will default to the object texture. Any shapes in the union without a specified texture will default to the object texture. The basic shapes in a union can be textured, but the union itself cannot be textured directly. These rules apply for all CSG shapes. As you have already seen, the individual shapes in a union can be given any texture. This allows you to create complex CSG shapes with a variety of textures on one shape. It also allows interesting effects when you use intersection, another CSG technique.

INTERSECTIONS

As the union might be the CSG carpenter combining shapes into one object, the intersection is the CSG sculptor. Where union combines all shapes into one, intersection makes a shape out of the places where the shapes overlap.

Intersections are a bit more difficult to grasp than unions, but they are far simpler than the easy tax forms you suffer each April. The syntax for `inter-section` is identical to `union`:

```
object {
    intersection {
      shape_1
      shape_2
      shape_3...
    }
}
```

For example,

```
object {
    intersection {
      sphere { <0 0 0> 1 }
      box   { <0 0 0> <1 1 1> }
    }
  texture { Guava }
}
```

Use the `intersection` keyword to start the shape block, and then list all the shapes that are part of the intersection. This intersection has only two shapes, but, as with unions, there is no limit to the number of shapes you can use in an intersection. Notice, though, that all the shapes in the intersection must overlap. If even one component doesn't overlap, the program will not be able to create a visible shape.

When all the shapes are intersecting, every shape listed in an intersection block won't necessarily be visible in the rendered shape. Only the space where *all* of the shapes in the intersection overlap will be visible. The resulting shape often looks nothing like the original shapes.

Like the union, almost any type of shape may be used in an intersection. For example:

```
object {
  intersection {
    sphere { <0 0 0> 1 }
    quadric { Ellipsoid scale <3 1 1> translate <0 1 0> }
    box { <-2 -1 -2> <2 1 2> }
  }
```

```
        texture { color red .35 green .6 blue .01 }
}
```

Like any other basic shape, intersections may be transformed, and the individual components of the intersection may be transformed separately.

Figures 5-11 and 5-12 show how an intersection of two circles can make a sort of eyeball shape. Listing 5-6 is a scene file using two spheres to re-create Figure 5-4 in three dimensions.

Listing 5-6 INTER.POV

```
// Ray Tracing Creations
// Chapter 5
// This scene file demonstrates CSG shape techniques
//

#include "colors.inc"
#include "textures.inc"

camera {
    location    <0    10 -20>
    direction   <0     0   3>
    up          <0     1   0>
    right       <1.33 0   0>
    look_at     <0     0   0>
}
// Light source
object {   light_source { <15 25 -30> color red 1.5 green 1.5 blue 1.5 } }

// This object uses CSG techniques
object {
    intersection {
      sphere { <0 0 0> 3.5  }
      sphere { <1.8 0 0> 3.5 }
    }
    texture {
      Cork
      scale <1.5 1 1>
    }
}
```

Render and view INTER.POV. Figure 5-11 shows the result.

From this angle, the shape in Figure 5-11 looks a bit like a big cork football. The "cork football" is actually closer in shape to a magnifying glass. Let's move the camera to one side so you can see the shape from a different angle. Change the camera description in Listing 5-6 so the location is 10 units to the right of the original location. In other words, add 10 to the X value of the location.

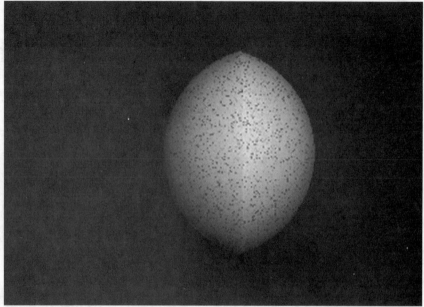

Figure 5-11 Intersection of Two Spheres

Figure 5-12 A Different Perspective on the Intersection

The new camera block should look like Listing 5-7. Save the new file as INTER2.POV, render, and view the scene. Figure 5-12 shows the shift in perspective.

Listing 5-7 Camera Block from INTER2.POV

```
...
#include "textures.inc"

camera {
    location    <10    10    -20>
    direction   <0     0      3>
    up          <0     1      0>
    right       <1.33  0      0>
    look_at     <0     0      0>
}
// Light source
...
```

Now you can see the spherical origins of this unusual shape. When experimenting, it's often helpful to change the camera's location to look at the object or scene being created from a fresh point of view.

TEXTURING AN INTERSECTION

Let's take this shape and apply two different textures to it. We'll start simple and change one of the spheres to a solid blue material. The other sphere we'll leave as cork.

Load INTER.POV, modify it so the right sphere is a solid blue material, and save this new file as INTER3.POV. The right sphere has its center at 1.8 units on the *x* axis. Be sure to put the blue texture inside the sphere description. If the texture is outside the sphere block it will generate an error message when you render the file. Listing 5-8 shows INTER3.POV.

Listing 5-8 INTER3.POV

```
// Ray Tracing Creations
// Chapter 5
// This scene file demonstrates CSG shape techniques
//

#include "colors.inc"
#include "textures.inc"

camera {
```

```
    location      <0     10    -20>
    direction     <0     0     3>
    up            <0     1     0>
    right         <1.33  0     0>
    look_at       <0     0     0>
}
// Light source
object {    light_source { <15 25 -30> color red 1.5 green 1.5
blue 1.5 } }

// This object uses CSG techniques
object {
   intersection {
      sphere { <0 0 0> 3.5  }
      sphere { <1.8 0 0> 3.5 texture { color Blue }}
   }
   texture {
      Cork
      scale <1.5 1 1>
   }
}
```

Figure 5-13 An Intersection with Different Textures

Render and view INTER3.POV. Figure 5-13 shows the result.

This image shows the same football-ish shape as INTER.GIF, but the left side of this shape is solid blue instead of cork. Though this is a single CSG shape, the ray tracer remembers what texture was specified for each component of the shape and determines how to color and shade each point by looking at the texture attached to that component. If a component doesn't have a texture attached to it specifically, the program uses the object texture. Because we used intersection, only a portion of the original spheres is visible.

INTER3 clearly demonstrates that textures can be assigned to the individual components of a CSG shape. INTER4.POV uses the same CSG shape to create a special effect with the cloud texture. Listing 5-9 shows INTER4.POV.

Listing 5-9 INTER4.POV

```
// Ray Tracing Creations
// Chapter 5
// This scene file demonstrates CSG shape techniques
//

#include "colors.inc"
#include "textures.inc"
camera {
    location    <10   5    -20>
    direction   <0    0    3>
    up          <0    1    0>
    right       <1.33 0    0>
    look_at     <0    0    0>
}
// Light source
object {   light_source { <35 10 -30> color red 1.5 green 1.5 blue 1.5 } }

// This object uses CSG techniques
object {
    intersection {
        sphere { <0 0 0> 3.5 texture { Clouds scale <.1 2 .1> } }
        sphere { <1.8 0 0> 3.5 texture { Clouds scale <2 .1 2> } }
    }
}

object { plane {<0 1 0> -3.5 texture { Cork } } }
```

Render and view INTER4.POV. Figure 5-14 shows the result.

The clouds texture is applied to both spheres with different scale values for each. The left side of the shape has horizontal cloud stripes because the texture was scaled smaller on its y axis and larger on the x and z axes. The right side of the shape has vertical stripes because we reversed the scaling: larger on

Figure 5-14 Applying Different Versions of a Texture

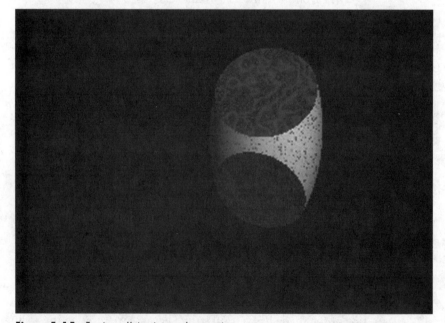

Figure 5-15 Turning a Union into an Intersection

the *y* axis and smaller on the *x* and *z* axes. The transparency in the clouds texture allows the entire surface shape to be seen. The horizontal and vertical cloud stripes create a strange and interesting pattern on the surface of the CSG shape. The cloud stripes also create an unusual shadow behind the shape that enhances the image.

Another interesting shape is created in INTER5.POV: the same box and ellipsoid from UNION3.POV, with `intersection` as the CSG type rather than `union`. The shape shown in Figure 5-15 is radically different from the original.

INSIDE OUT SHAPES

There is a character in Douglas Adams' book *So Long, and Thanks for All the Fish* named Wonko the Sane. He lives in a house that has been turned inside out. The furniture and carpet are on the "outside," and he has grass and trees "inside" the house. Of course, Wonko sees it differently. To him, the rest of the world is now "inside" the house he built for them and he is safe "outside" the insane asylum of the modern world. The next step in CSG requires the same kind of reasoning that spawned Wonko's inside out house.

We saw earlier how important the concept of a shape's inside and outside was to creating CSG shapes. Because the program knows what the inside of a sphere is, it can create shapes like the one in INTER.POV. This shape was made up of every place where the insides of the two spheres intersected or overlapped. What would happen though, if one of the spheres were turned *inside out*? The sphere's inside becomes the outside and the outside becomes the inside. This isn't just a surrealistic fantasy; it can be done easily in POV-Ray. Let's start in two dimensions to explain how an inside out or *inverse* shape works. Figure 5-16 shows two circles and a set of points inside and outside the circles.

Look at the normal circle on the left. Points C and D are inside the circle and points A, B, E, and F are outside the circle. This is the way you've been taught to perceive inside and outside, and it seems natural. Now look at the inverse circle on the right. What was the inside is now the outside and vice versa. Points C and D are outside of the inverted circle and points A, B, E, and F are inside of it. This challenges everything you've ever been taught about shapes. Every point that was considered outside is now called inside. The points didn't move, the circle didn't change at all. Only the way it is perceived has been changed, just as Wonko changed his perception of the world.

What happens when an inverted shape is used in an intersection? Figure 5-17 shows two pairs of intersecting circles and the shapes they create with CSG. The first pair is normal while the second pair has one normal circle and one inverse circle.

The first pair is essentially the same as the pair in Figure 5-2. Point A is outside both circles, points B and D are inside one circle, and point C is inside both circles. All the points that are inside both circles make up the shape below the two circles.

The second pair uses the same two circles, but the second one is inverted. Point A is now outside of circle 1 but *inside* of circle 2. Point B is now inside both circles. Point C is inside circle 1, but outside of the inverted circle 2. Point D is outside of both circles.

The shape created by this combination of a normal and an inverted circle is circle 1 with a curved piece cut out of it. This shape is still just the intersection, or overlap, between the two circles. The difference is circle 2 is now inverted and intersecting with every point that is not between its center and its surface.

Now let's try using an inverse shape in three dimensions. All that is required to invert any shape in POV-Ray is to include the keyword `inverse` in the shape's description. For example, here is a normal box shape:

```
box { <0 0 0> <1 1 1> } // Normal box
```

and here is an inverted box:

```
box { <0 0 0> <1 1 1> inverse } // Inverse box
```

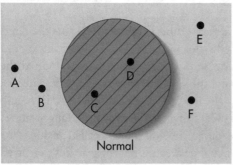
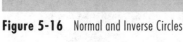
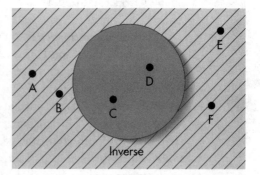

Figure 5-16 Normal and Inverse Circles

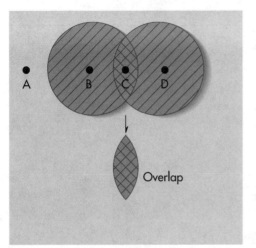

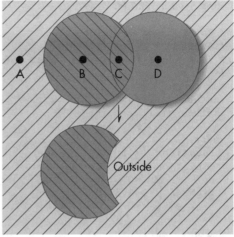

Figure 5-17   Intersecting Circles

No Inside or Outside?

Not all shapes have a clearly defined inside or outside. Consider a triangle. It is actually a two-dimensional shape being thrust into a three-dimensional world. It doesn't encompass three-dimensional space, nor does it cut space in half like a plane. Consequently, triangles don't make very interesting additions to CSG shapes. In fact, all shapes that are created from groups of triangles have no clear inside and outside. These shapes include the ordinary triangles, smooth triangles, Bicubic\Bezier patches, and Height-Fields (the latter are discussed later in this chapter).

This doesn't mean these shapes can't be used in a CSG shape. Union is the preferred method for combining a large group of triangles and there are many occasions where it is convenient to combine a Height-Field with several other shapes in a union. It does mean you can't expect to use a triangle-based object to "cut out" a shape from another shape using intersection or difference.

That's all there is to it. Any shape may be inverted, including a CSG shape like a union or an intersection. Listing 5-10, INTER5.POV, is a scene with an intersection of two spheres, one normal and one inverted.

Listing 5-10 INTER5.POV

```
// Ray Tracing Creations
// Chapter 5
// This scene file demonstrates CSG shape techniques
//

#include "colors.inc"
#include "textures.inc"

camera {
   location   <15    10    -20>
   direction  <0     0     3>
   up         <0     1     0>
   right      <1.33 0     0>
   look_at    <0     0     0>
}
// Light source
object {   light_source { <15 25 -30> color red 1.5 green 1.5 blue 1.5 }
}

// This object uses CSG techniques
object {
   intersection {
      sphere { <0 0 0> 3.5 }
      sphere { <2.8 1 0> 2.5 inverse }
   }
   texture {
      Cork
      scale <1.5 1 1>
   }
}
```

These two spheres are similar to the ones in the earlier INTER scenes, but the sphere on the right has been modified to highlight the effect of inverting it. It is inverted, of course, and it has been moved up and farther to the right. This sphere will, in effect, cut a chunk out of the sphere on the left. Render and view INTER5.POV. The Cork texture is used for consistency, but you can change it to any texture from TEXTURES.INC that you find more interesting. Figure 5-18 shows INTER5.GIF.

A small "dish" has been removed from the left sphere by the inverse right sphere. Figure 5-19 shows what the two spheres would look like if the shape were two normally unioned spheres. You can see that the dish cut out of the left sphere in Figure 5-18 is the intersection between the two shapes.

What happens when an inverse shape and a normal shape being intersected have different textures? This shape is treated just as any intersection

176

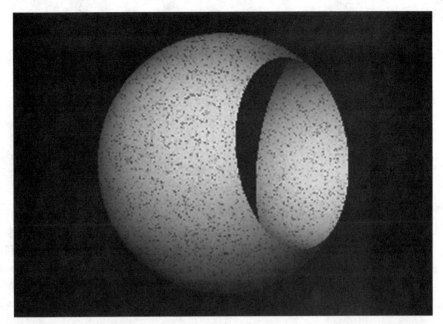

Figure 5-18   Intersection with an Inverted Circle

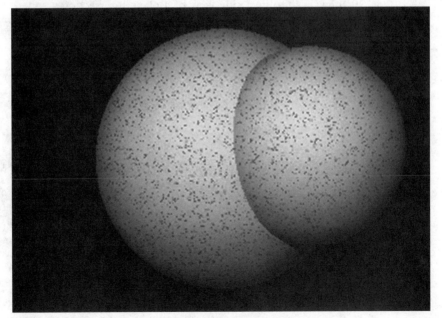

Figure 5-19   Union of the Two Spheres from Figure 5-18

with more than one texture is treated. Each portion of the CSG shape will have the texture that corresponds to the shape that makes up that bit of surface. So, the areas cut out of the original shape by the inverse shape will be the texture of the inverse shape.

The internal logic for an inverted shape is the same as that for a normal shape. Its surface is shaded the same, the program just treats the space inside and outside the shape differently. You can verify this by taking a simple scene with no CSG and adding the `inverse` keyword to one or more of the objects and rendering the scene. It won't change the scene at all: An inverse sphere is still a sphere.

INTERSECTING OTHER SHAPES

So far, the plane shape has only been used as a floor. It works great for this purpose, but you can do many more interesting things with a plane in CSG. A plane is an infinite shape, but for the purposes of ray tracing we can treat it as if it had an inside and outside. Consider everything on the side of the plane the normal is on as outside the plane and everything on the other side as inside the plane.

Using the intersection of a plane and a sphere demonstrates this. Figure 5-20 shows a simplified side view of a plane intersecting a sphere. The arrow pointing upward represents the plane's normal. This is the outside side of the

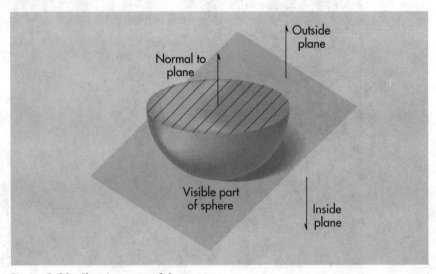

Figure 5-20 Plane Intersecting Sphere

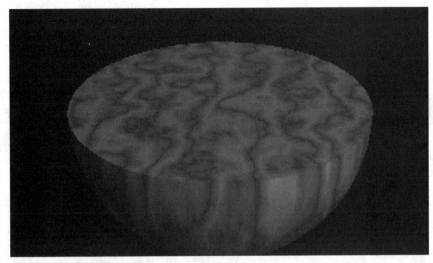

Figure 5-21   Rendering of Plane Intersecting Sphere

plane. The sphere and the inside of the plane intersect in the shaded area. Only the bottom half of the sphere will appear when this shape is rendered. The file INTPLANE.POV creates a hemisphere by intersecting a plane with a sphere. Render and view INTPLANE.POV; Figure 5-21 shows the result.

DIFFERENCES

What's the difference? A CSG difference is a base shape with other shapes cut out of it. This doesn't fit the classic definition of a logical difference, but it is an appropriate name for this shape. Figure 5-22 shows the difference between a sphere and a box. The sphere is the base and the box is cut out of the sphere.

Look familiar? It should, a CSG difference shape is just an intersection of one normal shape and one or more inverse shapes. The program does the work of making the extra shapes inverse when you specify difference. The syntax for difference is

```
object {
   difference {
      shape_1 // This first shape is the base shape
      shape_2 // The following shapes are made inverse and "cut out" of the
      shape_3... // base shape.
   }
}
```

CREATIONS

For example,

```
object {
   difference {
      sphere { <0 0 0> 2 }
      box    { <-1 -1 -1> <1 1 3> } // This box will be cut out of the sphere
   }
   texture { Guava }
}
```

This same shape could also be expressed with an intersection as

```
object {
   intersection {
      sphere { <0 0 0> 2 }
      box    { <-1 -1 -1> <1 1 3> inverse } // This box will be cut out of the sphere
   }
   texture { Guava }
}
```

The difference shape saves you a few keystrokes by automatically setting the other shapes as inverse. Why use difference at all if intersection can be used

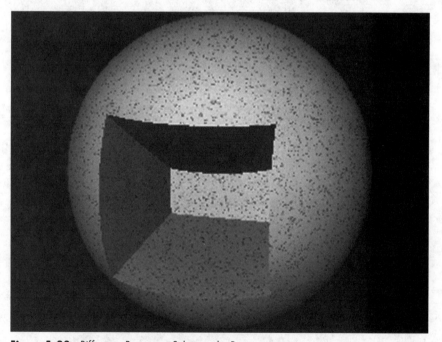

Figure 5-22 Difference Between a Sphere and a Box

the same way? Many people are better able to visualize the effects of the difference since it is less flexible than intersection.

Let's use difference to poke some holes in a wooden cube. Listing 5-11 shows DIFF.POV, which is a difference between a box and a cylinder.

Listing 5-11 DIFF.POV

```
// Ray Tracing Creations
// Chapter 5
// This scene file demonstrates CSG shape techniques
//

#include "colors.inc"
#include "textures.inc"
#include "shapes.inc"
camera {
   location  <9     8      -20>
   direction <0     0      2>
   up        <0     1      0>
   right     <1.33  0      0>
   look_at   <0     0      0>
}
// Light source
object {   light_source { <25 25 -30> color red 1.5 green 1.5 blue 1.5 } }

// This object uses
object {
   difference {
      box {
         <-4 -4 -4> <4 4 4>
      }
      quadric { Cylinder_Z scale <3 3 3> }
   }
   texture {
      DMFLightOak
      scale <1.5 1 1>
   }
}
// The checkered floor
object {
  plane { <0 1 0> -4  }
   texture { checker color Blue color White scale <5 5 5> }
}
```

The *z* axis cylinder will pierce the box and put a hole through its center. The quadric cylinder is infinite, but since it won't be visible, we don't need to use the disk shape. Render and view DIFF.POV. Figure 5-23 shows the result of DIFF.GIF. A large hole goes through the wood textured box. The hole is where the cylinder would be if it were not being used as a "carving" shape. Figure 5-24 illustrates what the cylinder would look like if this CSG shape were a union instead of a difference.

Here is a technique for testing a difference or intersection that isn't working as expected. Make the shape a union, and if the shape is complex, comment-out the original textures and make all the shapes in the CSG a different color. Then render the image again. Often this will ferret out a misplaced or off-sized shape that wasn't visible previously.

Notice that the base shape in a difference is not automatically carved by the succeeding shapes. If the succeeding shapes don't overlap the base shape, they won't cut a piece out of the shape.

Now, let's add x and y axes cylinders to the difference to cut out holes on the other four sides of the box. Listing 5-12 shows DIFF2.POV, which includes the extra cylinders in the difference.

Listing 5-12 DIFF2.POV

```
// Ray Tracing Creations
// Chapter 5
// This scene file demonstrates CSG shape techniques
//

#include "colors.inc"
#include "textures.inc"
#include "shapes.inc"
camera {
    location    <9     8      -20>
    direction   <0     0       2>
    up          <0     1       0>
    right       <1.33  0       0>
    look_at     <0     0       0>
}
// Light source
object {   light_source { <25 25 -30> color red 1.5 green 1.5
blue 1.5 } }

// This object uses CSG techniques
object {
    difference {
        box {
            <-4 -4 -4> <4 4 4>
        }
        quadric { Cylinder_Z scale <3 3 3> }
        quadric { Cylinder_Y scale <3 3 3> }
        quadric { Cylinder_X scale <3 3 3> }
    }
```

```
    texture {
      DMFLightOak
      scale <1.5 1 1>
    }
}
// The checkered floor
object {
  plane { <0 1 0> -4  }
    texture { checker color Blue color White scale <5 5 5> }
}
```

Render and view DIFF2.POV. Figure 5-25 shows the result.

This shape is very interesting and highlights the power of CSG and the ease with which complex shapes can be created with only a few shapes. Notice that when we created the CSG shape we made sure all the component shapes were centered on the origin. It's always best to create shapes this way so they can be easily transformed. It is tempting to create shapes where they will be positioned in the image, but this makes it very difficult to reposition them later. Shapes that are centered on the origin <0 0 0> can be easily scaled, rotated, and translated into their proper positions later, and they can be easily reused in other scenes in the future.

Figure 5-23 Difference Between a Box and a Cylinder

183

Figure 5-24   Union Instead of Difference

Figure 5-25   Difference with Multiple Cylinders

NESTING CSG SHAPES

Any shape type can be used in a CSG union, intersection, or difference. A CSG shape is treated by POV-Ray like any other shape, so you can use CSG shapes inside of a CSG shape. This allows easy creation of complex shapes.

Let's modify the shape we created with difference and then use it to create another shape by using CSG in CSG. The cylinders in DIFF2 go through the center of the box. It would be interesting to see what they would look like moved up a bit. Each cylinder could be translated individually, but it's much easier to put all three cylinders into a union and then translate the union. Listing 5-13 shows DIFF3.POV in which this has been done.

Listing 5-13 DIFF3.POV

```
// Ray Tracing Creations
// Chapter 5
// This scene file demonstrates CSG shape techniques
//


#include "colors.inc"
#include "textures.inc"
#include "shapes.inc"
camera {
    location    <9     8      -20>
    direction   <0     0      2>
    up          <0     1      0>
    right       <1.33  0      0>
    look_at     <0     0      0>
}
// Light source
object {   light_source { <25 25 -30> color red 1.5 green 1.5 blue 1.5 } }

// This object uses CSG techniques
object {
    difference {
        box {
            <-4 -4 -4> <4 4 4>
        }
        union {
            quadric { Cylinder_Z scale <3 3 3> }
            quadric { Cylinder_Y scale <3 3 3> }
            quadric { Cylinder_X scale <3 3 3> }
            translate <0 4 0>
        }
```

```
        }
        texture {
            DMFLightOak
            scale <1.5 1 1>
        }
    }
    // The checkered floor
    object {
      plane { <0 1 0> -4  }
      texture { checker color Blue color White scale <5 5 5> }
    }
```

The union includes all three cylinders and has been translated up the *y* axis by 4 units. Render and view DIFF3.POV. Figure 5-26 shows the result. Is it what you expected?

The X and Z cylinders are now cutting off the top of the box. The Y cylinder stretches infinitely up and down, so moving it up by 4 units doesn't change its affect on the box. Notice that the program now sees the three cylinders as

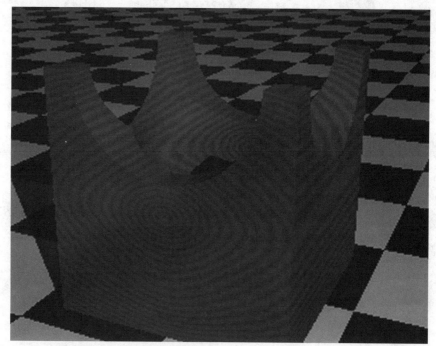

Figure 5-26 Unionizing and Translating

one CSG union shape. The final shape is now a CSG difference between a box and a union, not a box and three cylinders. This shape is still relatively simple to visualize, but as more shapes are added it becomes more difficult to read the file and to visualize the final shape. Let's use `declare` to make this file easier to read. Listing 5-14 shows DIFF4.POV, which declares the union of cylinders as XYZ_Cylinders. That union name is used in the CSG difference rather than the individual shapes. This makes the file easier to read, and the declared shape can be used later in the scene with other shapes.

Listing 5-14 DIFF4.POV

```
// Ray Tracing Creations
// Chapter 5
// This scene file demonstrates CSG shape techniques
//

#include "colors.inc"
#include "textures.inc"
#include "shapes.inc"
camera {
    location    <9    8    -20>
    direction   <0    0    2>
    up          <0    1    0>
    right       <1.33 0    0>
    look_at     <0    0    0>
}
// Light source
object {   light_source { <25 25 -30> color red 1.5 green 1.5 blue 1.5 } }

#declare XYZ_Cylinders =
    union {
        quadric { Cylinder_Z scale <3 3 3> }
        quadric { Cylinder_Y scale <3 3 3> }
        quadric { Cylinder_X scale <3 3 3> }
        translate <0 4 0>
    }

// This object uses
object {
    difference {
        box { <-4 -4 -4> <4 4 4> }
        union { XYZ_Cylinders}
    }
    texture {
        DMFLightOak
        scale <1.5 1 1>
    }
}
```

CREATIONS

```
// The checkered floor
object {
  plane { <0 1 0> -4 }
    texture { checker color Blue color White scale <5 5 5> }
}
```

This scene will produce the same image as DIFF3.POV, so there is no need to render it. If you did, though, you'd find that using a declare does not cause the rendering to slow down.

Let's go one step further with this shape and place the entire box-cylinder shape into an intersection with a sphere. We'll place a large sphere so that it encompasses the interesting carved part of the box. Figure 5-27 uses a slightly transparent sphere to demonstrate how such a sphere can be positioned. The intersection between the sphere and the CSG difference results in a shape that has all the points inside the sphere and the carved box.

Listing 5-15 shows DIFF5.POV, an intersection between a sphere and the carved box.

Listing 5-15 DIFF5.POV

```
// Ray Tracing Creations
// Chapter 5
// This scene file demonstrates CSG shape techniques
//

#include "colors.inc"
#include "textures.inc"
#include "shapes.inc"
camera {
    location    <9     8     -20>
    direction   <0     0     2>
    up          <0     1     0>
    right       <1.33  0     0>
    look_at     <0     0     0>
}
// Light source
object {   light_source { <25 25 -30> color red 1.5 green 1.5 blue 1.5 } }

// This object uses CSG techniques
object {
    intersection {
      sphere { <0 2 0> 5}
      difference {
        box {
          <-4 -4 -4> <4 4 4>
        }
        union {
          quadric { Cylinder_Z scale <3 3 3> }
```

188

```
            quadric { Cylinder_Y scale <3 3 3> }
            quadric { Cylinder_X scale <3 3 3> }
            translate <0 4 0>
        }
      }
   }
   texture {
      DMFLightOak
      scale <1.5 1 1>
   }
}
// The checkered floor
object {
   plane { <0 1 0> -4  }
   texture { checker color Blue color White scale <5 5 5> }
}
```

Render and view DIFF5.POV. Figure 5-28 shows the result.

This shape is very different from the shapes used to create it. CSG techniques enable you to use the basic primitives to create far more complex and interesting shapes than are possible by simply adding more shapes.

Figure 5-27 Transparent Sphere Demonstrates Intersection

CREATIONS

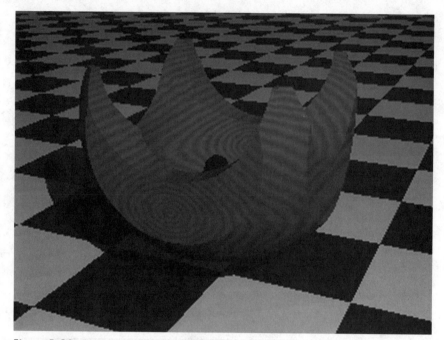

Figure 5-28 Intersection Between a Sphere and a Carved Box

COMPOSITE OBJECTS

The composite object is aptly described by its name. It is an object that is made up of a collection or composite of other objects. The syntax for a composite object is

```
composite {
    object { ... }
    object { ... }
    object { ... }
    [TRANSFORMATIONS...]
}
```

For example:

```
composite {
    object { sphere { <-6 0 0> 3 texture { color red 1 } }
    object { sphere { < 6 0 0>  3 texture { color red 1 } } }
    object { box    {<-5 -3 0> <5 3 0>}  texture {color blue 1}}
    rotate <0 30 0>
    translate <0 4 0>
}
```

Composite objects are used for applications similar to those of unions. Composites may be transformed as a whole. Unlike unions, they cannot be used in CSG since they are objects, not shapes. Composite objects may use composite objects. For example,

```
composite {
    object { sphere { <-6 0 0> 3 texture { color red 1 } }
    composite {
        object { sphere { <6 0 0>  3 texture { color red 1 } }
        object { sphere { <1 12 0> 3 texture { color red 1 } }
    }
    object { box    {<-5 -3 0> <5 3 0>}  texture {color blue 1}}
    scale <2 2 8>
    translate <0 7 10>
}
```

Composite objects cannot be textured. Each object in a composite should have its own texture, otherwise it will use the default texture.

PRIMITIVES

USING DESIGN PROGRAMS WITH POV-RAY

You may be wondering whether you can use drawing and rendering programs to create the scene files for POV-Ray. After all, it might be easier in many cases to draw an object interactively than to design it directly using POV scene files. The answer is "yes, you can."

In most commercial rendering programs, triangles are the only primitive shape. These programs use triangles to create all of the other shapes used in the program. There are advantages and disadvantages to this approach.

On the plus side, using only triangles simplifies the job of the programmer. With only one primitive to worry about, she can work on optimizing that shape. It is also easier to create objects like 3D text when using triangles. Graphic front ends are easier to write for triangles. And usually object files can be easily converted to other formats since triangles are so simple.

Conversely, it can require many thousands of triangles to create something as simple as a perfectly smooth sphere. The solid shapes in POV-Ray can be scaled to any size without degrading image quality, but shapes created from triangles must contain many, many triangles to even approach this high quality. These massive numbers of triangles take up huge amounts of memory and can

191

be very slow to render even with the best optimization. Scene files can be large and unwieldy. Also, constructive solid geometry is very difficult to manage with triangle-based shapes. Very few rendering programs even attempt this feature.

POV-Ray is widely used to render solid shape primitives, but it can handle triangles with equal grace. Complex shapes made out of triangles for POV-Ray are almost always created with a utility program or converted from another format.

One popular commercial rendering program is 3D Studio (3DS) by Autodesk (not included with this book). This three-dimensional design and animation program is highly regarded by reviewers and users. It has a sophisticated graphical front end that allows the user to create highly complex objects, scenes, and animations. It is highly optimized for commercial use and can quickly render high-quality images for use on the PC or on broadcast television. 3DS does make tradeoffs for its speed, though. It is a scan-line renderer, not a ray tracer. In plain terms, this means 3DS cannot do true reflections, shadows, refractions, or other effects that are the forte of ray tracers like POV-Ray.

Fortunately, you can convert 3DS files for use with POV-Ray since all 3DS objects are made up of triangles. The program 3DS2POV.EXE is included on the bundled disk for just this purpose. Note that 3DS2POV requires a math coprocessor to run.

The converter is usually used for two purposes. One is to convert individual objects created in 3DS and use these objects in POV-Ray scene files. The modeler in 3DS is excellent and it can make object creation much easier. The second use is to convert an entire 3DS scene—objects, lights, cameras, and all. POV-Ray is used to render a high-quality version of the scene with true reflections, lighting effects, shadows, refraction, and so on. It takes longer, but the result is worth the wait.

3DS2POV converts from 3D Studio ASCII format into a POV-Ray scene file. Therefore you must first run 3D Studio, load the file you wish to convert, and then choose the "SAVE AS ASCII" option from the file menu. If you wish to convert an object only, be sure that the object is the only item in the scene before saving.

The example is a conversion of an entire scene. Since it wasn't possible to include 3DS on the bundled disk, we've included a scene already saved in ASCII format. Let's use 3DS2POV to convert the 3DS file, MARBVASE.ASC, to the POV-Ray file, MARBVASE.POV.

At the command line, type

```
C:\POVRAY\CHAPTER5> 3DS2POV MARBVASE.ASC MARBVASE.POV (ENTER)
```

3DS2POV will work for a while converting the thousands of triangles to a POV-Ray format scene file. When it finishes there should be two new files created, MARBVASE.INC and MARBVASE.POV. Listing 5-16 shows MARB-VASE.POV.

Listing 5-16 MARBVASE.POV

```
#include "colors.inc"
#include "shapes.inc"
#include "textures.inc"

/* Camera: Camera01 */
camera {
    location <-142.2507 -769.0851 379.6377>
    direction <0 2.42 0>
    up <0 0 1>
    sky  <0 0 1>
    right <1.33 0 0>
    look_at <-7.4766 -48.4126 26.5369>
}


/* Light: Light01 */
object {
    light_source {
        <262.5925 -320.3238 255.3331> color red 0.90 green 0.86 blue 0.86
        spotlight
        point_at <18.1071 -6.0438 7.5527>
        tightness 0
        radius 0.50
        falloff 23.62
    }
}

#declare MARBLE_TEAL_2S = texture {
    ambient 0.1 diffuse 0.7
    phong 1.0 phong_size 70.0
    color White
}

#declare MARBLE_TEAL = texture {
    ambient 0.1 diffuse 0.7
    phong 1.0 phong_size 70.0
    color White
```

```
}

#declare DARKER_LIGHTWOOD = texture {
    ambient 0.1 diffuse 0.7
    phong 1.0 phong_size 70.0
    color White
}

#declare LIGHT_GRANITE = texture {
    ambient 0.1 diffuse 0.7
    phong 1.0 phong_size 70.0
    color White
}

#declare SHINYBLAK_MIRROR = texture {
    ambient 0.1 diffuse 0.7
    phong 1.0 phong_size 70.0
    color White
}

#declare SHINYBLACK = texture {
    ambient 0.1 diffuse 0.7
    phong 1.0 phong_size 70.0
    color White
}

#declare Default = texture {
    ambient 0.1 diffuse 0.7
    phong 1.0 phong_size 70.0
    color White
}

composite {  /* All Objects */
    #include "marbvase.inc"

    bounded_by {
    box { <-524.4711 -807.0038 -107.3164> <522.1447 357.6435 122.3808> }
    }

    /*
        Scene extents
        X - Min: -524.4711  Max: 522.1447
        Y - Min: -807.0038  Max: 357.6435
        Z - Min: -107.3164  Max: 122.3808
    */
}
```

Notice that the texture names are correct, but all the textures are set to a shiny white material. Textures do not convert from 3DS to POV-Ray, so they must be handled manually or with texture libraries. Texture libraries are specified with the -L(libname) option. Note 3DS2POV uses only minus signs in command-line switches. You cannot use +L(libname). Try this example:

`C:\POVRAY\CHAPTER5> 3DS2POV MARBVASE.ASC MARBVAS2.POV -LVASELIB.INC` ⸢ENTER⸣

A texture library is a POV-Ray include file. If 3DS2POV comes across the same texture name in the 3DS file and the POV-Ray library, it will use that texture instead of the default shiny white texture. It's possible to create comprehensive libraries and fully automate your conversion process, but for this example, we'll edit the textures by hand.

Listing 5-17 shows the modified textures saved in MARBVAS2.POV.

Listing 5-17 Excerpt from MARBVAS2.POV

```
...
#declare MARBLE_TEAL_2S = texture {
    PinkAlabaster
    ambient 0.1 diffuse 0.7
    phong 1.0 phong_size 70.0
}

#declare MARBLE_TEAL = texture {
    PinkAlabaster
    ambient 0.1 diffuse 0.7
    phong 1.0 phong_size 70.0
}
#declare DARKER_LIGHTWOOD = texture {
    DMFWood4
    ambient 0.1 diffuse 0.7
    phong 1.0 phong_size 70.0
}

#declare LIGHT_GRANITE = texture {
    White_Marble
    ambient 0.1 diffuse 0.7
    phong 1.0 phong_size 70.0
}

#declare SHINYBLAK_MIRROR = texture {
    color Gray20
    reflection .5
    ambient 0.1 diffuse 0.7
    phong 1.0 phong_size 70.0
}

#declare SHINYBLACK = texture {
    color Gray20
    ambient 0.1 diffuse 0.7
    phong 1.0 phong_size 70.0
```

```
}

#declare Default = texture {
    ambient 0.1 diffuse 0.7
    phong 1.0 phong_size 70.0
    color White
}
...
```

Render and view MARBVAS2.POV. Figure 5-29 shows the result.

This scene renders relatively quickly considering the large number of triangles contained in it. This is due to the optimized bounding shapes that 3DS2POV automatically creates. Quite complex and interesting 3D Studio shapes and scenes can be effectively rendered with POV-Ray due to this excellent utility.

Let's move on to some advanced techniques with the complex primitives. The POV-Ray features used may be a bit hard to understand at first, but fortunately you don't have to understand everything to begin to experiment with and enjoy them! We'll start with "height fields."

Figure 5-29 Scene Data from 3D Studio Ray Traced with POV-Ray

COMPLEX PRIMITIVES

HEIGHT-FIELDS

The Height-Field is one of the slickest primitives in POV-Ray and images using one have a high "Wow" factor. A Height-Field is a mesh of triangles where the height of the triangles is determined by the values in a graphic image file. Figure 5-30 shows a Height-Field rising out of rippling waters.

The Height-Field in this image is a fractal landscape, which is a popular and impressive use for the shape. Height-Fields can also be used for great-looking 3D text, graphing mathematical functions, bas-relief effects, and more.

The syntax for a Height-Field is

```
object {
   height_field {
      IMAGE_TYPE              //(gif, pot, or tga)
      "image.ext"
      [water_level value]    // value in range 0-255
   }
   texture { ... }
}
```

For example,

```
object {
   height_field { gif "plasma.gif"  }
   texture { Brown_Agate}
}
```

or,

```
object {
   height_field {
     tga "sombrero.tga"
     water_level 5
   }
   texture {
     color Blue
     reflection .7
     ripples .5
   }
   scale <3 1 3>
   rotate <-30 0 0>
}
```

Figure 5-30 Height-Field Rising Out of Rippling Waters

A Height-Field is a 1-unit wide by 1-unit long box made up of many small triangles. The height of each triangle making up the box is taken from the palette index or color value of the pixels in a graphic image file like GIF or Targa. Image files can store color information in one of two ways: palette based or true color.

Image formats like GIF use a *palette-based* method. The image file contains a table of up to 256 colors that are used in the image. This table is called the palette. Following the palette is the image data. For each pixel in the image a palette number is stored. If palette entry 5 is the color red, then the file will contain a number 5 for each red pixel in the image. When a GIF file is used in a height field, the palette number is used for the height, not for the color. Every pixel with palette entry 0 will have no height, and every pixel with palette entry 255 will be 1 unit high.

The optional *water_level* parameter tells the program to use triangles below a certain height. For the default value of 0, all triangles are used, and legal values are between 0 and 255. For example, "water_level 128" tells POV-Ray to render only the top half of the Height-Field. The other half is "below the water" and shouldn't be rendered. This term comes from the popular use of Height-Fields to render landscapes. A Height-Field is used to create islands and another shape like a plane is used to simulate water around the islands. A large portion of the Height-Field is obscured by the "water" so the *water_level* parameter was introduced to allow the program to ignore the unseen parts of the Height-Field. *Water_level* can also cut away unwanted lower values in a Height-Field. For example, if you have an image of a fractal on a solid colored background (palette entry 0), you can remove the triangles that correspond to the background in the Height-Field by specifying *water_level 1*. (Future versions of POV-Ray may use a water-level range of 0.0 to 1.0; check your documentation on disk.)

Image formats like Targa store colors directly for each pixel. This is called the *true color* method, and more storage space is required for the image. Three bytes of color information are stored for each pixel. This is referred to as 24-bit color because a byte has 8 bits. POV-Ray uses Targa files as numeric data files rather than for graphic images. The red is multiplied by 256 and added to the green value to represent a number between 0 and 65,535. (The blue value is ignored.) This allows creation of a much smoother Height-Field than the palette-based method. True-color Height-Field files cannot be created manually with a paint program, but must be generated with a utility.

You use the POT file format generated by Fractint (see *The Waite Group's Fractal Creations*) the same way you use a Targa file. The mesh of triangles corresponds directly to the pixels in the image file. There are two triangles for each pixel. The x and z axes position of the triangles is determined by the corresponding pixel location. The lower-left pixel creates two triangles near $x=0$, $z=0$. The upper-right pixel creates two triangles near $x=1$, $z=1$. The resolution of the image file does not change the size of the Height-Field, only the number of triangles in the shape. The y-axis (height) component of the triangles at each pixel is determined by the pixel data as described earlier. The higher the number, the higher the Y value of the triangles. The maximum height of an unscaled Height-Field is 1 unit. The minimum height is 0 units.

Because each pixel in the image corresponds to two triangles, the higher the resolution of the image file used to create the Height-Field, the smoother it will look. A 640x480 GIF has the potential to create a smoother Height-Field than a 320x200 GIF.

Let's use a GIF file included on the bundled disk to demonstrate creating 3D text with the height field. The image file LOGO.GIF was created using a Windows paint program. Figure 5-31 shows the rendering of the resulting

Figure 5-31 LOGO. GIF Created with Paint Program and Smoothed Using PICLAB

Height-Field. The paint program's text tool was used to create large, bold white text on a black background. This image was saved as a GIF file and then loaded into Piclab. In Piclab, the image was mapped to a grayscale palette and smoothed several times.

The scene HFLOGO.POV (Listing 5-18) uses LOGO.GIF to create an impressive POV-Ray 3D logo. Render and view it. Figure 5-32 shows the result.

Listing 5-18 HFLOGO.POV

```
// Simple Height field
camera {
  location <0 6 -20>
  direction <0 0 3>
  look_at <0 5 5>
}
object {
  height_field { gif "logo.gif" translate <-.5 0 -.5> }
  scale <8 1 8>
  rotate <-50 0 0>
  translate <0 5 5>
  texture { color red 1 phong 1}
}
object {
  plane { <0 1 0> 0  }
    texture { color green 1 }
 }
object {
 sphere { <0 0 0> 1000 }
 texture { color blue 1 green .25 ambient 1 diffuse 0 }
}
```

```
object {
  light_source { <8 22 -23> color red 1 green 1 blue 1 }
}
```

Height-Fields may be rotated, translated, and scaled like any other shape. Height-Fields cannot be used as true CSG shapes, though they are allowed in CSG shapes.

BICUBIC PATCHES

A way to create interesting curved surfaces, a Bicubic or Bezier patch is a 3D curved mesh of triangles defined by 16 control points. The control points determine the shape of the 3D curve by "pulling" at the mesh in the direction of the points. Figure 5-33 shows a Bezier patch.

Since the patch is defined by a curve, the actual number of triangles can be changed without changing the basic shape of the patch. This is useful for creating smooth curved surfaces. You can do testing with very few triangles and then give your final draft many triangles for maximum smoothness.

The syntax for a bicubic patch is

Figure 5-32 Logo Rendered by POV-Ray

201

Figure 5-33 Bicubic/Bezier Patch

```
object {
   bicubic {
      patch_type [flatness_val with types 2 and 3] u_steps v_steps
      <control point  1> <control point  2> <control point  3> <control point  4>
      <control point  5> <control point  6> <control point  7> <control point  8>
      <control point  9> <control point 10> <control point 11> <control point 12>
      <control point 13> <control point 14> <control point 15> <control point 16>

   }
}
```

We will be using only patch type 1 here. It does not require a flatness value. Information on other patch types can be found in the appropriate reference entries in Chapter 7. The number of triangles making up the patch is u_steps * v_steps. Other patch types may generate even more triangles.

U_steps and v_steps are usually the same value. For example, if they equal 5, then the patch will have 25 triangles. More triangles will make the patch look smoother but it will render more slowly. Use low numbers for quick tests and high numbers for final drafts.

For example:

```
object {
  bicubic_patch {
    1 4 4
    <0 0 0> <1 0 0> <2 0 0> <3 0 0>
    <0 0 1> <1 3 1> <2 3 1> <4 0 1>
    <0 0 2> <1 0 2> <2 1 2> <4 0 2>
    <0 0 3> <1 0 3> <2 0 3> <3 0 3>
  }
  texture { Guava }
}
```

Bicubic patches are rarely created manually. This task is usually left up to an external utility. Presently, there are no utilities available to create bicubic patches on the IBM-PC, but you can try out this shape type by modifying BEZIER.POV, which has one simple bicubic patch clearly displayed. Try changing the *u* and *v* steps to make the patch smoother or rougher. Try changing the control points that "pull" at the mesh. The patch can assume wildly different shapes depending on where you place the control points.

A more impressive demonstration of bicubic patches is TEAPOT.POV. The teapot is the classic three-dimensional object used to test new ray tracers and POV-Ray wouldn't be complete without one. The patches in TEAPOT.POV were converted from the classic Utah teapot data and they create a beautiful shape. Figure 5-34 shows the rendered image.

Because of the large amount of data TEAPOT.INC contains, it can render very slowly. You can make the image render more quickly by giving up some of the shape quality. Edit TEAPOT.INC and change the lines

```
#declare u_steps = 8
#declare v_steps = 8
```

to a smaller value. Or if you have a speedy machine you may want to try a higher value to make the teapot smoother.

Bicubic/Bezier patches cannot be used effectively in CSG shapes since they have no clear inside or outside. They can be translated, scaled, and rotated like any other shape.

QUARTICS

Quartics are fourth-order surfaces that can be used to describe a large class of shapes, including the torus (donut), the lemniscate, and the piriform. Figure 5-35 shows a few quartic shapes.

Don't be intimidated by a term like "fourth-order surface." There are ways to use quartics without taking a class in higher math. First, there is the standard

Figure 5-34 The Classic Teapot

include file SHAPESQ.INC, which contains many quartics that you can easily use in scenes. SHAPESQ.INC is a unique collection of shapes that can be very effective when properly applied. Like using the quadrics in the SHAPES.INC file, you just use the name of the quartic you want in a `quartic` block. For example:

```
#include "shapesq.inc"
...
object {
   quartic { Folium }
   texture { color red 1 phong 1 }
   translate < 3 1 0>
}
...
```

Quartics are not as well behaved as the quadrics, though. The internal calculations for quartics are very complex and not all quartics will render perfectly because of the limited accuracy of math operations on IBM-PCs. You can use a slower alternate calculation method for quartics if you run into speckled sur-

Figure 5-35 Quartic Shapes

faces due to math errors. The method is called *sturm* and you invoke it by placing the word sturm in the quartic definition after the other parameters. For example, you can use the sturm solver like this:

```
object {
    quartic { Folium sturm }
    texture { color red 1 phong 1 }
}
```

Like quadrics, some of the quartics will need to be scaled, rotated, intersected, or otherwise modified before they are truly useful in your scenes. Try them unmodified first to determine if you need to change them.

Another way to create a quartic is to use a utility. The most popular shape created with quartics is the donut-like torus. The bundled disk contains a utility for determining the quartic parameters of a particular torus. Truman's Torus Generator (TTG) generates an include file containing a torus whose inner and outer radius you supply. The syntax for this command-line utility is

```
ttg inner_radius outer_radius output_filename
```

For example,

```
C:\>ttg 3 6 torus.inc  ENTER
```

will create a torus with an inner radius of 3 units and an outer radius of 6 units, and it will place the definition in a file named TORUS.INC. Figure 5-36 shows the inner and outer radii.

The inner radius is the distance from the center of the torus to the inner edge. The outer radius is the distance from the center of the torus to the outer edge. The thickness of the torus midsection is equal to the outer radius minus the inner radius. In the case of the earlier example, this is 6–3, or 3 units. And the entire torus is 12 units wide.

Use TTG to create a torus that has an inner radius of 3 and an outer radius of 6. Place the output in a file called TORUS.INC. At the command line, type

```
C:\>ttg 3 6 torus.inc  ENTER
```

TTG will report that the output file was generated as TORUS.INC. Now you can use the torus defined in TORUS.INC in a scene. The scene TORUS.POV described in Listing 5-19 demonstrates how to use the TTG-generated torus.

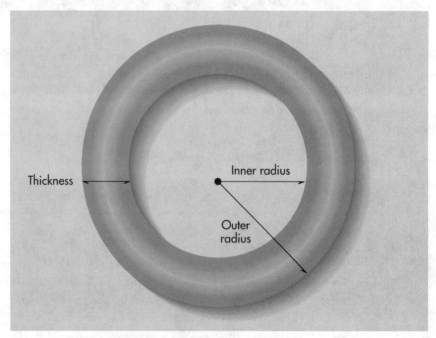

Figure 5-36 Torus' Inner and Outer Radii

Listing 5-19 TORUS.POV

```
// Ray Tracing Creations
// Chapter 5
// Torus Example

#include "colors.inc"
#include "textures.inc"
#include "torus.inc"

camera {
   location <9.0  2.0  -25.0>
   direction <0.0 0.0  2>
   up  <0.0  1.0  0.0>
   right <1.33333 0.0 0.0>
   look_at <0 6 5>
}
// Light source
object {
   light_source { <10 20 -30> color White }
}

// Sky sphere
object {
   sphere { <0 0 0> 1000 }
   texture {
      Blue_Sky3 scale <100 1000 100>
      ambient 1.0
      diffuse 0.7
      //color blue 1
   }
}

// Floor plane
object {
   plane { <0.0 1.0 0.0> 0.0 }
   texture {
      White_Marble
      //ripples .1
      //reflection .4
      scale <3 3 3>
   }
}

// torus
object {
   quartic {
      torus
      rotate <0 0 90> // Turn horizontal torus vertical
```

```
    }
     texture {
        color Green
        phong 1
        phong_size 50
        brilliance 2
     }
   rotate <0 45 0>
   rotate <-45 0 0>
   translate <0 6 5>
}
```

The file TORUS.INC is included before the torus is used in the scene. The torus is defined with its breadth on the *x-z* axis. Its side faces the camera, so it is rotated 90 degrees on the *z* axis to make it more visually interesting. It is also rotated 45 degrees on the *y* and *x* axes to improve its display. Render and view TORUS.POV. Figure 5-37 shows the resulting torus.

The quartic torus, like most shapes, can be used effectively in a CSG shape. The TORUS2.POV scene uses the same torus three times in a union. Listing 5-20 shows TORUS2.POV.

Figure 5-37 A Torus

Listing 5-20 TORUS2.POV

```
// Ray Tracing Creations
// Chapter 5
// Torus Example

#include "colors.inc"
#include "textures.inc"
#include "torus2.inc"

camera {
    location <9.0  2.0  -25.0>
    direction <0.0 0.0  2.5>
    up  <0.0  1.0  0.0>
    right <1.33333 0.0 0.0>
    look_at <0 6 5>
}

// Light source
object {
    light_source { <10 20 -30> color White }
}

// Sky sphere
object {
    sphere { <0 0 0> 1000 }
    texture {
        Blue_Sky3 scale <100 1000 100>
        ambient 1.0
        diffuse 0.7
        //color blue 1
    }
}

// Floor plane
object {
    plane { <0.0 1.0 0.0> 0.0 }
    texture {
        White_Marble
        //ripples .1
        //reflection .4
        scale <3 3 3>
    }
}

// tori
object {
  union {
    quartic {
      torus
```

209

```
        rotate <0 0 90>
      }
      quartic {
        torus
        rotate <0 0 90>
        rotate <0 90 0>
        texture {
          color Red
          phong 1
          phong_size 80
          brilliance 2
        }
      }
      quartic {
        torus
        texture {
          color Green
          phong 1
          phong_size 80
          brilliance 2
        }

      }
    }
    texture {
      color Orange
      phong 1
      phong_size 80
      brilliance 2
    }
    rotate <0 45 0>
    rotate <-45 0 0>
    translate <0 6 5>
}
```

Render and view TORUS2.POV. Figure 5-38 shows TORUS2.GIF.

The torus was created with TTG and has an inner radius of 5 and an outer radius of 6. The union CSG shape of a torus can be conveniently scaled, translated, and rotated as one object.

If you include more than one TTG-generated torus in the same scene file, be sure to edit the torus include file and give each torus a unique name.

The other way to create quartics is to fill in the correct parameters for the quartic equation of a certain shape. Teaching this level of mathematics is well beyond the scope of this text, but you can find references in the bibliographical section of POVRAY.DOC to help you explore this fascinating subject.

Figure 5-38 A Torus "Pretzel"

BLOBS

A blob is an organic-looking shape created from two or more "flexible" spheres. Spherical components of the blob actually stretch out smoothly and connect to each other. The spheres' surfaces stretch out smoothly and connect, as if coated in putty and pulled apart. Figure 5-39 shows a blob shape created with three components.

The syntax for a blob is

```
object {
   blob {
      threshold #
      component strength_val radius_val <center>
      component strength_val radius_val <center>
      (more components)
      [sturm]
   }
}
```

For example,

211

```
object {
  blob {
    threshold .6
    component 1 1 < 0 0 0>
    component 1 1 <.5 0 0>
    component 1 1 <.5 .3 0>
  }
  texture { Sapphire_Agate }
}
```

Blobs can be used in CSG shapes and they can be scaled, rotated, and translated. They may contain any number of components. Because the calculations for blobs need to be highly accurate, and the IBM-PC's math is not always highly accurate, blobs sometimes may not render correctly. If this happens, try using the `sturm` keyword in the blob block for more accurate but slower calculations.

Component strength may be positive or negative. A positive value will make that component attract other components. Negative strength will make that component repel other components.

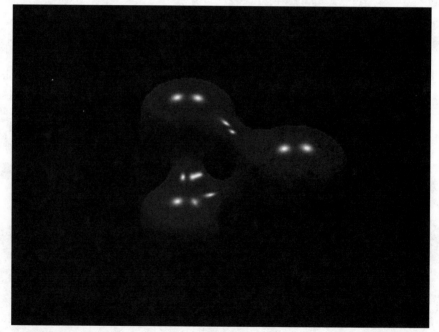

Figure 5-39 Blob Shape

Listing 5-21 shows BLOB2.POV, a very simple blob shape with only two components.

Listing 5-21 BLOB2.POV

```
// Ray Tracing Creations
// Chapter 5
// Blob shapes

#include "colors.inc"
#include "textures.inc"

camera {
   location <0.0  3.0  -10.0>
   direction <0.0 0.0  3>
   up  <0.0  1.0  0.0>
   right <1.33333 0.0 0.0>
   look_at <1.5 2 5>
}


// Light source
object {
   light_source { <10 20 -30> color White }
}


// Sky sphere
object {
   sphere { <0 0 0> 1000 }
   texture {
      Blue_Sky3 scale <1000 1000 1000>
      ambient 1.0
      diffuse 0.7
      //color blue 1
   }
}


// Floor plane
object {
   plane { <0.0 1.0 0.0> 0.0 }
   texture {
      checker  color red 1  color blue 1
      ripples .1
//      reflection .4
```

```
      scale <5 5 5>
   }
}
// blobs
object {
  blob {
    threshold .5
    //          Strength  Radius     Center
    component    1          1        <0 0 0>
    component    .66        1        <1 0 0>
    scale <2 2 2>
  }

  texture {
    ambient 0.2
    diffuse 0.7
    color Orange
    phong 1
    phong_size 80
    brilliance 2
  }
  translate <0 2 5>
}
```

Render and view this scene. Figure 5-40 shows the resulting blob.

This simple blob shape is useful for experimenting with blob behavior. Try changing the threshold value and rendering quick, small versions of the scene. Higher threshold values will make the blob smaller until it eventually disappears, lower threshold values will make the blob larger.

Try changing the strength values, also. Higher strength values will make the component larger. Lower values will shrink the size and influence of a component.

Be sure to try changing the position and radius of the two components in this scene. It's easy to get started using blobs and throw in many components just to see what happens. But it becomes difficult to tell how the parameters are affecting the shape when many components are involved. Some constructive play with this simple object will prove valuable.

Negative-Strength Components

Negative-strength components are not visible in a blob shape, but their influence is. Negative-strength components will "dent" nearby positive-strength compo-

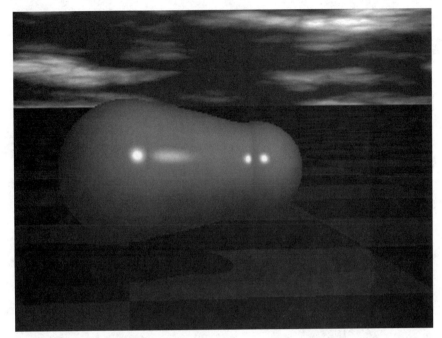

Figure 5-40 A Blob with Two Components

nents. The BLOBNEG.POV scene contains examples of negative-strength blobs. Listing 5-22 shows BLOBNEG.POV. Render and view this scene.

Listing 5-22 BLOBNEG.POV

```
// Ray Tracing Creations
// Chapter 5
// Blob shapes


#include "colors.inc"
#include "textures.inc"

camera {
   location <0.0  3.0  -10.0>
   direction <0.0 0.0  3>
   up  <0.0  1.0  0.0>
   right <1.33333 0.0 0.0>
   look_at <0 2 0>
}

// Light source
```

```
            object {
                light_source { <10 20 -30> color White }
            }

            // Sky sphere
            object {
                sphere { <0 0 0> 1000 }
                texture {
                    Blue_Sky3 scale <1000 1000 1000>
                    ambient 1.0
                    diffuse 0.7
                    //color blue 1
                }
            }

            // Floor plane
            object {
                plane { <0.0 1.0 0.0> 0.0 }
                texture {
                    checker  color red 1  color blue 1
                    scale <5 5 5>
                }
            }

            // blobs
            object {
                blob {
                    threshold .3
                    component 1 .9 <0 .6 0>
                    component 1 .7 <.4 -.4 0>
                    component 1 .7 <-.4 -.4 0>

                    component -1 .6 <0 .1 -.5>
                    component -1 .4 <0 .4  -.3>
                    component -1 .6 <0 .7 -.5>

                }
                texture {
                    ambient 0.2
                    diffuse 0.7
                    color Orange
                    phong 1
                    phong_size 80
                    brilliance 2
                }
                scale <1.5 1.5 1.5>
                translate <0 2 5>
            }
```

Figure 5-41 shows the result.

Try commenting-out the negative blobs and rendering the image. Then uncomment each negative component one at a time to see the influence of the negative component.

How Blobs Work

Now that you've seen something of what you can do with blobs, we'll look at their operation in a bit more detail. Picture each blob component as a point floating in space. Each point has a spherical field around it that starts very strong at the center and drops off to zero at the radius value. To create a shape from these fields, POV-Ray looks for the places where the strength of the fields combined is exactly the same as the specified threshold value. Figure 5-42 depicts this concept.

If you were to use only a single blob component, the surface of the blob would look just like a sphere since no other components would be nearby to push or pull it. The radius of this sphere would depend on the blob's threshold and component strength. It would be somewhere inside the radius value you specified for the component.

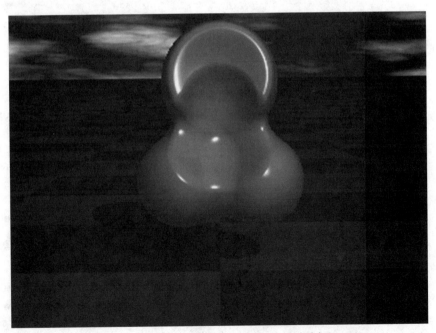

Figure 5-41 Negative-Strength Blob Components "Dent" Normal Blob Components

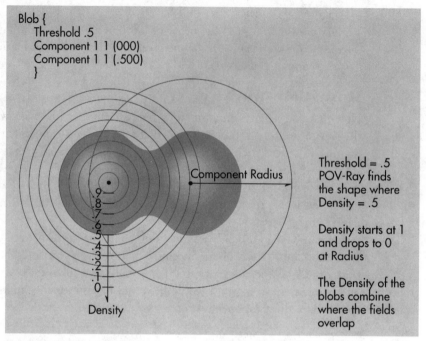

```
Blob {
    Threshold .5
    Component 1 1 (000)
    Component 1 1 (.500)
    }
```

Component Radius

Threshold = .5
POV-Ray finds
the shape where
Density = .5

Density starts at 1
and drops to 0
at Radius

The Density of the
blobs combine
where the fields
overlap

Density

Figure 5-42 How Blobs Work

Each component has a radius of influence. The component can only affect space within its radius. The field of each component should overlap at least one other component's field. If a component is within the radius of another component, the two components start to affect each other. At first there is only a small bulge outwards on each of the two components, but as they get closer they bulge more and more until they attach at a smooth neck. If the centers of the components are on top of each other, the blob surface will be a sphere. This is just like having a component of more strength at this point, which is bigger than the size of each of the component radii.

Blobs can be transformed and textured like any other shape. Blobs can also be used in CSG shapes.

Figure 5-43 shows the image generated from the BLOBBY.POV scene, a more complex blob created with many components.

This scene file is included in the \POVRAY\CHAPTER5 directory for you to modify and experiment with. A good modification to this scene would be to change the texture to something more sophisticated. The next section on advanced textures should help you create better textures and spice up your shapes.

Blob Tips
- Keep the blob components close together so their fields overlap.
- If the spherical component fields do not overlap, the blob will not have any "blobbiness." The components will just appear to be unconnected spheres.
- The threshold must be greater than zero. POV-Ray only looks for positive densities.
- If the threshold is greater than the strength of a component, then the component will disappear, but it will still influence nearby components.
- Higher threshold values create smaller blobs that are closer to the centers of the components.
- Lower threshold values create larger blobs that are closer to the radius of the components.
- Strength may be positive or negative. Zero is a bad value, as the net result is that no density is added. A zero-strength component does not affect the blob.
- The radius must be larger than zero.
- As the radius increases, the apparent size of the component will increase.
- Separate blob shapes do not affect each other.

Well, by now you're probably a bit overwhelmed by the possibilities of combining shapes with CSG techniques, using features like Height-Fields and Bezier patches, and exploring the weirdly fascinating world of blobs. Fortunately, it's easy to modify and experiment with just about anything in this chapter. We'll end the chapter by adding a few more textures to your repertoire.

ADVANCED TEXTURES

This section describes some techniques for creating more sophisticated materials.

TILES

The tiles texture is very much like checker, except that instead of creating a checkerboard of alternating colors it creates a checker board of alternating *textures*. First, let's look at the syntax for tiles and then we'll create a tiles texture:

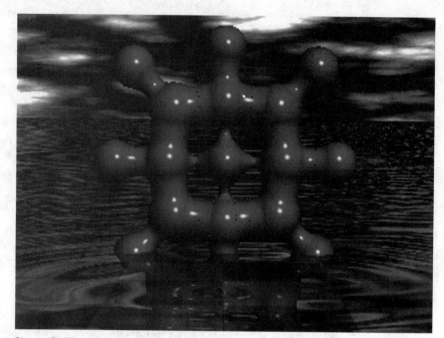

Figure 5-43 A More Complex Blob

```
texture {
  tiles {
    texture { ... }
  tile2
    texture { ... }
  }
}
```

For example:

```
texture {
  tiles {
    texture  { DMFWood4 scale <.5 .5 .5> }
  tile2
    texture { Blue_Sky scale <.5 .5 .5>}
  }
  scale <3 3 3>
}
```

You can use any texture in a tile, but only the color pattern of the tile will be used in the image. Effects like reflection do not work with tiles.

The white and jade tile checkerboard is easy to create using this syntax. The first texture will be the jade from TEXTURES.INC and the second texture will be a solid white color.

```
texture {
   tiles {
      texture  { Jade scale <.1 .1 .1> }
      tile2
         texture { color White }
      }
      scale <5 5 5>
}
```

The jade is scaled down locally *before* the global scale so that the pattern won't be too large to see. Any modifications to the tile textures other than transformations must be done in the local texture definition. Before we add this texture to a shape and render it, let's discuss some more texture features we can use in this scene.

TRANSPARENCY

Transparency is one of ray tracing's best-known features. POV-Ray can accurately render transparent and refractive shapes because it does the work of following the light rays through 3D space. Other rendering methods like z-buffer or scan-line aren't able to do high-quality transparent and refractive textures like a ray tracer is able to do.

Alpha

The keyword `alpha` is part of the color component like red, green, or blue. `alpha` tells POV-Ray how transparent a color is. The syntax for `alpha` is the same as the syntax for red, green, or blue:

```
color red #  green # blue # alpha #
```

Higher values of `alpha` make a color more transparent. Lower values of `alpha` make a color more opaque. `Alpha` defaults to zero if it isn't specifically added to a color.

The scene TILES.POV uses the jade and white tiles texture on the floor and has a transparent sphere using `alpha` as the center of attention. Listing 5-23 shows TILES.POV.

Listing 5-23 TILES.POV

```
// Ray Tracing Creations
// Chapter 5
// This scene file demonstrates texture creation
//

#include "colors.inc"
```

221

```
#include "textures.inc"

camera {
   location   <0    5   -20>
   direction  <0    0    2>
   up         <0    1    0>
   right      <1.33 0    0>
   look_at    <0    2    0>
}
// Light source
object {   light_source { <5 10 -10> color red 1.5 green 1.5
blue 1.5 } }

// Transparent sphere
object {
   sphere { <0 3 0> 3}
   texture {
     color White alpha .7 // 70% transparent
     phong 1
   }
}

// Floor
object {
   plane {
     <0 1 0> 0
     texture {
       tiles {
           texture {
              Jade
              scale <.1 .1 .1>
              ambient .4
           }
           tile2
           texture {
             color White
             ambient .4
           }
       }
       scale <5 5 5>
     }
   }
}
```

Render and view this scene. Figure 5-44 shows the result.

The sphere looks like a soap bubble left on the ballroom floor after a Lawrence Welk performance. This texture can be made more or less transparent by changing the value following alpha.

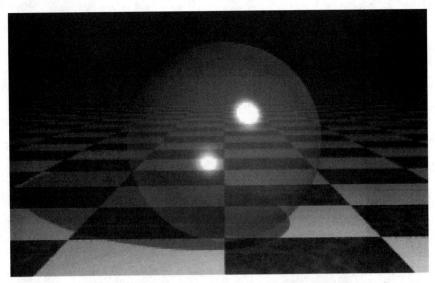

Figure 5-44   An Example Using Tiles

Alpha actually causes light to be filtered through the color. This is different from just making the color transparent. When the light is filtered, only the light that matches the color is passed through the filter; all other light is blocked. A green filter will allow only green light. A blue filter will pass only blue. A white filter is made up of all colors, so any color of light can pass through it. Let's modify the color of the sphere to demonstrate.

Change the sphere's color from white to red. This has already been done in the TILES2.POV scene. Render and view this scene. The effect is too subtle for the black and white figures of this book, so you'll have to view it on your monitor.

The sphere is a beautiful deep red. Notice that the shadow is also red because only red light is allowed to pass through the sphere. Look at the places where the green jade tile is visible through the sphere. The green light reflected off the jade tiles can't make it through the red filter. We would have to add some green to the sphere's color if we wanted to see the color of the jade tile. The white tile has equal parts red, green, and blue, so we can see the red component of that tile through the sphere.

How does the filtering quality of alpha transparency affect your scene creation?

A transparent black texture cannot be created. This is a common mistake; the artists want black glass so they take a black texture and add alpha to it.

223

Unfortunately, though, a black filter has no color and will not let any light pass through it. You should use a dark gray instead so some light can make it through.

White is the only color that can be made completely transparent. The color Clear is defined in COLORS.INC as "color red 1 green 1 blue 1 alpha 1." Any other combination would not allow all light through.

Since shadows are affected by the filtered light, realistic stained-glass window effects are possible.

REFRACTION AND IOR

Refraction is the bending of light when it passes through a solid transparent material like water or glass. POV-Ray can accurately simulate refraction for realistic creation of water, glass, diamond, and other transparent, refracting materials.

Place a straight straw in a glass of water and it appears to be bent at the water level. This is due to the effects of refraction. Refraction occurs when the path of a light ray is bent by the material it is passing through. The more dense the transparent material, the more it bends the light.

The syntax for `refraction` is

```
texture {
  //(texture must have some alpha)
  ...
  refraction 1 // Turn on refraction
  ior #        // How much will the light bend?
  ...
}
```

The color of the texture must have some degree of `alpha` for refraction to work. If the texture isn't transparent, light can't be bent while passing through it. Ior is the index of refraction, specifying the amount the light will bend. An ior of 1 means that light is not refracted at all, increasingly higher values will make the light bend more. All transparent materials have an index of refraction. The more dense an object is, the higher its ior. For example, the ior for water is 1.33, the ior for diamond is 2.47, and the ior for air is 1.000292. These and several other values for ior are included in IOR.INC.

We'll use `refraction` to transform the "soap bubble" into a large drop of water. And we'll add a blue sky textured sphere as a background to the tiles scene so the water drop will have something interesting to refract. Listing 5-24 shows TILES3.POV, which contains these modifications.

Listing 5-24 TILES3.POV

```
// Ray Tracing Creations
// Chapter 5
// This scene file demonstrates texture creation
//

#include "colors.inc"
#include "textures.inc"
#include "ior.inc"

camera {
   location     <0     3     -20>
   direction    <0     0      2>
   up           <0     1      0>
   right        <1.33 0       0>
   look_at      <0     3      0>
}
// Light source
object {   light_source { <5 10 -10> color red 1.5 green 1.5 blue 1.5 } }

// Transparent sphere
object {
   sphere { <0 3 0> 3}
   texture {
      color White alpha .7 // 70% transparent
      refraction 1         // Turn on refraction
      ior Water_Ior        // Set index of refraction to simulate water
      phong 1
   }
}
// Blue Sky background for refraction demonstration
object {
   sphere { <0 3 0> 1000}
   texture { Blue_Sky scale <100 50 100> ambient 1 }
}

// Floor
object {
   plane {
     <0 1 0> 0
     texture {
       tiles {
          texture {
             Jade
             scale <.1 .1 .1>
             ambient .4
          }
          tile2
          texture {
```

```
            color White
            ambient .4
        }
    }
    scale <5 5 5>
    }
    }

}
```

Render and view this scene. Figure 5-45 shows the result.

As if it were made of water, the sphere is now refracting the floor and background. In this case, the image through the sphere is flipped over by the refraction, similar to the way the lens in a camera turns an image upside down. Refraction can be used to create working lenses that magnify or shrink the image passing through them. Notice also the way the tiles seen through the sphere are curved at the edges. This is caused by the refraction.

POV-Ray does a highly accurate simulation of real-world refraction, but it does not do light-spectrum effects like light passing through a prism and creating a rainbow. The color information stored for each light ray is not sophisticated enough yet to re-create this real-world phenomenon.

LAYERED TEXTURES

Although the procedural textures in POV-Ray allow you to create great-looking materials, it's possible to create even more interesting and subtle effects using layered textures.

A layered texture has several textures that are partially transparent laid on top of each other to create a more complex texture. The different texture layers show through the transparent portions to create the appearance of one texture that is a combination of several textures.

You create layered textures by listing two or more textures one right after the other. The last texture listed will be the top layer; the first one listed will be the bottom layer. Other than the bottom layer, all textures in a layered texture should have some transparency.

The syntax for a layered texture is

```
texture { ... } // Bottom layer
texture { ... } // Next layer up must have transparency
texture { ... } // Next layer up must have transparency
...
```

Figure 5-45 Tiles with Refraction

Layers will be added until POV-Ray parses a keyword other than texture. Surface patterns like bumps and dents will only work on the top layer
but other properties such as ambient or Phong will show through. Here's an
example of a layered texture:

```
object {
    sphere { <0 0 0> 2 }
    texture { color Red } // Bottom layer
    texture { Clouds }     // The red bottom layer will show through the clouds
    texture {              // The red and cloud layers will show through the
        checker            // Clear portion of the checker texture
            color Blue
            color Clear
        phong 1
    }
    scale <2 2 2> // This transform will affect all layers
```

The first texture listed is a solid red color; this will be the bottom layer
upon which the other textures are placed. The next texture is clouds, which has
white clouds surrounded by transparency. The red bottom layer will show
through any transparent portions of the cloud texture. The third and top layer
is a blue and clear checker. The other two layers will show through the clear
portions of the checker. The Phong highlight set for the top layer will work for
the entire material. Now we'll create a simple layered texture.

You can use predefined textures in layered textures, so we'll start with rust as the first layer. It would be nice to have thin lines of green corrosion mixed in with the rust, so we'll use a gradient to make the top layer thin green lines on a transparent background. Listing 5-25 shows LAYER.POV, which contains the new layered texture.

Listing 5-25 LAYER.POV

```
// Ray Tracing Creations
// Chapter 5
// This scene file demonstrates texture creation
//

#include "colors.inc"
#include "textures.inc"

camera {
    location      <0    3    -20>
    direction     <0    0    2>
    up            <0    1    0>
    right         <1.33 0    0>
    look_at       <0    3    0>
}
// Light source
object {    light_source { <5 10 -10> color red 1.5 green 1.5 blue 1.5 } }

#declare Layered_Texture =
    texture { Rust }
    texture { // Put dark green stripes across the rust
        gradient <0 1 0>
        color_map {
            [0  .5  color Clear color Clear ]
            [.5 .6  color Clear color green .3 ]
            [.6 .7  color green .3 color green .3 ]
            [.7 .8  color green .3 color Clear ]
            [.8 1   color Clear color Clear ]
        }
    }


// Sphere with layered texture
object {
    sphere { <0 3 0> 3}
    texture {
        Layered_Texture
    }
}
// Blue Sky background for refraction demonstration
object {
```

```
   sphere { <0 3 0> 1000}
   texture { Blue_Sky3 scale <200 140 200> ambient 1 }
}

// Floor
object {
   plane {
     <0 1 0> 0
     texture {
       tiles {
         texture {
           Jade
           scale <.1 .1 .1>
           ambient .4
         }
         tile2
         texture {
           color White
           ambient .4
         }
       }
     scale <5 5 5>
     }
   }
}
```

We used `declare` to call this texture "Layered_Texture." It is used as the other textures you see in the sphere block. The vertical gradient texture is fairly simple—it is primarily made up of the clear color with a small percentage of dark green in the middle. The horizontal green lines can be made thicker or thinner by changing the amount of green in the color map. Render and view this scene. Figure 5-46 shows the result.

The green lines look pretty good on top of the rust, but they are a bit too straight. Some turbulence added to the top layer should help things. Add the line "turbulence .6" after the color map in the gradient texture block. The file LAYER2.POV contains this modification. Render and view this scene. Figure 5-47 shows LAYER2.POV.

That looks more like real corrosion. Use this scene as a starting point for experimenting with layered textures. Start simple: You can achieve quite a bit with only two layers, and the more layers you add, the longer the texture will take to render.

STONES.INC contains some terrific examples of sophisticated layered textures. It is a well-organized file in which each *portion* of the textures to be

Figure 5-46 Layered Textures

Figure 5-47 Layers with Turbulence

layered is defined so you can reuse the different components in creating textures, as well as plugging the complete textures in your scenes.

Thus far, we have explored an intricate but static world of ray traced images. In the next chapter, you will learn how to use a simple tool called Ani-batch to create *animated* ray traced scenes.

SUMMARY

This chapter presented a variety of features and advanced techniques. The basic theme was how to combine shapes in various ways. Compound shapes using CSG (Constructive Solid Geometry) can be combined to form unions or intersections.

- In a union, the resulting shape consists of everything in any of the component shapes. The syntax for a union is

```
object {
   union {
      SHAPE_1
      SHAPE_2
      SHAPE_3...
   }
}
```

- A useful feature of unions is that they allow a group of objects to be transformed as a single object.
- Textures aren't applied directly to a union. You can apply the texture to each individual shape in the union or you can apply it to the object containing the union.
- An intersection includes only the area common to two or more figures (that is, the area where the figures overlap). The syntax for intersection is the same as for union

```
object {
   intersection {
      shape_1
      shape_2
      shape_3...
   }
}
```

- You can texture the component objects of an intersection separately.
- You can use the `inverse` keyword to turn shapes "inside out." The same rules for union and intersection apply to inverted figures, but the results can be startling.

- A difference is what is left when one object "cuts" another. It is the same as an intersection with a figure's inverse, but the difference may be easier to visualize. The syntax for a difference is

```
object {
   difference {
      SHAPE_1      // This first shape is the base shape
      SHAPE_2      // The following shapes are made inverse and "cut out" of the
      SHAPE_3...   // base shape.
   }
}
```

- CSG shapes can be "nested" in other shapes, and manipulated with an intersection, union, and difference.
- A composite object is a collection of individual objects. The syntax for a composite is

```
composite {
    object { ... }
    object { ... }
    object { ... }
    [transformations...]
}
```

- Composites, like unions, can be transformed as a whole. Because they are objects, not shapes, composites cannot be used with CSG. Composite objects can contain other composite objects.
- You can use design programs such as 3D Studio to create scene files for POV-Ray. A utility for converting 3D Studio files, called 3DS2POV, is included on the disk.
- Height-Fields convert the colors in graphic images to triangles with a height corresponding to the color. You can use Height-Fields to produce realistic fractal landscapes. The "water level" determines how much of the triangles is shown.
- Bicubic/Bezier patches create a "mesh" of triangles "pulled" around specified points. They can be used to create smooth curved surfaces.
- The torus and other quartic shapes are mathematically complex, but you'll find it easy to experiment with the included quartics in SHAPES.INC. If quartics lead to math errors in rendering, you can use the keyword sturm to specify a slower but more accurate method of rendering.
- Blobs are organic-looking shapes whose components stretch according to their specified strength. Positive strength causes components to be

attracted and stretched toward each other, while negative strength causes repulsion and denting.

- Advanced POV-Ray texture techniques include tiling (where you have a checkerboard of alternating textures). The syntax for tiling is

```
texture {
    tiles {
        texture { ... }
    tile2
        texture { ... }
    }
}
```

- Transparency can be controlled through the alpha component of color. Alpha tells POV-Ray how transparent a color is: higher values are more transparent, lower values more opaque. Alpha is treated just like a color for syntax purposes.

- Refraction is the amount by which light bends when it passes through a solid transparent material. You introduce refraction by using the syntax

```
refraction 1 // Turn on refraction
ior #        // How much will the light bend?
```

For refraction to work, the color of the texture must include some degree of alpha. An ior (index of refraction) of 1 means no bending; the higher the value above 1, the more the light bends.

- You can layer textures by specifying the layers from the bottom up:

```
texture { ... } // Bottom layer
texture { ... } // Next layer up must have transparency
texture { ... } // Next layer up must have transparency
...
```

- Underlying textures will show through transparent upper ones, and properties such as ambience of light and Phong will show through the various layers.

" ... Glorious, stirring sight!" murmured Toad. . ."The poetry of motion!"

—Kenneth Grahame

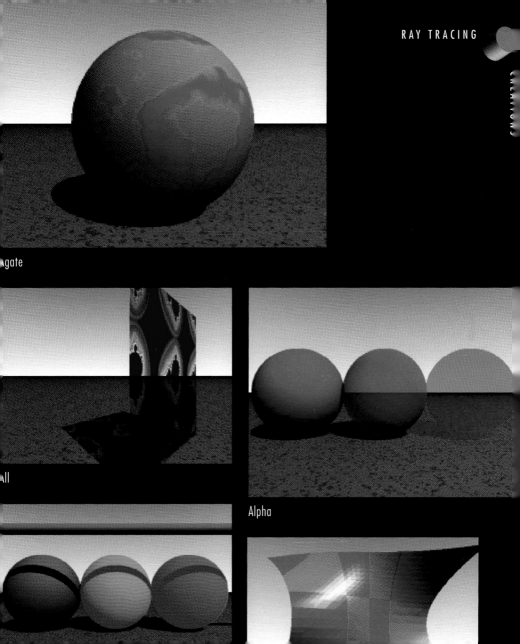

gate

ll

Alpha

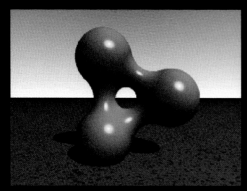

Blob

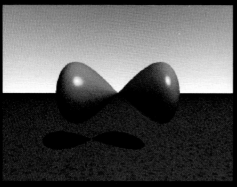

Bounded_By

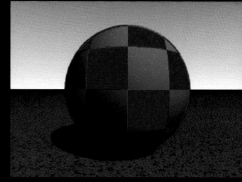

Blue

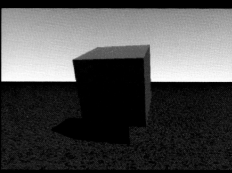

Box

Brilliance

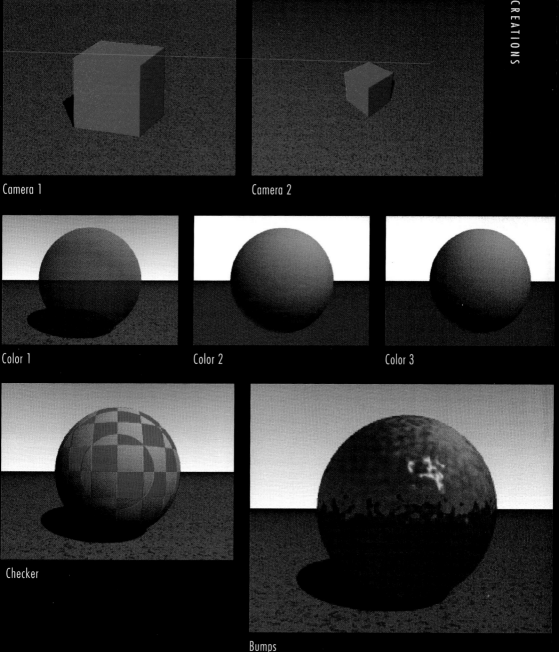

Camera 1

Camera 2

Color 1

Color 2

Color 3

Checker

Bumps

Composite

crand_value

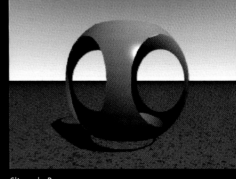

Component

Clipped_By

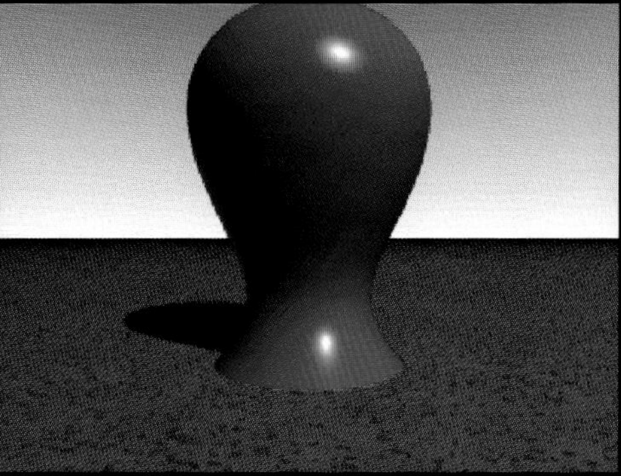

Cubic

Declare

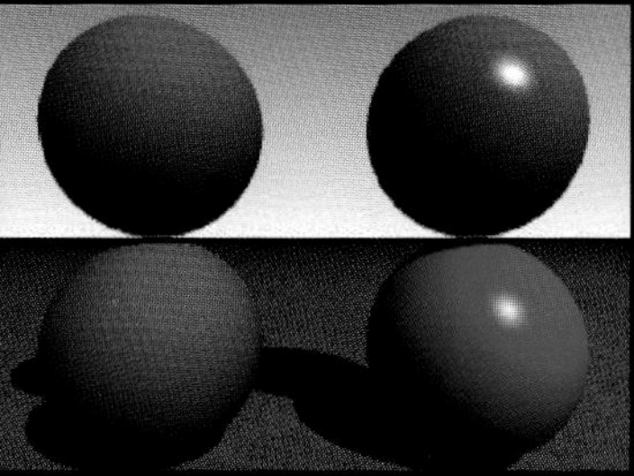

Default

Dents

Difference

Direct 1

Direct 2

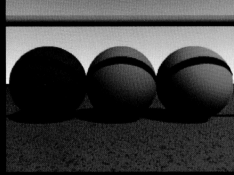

Diffuse

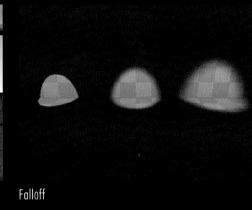

Falloff

Gradient

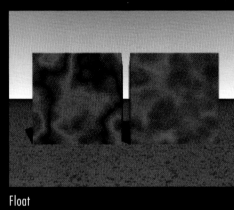

Float

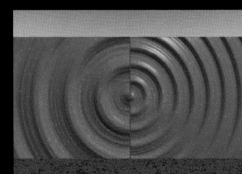

Frequency

Granite

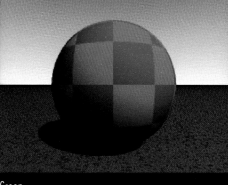

Green

Height_Field

Image_Map

Include

Interpolate

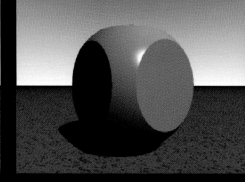

Intersect

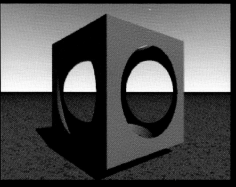

Inverse

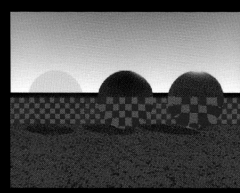

Ior

Leopard

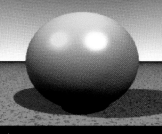

Light 1

Light 2

Light 3

Location

Look_At

Map_Type

Marble

Max_Trace_Level

Material_Map

RAY TRACING CREATIONS

Metallic

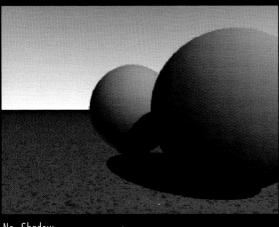

No_Shadow

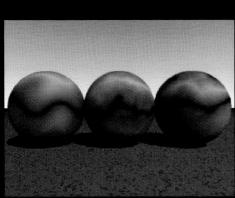

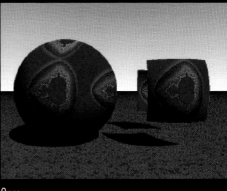

Object

Once

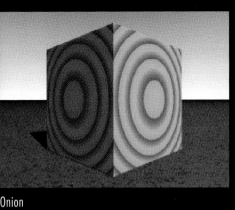

Onion

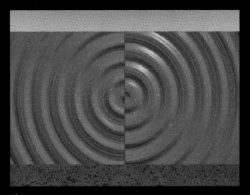

Phase

Phong

Phong_Size

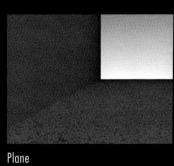

Plane

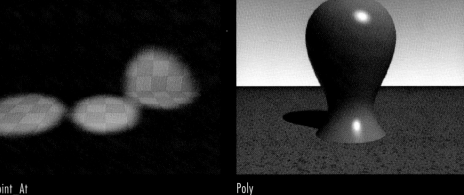

Point_At

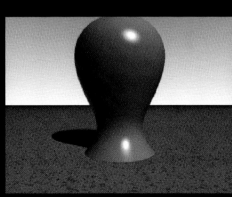

Poly

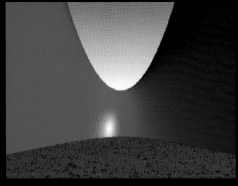

Quadric

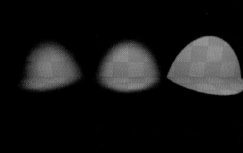

Radius

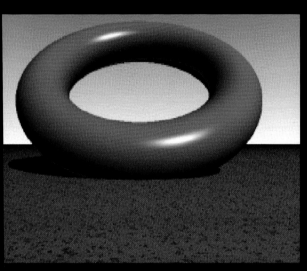

Quartic

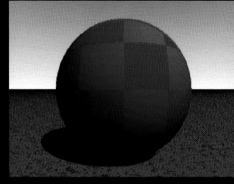

Red

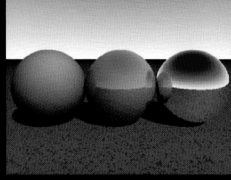

Reflection

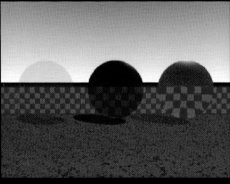

Refraction

Right

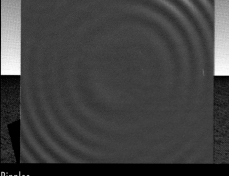

Ripples

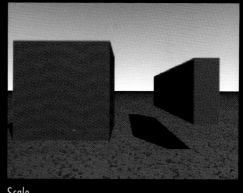

Rotate

Scale

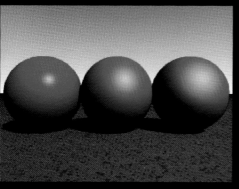

Roughness

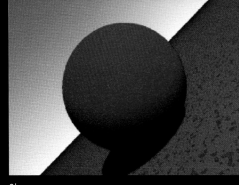

Sky

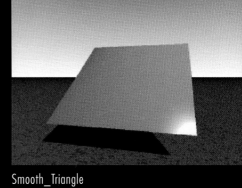

Smooth_Triangle

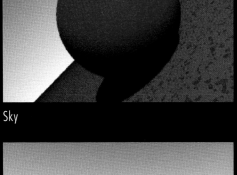

Specular

Texture

Spotlight

Spotted

Sphere

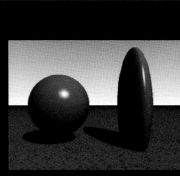

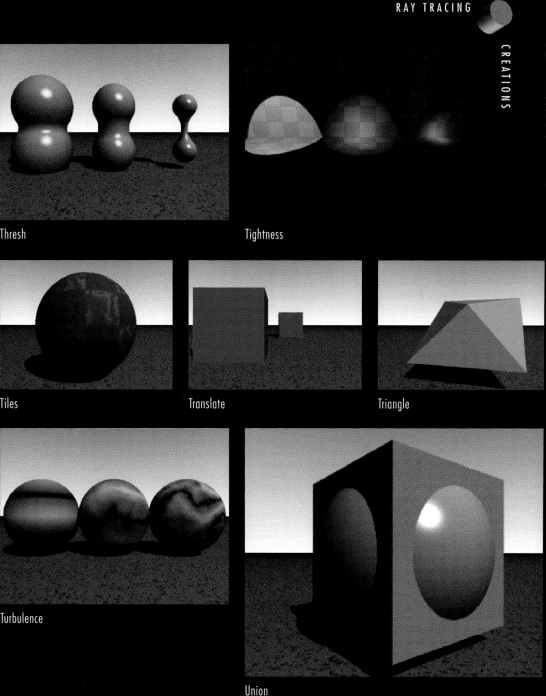

Thresh

Tightness

Tiles

Translate

Triangle

Turbulence

Union

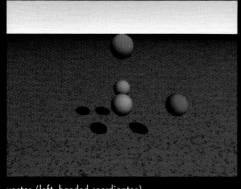

vector (left -handed coordinates)

Vector (right-handed coordinates)

Water_Level

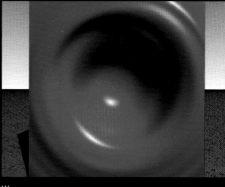

Waves

Wrinkles

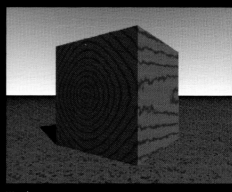

Wood

6

Building a Ray Traced Animation

If ray tracing can be said to add a third dimension to images, then animation adds the fourth dimension—time—to them. If ray tracing creates the illusion of reality within the computer, then animation adds another convincing element—realistic movement. Just as cinematography adds realism to still photography, animation techniques can bring realism and life to the images rendered by ray tracing. In this chapter, you will be introduced to some methods for extending your POV-Ray images into the realm of time through the use of animation. The simple utility programs provided on the bundled disk will get you started. The results can be striking!

WHAT IS ANIMATION?

An animation is built from a series of static images, each displaying the position of objects in space at a moment in time. When the images are displayed quickly enough, the brain fuses them into the perception of fluid motion. Broadly speaking, cartoons, movies, and television all can be considered forms of animation. In recent years, a new form of animation has been making increasingly frequent appearances in the movies and on television, and it is done with computers, using programs similar to POV-Ray.

A BRIEF HISTORY

While you are undoubtedly familiar with the Disney cartoons developed during the mid-twentieth century, various forms of animation were explored, more as curiosities than anything else, much earlier than that.

One of the earliest forms of animation was the *flip book*. Flip books are short, simple animation sequences drawn on successive pages of a small booklet. To view the animation in action, the viewer thumbs through the pages in rapid succession, giving the appearance of objects moving in time. You can easily create a simple flip-book animation yourself by drawing a series of simple shapes—say, circles—in the upper-right corner of successive pages of a writing tablet, each a bit lower than the circle on the previous page, as shown in Figure 6-1. By flipping through the pages, you will get the illusion that the circle is falling. This is the basis of all animation, from the early Mickey Mouse and Betty Boop cartoons to the highest-tech computer-generated animations of today.

There really is little difference in how flip books, animated cartoons, movies, and computer animations do their magic. All work by showing a succession of pictures quickly enough to melt into a smooth flow of motion to the viewer.

PERSISTENCE OF VISION

What allows this perception of motion to occur? When light strikes the retina at the back of the eye, a chemical and electrical reaction takes place. While this reaction is extremely fast, it is not quite instantaneous. There is a very slight lag

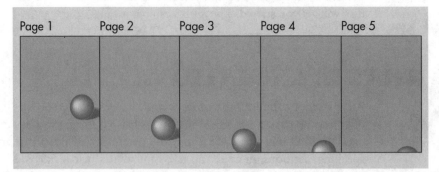

Figure 6-1 A Simple Flip-Book Animation

before the eye updates the brain with the new information it has received. Persistence of vision is the retina's ability to remain excited during this lag. The image persists on the retina for a short time and smooths the perception of motion. We also experience persistence of vision as an *after image*, that shadowy image that remains after looking at a bright light or other strong visual stimuli.

It is this time delay, or blending period of vision, that lets us display a series of related static images in rapid succession and perceive them as continuous motion. This continuity is enhanced by displaying more images over a given period of time. In this way, each image represents a smaller "slice of time," resulting in a smoother appearance to the viewer.

THE TRADITIONAL APPROACH TO ANIMATION

Historically, cartoon-style animations have been painstakingly hand drawn, one picture at a time. The traditional approach used a static background image, with overlays drawn onto sheets of clear celluloid to represent the moving portions of the image during a particular "slice of time." Each of these images was known as a *frame* or a *cel,* terms that are in use today, even with computer animation.

Once the first frame of a scene was drawn, another sheet of celluloid was laid on top of the first, and the entire image was redrawn, changing only those parts that would be in a different position at that particular moment in time. These celluloid frames were then placed, in succession, on top of the background image, and transferred onto movie film. Since even a short cartoon would consist of hundreds or thousands of frames, creating a traditional animation is a time-intensive and expensive process.

ANIMATION ON YOUR PC

As with most highly repetitive tasks, the personal computer lends itself beautifully to the animation process. Modern variations of the traditional methods have evolved, and new variations using modern rendering techniques such as ray tracing have expanded the field into areas never before dreamed of.

Traditional cartoon animation is now assisted by the computer's ability to easily modify portions of a hand drawn image. Once a frame has been drawn and saved, it can then be reloaded into the computer and used as a reference for the next frame in the sequence, changing only those portions that need to be different.

The advent of photo-realistic computer rendering, with its automatic perspective and highly detailed reflection, refraction, and shading calculations, has spawned a whole new era of animation that blurs the distinction between what is real and what is imagined. Architects are now using computer-generated "walkthroughs" of buildings that exist only within the computer; and scientists are now graphically able to portray the movement of glaciers and the interaction of molecules. Artists are creating convincing worlds that never existed and are letting their imaginations go wild exploring these through animation.

And yet, perhaps best of all, this technology is now available to anyone with a personal computer. The images that you have been creating with POV-Ray can very easily be turned into stunning animations, whose detail and complexity are only limited by your imagination. Let's see just how this is done.

WHAT IS NEEDED FOR ANIMATION?

The primary requisite for ray traced animation is a fast computer or a considerable amount of time and patience. This requirement can be minimized to a degree by keeping image resolution low and by avoiding techniques such as transparency and turbulence that add significantly to overall rendering times.

Besides POV-Ray, you will need a method to create the scene files required for each frame, a means to compile the series of images into a "film strip," and a program that will allow you to display this virtual film strip on your computer. The disk accompanying this book contains programs to do all of these tasks. Here's an overview of what each program does.

ANIBATCH

The examples in this chapter were created with the assistance of a program written by Dan Farmer, called ANIBATCH.EXE. This is a simple, but useful program that helps you create DOS batch files that ease the process of rendering animations by calling POV-Ray with the proper parameters required for each frame. This chapter will not concentrate on the use of Anibatch, but rather on helping you to understand the method that Anibatch uses. (Anibatch comes with its own documentation on disk.)

DAVE'S TARGA ANIMATOR

To compile your images into an animation, you will be using the program DTA.EXE ("Dave's Targa Animator"), written by David K. Mason. This program will take the Targa image files that POV-Ray creates and compile them into an FLI file. The FLI format was developed by Autodesk, Inc., for its Animator product. It uses a very efficient method of combining the images called *delta animation*. In delta animation, only differences, or deltas, between successive frames are stored and displayed. This speeds the process considerably by removing the task of loading complete images into the computer's memory for each frame displayed. It also has the desirable effect of compressing the size of the animation, which means that it will save a considerable amount of disk space.

DTA.EXE is a utility with a wealth of features. Not only can it convert TGA files to FLI animations, but with the correct command-line switches, it can also use GIF image files as input and it can create GIF images from Targa files. It can blend images to produce the illusion of motion blur. You can even use DTA to create red/blue "funny glasses" 3D stereo images. Most of the features of DTA.EXE are beyond the scope of this book, but we recommend that you read the documentation file, DTA.DOC, to learn about the many other exciting features.

PLAY

You will view the resulting FLI animation using Trilobyte's PLAY.EXE, which is also included. PLAY is a shareware program written by Graham Devine that very quickly loads and displays FLI-style animation files in both standard and SVGA display formats.

FROM SCENE TO ANIMATION

Creating an animation involves the following steps:

- Planning the animation
- Creating the basic scenes
- Rendering the scenes to create a series of Targa image files
- Compiling the image files into an FLI animation file
- Viewing the animation

The following sections discuss each of these steps in detail.

PLANNING THE ANIMATION

Even the simplest animation requires a little planning. Just as a motion picture producer has to adhere to a budget, you are faced with a budget of sorts regarding computing power, time, and your own abilities. You should have an idea

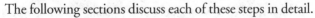

ahead of time as to the type of action you want to achieve, how many frames will be required to smoothly create that motion, and what the basic scene will look like. It is also helpful to know how long it will take POV-Ray to render the scenes you will be animating and how much disk space the resulting images will consume.

These variables are closely related and changing one will often affect the others. For example, if the type of motion you want happens to be a walk-through of a large building, you will have to generate a large number of frames for the motion to appear smooth. More frames, in turn, will require more time to render and consume more disk space.

Again, if the scene consists of finely detailed objects or textures, you will probably want to render the animation in a high-resolution format, which will also increase both the rendering time and the overhead of storing a number of large image files on the disk.

If your scene consists of computationally "expensive" shapes or textures, perhaps a number of glass quartic objects, you may very well decide to use a lower-image resolution or design the animation with a type of motion that will require fewer frames to be generated.

Careful planning is the key to successful animation rendering. There are a few tricks that we will be discussing that you can use to make interesting animations without leaving your computer inaccessible for other tasks for weeks or months at a time. Don't let this discussion of constraints and limitations discourage you, though. Start with simple, quick-rendering scenes and simple

---

Make sure there's enough disk space!
Each frame of an animation must be stored until all of the frames have been rendered. A 160x100 pixel Targa image file requires 48,018 bytes of storage. A 320x200 image requires 192,072 bytes. If you are planning a 20-frame, 320x200 animation, you need 192,072 x 20 = 3,841,440 bytes, or almost 4MB of disk space for the Targa images alone.

Before you begin, you should always make sure that you've got enough available storage to hold all of the images, plus the finished animation, plus any temporary files that the animation compiler may generate. Because of the nature of the FLI file format, it's not possible to predict the finished size of a FLI file, but as a rule of thumb when compiling the animation, make sure that you've got at least twice the space required for the Targa files alone.

motion. When you have an idea of how simple animations perform on your equipment, you will be ready to try more elaborate projects.

PLANNING THE SCENE

While any ray tracing has the potential for animation, not all scenes are equally good candidates. You wouldn't, for example, be likely to create a 50-frame animation of an image that takes your computer two days per frame to render unless you were planning an extended vacation. Your computer would be tied up for *over three months!* Of course, you could run this process as a background task from a multiprocessing environment such as Windows, but it would still require great patience.

Keep it simple. Animations do not have to be complicated to be good. Very effective animations can be made that contain only one or two primary objects in the scene. For example, a single sphere revolving around a larger central sphere as a moon around a planet can be extremely exciting and yet take very little time to create.

ANIMATING OBJECTS AND OTHER THINGS

Remember that you are not limited to moving only objects. With POV-Ray, you can actually animate just about everything that you can put in a scene file, including camera position, light source placement, textures, as well as the scale and placement of objects. You can animate things that would be impossible in the "real world." Imagine, for example, a glass cube gradually changing into a mirrored plane.

These ideas only touch on some of what you can modify for animation purposes. The possibilities are limited only by your imagination. The purpose here is to stimulate your thinking and to help you begin to explore some of the less obvious areas of animation potential. As you work with POV-Ray and animation, many more possibilities will make themselves apparent.

Object Position and Scale

Perhaps the most obvious type of animation is changing an object's position: objects being rolled, bounced, flown, or otherwise moved through a scene with translation and rotation commands. An object's size can be increased or decreased using scaling to give the appearance of growth or shrinkage. Height-Field mountain ranges can be "grown" by scaling the height.

Texture Position and Scale

Textures, too, can be animated. One example of transforming a texture throughout an animation would be to create a cloudy sky on a sphere and rotate the sphere on the *x* axis to give the effect of clouds advancing over the horizon on a windy day.

Texture Turbulence Amount

Varying the turbulence value of a texture can also be used effectively with cloudy skies. This effect is particularly nice when used in combination with rotation of the clouds. Surface textures such as marble and agate can be made to squirm and wiggle by adjusting the turbulence over time.

Specular, Roughness, and Brilliance Values

These surface characteristics can be manipulated for a variety of special effects. This is also a useful way for you to study the effects of changing these characteristics.

Reflection and Refraction Values

For an especially striking effect, a mirrored sphere can gradually become a glass sphere by slowly decreasing reflectivity and increasing refraction and alpha values in a texture.

Waves and Ripples

Both waves and ripples respond to the `phase` keyword, which can be incremented in small steps to move the waves through a complete cycle. This technique simulates the ripples on a pond or the waves on a lake.

Dent, Bump, and Wrinkle Values

These surface features would most likely be animated to achieve a particular special effect such as changing a smooth grape into a wrinkled raisin. Cycling through a range of values can make for a very strange, yet fascinating pulsating action.

Camera Settings

The `location` and `look_at` values of the camera can be changed to create "fly-through" animations where the camera moves through the scene. Increasing or decreasing the `direction` vector gradually will give the effect of a camera zoom. Moving the `look_at` value from left to right or up and down emu-

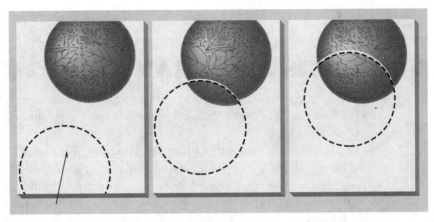

Figure 6-2 Using Animation to Understand The POV-Ray Feature of Difference

lates a camera's panning action. Take care when planning a fly-through, though, that the camera doesn't unintentionally pass through objects in the scene. Of course, there is nothing wrong with doing this as a special effect, but the effect can be rather disturbing when it is not intended.

One note of caution: Avoid moving the camera directly over the `look_at` position. Doing so can cause an error in POV-Ray that can stop the program!

Lights

POV-Ray's spotlights can be moved back and forth for very impressive "grand-opening" effects. Regular light sources can be dimmed by decreasing the values of the light's colors.

ANIMATION AS A CONCEPTUALIZING TOOL

Animation can be used as a tool for helping you to gain a better understanding of many of POV-Ray's features. For example, by modifying the `turbulence` value of a texture over successive frames, the effects of the turbulence can be dynamically observed. If you are having a difficult time understanding how CSG difference works, for example, you might create a simple animation that begins with a pair of spheres that do not quite touch. Then, through animation techniques, as shown in Figure 6-2, you could slowly move the spheres toward each other until they occupied the same physical space. Viewing the resulting animation would then help you gain a better understanding of the CSG process.

YOUR FIRST POV-RAY ANIMATION

For the first animation, we'll render a cube that rotates continuously about its *y* axis. Why a cube? For one thing, the cube primitive is an efficient object for POV-Ray to draw.

The cube offers one other advantage: symmetry. Because of a cube's symmetry, we can make it appear to rotate a full 360 degrees when, in reality, we just rotate it from one face to the next, or 90 degrees! In order to make this work, we will make the action *loop*, or start back at the beginning frame once the final frame has been displayed. This is one of the "tricks" that we can use to make animations that appear more complex than they actually are. If we were to rotate the cube by 10 degrees per frame—a fairly large amount for smooth motion—it would still require 36 frames to do a full 360 degrees. By taking advantage of the symmetry of the cube, however, and looping the animation back to the first frame, we can achieve the same results in only 9 frames! Of course, this will only work if the cube has the same color and pattern on all sides. Naturally, a cube is not the only shape that can be used in this manner. Figure 6-3 demonstrates this concept being used to rotate an eight-toothed

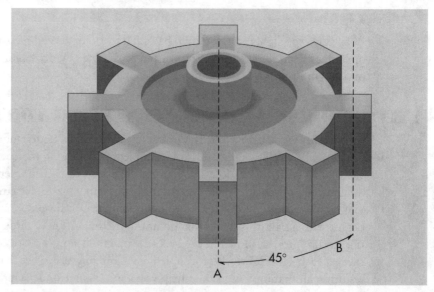

Figure 6-3 Taking Advantage of Object Symmetry for Fast Rotation

gear so that it would appear to be rotating continuously. Note that while a cube is symmetrical every 90 degrees, the gear is symmetrical every 45 degrees. Gears with more teeth would be symmetrical in fewer degrees. This means fewer frames would be needed to achieve smooth motion.

GETTING STARTED

That's enough theory for now. Let's get started. Take a look at the scene file, ANI0.POV, in the \POVRAY\CHAPTER6 directory (see Listing 6-1).

Listing 6-1 AN10.POV

```
// ANI0.POV
// Basic animation scene setup, without the animation.

        #include "colors.inc"
        #include "shapes.inc"
        #include "textures.inc"
        camera {
            location <6  6  -10>
            direction <0.0 0.0 2>
            up  <0.0  1.0  0.0>
            right <1.33333 0.0 0.0>
            look_at <0 -1 0>
        }

        object { light_source { < 50 10  -30>  color Gray90  } }

        object {
            box { <-1.0 -1.0 -1.0> <1.0 1.0 1.0>
                texture {
                    checker color Red color Yellow
                    translate <0.5 0.5 0.5>
                    scale <0.67 0.67 0.67>
                }
            }
        }

        object {
            plane { <0 1 0> -2 }
            texture {
                checker color White color Gray20
                scale <2 2 2>
                reflection 0.5
            }
        }
```

BUILDING A RAY TRACED ANIMATION

This listing sets up a simple scene with a single checker textured box and plane. It will be the basis for your first animation.

First, you need to set up the box rotation. This will mean inserting a rotate command in the texture description block for the box. If you will recall from Chapter 5, the placement of a transformation before or after a texture will give different results. Since the checker texture is to be rotated with the box, you will need to insert a rotate command *after* the texture has been applied. If you wanted the checkers to sit still while the box rotated "under them," you would put the rotate command first, followed by the texture block. For our current animation, however, we do want the texture to move *with* the box.

USING DECLARED CONSTANTS
IN AN ANIMATION

Before we make this change, however, let's think about this just a little more. You could render ANI0.POV just the way it is, save the image as FRAME001.TGA, edit the scene file to modify the rotation value for the next frame, render that frame, and so on, until the animation is finished. This might work fine for a three- or four-frame animation, but it is hardly an efficient method for more advanced projects. You could also create separate scene files for each frame of the animation. This would certainly work, but each file would have to be edited if you simply wanted to make one small change to the scene; again, not very convenient. Let's see if there is a better way.

You've already been introduced to declared constants in POV-Ray. We will discuss the reason for using them here in a moment, but for now, let's just say that we're going to use a declared constant for the rotation value. Load ANI0.POV into your editor and add the rotate command following the box's texture description, as shown in Listing 6-2. Also, add the #include command to the top of the file.

Listing 6-2 Changes to ANI0.POV

```
// ANI0.POV
// Basic animation scene setup, without the animation.

    #include "colors.inc"
    #include "shapes.inc"
    #include "textures.inc"
    #include "ani0.inc"            // add this line to animate
```

```
camera {
   location <6  6  -10>
   direction <0.0 0.0 2>
   up  <0.0  1.0  0.0>
   right <1.33333 0.0 0.0>
   look_at <0 -1 0>
}

object { light_source  { < 50 10  -30>  color Gray90  } }

object {
   box { <-1.0 -1.0 -1.0> <1.0 1.0 1.0>
      texture {
          checker color Red color Yellow
          translate <0.5 0.5 0.5>
          scale <0.67 0.67 0.67>
      }
   }
   rotate < 0 Angle 0 >    // add this line to animate
}

object {
   plane { <0 1 0> -2 }
   texture {
      checker color White color Gray20
      scale <2 2 2>
      reflection 0.5
   }
}
```

The new line, "rotate <0 Angle 0>" will use the constant named "Angle" to rotate the box along its y axis. But we haven't yet declared a value for Angle. This is what the include file, ANI0.ANI, will do.

Create a new file named ANI0.ANI and enter

```
#declare Angle = 45
```

Save this file and render ANI0.POV with the following command line:

```
POVRAY -IANIO.POV -OANIO_001.TGA
```

This command will create an image file named ANI0_001.TGA, which stands for "Animation 0, frame 001." Since this will actually be just a single frame and not a true animation at this point, calling it an animation is stretching the point a bit, thus the number *0*.

Now render and view the image. If you made the changes correctly, you should see a cube floating over a checkerboard floor. The cube should be positioned at a 45-degree angle toward the camera. POV-Ray read in the rotation value from the ANI0.ANI include file and used the value contained there to rotate the cube by 45 degrees.

AUTOMATING ANIMATION WITH A DOS BATCH FILE

What we've done so far is not much improvement over simply manually editing the scene file for each frame. You would still need to edit ANI0.ANI to update the constant values for each frame, and you would have to manually specify the output file name (FRAME001.TGA, FRAME002.TGA, etc.) for each frame in the animation. This method very quickly becomes unmanageable as the number of frames and animation variables increase.

Fortunately, DOS has a *redirection* feature that can be used to automate much of the process. We will use DOS redirection to create the include file for us. Redirection tells DOS to send its output somewhere other than to the screen. This is done by putting the > character, followed by the name of the *alternate output device* (in our case, simply a file name), after the DOS command that you wish to redirect. Our alternate device will be the ANI0.ANI file. Listing 6-3 shows a simple batch file for doing just this.

When DOS sees the > used in the way we are using it here, it always creates a brand new file, overwriting any existing file of the same name. The command to append to an existing file is >>. Thus, if you wanted to create an animation that contained two or more declared constants, you would still use the single > command for the first constant, but you would use the >> command for all future constants for that frame.

Listing 6-3 Simple Animation Batch File ANI0.BAT

```
rem ANI0.BAT
rem Listing 6-3  Simple animation batch file ani0.bat
rem _____

    echo #declare Angle = 45    > ani0.ani
    povray -Iani0.pov -Oani0_001.tga
```

Create this file with your text editor and save it with the name ANI0.BAT. When the batch file runs, the DOS Echo command will "type" the line "#declare Angle = 45" to a file named ANI0.ANI. POV-Ray then reads the ANI0.ANI file in when it parses ANI0.POV. It then replaces all occurrences of Angle with the value of Angle, or 45. Thus, the command rotate <0 Angle 0> becomes rotate <0 45 0>.

Since the POV-Ray command line is now included in this batch file, all you need to do to render it is to type *ANI0* (ENTER) from the directory that contains the files. Figure 6-4 graphically illustrates this process.

ESTIMATING TOTAL RENDERING TIME

When the render is complete, make a note of the rendering time shown on the statistics screen. Assuming that the rest of the frames will take approximately the same amount of time to render, you can simply multiply the rendering time by the number of frames in your animation to give an estimate of the time it will take, at that resolution and quality level, to create the full animation. This will, however, be a rough estimate in many cases. If, for example, you were going to render an animation of a glass sphere rolling toward the camera from a great distance, the first frame may take but a fraction of the time it would take to render the final frame, where the glass sphere would be covering the majority of the screen. In this case, rendering one of the middle frames would probably yield a more accurate estimate.

IMPROVING THE ANIMATION

Of course, a single frame does not make a very interesting "animation." Now that we've got the basic steps down, let's take this a bit further and produce a real animation by increasing the number of frames to four. Your \POVRAY\CHAPTER6 directory contains two files that both begin with the name of ANI1:

- ANI1.POV — The POV-Ray scene file. This will #include a file named ANI1.ANI.
- ANI1.BAT — The animation batch file. This will create the ANI1.ANI file and execute POV-Ray.

Listing 6-4, ANI1.POV, is basically the same as the edited, final version of ANI0.POV that you created for the single-frame ANI0 "animation." It already contains the `#include ani1.ani` command and the `rotate <0 Angle 0>` command, so you won't need to add them this time around.

Listing 6-4 ANI1.POV

```
#include "colors.inc"
#include "shapes.inc"
#include "textures.inc"
#include "ani1.ani"              // Animation constants file

camera {
```

```
     location <6  6  -10>
     direction <0.0 0.0 2>
     up   <0.0  1.0  0.0>
     right <1.33333 0.0 0.0>
     look_at <0 -1 0>
}


object { light_source  { <-50 60 -30>  color Gray50 } }
object { light_source  { < 50 10  -30>  color Gray90 } }

object {
    box { <-1.0 -1.0 -1.0> <1.0 1.0 1.0>
        texture {
            checker color Red color Yellow
            translate <0.5 0.5 0.5>
            scale <0.67 0.67 0.67>
        }
    }
    rotate < 0 Angle 0 >
}

object {
    plane { <0 1 0> -2 }
    texture {
        checker color White color Gray20
        scale <2 2 2>
        reflection 0.5
    }
}
```

Listing 6-5 shows the ANI1.BAT batch file that will create the animation. This file is a bit fancier than the ANI0.BAT that you created earlier, but it is still basically the same. It now has commands to render four frames instead of one. Since the rotation still ranges from 0 to 90 degrees, and the number of frames has increased, the rotation increments have been changed to 22.5-degree steps (90 / 4 = 22.5). This will yield values of 0, 22.5, 45, and 67.5 degrees. As mentioned earlier, we do not require a frame for the value of 90 degrees, since this view would be identical to the frame 0.

The output file names now range from ANI10001.TGA to ANI10004.TGA. By using a numbering method appended to a short *root* file name such as ANI1, batch operations can be performed on the files using DOS *wildcard* shorthand, making it easy to specify all frames with a single command. The call to DTA.EXE in the *COMPILE* section of the batch file makes use of this.

You may be relieved to learn that you're not going to have to write a long,

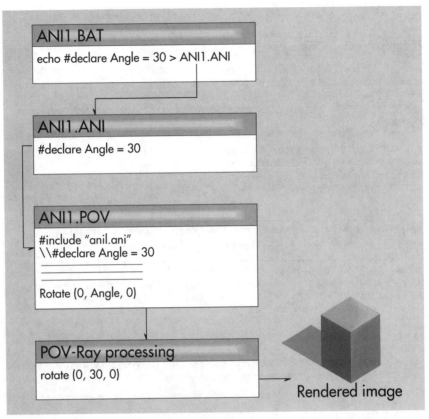

Figure 6-4 Changing Animation Variables Through the Use of Batch File Redirection

complicated batch file for each animation project. While we're going through these example batch files, you'll soon see how to automate the process with Anibatch. In fact, if you find the details of the batch files to be confusing or intimidating, just skip to the section on Anibatch and try the program out with the specifications for the cube animation given here.

Listing 6-5 ANI1.BAT

```
@echo off
rem  **********************************************************
rem  Animation batch file generated by Anibatch 2.1
rem  POV-Ray scene file : \povray\chapter6\ani1.pov
rem  Date : 02-11-1993
rem  Number of Frames :  4
rem  Number of declared constants :  1
```

251

```
rem  *************************************************************
rem
rem      Variable Name : Angle
rem         Start Value : 0
rem         Final Value : 67.5
rem     Incremented by : 22.5
rem
rem  *************************************************************


rem NOTE: Edit these lines to change the path/filename of your
rem POV-Ray and DTA executable files.
SET POV=\povray\povray.exe -w160 -h100 +d0 -v
SET DTA=\povray\dta.exe

rem _____
rem _This is a test to ensure the the executables actually    _
rem _exist where they are supposed to be found.               _
rem _____
if not exist %POV% echo %POV% doesn't exist!
if not exist %POV% goto BADEND
if not exist %DTA% echo %DTA% doesn't exist!
if not exist %DTA% goto BADEND


rem _____
rem _   Comment out the line below to skip the rendering portion and proceed    _
rem _   directly to the DTA compiling section if you only want to recompile the _
rem _   .tga frames without re-rendering them.                                  _
rem _____
     goto Render


rem _____
rem _   This next command is here as a method of jumping past the rendering  _
rem _   portion and allow you to go straight to the DTA compiling section. Use _
rem _   this if you need to recompile existing .tga files to a new .fli.      _
rem _____
     goto Compile

:Render
rem _____
rem _ This is the rendering portion.                  _
rem _ Edit the line below to jump to another frame.   _
rem _____
echo _
echo.
echo.
echo.
echo    About to render animation ani1.fli...
```

```
echo _____
echo _ If this is NOT what you want to do, then press CTRL/C now!      _
echo _____
pause
    goto Frame1
:Frame1
echo #declare Angle =       0.000000  > ani1.ani
%POV%  -i\povray\chapter6\ani1.pov -o\povray\chapter6\ani10001.tga -p

:Frame2
echo #declare Angle =      22.500000  > ani1.ani
%POV%  -i\povray\chapter6\ani1.pov -o\povray\chapter6\ani10002.tga -p

:Frame3
echo #declare Angle =      45.000000  > ani1.ani
%POV%  -i\povray\chapter6\ani1.pov -o\povray\chapter6\ani10003.tga -p

:Frame4
echo #declare Angle =      67.500000  > ani1.ani
%POV%  -i\povray\chapter6\ani1.pov -o\povray\chapter6\ani10004.tga -p


:COMPILE
rem _____
rem _ This is the compiling portion.              _
rem _ Edit the line below to change parameters.   _
rem _____
%DTA% \povray\chapter6\ani1*.tga /ff /oani1.fli
    goto endit
:BADEND
    echo Error: Raytrace aborted.
    goto endit
:ENDIT
SET POV=
SET DTA=
```

CUSTOMIZING THE BATCH FILE PATHS

You will notice a few other additions to this batch file. The first is the commands set POV=\povray\povray.exe and the similar command for the animation compiler, DTA, set DTA=\povray\dta.exe. These commands make it convenient to modify the batch file, should you need to change the name of the directories in which you keep your POV-Ray and DTA programs. Additional command-line switches can also be included on these lines if needed. In ANI1.BAT, for example, -W160 -H100 +d0 -v command-line switches are all set here for POV-Ray. DTA also has a number of optional command-line switches for various effects that you may wish to try.

You will also notice that the names for POV-Ray and DTA are changed to %POV% and %DTA% on the command lines for these programs. The **Set** command tells DOS to store the value that follows the command in environment variables called **POV** and **DTA**, respectively. It is much like the SET PATH= command in your computer's AUTOEXEC.BAT file. The %POV% command simply retrieves the stored value and substitutes it when executing the command. Thus, %POV% becomes "\povray\povray.exe" when DOS executes that line.

RECOMPILING EXISTING FRAMES

The lines that say *"goto Render"* and *"goto Compile"* in Listing 6-5 are there to let you skip over the calls to POV-Ray that produce the TGA files and jump straight to the DTA portion of the batch file. This is helpful when you have already rendered all of the frames and you want to experiment with different options with DTA. To do this, edit the file and type the word REM immediately before the *"goto Render."* Don't forget to undo this if you decide to re-render the images, however.

Listing 6-6 Recompiling Existing Frames

```
rem _____
rem _   Comment out the line below to skip the rendering portion and proceed    _
rem _   directly to the DTA compiling section if you only want to recompile the  _
rem _   .tga frames without re-rendering them.                                   _
rem _____
REM     goto Render


rem _____
rem _   This next command is here as a method of jumping past the rendering     _
rem _   portion and allow you to go straight to the DTA compiling section. Use   _
rem _   this if you need to recompile existing .tga files to a new .fli.         _
rem _____
    goto Compile
```

PUTTING IT ALL TOGETHER
WITH DAVE'S TARGA ANIMATOR

Finally, we have a command to compile our images into a viewable animation when the rendering process has completed. This is in the compile portion that we referred to above, and its function is to call DTA after all the frames have been rendered.

Caution About the Use of Wildcards

Having DTA called from the batch file is a handy feature, but there is one thing to be aware of: the command line that DTA is called with uses DOS wildcards to specify the input files. In the case of ANI1.BAT, *any and all files* with a .TGA file name extension that begin with the letters ANI10 will get compiled into the animation. If, for example, you had been experimenting with an idea that extended your animation to five frames, and then you later changed your mind and went back to four frames, the file, ANI10005.TGA, if you forgot to delete it, would also get compiled into the new ANI1.FLI. Be sure that you delete any unneeded TGA files after experimenting like this.

As mentioned earlier, DTA is a program to create an FLI format animation file from a series of Targa image files. The command line used to call DTA, `"%DTA% \povray\chapter6\ani1*.tga /ff /oani1.fli"`, tells DTA to read in all files that begin with the letters *ani1_* and end with the extension *.TGA*, and to convert these to a file of the .FLI format by the name of ANI1.FLI.

RENDERING ANI1

To create ANI1.FLI, type *"ANI1"* (ENTER) at the DOS command line. The rest will be automatic. DOS will place the `Angle` rotation values into ANI1.ANI for each frame, call POV-Ray to render the frame, and when all frames have been completed, it will tell DTA to put it all together.

VIEWING ANI1.FLI

When the animation is complete, type "PLAY ANI1.FLI "(you must include the .FLI extension with PLAY.EXE) and sit back and admire your work. You should see the checkered cube rotating clockwise on its *y* axis. As you are admiring it, you can be planning your next animation! The final frames of the animation are shown in Figures 6-5 through 6-8.

USING MULTIPLE DECLARED CONSTANTS

In the \POVRAY\CHAPTER6 directory is another variation on the rotating box theme called ANI2.POV. This image may be a bit more interesting than ANI1. The checkered pattern on the box has been changed to a metallic texture, and the box itself has been changed to rotate on the *x* axis instead of the *y*

Figure 6-5

Figure 6-6

Figure 6-7

Figure 6-8

axis. The checkered floor has been replaced by a reflective, wavy surface. This animation extends on your earlier project by not only rotating the cube, but also by animating the waves. Listing 6-7 shows ANI2.POV.

Listing 6-7 ANI2.POV

```
#include "colors.inc"
#include "shapes.inc"
#include "textures.inc"
#include "ani2.ani"                          // Animation constants file

camera {
  location <6  6  -10>
  direction <0.0 0.0 2>
  up  <0.0  1.0  0.0>
  right <1.33333 0.0 0.0>
  look_at <0 -1 0>
```

```
}

object { light_source { <-50 30 -30>  color Yellow  } }
object { light_source { < 50 60  -30>  color Blue   } }

object {
    box { <-1.0 -1.0 -1.0> <1.0 1.0 1.0>
        texture {
            Chrome_Metal
        }
    }
    rotate <Angle 0 0 >
no_shadow
}

object {
    plane { <0 1 0> -2 }
    texture {
        Metal
        color White
        waves 0.20
        phase -Wave_Phase        // negative values move waves outward
        frequency 5
        scale <0.75 1 0.75>
        translate <0 0 2>
        ambient 0.25
    }
}
```

Notice the `phase` keyword in the texture block for the plane. It indicates the position of the peak of the wave relative to the center of the source. By incrementing `phase` over time, we can move the waves either inward, toward the origin, or outward. Incrementing from phase 0 to phase 1 cycles the wave movement inward, while decrementing from 1 to 0 will move them outward. Since ANI2.POV has a negative sign preceding the `Wave_Phase` constant, the values will actually range from 0 to −1, and the waves will move outward in this example. Now, let's take a look at ANI2.BAT (Listing 6-8).

Listing 6-8 ANI2.BAT

```
@echo off
rem  ********************************************************
rem  Animation batch file generated by Anibatch 2.1
rem  POV-Ray scene file : \povray\chapter6\ani2.pov
rem  Date : 02-11-1993
rem  Number of Frames :  10
rem  Number of declared constants :  2
rem  ********************************************************
```

```
rem
rem      Variable Name : Angle
rem         Start Value : 0
rem         Final Value : 81
rem      Incremented by : 9
rem
rem      Variable Name : Wave_Phase
rem         Start Value : 0
rem         Final Value : 1
rem      Incremented by : .1111111
rem
rem      ********************************************************

rem NOTE: Edit these lines to change the path/filename of your
rem POV-Ray and DTA executable files.
SET POV=\povray\povray.exe -w160 -h100 +d0 -v
SET DTA=\povray\dta.exe

rem _____
rem _This is a test to ensure the the executables actually      _
rem _exist where they are supposed to be found.                 _
rem _____
if not exist %POV% echo %POV% doesn't exist!
if not exist %POV% goto BADEND
if not exist %DTA% echo %DTA% doesn't exist!
if not exist %DTA% goto BADEND

rem _____
rem _    Comment out the line below to skip the rendering portion and proceed   _
rem _    directly to the DTA compiling section if you only want to recompile the _
rem _    .tga frames without re-rendering them.                                  _
rem _____
      goto Render

rem _____
rem _    This next command is here as a method of jumping past the rendering   _
rem _    portion and allow you to go straight to the DTA compiling section. Use _
rem _    this if you need to recompile existing .tga files to a new .fli.       _
rem _____
      goto Compile

:Render
rem _____
rem _ This is the rendering portion.                     _
rem _ Edit the line below to jump to another frame.       _
rem _____
echo _
echo.
```

```
echo.
echo.
echo   About to render animation ani2.fli...
echo _____
echo _ If this is NOT what you want to do, then press CTRL/C now!    _
echo _____
pause
    goto Frame1
:Frame1
echo #declare Angle =       0.000000  > ani2.ani
echo #declare Wave_Phase =       0.000000  >> ani2.ani
%POV%  -i\povray\chapter6\ani2.pov -o\povray\chapter6\ani20001.tga -p

:Frame2
echo #declare Angle =       9.000000  > ani2.ani
echo #declare Wave_Phase =       0.111111  >> ani2.ani
%POV%  -i\povray\chapter6\ani2.pov -o\povray\chapter6\ani20002.tga -p

:Frame3
echo #declare Angle =      18.000000  > ani2.ani
echo #declare Wave_Phase =       0.222222  >> ani2.ani
%POV%  -i\povray\chapter6\ani2.pov -o\povray\chapter6\ani20003.tga -p

:Frame4
echo #declare Angle =      27.000000  > ani2.ani
echo #declare Wave_Phase =       0.333333  >> ani2.ani
%POV%  -i\povray\chapter6\ani2.pov -o\povray\chapter6\ani20004.tga -p

:Frame5
echo #declare Angle =      36.000000  > ani2.ani
echo #declare Wave_Phase =       0.444444  >> ani2.ani
%POV%  -i\povray\chapter6\ani2.pov -o\povray\chapter6\ani20005.tga -p

:Frame6
echo #declare Angle =      45.000000  > ani2.ani
echo #declare Wave_Phase =       0.555556  >> ani2.ani
%POV%  -i\povray\chapter6\ani2.pov -o\povray\chapter6\ani20006.tga -p

:Frame7
echo #declare Angle =      54.000000  > ani2.ani
echo #declare Wave_Phase =       0.666667  >> ani2.ani
%POV%  -i\povray\chapter6\ani2.pov -o\povray\chapter6\ani20007.tga -p

:Frame8
echo #declare Angle =      63.000000  > ani2.ani
echo #declare Wave_Phase =       0.777778  >> ani2.ani
%POV%  -i\povray\chapter6\ani2.pov -o\povray\chapter6\ani20008.tga -p

:Frame9
echo #declare Angle =      72.000000  > ani2.ani
```

```
echo #declare Wave_Phase =         0.888889  >> ani2.ani
%POV%  -i\povray\chapter6\ani2.pov -o\povray\chapter6\ani20009.tga -p

:Frame10
echo #declare Angle =       81.000000  > ani2.ani
echo #declare Wave_Phase =      1.000000  >> ani2.ani
%POV%  -i\povray\chapter6\ani2.pov -o\povray\chapter6\ani20010.tga -p


:COMPILE
rem _____
rem _ This is the compiling portion.              _
rem _ Edit the line below to change parameters.    _
rem _____
%DTA% \povray\chapter6\ani2*.tga /ff /oani2.fli
   goto endit
:BADEND
   echo Error: Raytrace aborted.
   goto endit
:ENDIT
SET POV=
SET DTA=
```

This file is still pretty much the same as ANI1.BAT. The number of frames has been increased to ten. The values for `Angle` have been incremented by one-tenth of 90 degrees, or 9 degrees, instead of the 22.5 degrees that we used earlier. Thus we will still encompass the full 90-degree rotation in the span of ten frames. Figures 6-9 through 6-11 show frames 1, 5, and 10 of this animation.

Notice that the `Wave_Phase` variable is created using the double >> redirection command to tell DOS to append this line to ANI2.ANI instead of over-writing it.

Once again, to build this animation, simply type "ANI2" (ENTER) and when it is complete, view it by typing "PLAY ANI2.FLI". I think you will agree that this is a rather interesting animation, yet it was done using some very simple techniques.

USING ANIBATCH TO CREATE ANIMATION BATCH FILES

Creating an animation with a batch file almost becomes an automatic process once the planning has been completed. But creating the batch file itself for a complex animation is still a daunting task. To ease this process, we have

Figure 6-9

Figure 6-10

Figure 6-11

included a program called Anibatch. While it is not capable of doing very sophisticated animation techniques, it works very nicely for simple linear incrementations of values like we have been using in the examples. In fact, Anibatch was used to create ANI1.BAT and ANI2.BAT. To run Anibatch, type "ANIBATCH" (ENTER) at the DOS prompt.

The program will first ask if you wish to restore from an Anibatch script file. Anibatch has the ability to save your keystrokes to a script file to make it easier to revise an animation. Since you are creating a new animation, you would enter (N) for "No." Later on, after you have answered all the necessary questions, you will be given the opportunity to save your responses to a script file. After you have done this, you can enter (Y) (for "Yes") to this prompt.

Anibatch will next ask you for the name of the file to animate. Since you are creating a new animation, enter the name of your POV-Ray scene file here.

Keep the file name to four characters, since it will also be used for the root portion of the rest of the files, just as ANI1.POV had its ANI1.BAT and output ANI10001.TGA.

When asked for the path and name of your POV-Ray and DTA executables, select the default value (option 1) if the name displayed there matches your setup. If not, select option 2 and enter the correct paths and names for the programs. You will only have to do this once for each animation as long as you save the script file.

You will then be taken through a series of questions dealing with the number of frames and the starting and ending values for each constant that you wish to define. Answer each of these prompts according to the needs of the animation you are designing.

Once you have declared starting and final values for all of your constants, Anibatch will ask if you want to save the Anibatch script. Type (Y) so that you can load the current values back in when you wish to change something.

Anibatch will then create a ready-to-run batch file with the same root name as the scene file (i.e., TEST.POV will have a batch file by the name of TEST.BAT). You should inspect the batch file first, however, to make sure that the file names and constant values look correct.

SUMMARY

In this chapter you have learned a bit about the history and early techniques of animation and created two simple animations of your own. You have been introduced to the fourth dimension of ray tracing: time.

You learned:

- how to create batch files that simplify the process of updating the animation variables,
- how use DTA to compile your images into an FLI format animation,
- how to use PLAY to view the final animation, and
- how to use Anibatch to create your own animation batch files and how to configure those batch files to suit your requirements.

Points to remember:

- Animation can be used as a tool to help you learn more about POV-Ray itself.

- Keep your animations simple, at least while starting out. Computer animation by ray tracing, while yielding spectacular results, is quite time-intensive. This can be minimized by careful planning and design.
- Think beyond simply moving objects around in a scene. There are many other effects that you can often add with little or no additional computer time required.

What we've covered here only touches the surface of what you can do with POV-Ray and a few other simple tools to create animations that are limited only by your own creativity. Happy exploring!

"Seek and ye shall find"

—Matthew 7:7

Reference

INTRODUCTION

This chapter constitutes a complete reference to the POV-Ray program. We begin with an overview of how the program works. Next we will discuss each of the command-line switches which control the way POV-Ray works. Then we give an overview of the scene-description language which specifies the objects, textures, and lighting to be rendered by POV-Ray. The chapter concludes with a detailed keyword reference section.

HOW POV-RAY WORKS

POV-Ray reads user-supplied text files and creates ray traced images from them. Figure 7-1 illustrates the steps involved in creating and viewing an image with POV-Ray. The main text file you supply (and others you may include) contains instructions written in POV-Ray's scene-description language. These input files describe the camera you will use to view the image, the objects seen in the image, the light sources that illuminate the scene, and other elements that tell the program how to do its job.

File input, processing, and screen and file output are controlled by various command-line switches that you specify when running the program. Default switch settings and groups of switches may also be specified through a DOS environment variable and/or a text file containing default switch settings.

The process of reading in your text file and interpreting it is called "parsing." The parser section of POV-Ray creates a model of your scene in memory.

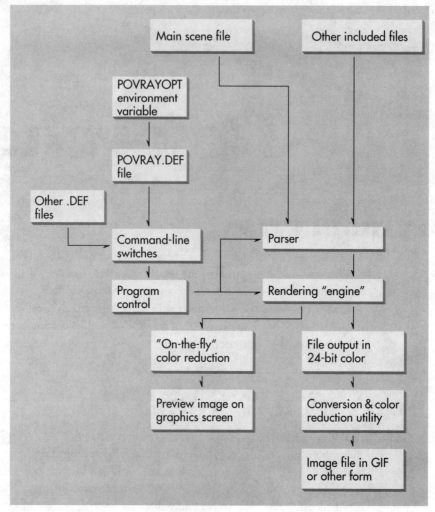

Figure 7-1 How POV-Ray Processes Information

The process of creating the image after parsing is complete is called either "rendering" or "tracing." The rendering engine in POV-Ray uses the internal memory model to create your image.

The output of POV-Ray is a file containing the resulting image and/or a preview of the image on your graphics screen. The preview image is only an approximation of what the final output looks like. The quality of this preview depends upon the quality of your graphics hardware. The output file will contain the full 24-bit color rendering of your scene. A separate conversion utility is generally used to translate the full color data file into a more useful format such as GIF. Such conversion utilities can often create an image that looks better than the on-the-fly color reduction that POV-Ray uses in displaying the preview image. When the program is finished, POV-Ray outputs a screen of statistics about the rendering. This statistics screen is detailed in the "+@ switch" section of this chapter.

COMMAND-LINE SWITCHES

From the DOS prompt, you invoke POV-Ray with a series of command-line switches to tell it how to do its job. Table 7-1 gives a brief list of the switches. Detailed descriptions are in the next section.

Switches are preceded by a "+" or "-" and are separated from each other by one or more spaces. For example,

```
C:\>POVRAY +Imyfile.pov +W640 +H480 +FT +Omyfile.tga
```

invokes POV-Ray with an input file MYFILE.POV, an image width and height of 640x480 pixels, and Targa format output to a file called MYFILE.TGA. Note that switches may not be joined. The +FT switch in the example above is the +F file switch with a suboption of T. It is not a +F switch followed by a +T switch.

POV-Ray reads the switches from left to right on your command line. Switches may be in either upper- or lowercase. When specifying switches that toggle options off or on, a + sign before a switch means turn this option on and a - sign means turn it off. In cases where the switch supplies a value and does not toggle an option, either a + or - will work the same. In general, if any switches appear more than once, the last setting encountered is the one used. The exception to this is the +L option that is used to define library paths. Multiple uses of the +L switch do not override previous specifications, but rather add additional search paths. Up to ten library paths may be defined in this way.

DEFINING DEFAULT SWITCH SETTINGS

Because it is inconvenient to type long lists of switches every time you run POV-Ray, you can define default sets of switches. Before reading any command-line switches, POV-Ray first looks for the environment variable POVRAYOPT. You can set this variable using the DOS Set command from

Table 7-1   Command-Line Switches

Switch	Action
+@filespec	Writes status file to disk while processing
+Annn	Controls adaptive antialiasing
+Bnnn	Sets output file buffer size in KB
+C	Continues an interrupted tracing
+Dnp	Controls graphics display
+Ennn	Terminates tracing before final line
+Ft	Sends image data to an output file
+Hnnn	Specifies height of image in pixels
+Ifilespec	Specifies input file name
+Lpath	Specifies path for libraries of files
+MSnnn	Sets various maximum values
+Ofilespec	Specifies output file name
+P	Causes a pause for keypress when rendering is complete
+Qn	Sets rendering quality level
+Snnn	Starts tracing at a particular line
+V	Turns line number display on and off
+Wnnn	Specifies width of image in pixels
+X	Allows rendering to be interrupted with a keypress

your AUTOEXEC.BAT file or from the DOS prompt. For example, if you always want output in Targa format and you want to specify a search path to a subdirectory of include files you could do the following:

```
C:\>SET POVRAYOPT= +FT +Lc:\povray\include
```

After processing the switches in the POVRAYOPT environment variable, POV-Ray searches your current directory for the file POVRAY.DEF. If the file is not in your current directory, your DOS path is searched. You may create this plain ASCII text file and POV-Ray will read any switches from it.

There is another way to pass groups of switches to the command line. If POV-Ray encounters a file name with no switches immediately preceding it on the command line, it assumes that it is a file similar to POVRAY.DEF. By convention, such files have an extension of DEF. POV-Ray searches the current directory and DOS path for that file and if it finds it, reads switches from it. After processing the DEF file, POV-Ray resumes scanning the command line. Only one such DEF file may be specified on the line. For example, if VGA.DEF contains the text +W640 +H480, then the earlier example could be invoked by

```
C:\>POVRAY +Imyfile.pov VGA.DEF +FT +Omyfile.tga
```

This would produce a 640 by 480 pixel image.

In summary, here is the order in which POV-Ray processes switch settings:

1) Starts with POV-Ray built-in defaults
2) Reads switches from POVRAYOPT environment variable if any
3) Reads switches from POVRAY.DEF text file if any
4) Reads switches from command line and insert switches from another DEF file if called for on the command line

The last specified setting of any switch (except for +L paths) overrides all previous settings. Some non-IBM versions of POV-Ray reverse steps 2 and 3 above and read the POVRAY.DEF file before reading the environment variable. Consult your version's documentation for details.

COMMAND-LINE SWITCH REFERENCE

This section describes the purpose, syntax, and use of each of POV-Ray's command-line switches. A "See Also" section under each switch directs your attention to related switches in this section as well as other topics in this chapter. In the examples given below, you should assume that no POVRAY-OPT environment variable has been set. Assume that a file named MYDEF.DEF has been created in the current directory and that it contains the following single line of text.

```
+W640 +H480 +Lc:\povray\include
```

+@

PURPOSE
Writes a status file to disk while processing. This file is designed to allow multi-tasking environments to monitor POV-Ray's status and to determine how the program terminated.

SYNTAX
-@   Turn off status file (DEFAULT)
+@   Send status to POVSTAT.OUT
+@*filespec*   Send status to specified file

DESCRIPTION
This switch is primarily for use with shell programs that invoke POV-Ray or for checking the status of POV-Ray when running it in the background in a multitasking environment. Used alone, the +@ switch will create a status file called POVSTAT.OUT on the current drive and directory or overwrite any previous file with that name. By putting a file specification after the +@ you can output to any file. The -@ switch disables any previous use of the +@ switch. The default is -@ for no status file.

When the +@ option is on, POV-Ray writes a line of text to a status file after tracing each line. This text line gives the current line number. The file is overwritten for every line. When rendering in a multitasking environment, you can examine the status file to determine the current status of POV-Ray. If a parsing or rendering error occurs, the error message is written to the status file.

Upon normal termination, POV-Ray displays a screen with statistics about the number of rays traced, number of intersections, time consumed, and other interesting information. When you use the +@ switch, this closing information is not displayed on the screen. It is redirected to the status file. Because the +@ switch causes the status file to be overwritten as every line is traced, it can add significant time to the rendering. If you do not need to monitor the progress of the program during rendering, the +@ is an inefficient way to capture this final screen display to a file. A more efficient method is to use DOS console Redirection as shown here:

```
C:\>POVRAY MYDEFS.DEF +IMYFILE.POV > SCREEN.TXT
```

Figure 7-2 shows a sample of the statistics from a typical successful rendering.

Persistence of Vision Raytracer Ver 1.0.ibmicb			

examp.pov statistics

Image Resolution 160 pixels wide x 100 pixels high
Rays Calculated   :   16000
Pixels Calculated   :   16000
Pixels Supersampled   :   0

Ray -/ Shape Intersection Tests			
Type	Tests	Succeeded	Percentage
Sphere	51969	31139	59.92
Plane	25561	8000	31.30

Calls to Noise Routine   :   34062
Calls to DNoise Routine   :   10

Shadow Ray Tests   :   39091
Blocking Objects Found   :   847

Rendering Time   :   0 hours   0 minutes   41.00 seconds

Figure 7-2 Typical Rendering Statistics Screen

SEE ALSO

+V

EXAMPLE

`C:\>POVRAY MYDEFS.DEF +Imyfile.pov +@status.txt`

creates "STATUS.TXT" in the current directory and outputs status information to it.

`C:\>POVRAY SPECIAL.DEF +Imyfile.pov -@`

assuming SPECIAL.DEF contains a +@ switch then the -@ switch turns it off.

+A

PURPOSE

Controls adaptive antialiasing. Antialiasing is a method of smoothing out the jagged "stair-step" look of diagonal lines in computer-generated images.

SYNTAX

-A   Do not use antialiasing (DEFAULT)
+A   Use antialiasing with default threshold 0.3
+A*nnn*   Use antialiasing with specified threshold

DESCRIPTION

Any images made of rows and columns of pixels (not just ray traced images) often have a jagged or "stair-step" appearance where there are diagonal lines. This phenomenon is a type of aliasing. The word comes from the root "alias" because the line looks like one thing (a jagged line) when it is in reality something else (a smooth line). Any method of compensating for aliasing is called antialiasing.

POV-Ray has an optional antialiasing feature called "adaptive jittered super-sampling" to smooth out these jagged lines. When antialiasing is on, POV-Ray checks the colors of pixels above and to the left of the current pixel. The colors of these pixels are compared to the current pixel. If the difference between the pixels exceeds the threshold value, POV-Ray antialiases those pixels. The method is called "adaptive" because it does not antialias in smooth areas where adjacent pixels have a similar color. Antialiasing only kicks in where there are abrupt changes between pixels that need smoothing.

Normally POV-Ray traces only one ray per pixel. The antialiasing of an individual pixel is done by sending nine extra rays through the pixel's area in a three-by-three grid within the space of the pixel. This is called "super-sampling" a pixel. Each ray of the sample is also "jittered" or wiggled a tiny random amount. The colors of all nine of these jittered super samples are averaged in order to determine the final color of the pixel.

The +A command-line switch turns on antialiasing. The -A switch can be used to turn off any previous +A setting. The number following the +A is the threshold amount. If +A is specified with no threshold, a default threshold of 0.3 is used. A threshold of 0.0 antialiases all pixels. A threshold of 1.0 antialiases none.

EXAMPLE

```
POVRAY MYDEFS.DEF +Imyfile.pov +A0.2
```

renders MYFILE.POV with antialiasing on and a threshold value of 0.2.

+B

PURPOSE

Sets the number of 1024-byte (1KB) blocks to use for file output.

SYNTAX

-B*nnn* or +B*nnn*

DESCRIPTION

The +B switch causes POV-Ray to write to the output file with a buffer of the size specified. (File output must first be enabled with the +F switch.) The number you specify after the +B is the number of 1024-byte (1KB) blocks of memory to use. If you specify a number lower than the default buffer size, your specification is ignored and the default size is used. The default size depends upon which POV-Ray version you are using and upon the compiler used to create it. The default is usually 8–10KB. The maximum size of this buffer depends on how much memory you have and how much free disk space you have available for a swap file created by the virtual memory manager. Further guidance on managing memory is available in the machine-specific documentation for POV-Ray.

Note that the -B switch does not turn buffering off; it works exactly like the +B switch.

Normally, POV-Ray flushes the output file at the end of each line of pixels. This ensures that an interrupted tracing has had as much data as possible safely written to disk. When running POV-Ray in background under multitasking environments such as Windows or DesqView, this line-by-line flush lets you have access to partially completed traces without interrupting the program. The disadvantage to this is it can slow down tracing. By using the +B switch, you tell POV-Ray to use an output buffer and not to flush after each line. Buffered disk writes are less frequent so less time is used. If the trace abnormally terminates, however, you may lose up to a buffer's worth of data.

The +X switch allows you to interrupt a trace by pressing a key. Such an interruption does not cause loss of data.

SEE ALSO

+F, +O, +X

EXAMPLE

```
POVRAY MYDEF.DEF +Imyfile.pov +B64
```

tells POV-Ray to run with a 64KB buffer for the output file.

+C

PURPOSE

Continues an interrupted tracing by reading the previous output file to determine where the program was interrupted. Does not work if no file output has been used.

SYNTAX

-C   Do not continue from previous session (DEFAULT)
+C   Continue from previous session

DESCRIPTION

A tracing session that was interrupted with the +X switch enabled, or that was set up to partially complete with the +E switch, can be continued by rerunning POV-Ray with the +C switch. This will only work if the +F switch has been used to turn on file output.

When POV-Ray is restarted with the +C switch it will read the specified output file to determine where tracing stopped. It will continue tracing at the next line. If no output file is found with the proper name, then POV-Ray will create the file and render the image from the first line. If the file is found and the rendering has already been completed, POV-Ray will terminate. If the +D display is turned on, POV-Ray will display the already completed part of the image before continuing.

It is important that you use switches that will produce a rendering identical to the original or the results will be unpredictable. You may use other switches, such as +D, +V, and +X, for the continued tracing without any adverse effects because such switches do not affect the image itself. However such other switches as +W or +H must not be changed. Note: Do not use the +S switch in combination with +C.

SEE ALSO

+E, +F, +O, +S, +X

EXAMPLE

Suppose that a trace is started

```
POVRAY MYDEFS.DEF +Imyfile.pov +Omyfile.tga +FT +X
```

Part of the way through the tracing, a key is pressed to interrupt the program. Later the tracing may be resumed with

```
POVRAY MYDEFS.DEF +Imyfile.pov +Omyfile.tga +FT +X +C
```

It should not be restarted with just the +C switch like this:

```
POVRAY +C
```

POV-Ray does not record previous settings, so the example above uses default switches such as +Iobjects.pov +Odata.raw and others, which were not the same as originally specified. Unless OBJECTS.POV existed, POV-Ray would terminate with an error message about a missing input file.

Now assume that a tracing is run as follows:

```
POVRAY MYDEFS.DEF +Imyfile.pov +Omyfile.tga +FT +X −D +V
```

After interruption you could change to

```
POVRAY MYDEFS.DEF +Imyfile.pov +Omyfile.tga +FT +X +D −V +C
```

Eliminating the +V and adding the +D display will not hurt anything.

+D

PURPOSE

Controls graphics display for the preview image. You may autodetect the hardware type or manually select it. You may select palettes for the preview image.

SYNTAX

-D   Do not use graphics display (DEFAULT)
+D   Turn graphics display on and autodetect hardware type
+D*n*   Turn graphics on for the specified video type
+D*np*   Turn graphics on for the specified video and palette type

DESCRIPTION

POV-Ray can display a preview version of the image being rendered on the graphics screen as it is working. (Note: This section assumes you are using an IBM version of POV-Ray. Other versions may not implement graphics. Some have graphics but the options are different. Consult the machine-specific documentation for your version of POV-Ray for further information.)

The default -D means no display. The +D switch turns graphics on. Typically, while not essential, the -V switch is used to turn off the reporting of line

275

numbers when +D is used. Also the +P switch is generally used to keep the screen from clearing when the tracing is complete.

A number of suboptions may follow the +D switch. The character immediately after the +D selects the type of video hardware. If no hardware type is specified, POV-Ray attempts to autodetect the type. Hardware support settings are summarized in Table 7-2. Unless otherwise specified, the cards will support up to 640x480 pixels. The highest supported resolution mode is listed. However if the image will fit in a supported lower resolution mode, it will be used. Only

Table 7-2	Video Hardware Selection with the +D Switch
Switch and Suboption	**+D or VGA and SVGA**
+D0	Autodetect VGA or SVGA type
+D1	Standard VGA at 320x200
+D2	Standard VGA at 360x480
+D3	Tseng Labs 3000 up to 800x600
+D4	Tseng Labs 4000 up to 1024x768 (800x600 in HiColor)
+D5	AT&T VDC600 up to 640x400
+D6	Oak Technologies
+D7	Video 7 SVGA
+D8	Video 7 Vega (Cirrus) VGA 360x480
+D9	Paradise SVGA
+DA	Ahead Systems Ver. A SVGA
+DB	Ahead Systems Ver. B SVGA
+DC	Chips & Technologies SVGA
+DD	ATI SVGA up to 1024x768
+DE	Everex SVGA
+DF	Trident SVGA
+DG	VESA Standard SVGA Adapter (any VESA supported mode)
+DH	ATI XL display card

256-color VGA systems are supported. (No other video systems such as original Hercules monochrome, CGA, EGA, or 16-color VGA are supported.)

An optional third character selects the palette type. Palette options are shown in Table 7-3. Internally POV-Ray uses floating-point values for colors of countless variety. These values are rounded to 8 bits for each of the red, green, and blue color components for a total of 24 bits of color information per pixel in the output file. This represents over 16 million possible colors per pixel. This wide variety of colors cannot be displayed on VGA systems. Some form of color reduction must be performed. These palette options let you pick the color-reduction method you prefer. This color reduction only affects the display. The file output remains in full 24-bit color in any case. POV-Ray's color reduction is "on-the-fly" and is not as accurate as color-reduction methods used by file conversion utilities, which can look at the entire completed output and calculate an optimum palette.

If none is specified, the default palette is the 332 palette. The 332 palette may also be specifically selected using the character 3. The 332 palette is a fixed set of 256 VGA colors consisting of 3 bits of red data, 3 bits of green data, and 2 bits of blue data.

The 0 option, like the 3 option, uses a fixed palette of 256 colors, but it has been specially selected to balance the hue, saturation, and value (HSV) of the colors. An HSV color system such as this converts red, green, and blue component values into HSV values that define colors in terms of hue (color tint), saturation (amount of pure color compared to whiteness or degree of pastel), and value (the brightness or intensity of the shade). HSV color reduction chooses colors by giving greater consideration to what hue the color is and less consideration to how light or dark, or pure colored or pastel a color is.

Table 7-3 Palette Selections with the +D Switch

Switch and Suboption	Palette
+Dn3	Use 332 palette with dithering (DEFAULT)
+DnH	Use HiColor option; uses 32,000+ colors with dithering
+Dn0	Use HSV palette option for VGA display
+DnG	Use Gray scale palette option for VGA display

The H option selects the HiColor option on specially equipped Tseng 4000 and ATI XL systems. HiColor modes use a fixed palette of over 32,000 colors with 5 bits each of red, green, and blue.

The G option converts the color to grayscale and uses a fixed VGA palette of 64 shades of gray.

All of these methods also use dithering, the process where two different-color pixels are plotted next to each other to simulate an unavailable color that is between the two available colors.

SEE ALSO

+P, +V

EXAMPLE

```
POVRAY MYDEF.DEF +Imyfile.pov +D +P
```

renders MYFILE.POV and autodetects the hardware. Uses 332 palette and pauses when finished.

```
POVRAY MYDEF.DEF +Imyfile.pov +D4H +P
```

specifically selects the HiColor option on a Tseng 4000 based card.

```
POVRAY MYDEF.DEF +Imyfile.pov +D9G +P +FT +Omyfile.tga
```

renders on a system with Paradise VGA using a grayscale palette. Also outputs full color data in Targa 24-bit format to MYFILE.TGA.

+E

PURPOSE

Terminates tracing before the final line of the image is rendered. This is used to render a partial image that may be resumed later.

SYNTAX

-E*nnn* or +E*nnn*

DESCRIPTION

If you wish to render only part of an image you can use the +E switch to tell POV-Ray the line at which to end. Lines are numbered from the top down, beginning with line 1. The +E switch tells POV-Ray to quit after rendering the specified line. Tracing can be restarted later using the +C switch.

SEE ALSO
+C, +S

EXAMPLE
```
POVRAY MYDEFS.DEF +Imyfile.pov +Omyfile.tga +E50
```

causes POV-Ray to quit after rendering the 50th line from the top. To restart the tracing from line 51 onward, you would use the +C switch:

```
POVRAY MYDEFS.DEF +Imyfile.pov +Omyfile.tga +C
```

+F

PURPOSE
Sends the image data to an output file for later processing or viewing.

SYNTAX
-F   Do not output to a file
+F   Create output file in default format (DEFAULT)
+FD   Create output file in dump format
+FR   Create output file in raw format
+FT   Create output file in Targa 24 format (IBM DEFAULT)

DESCRIPTION
The +F switch tells POV-Ray to output its image data to a disk file. The optional second character specifies dump (D), raw (R), or Targa (T) format. The IBM default is +FT for Targa, but other versions may have other defaults. Dump format is that used by the QRT ray tracer, another widely available program for ray tracing. Raw format is used by the image processing program PICLAB. Targa 24 is a format used originally for Targa brand 24-bit hardware made by Truevision, Inc., but it is now a popular standard for full color files. When the +F is used, the output is sent to a file with a default name of DATA.TGA. A different output file name is usually specified with the +O switch.

Note that if -F is used you cannot use +C to resume an interrupted trace. If both the -F and -D switches are specified, POV-Ray calculates the tracing but otherwise produces no output of any kind.

+C, +D, +O

EXAMPLE

```
POVRAY MYDEFS.DEF +Imyfile.pov +Omyfile.tga +FT
```

outputs image in Targa 24 format to MYFILE.TGA.

+H

PURPOSE

Specifies the height of the rendered image in pixels.

SYNTAX

-H*nnn* or +H*nnn*

DESCRIPTION

The height of the rendered image in rows of pixels is specified by the +H switch. Either -H or +H may be used. The switch must be followed by a number. If no +H switch is given, the default value of +H100 is used. (The +W switch specifies the width of the image. See the `camera` and `right` keywords for information on the +H and +W switches and image aspect ratio.)

SEE ALSO

+W, Keywords `camera`, `right`

EXAMPLE

```
POVRAY MYDEFS.DEF +Imyfile.pov +Omyfile.tga +W320 +H200
```

changes the 640x480 specification in MYDEFS.DEF to 320x200.

+I

PURPOSE

Specifies the name of the input file.

SYNTAX

-I*filespec* or +I*filespec*

DESCRIPTION

POV-Ray requires an input file in ASCII text to describe the image to be rendered. Use the +I switch to give the file specification for the input file, including drive and path if necessary. By convention, input files have the extension .POV. If the file is not found on the current drive, any library paths specified by the +L switch are searched. If no file is specified with the +I switch, POV-Ray uses the default name OBJECT.POV.

SEE ALSO

+L, Scene-Description Language, and `include` Keyword

EXAMPLE

`POVRAY MYDEFS.DEF +Imyfile.pov`

runs POV-Ray with the file "MYFILE.POV" used for input.

+L

PURPOSE

Specifies the search path for libraries of files.

SYNTAX

-L*path* or +L*path*

DESCRIPTION

POV-Ray comes with standard include files full of shapes, textures, and objects which you can use in your scenes. You will probably want to create your own libraries of files for use with POV-Ray. The +L switch allows you to better manage your files by placing them in separate directories and specifying a path where they can be found. Multiple uses of the +L switch do not override earlier paths, but simply add the specified path to the list. You can specify up to ten library paths per run, counting those in the POVRAYOPT environment variable and any DEF files.

When POV-Ray looks for an input file specified with the +I switch, an INC file in an `#include` directive, or files for `image_map`, `bump_map`, `material_map` or `height_field` statements, it does the following:

- Uses the full drive, path and file name, if given

- Searches the current drive and directory if only the file name is given
- Searches the paths specified with the +L switch

SEE ALSO

+I, Keywords: `image_map`, `bump_map`, `material_map`, `height_field`

EXAMPLE

`POVRAY MYDEFS.DEF +Lc:\povray\maps +Imyfile.pov`

adds C:\POVRAY\MAPS to the paths searched when looking for .POV, .INC, or map files.

+M

PURPOSE

Sets various maximum values.

SYNTAX

-MS*nnn* or +MS*nnn*

DESCRIPTION

The +M switch is designed to allow the setting of a variety of values. Currently only the +MS setting is implemented: It sets the maximum number of symbols in the symbol table for identifiers. Every use of the `#declare` language directive creates one entry in the symbol table. The default value is 500.

SEE ALSO

Keyword `declare`

EXAMPLE

`POVRAY MYDEFS.DEF +Ibigfile.pov +MS800`

renders BIGFILE.POV with 800 symbol table slots available.

+O

PURPOSE

Specifies the name of the output file.

SYNTAX

-O*filespec* or +O*filespec*

DESCRIPTION

When the +F switch is specified, POV-Ray outputs 24-bit color data for the rendered image to a disk file called by default DATA.TGA. You may override this file name and supply your own output file name with the +O switch. Note that -O does not turn output off, but works just like +O. You should use -F if you wish to disable file output.

SEE ALSO

+F

EXAMPLE

```
POVRAY MYDEFS.DEF +Imyfile.pov +FT +Omyfile.tga
```

renders MYFILE.POV and output data to MYFILE.TGA in Targa format.

+P

PURPOSE

Pauses for a keypress when rendering is complete.

SYNTAX

-P   Do not pause when finished (DEFAULT)
+P   Pause for keypress when finished

DESCRIPTION

The +P switch causes POV-Ray to pause for a keypress before displaying the final statistics. This is generally used with the +D display switch so that the completed rendering remains on the screen. The default is -P, which does not pause.

SEE ALSO

+D

EXAMPLE

```
POVRAY MYDEFS.DEF +Imyfile.pov +D0 +P
```

renders MYFILE.POV with graphics display on and pauses when finished.

+Q

PURPOSE

Sets rendering quality level. Low levels are used for faster, less detailed test renderings.

SYNTAX

-Q*n* or +Q*n*

DESCRIPTION

The +Q switch causes POV-Ray to take shortcuts to speed the rendering of test images. Table 7-4 describes the various settings. By eliminating some of the time-consuming texture and reflection calculations you can quickly get a rough idea of objects' positions. This can be helpful when developing complex images with many objects. Then you can render the scene with the default quality level +Q9 which performs all calculations at full quality. Each higher level adds to the features of the lower levels except for "quick colors." The "quick colors" in +Q0 through +Q5 are in place of the color pattern. Levels +Q6 through +Q9 use the full color pattern. Color patterns are discussed in the language reference later in this chapter. Quick colors are discussed in the keyword reference under `color`.

Table 7-4 Rendering Quality Settings with +Q	
Switch and Suboptions	**Action**
+Q0 or +Q1	Just show quick colors; full ambient lighting only
+Q2 or +Q3	Show diffuse and ambient lighting
+Q4 or +Q5	Trace shadow rays to render shadows
+Q6 or +Q7	Render surface textures including full color patterns
+Q8 or +Q9	Render full quality with reflected, refracted, and transmitted rays

Note: The duplication of values in the table allows for future expansion of this option.

SEE ALSO

Keyword color

EXAMPLE

```
POVRAY MYDEFS.DEF +Imyfile.pov +D0 +W80 +H50 +Q2
```

renders a small version of MYFILE.POV with graphics display on and shows only quick colors, and ambient and diffuse lighting.

+S

PURPOSE

Begins tracing at a specified line.

SYNTAX

-S*nnn* or +S*nnn*

DESCRIPTION

If you wish to render only part of an image, you can tell POV-Ray which lines to start and end with by using the +S and +E switches, respectively. Lines are numbered from the top down beginning with line 1. The +S switch tells POV-Ray to start rendering *after* the specified line. The default value of +S0 starts rendering line 1. This numbering is somewhat odd because the switch was originally used to resume partial traces with the +E switch. Therefore a rendering with +E50 could be restarted with +S50. Unfortunately the interrupted tracings required piecing together files with special utilities. Now tracing may be restarted using the +C switch.

The +S switch is somewhat obsolete but still useful for making partial test renderings.

SEE ALSO

+C, +E

EXAMPLE

```
POVRAY MYDEFS.DEF +Imyfile.pov +Omyfile.tga +S50
```

causes POV-Ray to start by rendering the 51st line from the top.

+V

PURPOSE

Turns line number display on and off. Line number display is useful for monitoring the progress of a tracing, especially if no graphics display is used.

SYNTAX

-V   Display no line numbers during rendering (DEFAULT)
+V   Display line numbers while rendering

DESCRIPTION

The +V switch turns on the display of the number of lines that have completed rendering. The input and output file names are also shown. The default value is -V for no displayed numbers. Typically, -V is used with +D graphics on and +V is used with -D graphics off. Any combination is valid, however.

SEE ALSO

+D

EXAMPLE

```
POVRAY MYDEFS.DEF +Imyfile.pov -D +V
```

renders MYFILE.POV with graphic display off and line number status on.

+W

PURPOSE

Specifies the width of the rendered image in pixels.

SYNTAX

-W*nnn* or +W*nnn*

DESCRIPTION

The width of the image in columns of pixels is specified by the +W, or -W, switch. The switch must be followed by a number. If no +W switch is given, the default value of +W100 is used. (The +H switch specifies the height. See the `camera` and `right` keywords for information on the +H and +W switches and image aspect ratio.)

SEE ALSO

+H, Keywords `camera`, `right`

EXAMPLE

`POVRAY MYDEFS.DEF +Imyfile.pov +Omyfile.tga +W320 +H200`

changes the 640x480 specification in MYDEFS.DEF to 320x200.

+X

PURPOSE

Allows rendering to be interrupted with a keypress.

SYNTAX

-X   Do not allow interruption (DEFAULT)

+X   Allow interruption with keypress

DESCRIPTION

The +X option causes POV-Ray to permit interruption of rendering by simply pressing a key. The tracing may be resumed at the last full line using the +C (continue) switch, provided that file output has been enabled with the +F switch. The default setting is -X, which allows no interruption. The +X switch is only available in the IBM version of POV-Ray.

SEE ALSO

+C

EXAMPLE

`POVRAY MYDEFS.DEF +Imyfile.pov +X +FT`

renders MYFILE.POV with Targa file output and enables keypress interruption. An interrupted rendering may resume with

`POVRAY MYDEFS +Imyfile.pov +C +FT`

SCENE-DESCRIPTION LANGUAGE REFERENCE

POV-Ray has its own language that you use to describe the image you want to create. Using this language, you describe the scene by typing statements into an ASCII text file using a text editor of your choice. POV-Ray reads that file as input and creates an internal model of the scene. It then uses that model to create the image.

When you start POV-Ray it looks for the command-line switch +I*filespec* to find your input text file containing the language statements. If no +I switch is given, POV-Ray will look for the default input file OBJECT.POV. It is standard practice that scene-description files have the .POV extension.

The input file may contain one or more `#include` directives that reference other text files containing POV-Ray statements. It is standard practice to give these files the .INC extension. POV-Ray has a number of standard include files such as SHAPES.INC and TEXTURES.INC that contain `#declare` directives defining commonly used shapes and textures. POV-Ray begins parsing your input file at the first line and continues processing it line-by-line to the end. You may put an `#include` directive anywhere in the file. The form is

```
#include "file.inc"
```

where "FILE.INC" is the name of a file containing POV-Ray statements.

POV-Ray remembers where it is in the current file and begins processing text from FILE.INC as if its contents had been copied into the main file at that point. When POV-Ray has finished processing the include file, it picks up where it paused and processes the remainder of the earlier file. You may nest `#include` directives ten levels deep while there is no restriction on the number of non-nested include files you use.

The text you create in the scene file is free form. Use blanks, tabs, or new lines as needed to arrange the text for readability.

If you are familiar with programming languages you will notice that there are no flow control, looping, or conditional statements in the language. POV-Ray simply starts at the top and reads statements one by one in a single pass. This is because POV-Ray doesn't execute the statements as a typical programming language does. All of your statements in the scene file are declarations that describe objects or parts of objects. This is similar to structure and variable declarations in a standard programming language.

Many times you will declare pieces of objects and then assemble them into bigger pieces. Because parsing occurs in a single pass, you must declare the pieces before you can use them to define other pieces. If the piece you are describing is not made up of other pieces then their order in the file does not matter.

In general, a statement is specified by a keyword followed by one or more items enclosed in curly brackets: `texture {MyTexture}`, for example. The items may be other statements, vectors, floating-point values, or keywords followed by a vector or float value. The grammatical rules of the language are defined in the "Complete Syntax Reference" section later in this chapter. It defines how you can combine values, keywords, and statements to describe your scene.

POV-Ray scene descriptions are made up of comments, literals, special characters, identifiers, and reserved keywords. Here is a brief summary of those language elements.

COMMENTS

You use comments to document the statements that make up your scene. Any text after a double slash through the end of a line is considered a comment. For example:

```
object { // The text after two slashes is a comment.
  MyObject // Reference previously defined object
  translate <4 5 1>      // move it into place.
}
```

Also any text found between /*and */ characters is also treated as a comment. This allows multiline comments to be easily included. For example:

```
/*
    This is an extended multiline comment.
    POV-Ray ignores everything up until the next line.
*/
```

The /* and */ pairs may be nested. This makes it easy to comment-out sections of a file without worrying about comments that are already there.

LITERALS

You can use two types of literals: numeric literals and character string literals. Examples of numeric literals are `1.0`, `123.456`, `.5`, `100`, `-123`, `+321`,

-1.234e-2. Note that a leading zero is not required. Plus or minus signs may be used. Integer values do not require a decimal point. Scientific notation in "e" format may be used, as shown above.

String literals are any printable ASCII characters between a pair of double quotes. Strings many not contain a double quote. Currently strings are only used for file names in #include directives, image maps, bump maps, material maps, and Height-Fields.

SPECIAL CHARACTERS

All printable ASCII characters are reserved for use by POV-Ray but not all have uses defined yet. The ones currently used are given in Table 7-5.

IDENTIFIERS AND KEYWORDS

POV-Ray allows you to declare identifiers as names for objects, shapes, textures, values, and other language constructs. Identifiers must begin with a letter or an underscore. They may contain letters, digits, or underscores and may be

Table 7-5 ASCII Characters Used in POV-Ray

ASCII Characters	Usage
{ and }	Delimit statements; for example: texture {MyTexture}
+ and −	Specifies sign used in numeric literals and identifiers
=	Declare identifiers in #declare directive
#	Used before many language directives; for example: #include or #declare
< and >	Begin and end vectors; for example: scale <5 4 2>
[and]	Begin and end entries in a color_map statement
//	Begin single-line comments
/*	Begin multiline comments
*/	End multiline comments
"	Delimit string literals

from 1 to 40 characters long. Identifiers are case sensitive. Thus "MyThing" and "mything" have two different meanings. See the #declare directive for details on declaring identifiers.

POV-Ray reserves a number of identifiers as keywords that cannot be used as identifiers by the user. All keyword characters are lowercase. Therefore using an identifier with at least one uppercase letter assures it is not reserved by POV-Ray as a keyword. For example, you could declare Texture as an identifier and it would be distinct from texture the reserved keyword. Such practices can be confusing, however, and are discouraged. The reserved keywords are listed in Table 7-6.

POV-Ray permits the Canadian spelling "colour" in any keyword that has "color" as any part of it.

SYNTAX NOTATION

Literals, special characters, keywords, and identifiers are pieced together to form larger language elements such as shapes, objects, and textures. The rules for combining these pieces are described in a special notation. These rules and the notation used to describe them are called a "formal language grammar." Although it may look intimidating, such notation is not very complicated and it can help you understand exactly what combinations of statements, keywords, and values are allowed.

Table 7-7 details the notation used in the complete syntax summary and in the syntax section of each entry of the keyword reference.

For example, here is how the notation is used in the rules that define a color in the POV-Ray language:

COLOR =
   color *[COLOR_COMPONENT...]*
COLOR_COMPONENT =
   red *red_amount* | green *green_amount* | blue *blue_amount* |
   alpha *alpha_amount* | *COLOR_IDENTIFIER*

The first rule says that color is defined as the keyword color optionally followed by zero or more occurrences of a *COLOR_COMPONENT*. The second rule says that *COLOR_COMPONENT* is defined as a choice of one of five different things: the keyword red followed by a floating-point value that specifies the *red_amount*; or the green, blue, or alpha keywords followed by an amount; or a *COLOR_IDENTIFIER*. Note that you would not type *COLOR=*. As an example, the following two POV-Ray statements conform to these rules.

Table 7-6   Reserved Keyword List

agate	difference	material_map	scale
all	diffuse	metallic	sky
alpha	direction	no_shadow	smooth_triangle
ambient	dump	object	
bicubic_patch	falloff	octaves	specular
blob	fog	once	sphere
blue	frequency	onion	spotlight
bounded_by	gif	phase	spotted
box	gradient	phong	sturm
bozo	granite	phong_size	texture
brilliance	green	plane	tga
bump_map	height_field	point_at	threshold
bump_size	iff	poly	tightness
bumps	image_map	pot	tile2
camera	include	quadric	tiles
checker	interpolate	quartic	translate
clipped_by	intersection	radius	triangle
color	inverse	raw	turbulence
color_map	ior	red	union
component	leopard	reflection	up
composite	light_source	refraction	use_color
cubic	location	right	use_index
declare	look_at	ripples	waves
default	map_type	rotate	wood
dents	marble	roughness	wrinkles

Table 7-7 Notation Usage

`Keyword`	Monospaced font means a reserved keyword or required special characters.
value	Lowercase italic means a floating-point literal or float identifier.
ITEM	Uppercase italic means a language construct of type "item."
ITEM = `keyword` *value*	Equal sign means the definition of *ITEM* follows. In this example, *ITEM* is defined as `keyword` followed by *value*.
ITEM = *THIS* | *THAT*	A bar between items means a choice of items. Thus *ITEM* may be a single occurrence of either *THIS* or *THAT*.
ITEM = *A B* | *C D*	This means either that *ITEM* can be *A* followed by *B* or *ITEM* can be *C* followed by *D*. It does not mean *A* followed by one of *B* or *C* and that followed by *D*.
ITEM...	An ellipsis means one or more occurrences is required.
[ITEM]	Italic square brackets mean an optional item. That is zero or one occurrence but no more than one.
[ITEM...]	An ellipsis inside italic square brackets means zero or more occurrences of *ITEM* are legal.
<vector>	Lowercase italic between angle brackets means a three-component vector or a vector identifier. See *VECTOR*.
`[ ] <>`	Monospaced font, nonitalic brackets means that the literal brackets are used. Take care not to confuse these with brackets in italics, which are part of the syntax notation.
ITEM_IDENTIFIER	An identifier of type "item" that was previously defined in a `#declare` directive.
FILESPEC	A string of ASCII characters specifying a file specification.

```
color red 1.0 green 0.5 alpha 1.0
color Hot_Pink alpha 0.5
```

The names of language constructs have been chosen to be as self-explanatory as possible. For example, an *OBJECT* defines an `object` statement, an *OBJECT_MODIFIER* is an item that modifies an *OBJECT*, and a *TEXTURE_ITEM* is an item that can appear in a `texture` statement.

COMPLETE SYNTAX REFERENCE

Below is the complete set of rules for the POV-Ray language. It begins by defining a *SCENE_ITEM*, which is the most fundamental part of the language. Your input file must contain one or more scene items. Except for *SCENE_ITEM*, none of the language elements may appear alone. All other elements are in some way a part of a scene item. For example, a `box` statement is not a *SCENE_ITEM* so it cannot appear alone in the file. An *OBJECT* is a legal *SCENE_ITEM* and, in turn, the rule for *OBJECT* says it may contain a *SHAPE*. Finally, a *SHAPE* may be a *BOX*. Therefore if you want a box in your scene you must make it part of an `object` statement.

Here are the rules for the POV-Ray language:

- *SCENE_ITEM* =
  CAMERA | *FOG* | *OBJECT* | *COMPOSITE* | *LANGUAGE_DIRECTIVE*
- *CAMERA* =
  `camera` { *[CAMERA_ITEM...]* }
- *CAMERA_ITEM* =
  `location` *<point>* | `direction` *<vector>* | `up` *<vector>* |
  `right` *<vector>* | `sky` *<vector>* | `look_at` *<point>* |
  TRANSFORMATION | *CAMERA_IDENTIFIER*
- *FOG* =
  `fog` { *[FOG_ITEM...]* }
- *FOG_ITEM* =
  COLOR | *distance_value*
- *OBJECT* =
  `object` { *OBJECT_IDENTIFIER [OBJECT_MODIFIER...]* } |
  `object` { *SHAPE [OBJECT_MODIFIER...]* }
- *OBJECT_MODIFIER* =
  SHAPE_MODIFIER | `no_shadow` | *CLIPPED_BY* | *BOUNDED_BY*
- *CLIPPED_BY* =
  `clipped_by` { *SHAPE...* }
- *BOUNDED_BY* =
  `bounded_by` { *SHAPE...* }
- *COMPOSITE* =
  `composite` { *COMPOSITE_IDENTIFIER [COMPOSITE_MODIFIER...]* } |

`composite {` *COMPOSITE_ITEM... [COMPOSITE_MODIFIER...]* `}`
- *COMPOSITE_ITEM =*
  COMPOSITE | OBJECT
- *COMPOSITE_MODIFIER =*
  CSG_MODIFIER | BOUNDED_BY | CLIPPED_BY
- *LANGUAGE_DIRECTIVE =*
  `#declare` *IDENTIFIER = DECLARE_ITEM |*
  `#include` *"FILESPEC" |*
  `#default {` *TEXTURE...* `} |*
  `#max_trace_level` *level*
- *DECLARE_ITEM =*
  CAMERA | COLOR | COMPOSITE | FLOAT |
  OBJECT | SHAPE | TEXTURE... | VECTOR
- *SHAPE =*
  BICUBIC_PATCH | BLOB | BOX | CUBIC | HEIGHT_FIELD |
  LIGHT_SOURCE | PLANE | POLY | QUADRIC | QUARTIC |
  SMOOTH_TRIANGLE | SPHERE | TRIANGLE | CSG_SHAPE
- *CSG_SHAPE =*
  INTERSECTION | DIFFERENCE | UNION
- *INTERSECTION =*
  `intersection {` *INTERSECTION_IDENTIFIER [CSG_MODIFIER...]* `} |*
  `intersection {` *SHAPE... [CSG_MODIFIER...]* `}`
- *DIFFERENCE =*
  `difference {` *DIFFERENCE_IDENTIFIER [CSG_MODIFIER...]* `} |*
  `difference {` *SHAPE... [CSG_MODIFIER...]* `}`
- *UNION =*
  `union {` *UNION_IDENTIFIER [CSG_MODIFIER...]* `} |*
  `union {` *SHAPE... [CSG_MODIFIER...]* `}`
- *CSG_MODIFIER =*
  TRANSFORMATION | `inverse`
- *BICUBIC_PATCH =*
  `bicubic_patch {` *BICUBIC_PATCH_IDENTIFIER [SHAPE_MODIFIER...]* `} |*
  `bicubic_patch {`
    type [flatness] u_steps v_steps <point1> <point2>... <point16>
      [SHAPE_MODIFIER...]
  `}`

   Note: flatness is used only if *type*=2 or *type*=3. It is required for those types.

RAY TRACING

- *BLOB =*
  blob { *BLOB_IDENTIFIER [POLY_MODIFIER...]* } |
  blob { *BLOB_ITEM... [POLY_MODIFIER...]* }
- *BLOB_ITEM =*
  component *strength radius <center>* |
  threshold *value*
- *BOX =*
  box { *BOX_IDENTIFIER [SHAPE_MODIFIER...]* } |
  box { *<corner1> <corner2> [SHAPE_MODIFIER...]* }
- *CUBIC =*
  cubic { *CUBIC_IDENTIFIER [POLY_MODIFIER...]* } |
  cubic { *POLY_3_IDENTIFIER [POLY_MODIFIER...]* } |
  cubic { *< term1 term2 term3 term4... term_20 > [POLY_MODIFIER...]* }
- *HEIGHT_FIELD =*
  height_field { *HT_FIELD_IDENTIFIER [HT_FIELD_MODIFIER...]* } |
  height_field { *HT_FIELD_TYPE "FILESPEC" [HT_FIELD_MODIFIER...]* }
- *HT_FIELD_TYPE =*
  gif | pot | tga
- *HT_FIELD_MODIFIER =*
  SHAPE_MODIFIER | water_level *amount*
- *LIGHT_SOURCE =*
  light_source { *LIGHT_SRC_IDENTIFIER [LIGHT_SRC_MODIFIER...]* } |
  light_source { *<location> COLOR [LIGHT_SRC_MODIFIER...]* }
- *LIGHT_SRC_MODIFIER =*
  spotlight | point_at *<location>* |
  falloff *degrees* | radius *degrees* | tightness *value* |
  TRANSFORMATION | *COLOR*
- *PLANE =*
  plane { *PLANE_IDENTIFIER [SHAPE_MODIFIER...]* } |
  plane { *<normal> displacement [SHAPE_MODIFIER...]* }
- *POLY =*
  poly { *POLY_IDENTIFIER [POLY_MODIFIER...]* } |
  poly { *order < term1 term2 term3... term_m > [POLY_MODIFIER...]* }
    (total of "m" terms where m=(order+1)*(order+2)*(order+3)/6)
- *POLY_MODIFIER =*
  SHAPE_MODIFIER | sturm
- *QUADRIC =*
  quadric { *QUADRIC_IDENTIFIER [SHAPE_MODIFIER...]* } |

```
quadric {
```
<square_terms> <mixed_terms> <single_terms> constant
    [SHAPE_MODIFIER...]
```
}
```

- *QUARTIC =*
  ```
  quartic {
  ```
  QUARTIC_IDENTIFIER [POLY_MODIFIER...]} |
  ```
  quartic {
  ```
  POLY_4_IDENTIFIER [POLY_MODIFIER...]} |
  ```
  quartic {
  ```
  < term1 term2 term3 term4... term_35 > [POLY_MODIFIER...]}

- *SMOOTH_TRIANGLE =*
  ```
  smooth_triangle {
  ```
  SM_TRIANGLE_IDENTIFIER [SHAPE_MODIFIER...]} |
  ```
  smooth_triangle {
  ```
      <vertex_1> <normal_1>   <vertex_2> <normal_2>   <vertex_3> <normal_3>
      [SHAPE_MODIFIER...]
  ```
  }
  ```

- *SPHERE =*
  ```
  sphere {
  ```
  SPHERE_IDENTIFIER [SHAPE_MODIFIER...] } |
  ```
  sphere {
  ```
  <center> radius [SHAPE_MODIFIER...] }

- *TRIANGLE =*
  ```
  triangle {
  ```
  TRIANGLE_IDENTIFIER [SHAPE_MODIFIER...]} |
  ```
  triangle {
  ```
  <vertex_1> <vertex_2> <vertex_3> [SHAPE_MODIFIER...]}

- *SHAPE_MODIFIER =*
  TRANSFORMATION | COLOR | TEXTURE... | `inverse`

- *TEXTURE =*
  ```
  texture {
  ```
  TEXTURE_ITEM... }

- *TEXTURE_ITEM =*
  COLOR_PATTERN | COLOR_PATTERN_MODIFIER |
  NORMAL_PATTERN | NORMAL_PATTERN_MODIFIER |
  FINISH_PARAMETER | SPECIAL_TEXTURE |
  TRANSFORMATION | TEXTURE_IDENTIFIER

- *COLOR_PATTERN =*
  ```
  agate | bozo | granite | leopard | marble | onion |
  spotted |
  wood | checker
  ```
  COLOR COLOR | `gradient` *<vector>* | *COLOR* |
  ```
  image_map {
  ```
      [MAP_PREFIX...] MAP_FILE_TYPE "FILESPEC"
      [IMAGE_MAP_MODIFIER...]
  ```
  }
  ```

- *COLOR_PATTERN_MODIFIER =*

turbulence *turb_amount* | octaves *octave_number* | *COLOR_MAP*
- *NORMAL_PATTERN* =
  bumps *amount* | dents *amount* | ripples *amount* | waves *amount* |
  wrinkles amount |
  bump_map {
      [MAP_PREFIX...] MAP_FILE_TYPE "FILESPEC"
      [BUMP_MAP_MODIFIER...]
  }
- *NORMAL_PATTERN_MODIFIER* =
  phase *amount* | frequency *amount*
- *FINISH_PARAMETER* =
  crand_value | metallic | ambient *value* | diffuse *value* |
  specular *value* | roughness *value* | phong *value* | phong_size *size* |
  brilliance *value* | ior *index_of_refraction* | refraction *amount* |
  reflection *amount*
- *SPECIAL_TEXTURE* =
  tiles { *TEXTURE...* tile2 *TEXTURE...* } |
  material_map {
      [MAP_PREFIX...] MAP_FILE_TYPE "FILESPEC"
      TEXTURE...
      [MATERIAL_MAP_MODIFIER...]
  }
- *IMAGE_MAP_MODIFIER* =
  once | interpolate *type* | map_type *type* |
  alpha all *alpha_amount* | alpha *index alpha_amount*
- *BUMP_MAP_MODIFIER* =
  once | interpolate *type* | map_type *type* |
  use_color | use_index | bump_size *bump_amount*
- *MATERIAL_MAP_MODIFIER* =
  once | interpolate *type* | map_type *type*
- *MAP_PREFIX* =
  map_type | *<orientation_vector>*
- *MAP_FILE_TYPE* =
  iff | gif | dump | tga
- *COLOR* =
  color *[COLOR_COMPONENT...]*
- *COLOR_COMPONENT* =
  red *red_amount* | green *green_amount* | blue *blue_amount* |
  alpha *alpha_amount* | *COLOR_IDENTIFIER*

- *COLOR_MAP =*
  `color_map { [COLOR_MAP_ENTRY...] }`
- *COLOR_MAP_ENTRY =*
  [*low_value high_value COLOR COLOR*]
- *TRANSFORMATION =*
  `translate` *<vector>* | `rotate` *<angles>* | `scale` *<amount>*
- *VECTOR =*
  <x_value y_value z_value>
- *FLOAT =*
  [SIGN] [DIGIT...] [POINT] DIGIT... [EXP [SIGN] DIGIT...] |
  [SIGN] FLOAT_IDENTIFIER
- *DIGIT =*
  `0` | `1` | `2` | `3` | `4` | `5` | `6` | `7` | `8` | `9`
- *EXP =*
  `e` | `E`
- *SIGN =*
  `+` | `-`
- *POINT =*
  `.`

Note that an `#include` directive may appear virtually anywhere between two items but typically it is only used between other *SCENE_ITEMS*.

KEYWORD REFERENCE

This section provides a complete alphabetical reference for all POV-Ray keywords. It also provides details on several important language constructs. For example, *OBJECT* and *OBJECT_MODIFIER* are documented under the keyword `object`, and *TEXTURE* and *TEXTURE_ITEM* are described under the keyword `texture`. However, some important language constructs do not have a keyword directly associated with them. For this reason, you will also find entries for *COLOR_PATTERN, crand_value, CSG_SHAPE, FINISH_PARAMETER, FLOAT, NORMAL_PATTERN, SHAPE,* and *VECTOR*.

Each entry in the reference contains:

1) Keyword or language item name (`sphere`, `color`, *VECTOR*)
2) Type of language item described (*SHAPE, OBJECT*, etc.)
3) Purpose (What do you use it for?)

4) Syntax (How do you use it?)

5) Description (What does each part of the syntax mean, what options are available, and what are the end results?)

6) See also (What are some related keywords?)

7) Example code (What does a typical use of this keyword look like?)

Each code example is a complete POV-Ray scene you can render yourself; it is not an out-of-context fragment. Most of the examples include a grayscale reproduction of the image that the example code creates. Full color versions of these images can be found in the color plate insert of this book. The example code not only illustrates how to use a particular feature; it also illustrates the effects generated by that feature. For example, the sample code for the ambient keyword renders a scene with three objects, each with a different ambient lighting value applied to it.

Because POV-Ray scenes require a camera and light sources to make a complete scene, we provide two include files which contain a camera, light source, and background for the examples. The file EXAMP.INC is used for the majority of the scenes. A special background for illustrating spotlights is in SPOTBACK.INC. Listings 7-1 and 7-2 give the complete contents of these files. These files as well as all other files necessary to render the examples are in the POVRAY\CHAPTER7 directory.

Listing 7-1 EXAMP.INC

```
// Examp.inc
//
// This file is for use with the Ray Tracing Creations
// reference section examples.
// Place this file in your working directory or any directory
// referenced by a +L command-line switch.
// Then place a #include "examp.inc" statement in your sample
// file.
//

#include "shapes.inc"
#include "colors.inc"
#include "textures.inc"

// Camera definition
camera {
  location <0 0 -3>
  direction <0 0 1>
}

// Floor
object {plane { <0 1 0> -1.01}
```

```
        texture { Cork }
        color Tan // quick render color
}

// Sky
object {
 sphere { <0 0 0> 1 }
 texture {
   gradient <0 1 0>
   color_map {
    [0 1 color White color Blue]
   }
   ambient 1 diffuse 0
  }
 color White // quick render color
 scale <10000 10000 10000>
}

// Light
object { light_source { <30 50 -50> color White } }
```

Listing 7-2 SPOTBACK.INC

```
// Spotback.inc
//
// This file is for use with the Ray Tracing Creations
// reference section examples.
// Place this file in your working directory or any
// directory referenced by a +L command-line switch.
// Then place a #include "spotback.inc" statement in
// your sample file.
//

#include "shapes.inc"
#include "colors.inc"
#include "textures.inc"

// Camera definition
camera {
  location <0 3 -6>
  look_at <0 1 0>
}

// Floor
object {
 plane { <0 1 0> -1.01}
 texture {
   checker color White
           color Yellow
  }
```

```
  color White // quick render color
}

// Back wall
object {
 plane { <0 0 1> 4.99}
 texture {
   checker color White
           color Yellow
 }
 color White // quick render color
}
// very dim light so spotlights will show
object { light_source { <30 50 -50> color Gray25} }
```

agate

TYPE
COLOR_PATTERN

PURPOSE
Specifies an agate color pattern in a texture. This is a turbulent, marblelike pattern.

SYNTAX
texture { agate *[COLOR_PATTERN_MODIFIER...]*
[TEXTURE_ITEM...] }

DESCRIPTION
The `agate` keyword specifies a color pattern that is a turbulent, marblelike color pattern with a blotchy look to it. The agate pattern has its own built-in

turbulence function and the `turbulence` keyword has no effect on it. The `octaves` keyword does influence it.

A default color map is provided, but you will normally add a `color_map` of your own. Color patterns may be translated, rotated, or scaled. Only one color pattern may be specified in each `texture` statement.

SEE ALSO

`color_map`, *COLOR_PATTERN*, `octaves`, `texture`

EXAMPLE

```
// AGATE.POV
#include "examp.inc"
object {
  sphere { <0 0 0> 1 }
  texture {
    agate
    color_map {
      [ 0 .5 color Silver   color Silver]
      [.5 .6 color Silver   color White]
      [.6  1 color White    color Cyan]
    }
  }
}
```

all

TYPE
IMAGE_MAP_MODIFIER

PURPOSE

Specifies that all colors in an image map should have an alpha component to make them transparent.

SYNTAX

```
image_map { [MAP_PREFIX...] MAP_FILE_TYPE "FILESPEC"
 alpha all alpha_amount
 [IMAGE_MAP_MODIFIER]
}
```

DESCRIPTION

Because the supported image types do not allow for an alpha component value in the palette, you can use the `alpha` keyword as an image map modifier in order to add transparency to any or all colors in the image. Used with the `alpha` keyword, the `all` keyword specifies that all colors will have the given amount of transparency added to them. Values from 0.0 (no transparency) to 1.0 (fully transparent) may be used. Note that the red, green, and blue components of a color remain the same even when alpha is added. Thus the light passing through the surface or texture layer is filtered by the pixel color. Black pixels transmit no light regardless of the alpha value applied. Complete details can be found under `image_map`.

SEE ALSO

`alpha, image_map`

EXAMPLE

```
// ALL.POV
#include "examp.inc"
object {
  plane { <0 0 1> 0}
  clipped_by{box{UnitBox}}
  texture {
    image_map{
      gif "bumpmap_.gif"
      alpha all 0.9
//    alpha 1 0.9   // try this instead of all
    }
    translate <-0.5 -0.5 0> // center image
  }
  translate <0 0 -1>
  rotate <0 -50 0>
}
```

alpha

TYPE

COLOR_COMPONENT or *IMAGE_MAP_MODIFIER*

PURPOSE

Specifies how transparent a color will be.

SYNTAX

alpha *alpha_amount*

DESCRIPTION

All colors in POV-Ray consist of red, blue, green, and alpha components. The alpha keyword specifies the degree of transparency a given color has. The float value after the keyword can range from 0.0 (no transparency) to 1.0 (fully transparent). If no alpha value is given, then the default is alpha 0. The light let through an object with an alpha component is also filtered by the red, green, and blue components of the color. Therefore low values for red, green, and blue will not permit much light through. A common mistake is to attempt to specify a clear color such as

```
color alpha 1.0
```

The default red, green, and blue values are all 0.0, however. This results in a totally black filter. The correct way is

```
color White alpha 1.0
```

This filtering is especially important to consider when creating an image map with transparent areas. See the image_map statement and the all key-

305

word for details on how to use the alpha keyword as an *IMAGE_MAP_MODIFIER* to specify transparency in an image map.

Note that no refraction or bending of light occurs with transparent colors unless the refraction and ior keywords are used.

SEE ALSO

all, blue, color, green, image_map, ior, red, refraction

EXAMPLE

```
// ALPHA.POV
#include "examp.inc"  camera{location <0 0 -5>}

// Three different alpha values
object {sphere { <-2 0 0> 1 }
  texture {color Cyan alpha 0.0} // not transparent
}

object {sphere { <0 0 0> 1 }
  texture {color Cyan alpha 0.5} // part transparent
}

object {sphere { <2 0 0> 1 }
  texture {color Cyan alpha 1.0} // fully transparent
}
```

ambient

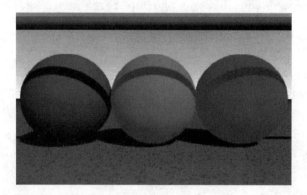

TYPE
FINISH_PARAMETER

PURPOSE

Controls the amount of illumination from ambient light on an object. Ambient light illuminates shadowed areas.

SYNTAX

```
texture { ambient amount [TEXTURE_ITEM...] }
```

DESCRIPTION

Use the `ambient` keyword to specify the amount of ambient light hitting a surface. Typically, ambient light is that which comes from all directions and illuminates shadowed areas in a scene. This is in contrast to diffuse light that comes directly from a light source. In the real world, ambient light is generated by diffuse light that is reflected off other objects and (more or less) uniformly illuminates all areas, including shadowed areas. POV-Ray cannot calculate the diffuse reflected light from every point on every object so it simulates this effect by ambient lighting. Values for ambient light can range from 0.0 (no ambient light, dark shadows) to 1.0 (fully ambient, glowing or luminous looking). The default value for ambient lighting is 0.1 for a small amount of ambient light and deep shadows.

Although ambient light is mostly noticed in shadowed areas, it does contribute to all areas equally. This can be seen in the example that follows. Increasing the `ambient` value brightens both shadowed and nonshadowed areas. To obtain the same brightness on nonshadowed areas, the `diffuse` value has to be decreased the same amount as the increased `ambient`. For realistic results, the values specified by the `ambient`, `diffuse`, and `reflection` keywords generally should not total more than 1.0.

Note that the ambient value is applied to individual objects. Some rendering software only applies one ambient setting to the entire scene.

SEE ALSO

`diffuse`, *FINISH_PARAMETER*, `no_shadow`, `reflection`, `texture`

EXAMPLE

```
// AMBIENT.POV
#include "examp.inc"  camera{location <0 0 -5>}

// First sphere has default values
object {sphere { <-2 0 0> 1 }
  texture {color NeonPink ambient 0.1 diffuse 0.6}
}
```

```
// Higher ambient increases both shadow and light
object {sphere { <0 0 0> 1 }
  texture {color NeonPink ambient 0.5 diffuse 0.6}
}

// Higher ambient with lower diffuse evens out
object {sphere { <2 0 0> 1 }
  texture {color NeonPink ambient 0.5 diffuse 0.2}
}

// This bar casts a shadow for effect
object {
  quadric {
    Cylinder_X scale <1 0.1 0.1> translate <0 1.2 -1.5>
  }
  texture {color Green}
}
```

bicubic_patch

TYPE
SHAPE

PURPOSE
Specifies a 3D curved surface using a bicubic patch shape in an object.

SYNTAX
bicubic_patch { *BICUBIC_PATCH_IDENTIFIER [SHAPE_MODIFIER...]* } |
bicubic_patch {
  type [flatness] u_steps v_steps <point1> <point2>... <point16>

308

[SHAPE_MODIFIER...]

}

DESCRIPTION

A `bicubic_patch` statement defines a shape that is a 3D curved surface created from a mesh of triangles. Currently Bezier patches are the only type of bicubic patches supported. The float value *type* specifies the type of patch, the shading characteristics of the patch, and the amount of storage used for mesh constants. The following types are supported:

0) Bezier patch, only sufficient storage is allocated to store the triangular vertices
1) Bezier patch, vertices, all plane equations defined by the triangulation of the patch into subpatches are stored
2) Bezier patch, using binary subdivision to find the point of surface intersection
3) Bezier patch, using binary subdivision, with vertices and all values precomputed and stored
4) Bezier patch, vertices, all plane equations, normals at each vertex of a subpatch are stored (to be used for a smooth triangle shading in each subpatch)

If patch type 2 or 3 is specified, then the next float value is a *flatness* value ranging from 0.01 to 1.0, with higher values giving coarser, less smooth results. Types other than 2 or 3 use a fixed flatness value of 0.1 and no user-defined value can be specified.

The next two float values *u_steps* and *v_steps* determine the number of rows and columns that are taken when subdividing the patch into triangles. The number of triangles for types 0, 1, and 4 is

$$number = 2* u\_ steps* v\_steps$$

The number of triangles for types 2 and 3 is at most

$$number = 2^{u\_steps* v\_steps}$$

For types 2 and 3, the number of triangles may be less than the maximum if the patch is flatter than the flatness value. The subpatches are compared to a plane that approximates the four corners of the subpatch. If the distance between the corners of the subpatch and the plane is less than the flatness value, no further subdivision is performed.

A set of 16 control points in a 4-by-4 array define the shape of the patch. The 3D coordinates of these points are specified by 16 vectors: *<point1>* through *<point16>*. The corners of the patch are *<point1>*, *<point4>*, *<point13>*, and *<point16>*. The shape will touch those four points. Intermediate points serve to pull the surface into shape but the surface probably will not pass through those points.

Because it is made from triangles, a bicubic patch cannot be used as a solid object in an `intersection` or `difference` statement nor can it be used in a `clipped_by` statement. A bicubic patch can be included in a `union` statement. A bicubic patch should not be used as a bounding shape.

Usually Bezier patches are created by external utilities such as CAD programs or other professional 3D design tools. Currently there are no bicubic patch-generating programs written specifically for use with POV-Ray; however, such utilities are reported to be in various stages of development.

In future, other types of patches besides Bezier may be implemented. In this case, new values of *type* will be defined for them.

SEE ALSO
CSG_SHAPE, `object`, *SHAPE*

EXAMPLE

```
// BICUBIC.POV
#include "examp.inc"  camera{location <0 0 -5>}

object {
   bicubic_patch { 3 0.01 6 6
     <0  0  2>  <1  0  0>  <2  0  0>  <3  0 -2>
     <0  1  0>  <1  1  0>  <2  1  0>  <3  1  0>
     <0  2  0>  <1  2  0>  <2  2  0>  <3  2  0>
     <0  3  2>  <1  3  0>  <2  3  0>  <3  3 -2>
     }
   texture { checker color Cyan color Yellow phong 1 }
   translate <-2 -1 0>
   rotate    <0 -45 0>
}
```

blob

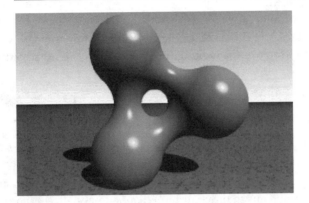

TYPE
SHAPE

PURPOSE
Specifies a blob shape in an object. A blob shape is made from spheres that flow and blend into each other smoothly to create a liquid effect.

SYNTAX
```
blob { BLOB_IDENTIFIER [POLY_MODIFIER...] } |
blob { BLOB_ITEM... [POLY_MODIFIER...] }
```

BLOB_ITEM =
    `component` *strength radius <center>* |
    `threshold` *value*

DESCRIPTION
The `blob` statement defines a shape that is made from spheres that flow and blend into each other smoothly to create a liquid effect. The individual components attract or repel each other and result in "blobby" organic-looking shapes.

For each component you must give a float value for the *strength*, a float value for the *radius,* and a vector that is the 3D coordinate of the center of the component. Positive strength values cause the blob components to attract and flow together. Negative strength values make invisible components that repel or make dents in other components. (See the `component` keyword for an example of negative strength components.) Radius values must be positive. A float value for `threshold` should also be given, but if it is not specified, a default value of 1.0 is used.

Mathematically, each component of the blob represents a field density function that starts at the center of the component at the strength value given and tapers off to zero at the radius given. The density falls off according to the function:

$$field\_strength = \left[\, 1 - \left[\, \frac{r}{radius} \,\right]^2 \,\right]^2$$

where *r* is the distance from the center of the component and *radius* is the radius where the density falls off to zero.

At every point, the densities of all components of the blob are added together. Components in different blob shapes do not affect each other. The surface of the blob is defined by all points in space with accumulated densities equal to the threshold value. Points with greater density are inside the blob. Points with lower density are outside the blob.

Blobs can be used in CSG shapes and they can be scaled, rotated, and translated as a whole. Individual components may not be independently translated, rotated, or scaled. Because the calculations for blobs need to be highly accurate, they will not always render correctly. If this happens, you can specify the `sturm` keyword to use POV-Ray's more accurate, but slower, Sturmian sequence root solver.

SEE ALSO

`object`, *SHAPE,* `sturm`

EXAMPLE

```
// BLOB.POV
#include "examp.inc"

object {
  blob {
    threshold 0.6
    component 1.0 1.0 < 0.75    0        0>
    component 1.0 1.0 <-0.375  0.64952 0>
    component 1.0 1.0 <-0.375 -0.64952 0>
  }
  texture {color Yellow phong 1 }
}
```

blue

TYPE
COLOR_COMPONENT

PURPOSE
Specifies the blue component of a color.

SYNTAX
`blue` *blue_amount*

DESCRIPTION
All colors in POV-Ray consist of red, blue, green, and alpha components. By using various combinations of red, blue, and green, you can specify nearly any color. Use the `blue` keyword to specify the amount of blue color. The alpha part of a color specification describes the degree of transparency a given color has.

The float value after the keyword can range from 0.0 (no blue) to 1.0 (full intensity blue). If no value is given for a component, then the default is 0.

SEE ALSO
`alpha, color, green, red`

EXAMPLE
```
// BLUE.POV
#include "examp.inc"
object {
  sphere { <0 0 0> 1 }
```

```
texture {
  checker
    color blue 1.0            // This check is pure blue.
    color blue 0.7 green 0.8  // This one is bluish green.
  scale <0.5 0.5 0.5>
  }
}
```

bounded_by

TYPE
OBJECT_MODIFIER or *COMPOSITE_MODIFIER*

PURPOSE
Defines an invisible shape around an object to speed ray-object intersection
tests.

SYNTAX
object { *SHAPE* bounded_by { *SHAPE...* } *[OBJECT_MODIFIER...]*} |
composite { *OBJECT...* bounded_by { *SHAPE...* }
    [COMPOSITE_MODIFIER...]}

DESCRIPTION
You can use the bounded_by statement to speed rendering of complex
objects. Rendering a scene involves complex and time-consuming calculations.
Ray-object intersection tests must be performed for every object in the scene.
These tests may be performed many times per pixel when antialiasing, shadow
rays, reflected rays, and refracted rays are involved. Some shapes, such as
spheres, boxes, and quadrics take relatively little time to perform ray-object

314

tests, while quartics, poly, and complex CSG shapes take much longer. By wrapping an object in a quickly tested shape you can avoid computing tests for rays that do not come near the object.

When performing a ray-object intersection test for an object with a bounding shape, POV-Ray first tests the ray against all bounding shapes specified for the object. If the ray fails to intersect any of the bounding shapes, the ray is not tested against the object itself.

Note that a `bounded_by` statement may be used as an object modifier or as a composite modifier but not as a shape modifier.

The fastest shape that can be used as a bounding shape is a sphere. A box shape may be faster if the box can be made to fit the object more closely than a sphere. Quadrics can also be used, but they are only cost effective if extremely slowly rendered objects are bound with them.

While all shapes can be used as bounding shapes, they may not all be cost effective. Multiple shapes may be given in the `bounded_by` statement but they generally slow things down.

It is up to the user to size and place a bounding shape so that the object lies entirely within the bounds. If part of the object extends outside the bounds, it does not necessarily mean that the protruding part will not be rendered. It's inclusion depends on the geometry of the ray and the object.

If the `translate`, `rotate`, or `scale` keywords appear after the `bounded_by` statement, then the bounding shapes move and scale along with the bounded object.

SEE ALSO

`clipped_by`, `composite`, `object`, *SHAPE*

EXAMPLE

```
// BOUNDED.POV
#include "examp.inc"
#include "shapesq.inc"  // Need slow quartic shape to test.

object {
  quartic { Lemniscate sturm }
  texture { color Yellow phong 1}
    bounded_by {sphere {<0 0 0> 1}}
//  bounded_by {box {<-1 -0.5 -0.5> <1 0.5 0.5>}}
}

/*
Try commenting out both bounded_by statements.  Then try
```

```
the sphere or the box individually.  Note the times to
trace.  On a 386/387 at 33mhz we noted these times for a
320 x 200 pixel test.
    no bounding shape     47 secs
    bounded_by box        38 secs
    bounded_by sphere     37 secs
Although the boxes fit more closely, the sphere was still
faster.  On a slower shape the box might be faster.
*/
```

box

TYPE
SHAPE

PURPOSE
Specifies a box shape in an object.

SYNTAX
box { *BOX_IDENTIFIER [SHAPE_MODIFIER...]* } |
box { *<corner1> <corner2> [SHAPE_MODIFIER...]* }

DESCRIPTION
The box statement specifies a shape that is a solid, right-angled prism shape
made of six plane surfaces. Opposite faces are parallel and adjacent faces are
at right angles to each other. Each side is parallel to a coordinate axis when
the box is defined. The box can be rotated to sit at any angle. Combinations

of rotations followed by scaling can skew the box so that adjacent sides are no longer perpendicular.

The vectors *<corner1>* and *<corner2>* are the 3D coordinates of opposite corners that define the shape. Particular corners must be chosen. Each X, Y, and Z component of *<corner1>* must be less that the corresponding X, Y, and Z component of *<corner2>*. Thus the following is illegal:

```
box { <1 0 0> <0 1 1> }
```

Instead you would specify the same size and shape like this:

```
box { <0 0 0> <1 1 1> }
```

Box shapes render faster than an equivalent shape made from an intersection of planes. The box-ray intersection calculation is fast enough to make it an excellent choice for `bounded_by` statements. Boxes can be used in CSG shapes and `clipped_by` statements, and they can be scaled, rotated, and translated.

SEE ALSO

`bounded_by`, `object`, *SHAPE*

EXAMPLE

```
// BOX.POV
#include "examp.inc"
object {
  box {<-0.5 -0.5 -0.5> <0.5 0.5 0.5> }
  texture {color Cyan}
  rotate <-20 15 0>
}
```

bozo

TYPE
COLOR_PATTERN

PURPOSE
Specifies a random "bozo" color pattern in a texture. This pattern is often used to create clouds.

SYNTAX
`texture { bozo` *[COLOR_PATTERN_MODIFIER...]*
[TEXTURE_ITEM...] `}`

DESCRIPTION
The `bozo` keyword specifies a blotchy, random color pattern most often used to create clouds. The pattern is created by a noise function in which points close to each other have similar values but points far from each other have random, unrelated values.

The `turbulence` and `octaves` keywords may be used to stir up the pattern. A default color map is provided but normally you would add a `color_map` of your own. Color patterns may be translated, rotated, or scaled. Only one color pattern may be specified in each `texture` statement.

SEE ALSO
`color_map`, *COLOR_PATTERN*, `octaves`, `texture`, `turbulence`

EXAMPLE

```
// BOZO.POV
#include "examp.inc"

object {
  sphere { <0 0 0> 1 }
  texture {
    bozo
    color_map {
      [0.0 0.3 color SkyBlue color SkyBlue]
      [0.3 0.6 color SkyBlue color White]
      [0.6 1.0 color White   color Gray60]
    }
  scale <1 0.3 0.3>
  }
}
```

brilliance

TYPE
FINISH_PARAMETER

PURPOSE
Controls tightness of diffuse lighting in a texture.

SYNTAX
```
texture { brilliance amount [TEXTURE_ITEM...] }
```

DESCRIPTION

You can adjust the appearance of an object's surface with the `brilliance` keyword. The amount of diffuse illumination a point receives is dependent upon the angle of incidence between the illuminating light ray and the surface normal and the `brilliance` amount. The intensity of diffuse illumination is computed by

$$intensity = cos\,(angle\_of\_incidence)^{brilliance}$$

The default `brilliance` value is 1.0. Higher values gives tighter illumination. Lower values give broader illumination. See the example image. When used with Phong or specular highlights, the brilliance adjustment can make objects look more metallic.

SEE ALSO

`diffuse`, *FINISH_PARAMETER*, `metallic`, `phong`, `specular`, `texture`

EXAMPLE

```
// BRILLIAN.POV
#include "examp.inc"   camera{location <0 0 -5>}

object {sphere { <-2 0 0> 1 }
  texture {color Yellow brilliance 0.25}
}

object {sphere { <0 0 0> 1 }
  texture {color Yellow brilliance 1} // default
}

object {sphere { <2 0 0> 1 }
  texture {color Yellow brilliance 3}
}
```

bumps

TYPE
NORMAL_PATTERN

PURPOSE
Makes a texture look bumpy by applying a normal pattern to it.

SYNTAX
`texture { bumps` *amount [TEXTURE_ITEM...]* `}`

DESCRIPTION
The `bumps` keyword specifies a surface normal perturbation pattern that modifies the surface normal to look like random irregular bumps. (See *NORMAL_PATTERN* for details on surface normals.) This pattern uses a noise function similar to the one used in the spotted color pattern. The required float value after the keyword specifies an apparent depth of the bumps. Values from 0.0 (no bumps) to 1.0 (high bumps) are typical. Each bump is about 1 or 2 units wide so for small objects a scale modifier is often used to alter the diameter of the bumps.

Note that the use of a normal pattern to perturb the surface normal does not actually change the shape of the object. It artificially modifies the surface normal so that lighting, reflections, refractions, and highlights look as though the surface were bumped. Only one normal pattern may be used in each `tex-ture` statement.

SEE ALSO
NORMAL_PATTERN, `texture`

EXAMPLE

```
// BUMPS.POV
#include "examp.inc"

object {
  sphere { <0 0 0> 1 }
  texture
   {Brass_Metal
    bumps 0.3
    scale <0.05 0.05 0.05>
   }
}
```

bump_map

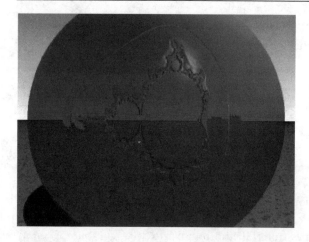

TYPE
NORMAL_PATTERN

PURPOSE
Makes a texture look bumpy or embossed by using a map file to apply a normal pattern to it.

SYNTAX

```
texture {
bump_map {
```
  [MAP_PREFIX...] MAP_FILE_TYPE "FILESPEC"
  BUMP_MAP_MODIFIER...]
  `}`
  [TEXTURE_ITEM...]
`}`

MAP_PREFIX =
 map_type | *<orientation_vector>*

MAP_FILE_TYPE =
 `iff` | `gif` | `dump` | `tga`

BUMP_MAP_MODIFIER =
 `once` | `interpolate` *type* | `map_type` *type* |
 `use_color` | `use_index` | `bump_size` *bump_amount*

DESCRIPTION

A `bump_map` statement specifies a surface normal perturbation pattern that modifies the surface normal to look like bumps are embossed onto the object. (See *NORMAL_PATTERN* for details on surface normals.) A map file is used to define the pattern of the bumps. The file is an image of pixels in IFF, GIF, TGA, or DUMP format. Rather than mapping the colors onto the object as with an image map, the pixels are used to define how the surface normal is perturbed.

A float value may be given at the start of the statement to specify the *map_type* but this usage is outdated. The `map_type` keyword should be used instead.

By default, the file will be mapped onto a square area of the X,Y plane from 0,0 to 1,1. The `texture` statement may contain `translate`, `rotate`, or `scale` keywords to adjust the position of the map. An optional *<orientation_vector>* may be used to change the orientation as well. One component of the vector must be positive. It specifies which of the three positive axes is used for the width of the map. Another component of the vector must be negative. It specifies which of the three positive axes is used for the height. Note that the positive axis is always used. The sign only specifies a plus for width and a minus for height. The remaining component must be zero. For example, <0 1 -1> means that the file is mapped with the width along the positive *y* axis because the *y* component is positive; the height is along the positive *z* axis because the *z* component is negative.

You must specify a file type using keywords `iff`, `gif`, `tga`, or `dump`, followed by the file specification in quotes. If the file is not found in the current directory, then any library paths specified with the +L command-line switch are also searched.

After the file specification is given, a number of options may follow. Use the `bump_size` keyword followed by a float value *bump_amount* to specify the apparent depth of the bumps. Values from 0.0 (no bumps) to 1.0 (high bumps) are typical. The default value is 0.0, so be sure not to omit this parameter.

If the bump map is too small to cover the entire object then it is repeated over and over, as with tiles. The `once` keyword turns this feature off so that the bump map only appears once.

Normally the bump map converts the color of the map pixel to grayscale and then uses the intensity of the pixel to determine the bump height at that point. The `use_index` keyword tells POV-Ray to use the index of the pixel rather than the color. On nonpalette-based file types that do not have index values, the `use_index` keyword is ignored. You can also give a `use_color` keyword to document that the color method is used.

A smoother look can be obtained by adding the `interpolate` keyword. The value after the keyword may be 0 for no interpolation, 2 for bilinear interpolation, or 4 for normalized distribution.

A bump map is a two-dimensional feature that must be applied to a three-dimensional object. The `map_type` keyword may be used to define how the map is wrapped around the object. The default is 0 for planar mapping; use 1 for spherical, 2 for cylindrical, and 5 for torus. Types 3 and 4 are under development. See `map_type` for details.

Note that the use of a normal pattern to perturb the surface normal does not actually change the shape of the object. It artificially modifies the surface normal so that lighting, reflections, refractions, and highlights look as though the surface were bumped. Only one normal pattern may be used in each `texture` statement.

SEE ALSO

`bump_size`, `interpolate`, `map_type`, *NORMAL_PATTERN*, `once`, `texture`, `use_color`, `use_index`

EXAMPLE

```
// BUMPMAP.POV
#include "examp.inc" camera{location <0 0 -2>}

object {
  sphere { <0 0 0> 1}
  texture {
    Copper_Metal
    bump_map {
       gif "bumpmap_.gif"
       once
       map_type 0    // planar
       interpolate 4        // normalized distribution
       use_color     bump_size 1.5
//     use_index     bump_size 0.1  // try this
    }
    translate <-0.5 -0.5 0> // center image
  }
}
```

bump_size

TYPE
BUMP_MAP_MODIFIER

PURPOSE
Specifies the apparent depth of bumps in a bump map.

SYNTAX
```
bump_map {
```

[MAP_PREFIX...] MAP_FILE_TYPE "FILESPEC"
`bump_size` *bump_amount [BUMP_MAP_MODIFIER...]*
}

DESCRIPTION

The `bump_size` keyword followed by a float value *bump_amount* should be used to specify the apparent depth of the bumps in a `bump_map` statement. Values from 0.0 (no bumps) to 1.0 (high bumps) are typical. The default value is 0.0 so be sure not to omit this parameter.

SEE ALSO

`bump_map`

EXAMPLE

See the example in `bump_map`.

camera

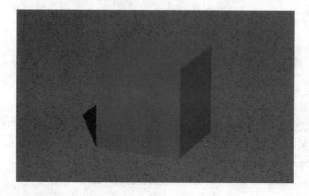

TYPE

SCENE_ITEM

PURPOSE

Defines the position and properties of the camera.

SYNTAX

`camera {` *[CAMERA_ITEM...]* `}`

CAMERA_ITEM =
    location *<point>* | direction *<vector>* | up *<vector>* |
    right *<vector>* | sky *<vector>* | look_at *<point>* |
    TRANSFORMATION | *CAMERA_IDENTIFIER*

DESCRIPTION

POV-Ray itself is an imaginary camera that views an imaginary scene. Use the camera statement to define the location, direction, orientation, and aspect ratio of the camera that POV-Ray is simulating.

The camera is an invisible point in the scene from which the rays are traced. The location keyword can be used to specify a vector to define the location. If a location is not given, the default value is location <0 0 0>. The translate, rotate, and scale keywords may also may be used to modify the camera location.

Rays start at the camera's location and travel outward towards an imaginary rectangular viewing window. The view window is divided into rows and columns of points that will become the pixels of the completed image. The number of pixels is controlled by the +W and +H command-line switches.

Use the three keywords—direction, up, and right—to specify vectors that fix the position of this view window relative to the camera's location.

The direction keyword defines the direction the camera is looking. The ray that is traced in the center of the image follows this vector. The default value is direction <0 0 1>. This means that the camera is looking in the positive *z* direction. The length of the direction vector also determines the distance of the view window from the camera location. This controls the field of view for the camera. A short direction vector gives a wide-angle view because the view window is close. A long direction vector zooms in for a narrower field of view. (See Figure 7-3 later, in the entry for the direction keyword.)

The up keyword defines which direction is "up" in the view window. The length of the up vector determines the height of the view window. The default value is up <0 1 0>.

The right keyword defines the horizontal direction and width of the view window but the vector does not always point to the right side of the window. The absolute value of the right vector does point to the right. The sign of the right vector determines the handedness of the coordinate system. A positive right vector means a left-handed system is used. A negative vector means right-handed coordinates are used. (See *VECTOR* for more on left- and right-handed coordinate systems.)

The default value is right <1.33 0 0>. Because this is a positive value, the coordinate system is left-handed by default. The default value of right <1.33 0 0>, when used with a default of up <0 1 0>, gives an aspect ratio (width-to-height ratio) of about 4:3. This ratio is typical of a landscape-oriented computer screen. You should specify up and right values in the ratio you want the overall image to have, independent of pixel size or video mode. This helps to preserve scene compatibility across hardware platforms. See the reference entry for the right keyword for a detailed explanation of the interaction between the up and right vectors and the +W and +H command-line switches.

The location, direction, up, and right vectors completely define the camera. Theoretically, that is all that is needed. However, it is very difficult to hand calculate the vectors for anything other than an orientation along an axis. The up, right, and direction vectors must be perpendicular to each other in order to avoid distortion. Typically, you will define a camera with the direction, up, and right vectors on an axis and then use rotate or look_at statements to turn the camera to the actual direction.

The translate and rotate keywords can be used to move and point the camera, but this can still be difficult because rotations are always relative to the coordinate axes.

The look_at keyword can be used to point the camera more easily. You should specify the camera location, up, right, and direction keywords and vectors first. Then use look_at to define the 3D coordinates of the point you want to look at. POV-Ray pans the camera left or right until the view window lines up with the "look at" point. It then tilts the camera up or down until it is pointed directly at the proper point.

Use the sky keyword to define the way the camera is panned when a "look at" rotation is performed. During such rotations, the camera is first rotated so that the up vector matches the sky vector. The default value is sky <0 1 0> so generally the camera is already in this orientation. The sky vector then becomes the axis of rotation for the panning. The tilting part of a "look at" rotation is also done in line with the sky vector. If the "look at" point lies directly along the sky axis then it cannot pan left or right to line up with it and a blank image results. The sky keyword only affects the way subsequent look_at operations work. It has no other effect.

A default camera is defined so you need not have any camera statement. All camera statements start with the system default values and proceed from there. If more than one `camera` statement is in a scene, any previous cameras are overwritten.

You may declare camera identifiers, letting you define multiple camera locations and orientations. You then choose one among them by inserting the proper identifier in the `camera` statement. A camera identifier in a `camera` statement completely overwrites all previous values of all of the vectors. Therefore, you should always place a camera identifier first in a `camera` statement.

SEE ALSO

+H, +W, `direction`, `location`, `look_at`, `right`, `sky`, `up`, *VECTOR*

EXAMPLE

```
// CAMERA1.POV
#include "examp.inc"

// Example 1
// Define something to look at
object {box {UnitBox} texture {color Cyan}}

// Define camera.
// Try different direction lengths and locations.
camera {
 right <4 0 0>          // View window 4 wide by
 up    <0 3 0>          //   3 tall.
 direction <0 0 20>     // Zoom way in with long direction.
 location  <12 10 -30>  // Position from bird's-eye view.
 look_at   <0 0 0>      // Pan & tilt to look at object.
}
///////////////////// Try these examples seperately /////
// CAMERA2.POV
#include "examp.inc"

// Example 2
// Define something to look at
object {box {UnitBox} texture {color Cyan}}

// Define 2 camera identifiers
#declare Wide_angle=
 camera {direction <0 0 0.8>}

#declare Zoom=
 camera {direction <0 0 3>}

//Pick a camera.  Try substituting Zoom.
camera {
 Wide_angle          //Identifier FIRST!
```

```
location   <5 5 -5>  //Place it.
look_at    <0 0 0>   //Point it.
}
```

checker

TYPE
COLOR_PATTERN

PURPOSE
Specifies a checker color pattern in a texture.

SYNTAX
`texture { checker` *COLOR COLOR* *[TEXTURE_ITEM...]* `}`

DESCRIPTION
The `checker` keyword specifies a color pattern consisting of a 3D pattern made of cubes of alternating colors. The cubes are one unit in all directions and are parallel to the coordinate axes.

Unlike other color patterns, a `color_map` is not used, nor do the `turbulence` or `octaves` keywords have any effect. Color patterns may be translated, rotated, or scaled. Only one color pattern may be specified in each `texture` statement.

SEE ALSO
`color`, *COLOR_PATTERN*, `texture`, `tiles`

330

EXAMPLE

```
// CHECKER.POV
#include "examp.inc"

object {
  sphere { <0 0 0> 1 }
   texture {
     checker color Magenta color White
     scale <0.3 0.3 0.3>
  }
}
```

clipped_by

TYPE
OBJECT_MODIFIER or *COMPOSITE_MODIFIER*

PURPOSE
Defines an invisible shape that clips away part of an object, letting rays inside.

SYNTAX
object { *SHAPE* clipped_by { *SHAPE...* } *[OBJECT_MODIFIER...]* } |
composite { *OBJECT...* clipped_by { *SHAPE...* }
        [COMPOSITE_MODIFIER...] }

DESCRIPTION
Although it is generally useful to think of most POV-Ray objects as solid, in fact they are hollow surfaces, which you can observe by placing texture state-

331

ments with some transparency in the individual shapes of a CSG intersection. This method is slow because clear surface textures require that more rays be traced. A `clipped_by` statement can be used more efficiently to create the same effect.

The ray-object intersection tests for the object are performed as usual, but any intersection points that are not inside the clipping shape are ignored. Multiple shapes may be given in the `clipped_by` statement. (Note that a `clipped_by` statement may be used on an object or a composite but not on a shape.)

Because bicubic patch, triangle, and smooth triangle shapes have no inside defined, they cannot be used in a `clipped_by` statement; however they can be clipped by other shapes.

If `translate`, `rotate`, or `scale` keywords appear after the `clipped_by` statement, then the clipping shapes will move and scale along with the clipped object.

SEE ALSO

`composite`, `object`, *SHAPE*

EXAMPLE

```
// CLIPPED.POV
// Compare with union, intersection and
//   difference examples.
#include "examp.inc"

object {
  sphere {<0 0 0> 1}  // Start with a sphere.
  clipped_by {         // Clip with a smaller box.
    box {<-0.8 -0.8 -0.8> <0.8 0.8 0.8>}
  }
  texture { color White phong 1}
  rotate <0 50 0>
}
```

color or colour

TYPE
COLOR_PATTERN (and other assorted uses)

PURPOSE
Defines the red, green, blue, and alpha components of a color.

SYNTAX
color *[COLOR_COMPONENT...]*

COLOR_COMPONENT =
    red *red_amount* | green *green_amount* | blue *blue_amount* |
    alpha *alpha_amount* | *COLOR_IDENTIFIER*

DESCRIPTION
All colors in POV-Ray are specified by using the color keyword (which can also be spelled colour). It may be followed by a color identifier and/or any of four color component keywords: red, green, blue, or alpha. The alpha component defines the degree of transparency. All colors in POV-Ray have these four components. The value of each component typically ranges from 0.0 (no color) to 1.0 (full intensity). If any of them is unspecified, the default value is 0. Therefore, the following two statements are identical.

```
color red 0.8
color red 0.8 green 0.0 blue 0.0 alpha 0.0
```

333

A color identifier contains all four values even if only a few are defined. Therefore, you should always put identifiers first so that previously defined values are not overwritten. For example:

```
#declare Medium_Red =
   color red 0.8  // this has default blue 0 green 0 alpha 0

#declare Medium_Violet =
   color blue 0.8 Medium_Red // WRONG! Overwrites blue

#declare Medium_Violet =
   color Medium_Red blue 0.8 // Right.
```

The `color` keyword has many uses. Color specifications appear in the definitions of `light_source`, `color_map`, and `checker`. For details on using color in these instances see their reference entries.

When a `color` statement is used as a shape modifier or object modifier and it is not inside the brackets of a `texture` statement, it is called a *quick rendering* color. Quick rendering color specifications are used with the +Q command-line switch. The +Q command-line switch controls the quality of the texture evaluation. A setting of +Q9 gives full quality but lower settings leave out some of the calculations so that test renderings will finish faster. Any setting of +Q5 or lower omits the color pattern calculations. This causes all objects to show up as medium gray. A `color` specification added as a shape modifier or object modifier lets you define a color that is used only at these lower quality settings. For settings +Q6 or higher this quick color is ignored and the texture's color pattern is used. Note that this feature cannot be used in CSG shapes or composites.

When used inside the brackets of a `texture` statement, the `color` keyword specifies a color pattern, which is really no pattern at all. It simply specifies texture consisting of one solid color. Typical color pattern modifiers such as `turbulence`, `octaves`, or `color_map` cannot be used with this type of color specification because there is no pattern to modify. Only one color pattern may be specified in each `texture` statement.

SEE ALSO

`alpha`, `blue`, `checker`, `color_map`, *COLOR_PATTERN*, `green`, `light_source`, `object`, `red`, *SHAPE*, `texture`

EXAMPLE

```
// Try each of these examples separately
// COLOR1.POV
#include "examp.inc"
```

```
//Example 1.    Color as a color pattern
//              inside a texture {...}
object {
  sphere { <0 0 0> 1 }
  texture {color red 1.0 green 0.8 blue 0.8 alpha 0.5}
}
/////////////////////////////////
// COLOR2.POV
#include "examp.inc"

//Example 2.    Color as a shape modifier,
//              run at +Q5 or lower
object {
  sphere { <0 0 0> 1 color Yellow}
  texture { bozo }
}
/////////////////////////////////
// COLOR3.POV
#include "examp.inc"

//Example 3.    Color as an object modifier,
//              run at +Q5 or lower
object {
  sphere { <0 0 0> 1 }
  texture { bozo }
  color Yellow
}
```

color_map or colour_map

TYPE
COLOR_PATTERN_MODIFIER

PURPOSE

Defines the blend of colors used in a texture color pattern.

SYNTAX

`color_map { [` *low_value high_value COLOR COLOR* `]... }`

DESCRIPTION

The `color_map` statement defines the colors to be used in agate, bozo, granite, leopard, marble, onion, spotted, wood, and gradient color patterns. Each of these patterns transforms the 3D coordinates of each point on the textured surface into a pattern function result value from 0.0 through 1.0. The color map provides a look-up table of colors for various ranges of these values.

You can specify up to 20 entries in a `color_map` statement. Each entry is enclosed in square brackets and contains a *low_value, high_value,* and two color definitions. POV-Ray evaluates the pattern function and obtains a result value. Then it searches the color map entries from the top down until it finds an entry such that the pattern result value is between *low_value* and *high_value* inclusive. If the pattern result value is equal to *low_value,* the first color is used. If it equals *high_value,* the second color is used. If the value is between, the color map interpolates the two colors proportionally.

It is up to the user to ensure that sufficient entries are given to cover all possible ranges of values from 0.0 through 1.0.

All of the pattern types listed above except gradient, have default color maps built in.

SEE ALSO

agate, bozo, color, *COLOR_PATTERN,* gradient, granite, leopard, marble, onion, spotted, texture, wood

EXAMPLE

```
// COLORMAP.POV
#include "examp.inc"

object {
  sphere { <0 0 0> 1 }
  texture {
    gradient <1 0 0>
    color_map {
      [0.0 0.2   color red 1
                 color red .7  blue .7]
      [0.2 0.4   color red .7  blue .7
```

```
                     color blue 1          ]
          [0.4 0.6   color blue 1
                     color blue .7 green .7]
          [0.6 0.8   color blue .7 green .7
                     color green 1          ]
          [0.8 1.0   color green 1
                     color green .7 red .7 ]
        }
     scale <0.5 0.5 0.5>
     }
}
```

COLOR_PATTERN

TYPE
TEXTURE_ITEM

PURPOSE
Specifies the pattern of color in a texture. In addition to using solid colors, ten different predefined patterns and the option to map an image file onto a surface are provided.

SYNTAX

```
texture {
  COLOR_PATTERN   [COLOR_PATTERN_MODIFIER...]
    [TEXTURE_ITEM...]
}
```

COLOR_PATTERN =
    agate | bozo | granite | leopard | marble | onion | spotted |
    wood | checker *COLOR COLOR* | gradient *<vector>* | *COLOR* |
    image_map {
      [MAP_PREFIX...] MAP_FILE_TYPE "FILESPEC"
        [IMAGE_MAP_MODIFIER...]
}

COLOR_PATTERN_MODIFIER =
    turbulence *turb_amount* | octaves *octave_number* | *COLOR_MAP*

DESCRIPTION

Textures consist of three basic types of parameters: color patterns, normal patterns, and finish parameters. You specify the color of a surface with a color pattern. It specifies the color the object actually "is" rather than how it "looks." For example, if you paint a wall white, then under normal circumstances it looks white. But if you shine a red light on it, the wall "looks" red even though it really "is" painted white. Therefore, a color pattern is sometimes called the *pigment* because it is the color that is built into the surface like the pigment in a coat of paint or the dyes in a piece of cloth. The color pattern is the part of the texture specification that does not consider how the surface is illuminated or what its reflective properties are.

The `color` keyword, with color components such as `red`, `green`, `blue`, and `alpha`, is used to specify a single solid color over the entire surface. (See the reference entry on `color` for details.)

The `checker` keyword uses two color specifications to define a checkered pattern.

The keywords `agate`, `bozo`, `granite`, `leopard`, `marble`, `onion`, `spotted`, `wood`, `checker`, and `gradient` specify built-in patterns that allow you to vary the color over the entire surface. These color patterns are used with a `color_map` statement. The pattern is actually a mathematical function that converts the 3D coordinates of each point on the textured surface into a pattern function result value from 0.0 through 1.0. The color map provides a look-up table of colors for various ranges of these values.

An `image_map` statement specifies an image file that is applied to a surface as a color pattern. The two-dimensional image is projected onto or wrapped around the three-dimensional surface.

Some pattern types respond to the `turbulence` and `octaves` keywords. The `turbulence` keyword stirs up the pattern. The `octaves` keyword controls how "jagged" the turbulence is. Color patterns can be translated, rotated, or scaled. You can only specify one color pattern in each `texture` statement.

For complete details see each of the keywords listed below.

SEE ALSO

`agate`, `bozo`, `checker`, `color`, `color_map`, *FINISH_PARAMETER*, `gradient`, `granite`, `image_map`, `leopard`, `marble`, *NORMAL_PATTERN*, `octaves`, `onion`, `spotted`, `texture`, `turbulence`, `wood`

EXAMPLE
See examples for the keywords listed above.

component

TYPE
BLOB_ITEM

PURPOSE
Specifies a spherical component in a blob shape. A blob shape is made from spheres that flow and blend into each other smoothly to create a liquid effect.

SYNTAX
```
blob {
  component strength radius <center>
  [BLOB_ITEM...] [POLY_MODIFIER...]
}
```

DESCRIPTION
The `component` keyword is used to specify the properties of a component in a blob shape. The components are spheres that flow and smoothly blend into each other to create a liquid effect. The individual components attract and repel each other and result in "blobby" organic-looking shapes.

For each component you must give a float value for the *strength*, a float value for the *radius*, and a vector that is the 3D coordinate of the center of the component. Positive strength values cause the blob components to attract and flow together. Radius values must be positive. Negative strength values make

invisible components that repel or make dents in other components. The example below shows how negative strength values create dents. See `blob` for more details.

SEE ALSO

`blob, threshold`

EXAMPLE

```
// COMPONENT.POV
#include "examp.inc"

object {
  blob {
    threshold 0.6

  // First component is main blob
    component  1.0 2.0 < 0 0 0>

  // These two smaller components have
  // negative strength which causes them
  // to dent into the main component
    component −0.4 0.2 <−0.3 0.4 −0.95>
    component −0.4 0.2 < 0.3 0.4 −0.95>
  }
  texture {color White phong 1 }
}
```

composite

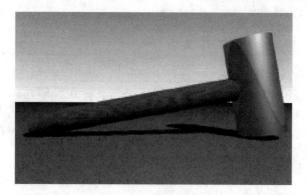

TYPE
SCENE_ITEM

PURPOSE
Provides a way to combine objects together to treat them as a unit.

SYNTAX
`composite {` *COMPOSITE_IDENTIFIER*
    [COMPOSITE_MODIFIER...] `}` |
`composite {` *COMPOSITE_ITEM... [COMPOSITE_MODIFIER...]* `}`

COMPOSITE_ITEM =
    COMPOSITE | *OBJECT*

COMPOSITE_MODIFIER =
    CSG_MODIFIER | *BOUNDED_BY* | *CLIPPED_BY*

DESCRIPTION
It is often convenient to group objects together so they may be translated, rotated, scaled, bounded, or clipped as a single unit. The `union` statement can be used for combining shapes but it cannot operate on complete objects. The `composite` statement works just like a `union` statement except `composite` operates on objects or other composites.

    The only legal composite modifiers are `translate`, `rotate`, `scale`, `inverse`, `bounded_by`, and `clipped_by`. Neither textures nor colors may be applied to a composite.

SEE ALSO
`bounded_by`, `clipped_by`, *CSG_SHAPE*, `inverse`, `object`, `rotate`, `scale`, `translate`, `union`

EXAMPLE
```
// COMPOSIT.POV
#include "examp.inc" camera {location <0 2 -20>}

/* First two examples of why "union" won't work
union {
  intersection {
    Disk_Z scale <1 1 10>
    texture {   // ERROR! intersection can't have texture.
```

```
        DMFWood4 turbulence 0.1 rotate <0 5 0>
    }
  }
  intersection {
    Disk_Y scale <2 4 2> translate <0 0 10>
    texture { Chrome_Metal }  // ERROR!  can't have texture.
  }
  rotate <0 90 0>
  rotate <0 0 10>
  translate <0 1.7 0>
}
// Now try putting texture in objects...
union {
  object { //  ERROR! union works on shapes, not objects
    intersection { ...

*/
// Use composite to stick objects together like this...
composite {
 object {
  intersection { Disk_Z scale <1 1 10>  }
  texture { DMFWood4 turbulence 0.1 rotate <0 2 0>}
 }
 object {
  intersection { Disk_Y scale <2 4 2> translate <0 0 10>}
  texture { Chrome_Metal }
 }
 rotate <0 90 0>
 rotate <0 0 10>
 translate <0 1.7 0>
}
```

crand_value

TYPE
FINISH_PARAMETER

PURPOSE
Adds a random, grainy look to a texture on a pixel-by-pixel basis.

SYNTAX
`texture {` *crand_value [TEXTURE_ITEM...]* `}`

DESCRIPTION
Any time a float value appears alone in a `texture` statement and is not associated with any keyword, it is specifying a color randomness value. The color of the pixel is computed and then adjusted by a small random amount proportional to the value. The default is 0.0 and typical values range from 0.01 up to 0.2 or more. The original intent of this value was to simulate tiny bumps or dents in the surface or to give it the look of a rough, grainy surface such as concrete. This random effect is applied on a pixel-by-pixel basis, however, and does not take into account the distance of the surface from the camera. Because it is pixel oriented, the resolution used in rendering has a dramatic effect on the results. In high-resolution renderings, the pixels are so small that the grain is too fine to see. In some circumstances this feature can improve the appearance of a surface, but in general it does not produce useful or realistic results.

SEE ALSO
FINISH_PARAMETER, `texture`

EXAMPLE
```
// CRAND.POV
#include "examp.inc"  camera{location <0 0 -5>}

// Three different crand values
object {sphere { <-2 0 0> 1 }
  texture {
    0.0           // default
    color White
  }
}

object {sphere { <0 0 0> 1 }
  texture {
    0.1           // some speckles
```

```
        color White
    }
}

object {sphere { <2 0 0> 1 }
    texture {
      0.2          // many speckles
      color White
    }
}
```

CSG_SHAPE

PURPOSE
Combines shapes into more complex shapes using constructive solid geometry.

SYNTAX

```
intersection { CSG_BODY [CSG_MODIFIER...] }   |
difference { CSG_BODY [CSG_MODIFIER...] }     |
union { CSG_BODY [CSG_MODIFIER...] }
```

CSG_MODIFIER =
        translate *<vector>* | rotate *<angles>* | scale *<amount>* | inverse

CSG_BODY =
        SHAPE... | *CSG_IDENTIFIER*

DESCRIPTION
POV-Ray provides a way to combine shapes into more complex shapes using "constructive solid geometry," or CSG for short. Three CSG shapes—intersection, difference, and union—are available. An intersection shape contains all and only the points that are inside all of its component shapes. A difference shape starts with a master shape and all points inside the other component shapes are cut away from it. A union shape is a way to group shapes together so that they may be treated as a single shape. Details on each of these CSG shapes are in their respective reference entries.

CSG shapes may contain regular shapes or other CSG shapes in any combination. However, bicubic patches, triangles, smooth triangles, and Height-

REFERENCE

Fields do not have clearly defined insides or outsides and thus will not work in intersection or difference shapes.

CSG shapes can only be modified by translate, rotate, scale, or inverse. A texture or quick-render color cannot be used on a CSG shape. Any texture or color modifiers must either be inside the component shape statements or in the object statement containing the CSG shape.

CSG shapes are made of shapes—not objects. The composite statement provides a way to group objects like a union statement does for shapes. Also a clipped_by statement provides a specialized type of intersection on objects and composites but there is no general way to perform CSG intersection or difference operations on objects.

These limitations on CSG are specific to POV-Ray 1.0. Future versions may include the extra programming required to implement complex nesting of textured shapes or objects in CSG.

SEE ALSO

clipped_by, color, composite, difference, intersection, inverse, object, rotate, scale, *SHAPE*, texture, translate

EXAMPLE

See examples under clipped_by, composite, difference, intersection, union.

cubic

TYPE
SHAPE

PURPOSE
Defines a third-order polynomial shape.

SYNTAX
```
cubic { CUBIC_IDENTIFIER [POLY_MODIFIER...] } |
cubic { POLY_3_IDENTIFIER [POLY_MODIFIER...] } |
cubic { < term1 term2 term3 term4... term_20 > [POLY_MODIFIER...] }
```

DESCRIPTION
The `cubic` statement is actually an alternate way to specify a third-order polynomial shape. The `poly { 3 <term1 term2... term20>}` statement creates the exact same representation internally in POV-Ray and produces the same results. The surface is defined by the equation:

$$A_1 x^3 + A_2 x^2 y + A_3 x^2 z + A_4 x^2 + A_5 xy^2 + A_6 xyz + A_7 xy + A_8 xz^2 + A_9 xz + A_{10} x +$$
$$A_{11} y^3 + A_{12} y^2 z + A_{13} y^2 + A_{14} yz^2 + A_{15} yz + A_{16} y + A_{17} z^3 + A_{18} z^2 + A_{19} z + A_{20} = 0$$

where A_1 through A_{20} are specified by *term1* through *term20*, respectively.

Points where the equation is less than 0 are defined as inside the shape.

Cubic shapes can be used in CSG shapes and cubics can be scaled, rotated, and translated. Because the calculations for cubics need to be highly accurate, sometimes they will not render correctly. If this happens, you may specify the `sturm` keyword to use POV-Ray's more accurate (but slower) Sturmian sequence root solver.

SEE ALSO
`object`, `poly`, *SHAPE*, `sturm`

EXAMPLE
```
// CUBIC.POV
#include "examp.inc"

// Try varying the y*y*y value from 3 down
// to 0.0 in small steps.
object {
  cubic {
//          x*x            + y*y*y + y*y        + z*z  −1 =0
```

```
    <0 0 0 1 0 0 0 0 0 0  0.45 0  1  0 0 0 0 1 0 -1>
      sturm
   }
   translate <0 1 1>
   texture {color LimeGreen phong 1}
}
```

declare

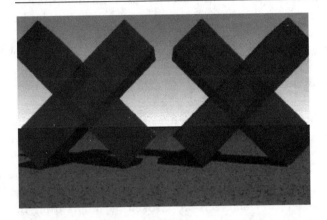

TYPE
LANGUAGE_DIRECTIVE

PURPOSE
Declares an identifier for later use.

SYNTAX
`#declare` *IDENTIFIER = DECLARE_ITEM*

DECLARE_ITEM =
    BICUBIC_PATCH | BLOB | BOX | CAMERA | COLOR |
    COMPOSITE | CUBIC | DIFFERENCE | FLOAT | HEIGHT_FIELD |
    INTERSECTION | LIGHT_SOURCE | OBJECT | PLANE |
    POLY | QUADRIC | QUARTIC | SMOOTH_TRIANGLE |SPHERE |
    TEXTURE... | TRIANGLE | UNION | VECTOR

347

DESCRIPTION

POV-Ray allows you to declare 23 types of identifiers. This helps you to modularize your scene descriptions and it makes them more readable. You might declare a complex object and then make multiple copies of that object translated, rotated, or scaled into different positions by simply invoking the identifier in several places. You can declare floating-point values or vectors describing various parameters. By using these parameters you need only change the one declaration to change all of the places it is used. Identifiers may be used anywhere that the items they represent could be used, including the declarations of other identifiers.

A declaration beginning with the `#declare` keyword is followed by the identifier to be declared. These are followed by an equal sign followed by the item to be declared. An identifier's declaration must appear in the file before it can be invoked.

Identifiers must begin with a letter or an underscore. They may contain letters, digits, or underscores and may be from 1 to 40 characters long. Identifiers are case sensitive. Thus "MyThing" and "mything" are two different things. Identifiers cannot match any reserved keywords. (See the keyword list in Table 7-6.)

Float and vector identifiers are invoked by simply using the identifier wherever a floating-point value or vector can be used. Do not enclose a vector identifier in angle brackets. For example:

```
#declare Radius = 2        // declare a float identifier
#declare Center = <1 5 3>  // declare a vector identifier
object {
  sphere { Center Radius }// same as "sphere {<1 5 3> 2}"
}                          // Note vector identifier has no <>
```

Float identifiers may also be preceded by a plus or minus sign. See the usage of the float identifier `Half_Length` in the example below.

A color identifier may appear after the `color` keyword. All other types of identifiers must be invoked by surrounding them with `{ }` braces with their type before it. For example, if MyObject is an object identifier, it is invoked by `object {MyObject}`. The type of the identifier must match the keyword.

The syntax for invoking a color identifier, camera identifier, or texture identifier allows for other items to appear before the identifier but you should never do this. An identifier completely defines the entire item and invoking it will overwrite all previous specifications, as shown in the examples below.

SEE ALSO

bicubic_patch, blob, box, camera, color, composite, cubic, difference, *FLOAT*, height_field, Identifiers and Keywords section, intersection, light_source, object, plane, poly, quadric, quartic, smooth_triangle, sphere, texture, triangle, union

VECTOR

EXAMPLE

```
// DECLARE.POV
#include "examp.inc"

// Declare some values, shapes, objects
#declare Left_X_Location = <-2 0.8 3>    // vector
#declare Right_X_Location = <2 0.8 3>    // vector
#declare Half_Length = 2                 // float
#declare MyPurple = color red 1 blue 1 green 0.2

#declare MyBox =
  box {<-Half_Length -0.5 -0.5> <Half_Length 0.5 0.5>}

#declare MyCross =
  union {
    box{MyBox}
    box{MyBox rotate <0 0 90>}
  }

#declare Big_Purple_X =
  object {
    union {MyCross}
    texture {
//      color alpha 0.5 MyPurple  // WRONG! Overwrites alpha
        color MyPurple alpha 0.5  // Right, adds alpha
    }
    rotate <0 0 45>
  }

// Now put it all together

// object {MyCross}   // ERROR! wrong type

object {Big_Purple_X translate Left_X_Location}
object {Big_Purple_X translate Right_X_Location}
```

default

TYPE
LANGUAGE_DIRECTIVE

PURPOSE
Defines default values.

SYNTAX
`#default { ` *TEXTURE...* ` }`

DESCRIPTION
All parameters in a POV-Ray texture have default values that are used if you do not specify a value. If you prefer other defaults, the `#default` language directive lets you define your own default texture values. Any `texture` statements following the `#default` directive will start out with the values you specify. That default stays in effect until changed by a subsequent `#default` directive. Note that the `texture` statements inside later `#default` directives begin with the previously defined defaults, not with POV-Ray's startup defaults.

The syntax for this directive allows for future versions of POV-Ray to enable user control of other defaults, but currently only textures are supported.

A texture identifier uses the set of defaults that were in effect when the identifier was declared, not the defaults in effect when it is invoked. In the example below, the upper left sphere has no Phong highlight because that is the POV-Ray default and no Phong was explicitly specified. The declaration for `NeonPink_Texture` has no Phong highlight for the same reasons. A

#default statement then makes Phong highlights part of the default texture. So the declaration for Cyan_Texture, which follows the #default statement, has the Phong highlight as a default, even though no phong keyword is used. The lower right object illustrates that Cyan_Texture does indeed have Phong highlights. The upper right object uses color NeonPink (not Neon-Pink_Texture) and it has the new default Phong highlight. The lower left object uses the texture identifier NeonPink_Texture which had no Phong highlight when it was declared. Therefore, it has no highlight when it is invoked even though the default has subsequently changed.

SEE ALSO

texture

EXAMPLE

```
// DEFAULT.POV
#include "examp.inc" camera{location<0 1 -5>}

// Create some objects with and without default
// texture settings
object {
   sphere {<-1.5 2 0> 1}        //upper left
   texture {color NeonPink}     //has no phong
}

#declare NeonPink_Texture =
   texture {color NeonPink} //no phong

#default {texture{phong 1.0}}  //make phong default

#declare Cyan_Texture =
   texture {color Cyan}  //has new default phong

object {
   sphere {<1.5 2 0> 1}         //upper right
   texture {color NeonPink}     //has new default phong
}

object {
   sphere {<-1.5 0 0> 1}        // lower left
   texture {NeonPink_Texture}   // identifier overwrites
}

object {
   sphere {<1.5 0 0> 1}         // lower right
   texture {Cyan_Texture}       // identifier has phong
}
```

dents

TYPE
NORMAL_PATTERN

PURPOSE
Makes a texture look dented or pitted by applying a normal pattern to it.

SYNTAX
`texture { dents` *amount [TEXTURE_ITEM...]* `}`

DESCRIPTION
The `dents` keyword specifies a surface normal perturbation pattern which modifies the surface normal to look like random irregular dents have been beaten in with a ball peen hammer. (See *NORMAL_PATTERN* for details on surface normals.) The required float value after the keyword specifies an apparent depth of the dents. Values from 0.0 (no dents) to 1.0 (deep dents) are typical. Each dent is about 1 or 2 units wide, so for small objects a scale modifier is often used to alter the diameter of the dents.

Note that the use of a normal pattern to perturb the surface normal does not actually change the shape of the object. It artificially modifies the surface normal so that lighting, reflections, refractions, and highlights look as though the surface were dented. Only one normal pattern may be used in each `texture` statement.

SEE ALSO
NORMAL_PATTERN, `texture`

EXAMPLE

```
// DENTS.POV
#include "examp.inc"

object {
  sphere { <0 0 0> 1 }
  texture
   {Chrome_Metal
    dents 0.4
    scale <0.07 0.07 0.07>
    }
}
```

difference

TYPE
SHAPE

PURPOSE
Creates a constructive solid geometry shape that cuts one or more shapes away from another shape.

SYNTAX
```
difference { DIFFERENCE_IDENTIFIER [CSG_MODIFIER...]} |
difference { SHAPE... [CSG_MODIFIER...] }
```

CSG_MODIFIER =
  TRANSFORMATION | `inverse`

DESCRIPTION

Use the `difference` keyword to define a shape that is an alternate to certain types of constructive solid geometry (CSG) intersection shapes. You must specify more than one shape; the first shape given is the "master" shape and all subsequent shapes are carved away from the first one. The same effect can be obtained by using intersection and specifying the `inverse` keyword for all shapes except the first. For example, the example under `inverse` uses `intersection` and `inverse` to create the exact same shape as the `difference` example below.

Like the intersection shape, the difference shape requires component shapes that have a well-defined inside and outside. Thus triangle, smooth triangle, and bicubic patch shapes cannot be used, and Height-Field shapes do not always work well with it.

As with all CSG shapes, `difference` can only operate on shapes; it cannot operate on objects. It cannot use `texture` or quick-render `color` specifications as a shape modifier. You can only use `translate`, `rotate`, `scale`, or `inverse` keywords with it.

SEE ALSO

CSG_SHAPE, `intersection, inverse, object,` *SHAPE*

EXAMPLE

```
// DIFFEREN.POV
#include "examp.inc"

// Compare with union, intersection, inverse
// and clipped_by examples.
// Start with box and throw away all
// parts in sphere.

object {
  difference {
    box {<-0.8 -0.8 -0.8> <0.8 0.8 0.8>}
    sphere {<0 0 0> 1}
  }
  texture { color White phong 1}
  rotate <0 50 0>
}
```

diffuse

TYPE
FINISH_PARAMETER

PURPOSE
Controls the amount of diffuse illumination on an object from light sources in a scene.

SYNTAX
`texture { diffuse` *amount [TEXTURE_ITEM...]* `}`

DESCRIPTION
The `diffuse` keyword controls the amount of illumination that comes directly from light sources. This is in contrast to ambient light that comes from all directions in a scene. The amount of diffuse light falling on each point of a surface is dependent upon the geometry of the surface and the light source. When diffuse light strikes at a shallow angle, the light is less intense than if it were striking at a steep angle. See the `brilliance` keyword for more on this aspect of diffuse light. When a shadow is created by an object blocking the path of light from a light source to a surface, it is the diffuse light that is blocked.

Values for diffuse light can range from 0.0 (no directional light, shadows only) to 1.0 (full diffuse light). The default value for diffuse lighting is 0.6.

SEE ALSO
`ambient`, *FINISH_PARAMETER*, `light_source`, `no_shadow`, `texture`

CREATIONS

RAY TRACING

EXAMPLE

```
// DIFFUSE.POV
#include "examp.inc"  camera{location <0 0 -5>}

// Three different diffuse values
object {sphere { <-2 0 0> 1 }
  texture {color NeonPink diffuse 0.2} //low
}

object {sphere { <0 0 0> 1 }
  texture {color NeonPink diffuse 0.6} //default
}

object {sphere { <2 0 0> 1 }
  texture {color NeonPink diffuse 0.8} //high
}

// This bar casts a shadow for effect
object {
  quadric {
    Cylinder_X scale <1 0.1 0.1> translate <0 1.2 -1.5>
  }
  texture {color Green}
}
```

direction

TYPE
CAMERA_ITEM

356

PURPOSE

Defines the direction the camera points and the angle of the field of view.

SYNTAX

```
camera { direction <vector> [CAMERA_ITEM...] }
```

DESCRIPTION

Three keywords—direction, up, and right—are used to specify vectors that dictate the position of the view window relative to the camera's location.

The direction keyword defines the direction the camera is looking. The ray that is traced in the center of the image follows this vector. The default value is direction <0 0 1>. This means that the camera is looking in the positive *z* direction. The length of the direction vector also determines the distance of the view window from the camera location (see Figure 7-3). This can be used to control the field of view for the camera. For fixed values of the up and right vectors, a shorter direction vector gives a wide-angle view because the view window is close. A longer direction vector zooms in for a narrower field of view.

The location, direction, up, and right vectors completely define the camera. Theoretically, that is all that is needed. However, it is very difficult to hand calculate the vectors for anything other than an orientation along an axis. The up, right, and direction vectors must be perpendicular to each other in order to avoid distortion. Typically, you will define a camera with the direction, up, and right vectors on an axis and then use rotate or look_at statements to turn the camera to the actual direction. For a complete discussion of the POV-Ray camera, see the camera keyword.

SEE ALSO

camera

EXAMPLE

```
// DIRECT1.POV
#include "examp.inc"

// Something to look at.
object {
  sphere { <0 0 0> 1 }
  texture {color NeonPink phong 1}
}
```

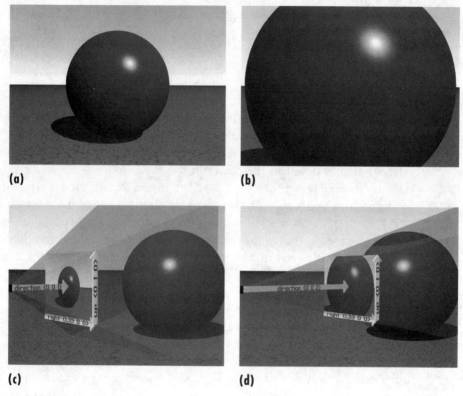

(a)

(b)

(c)

(d)

Figure 7-3 POV-Ray View Window

The illustrations in Figure 7-3 show how the up, right, and direction vectors define the size, shape, and location of the viewing window relative to the camera's location. Figures (a) and (b) are POV-Ray images of a sphere with radius 1 at the origin.

In both scenes, the camera is located at location <0 0 -3> and uses the default values up <0 1 0> and right <1.33 0 0>. However Figure (a) uses the default value direction <0 0 1> while Figure (b) uses direction <0 0 2>.

Figures (c) and (d) are depictions of what POV-Ray's imaginary camera and view window might look like while viewing scenes (a) and (b) respectively. The "black box" on the left is the camera. Rays are projected outwards through the window in a rectangular cone that is the camera's field of view. The up and right vectors define the height and width of the window. The direction vector determines the distance of the window from the camera. Figure (d) shows how the longer direction vector creates a narrower cone and a narrower field of view.

```
// Camera with wide view
camera {
  location <0 0 -3.5>
  direction <0 0 1>      // Try changing to <0 0 2>
                         // for narrower view.
}
```

dump

TYPE
MAP_FILE_TYPE

PURPOSE
Specifies a file type of DUMP in an image_map, bump_map, or material_map.

SYNTAX
dump *"FILESPEC"*

DESCRIPTION
POV-Ray uses files made of arrays of pixels for patterns in image maps, bump maps, and material maps. The dump keyword specifies that the dump format file is to be used. This format is used by QRT ray tracer, another popular program for ray tracing.

You specify a file type using the dump keyword followed by the file specification in quotes. If the file is not found in the current directory, library paths specified with the +L command-line switch are also searched. For complete details see the maps listed below. Note that Height-Field shapes cannot use dump files.

SEE ALSO
+F switch, bump_map, gif, iff, image_map, material_map, tga

EXAMPLE
See examples for bump_map, image_map, or material_map.

falloff

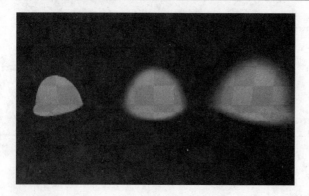

TYPE
LIGHT_SRC_MODIFIER

PURPOSE
Specifies the width of the cone of light produced by a spotlight. It is the angle away from the center line where the intensity falls off to zero.

SYNTAX
```
light_source {
  <center> COLOR
  spotlight falloff degrees
  [LIGHT_SRC_MODIFIER...]
}
```

DESCRIPTION
Normally light diffuses outward equally in all directions from a light source. However the `spotlight` keyword can be used to create a cone of light that is bright in the center and falls off to darkness in a soft fringe effect at the edge. Although the cone of light fades to soft edges, objects illuminated by spotlights still cast hard shadows.

The `falloff`, `radius`, and `tightness` keywords control the way that light tapers off at the edges of the cone. These three keywords apply only when you use the `spotlight` keyword.

The `falloff` keyword specifies the overall size of the cone of light. This is the point where the light falls off to zero intensity. The float value you specify is the angle, in degrees, between the edge of the cone and center line. The value should be in the range from 0 to 180. See Figure 7-7 later, under the `spotlight` keyword. The `radius` keyword specifies the size of the "hot-spot" at the center of the cone of light. The "hot-spot" is a brighter cone of light inside the spotlight cone and has the same center line. The `radius` value specifies the angle, in degrees, between the edge of this bright, inner cone and the center line. The light inside the inner cone is of uniform intensity. The light between the inner and outer cones tapers off to zero.

For example, with `radius 10` and `falloff 20` the light from the center line out to 10 degrees is full intensity. From 10 to 20 degrees from the center line the light falls off to zero intensity. At 20 degrees or greater there is no light. See the examples under the `radius` and `falloff` keywords. Note that if the radius and falloff values are close or equal the light intensity drops rapidly and the spotlight has a sharp edge. The default values for both `radius` and `falloff` is 70. Figure 7-8 later, shows the effect of various `falloff` values.

The `tightness` keyword is used to specify an additional exponential softening of the edges. See the reference entries for `light_source` and `spotlight` for further details.

SEE ALSO

`light_source, radius, spotlight, tightness`

EXAMPLE

```
// FALLOFF.POV
#include "spotback.inc"

// Three different falloff values
object {
  light_source {
    <-5 4 0> color White
    spotlight point_at <-5 -1 5>
    tightness 0 radius 10
    falloff 10  // small
  }
}

object {
  light_source {
    <0 4 0> color White
    spotlight point_at <0 -1 5>
    tightness 0 radius 10
    falloff 15  // medium
```

```
    }
  }

object {
  light_source {
    <5 4 0> color White
    spotlight point_at <5 -1 5>
    tightness 0 radius 10
    falloff 20  // large
  }
}
```

FINISH_PARAMETER

TYPE
TEXTURE_ITEM

PURPOSE
Specifies any of twelve parameters used in a texture to specify the surface finish and lighting properties of an object.

SYNTAX
`texture {` *FINISH_PARAMETER [TEXTURE_ITEM...]* `}`

FINISH_PARAMETER =
    crand_value | `metallic` | `ambient` *value* | `diffuse` *value* |
    `specular` *value* | `roughness` *value* | `phong` *value* |
    `phong_size` *size* |
    `brilliance` *value* | `ior` *index_of_refraction* |
    `refraction` *amount* | `reflection` *amount*

DESCRIPTION
Textures consist of three basic types of parameters: color patterns, normal patterns, and finish parameters. The finish parameters are various values that control how light reflects off of or passes through the surface of an object.

    The `ambient` and `diffuse` keywords control the way the surface is illuminated by general lighting in the scene (ambient lighting) and direct light from light sources (diffuse lighting). When diffuse light strikes a surface at a shallow angle it causes less illumination. The amount that diffuse light is diminished at shallow angles is controlled by the `brilliance` keyword.

The phong keyword controls the brightness of a Phong highlight and the phong_size keyword controls the size of the highlight. You can specify an alternative type of highlight with the specular keyword and control the size of a specular highlight with the roughness keyword. Normally any Phong or specular highlight has the same color as the light source that causes it. The metallic keyword causes these highlights to be filtered by the surface color, making them appear more metallic.

The reflection keyword controls the amount of light reflected off very smooth finishes such as mirrors or polished surfaces.

The refraction keyword controls the amount of light that passes through a transparent surface, and the ior keyword specifies the index of refraction, the amount that a ray of light is bent when passing through a surface.

For complete details, see the reference entry for each of the keywords listed below.

One finish parameter that has no keyword associated with it is the color randomness value. It is used to add a rough or grainy look to a surface. A future version of POV-Ray will use the keyword crand for this value. (See the reference entry under *crand_value* for details.)

SEE ALSO

ambient, brilliance, *COLOR_PATTERN*, *crand_value*, diffuse, metallic, *NORMAL_PATTERN*, phong, phong_size, reflection, refraction, roughness, specular, texture

EXAMPLE

See examples for the keywords listed above.

FLOAT

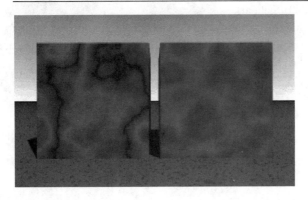

PURPOSE
Specifies a floating-point value.

SYNTAX
[SIGN] [DIGIT...] [POINT] DIGIT... [EXP [SIGN] DIGIT...] |
[SIGN] FLOAT_IDENTIFIER

DIGIT =
    0 | 1 | 2 | 3 | 4 | 5 | 6 | 7 | 8 | 9

EXP =
    e | E

SIGN =
    + | –

POINT =
    .

DESCRIPTION
Floating-point values are required many places in the language. In a syntax specification, any lowercase italic word, such as *red_amount,* is calling for a *FLOAT* to be given.

You can declare float identifiers. When you invoke a float identifier, you can add a plus or minus sign in front of it. Float literals can be specified in almost any format. For example: 1.0, 123.456, .5, 100, –123, +321, –1.234e-2. Note that a leading zero is not required. Integer values do not require a decimal point. Scientific notation in "e" format may be used, as shown above.

Any parameters that use integer values will accept a float value and will ignore the fractional part.

When a float value appears in a texture statement without an associated keyword it is used to specify a color randomness value to produce a grainy appearance. See the reference entry for *crand_value* for details.

SEE ALSO
crand_value, declare, *VECTOR*

EXAMPLE

```
// FLOAT.POV
#include "examp.inc" camera {location <0 0 -5>}

// Declare and use a float identifier
#declare Offset = 1.1

object {
  box{UnitBox} texture {White_Marble}
  translate <-Offset 0 0>  // offset left
}

object {
  box{UnitBox} texture {PinkAlabaster}
  translate <Offset 0 0>  // offset right
}
```

fog

TYPE
SCENE_ITEM

PURPOSE
Adds a colored fog effect to a scene.

SYNTAX
fog { *[COLOR] [distance_factor]* }

DESCRIPTION

You may add a fog effect to a scene by adding a `fog` statement anywhere between scene items. The effect applies to the entire scene. The effect is created by adding the fog color to the color of an object. The ratio of fog color to object color is

$$1 - e^{\left[\frac{-object\_distance}{fog\_distance}\right]}$$

When the distance to an object is equal to the fog distance factor, 63% of the color comes from the object and 37% comes from the fog color. A distance setting of 0.0 turns off the fog effect.

SEE ALSO

`color`

EXAMPLE

```
// FOG.POV
#include "examp.inc"

#declare Ball=
  object {sphere {<0 0 0> 1} texture{color Red}}

// Place objects at various distances
object{Ball translate <-3 0 2>}
object{Ball translate < 3 0 10>}
object{Ball translate <-3 0 20>}
object{Ball translate < 3 0 30>}
object{Ball translate <-3 0 40>}
object{Ball translate < 3 0 50>}
object{Ball translate <-3 0 60>}

// Add fog that is 80% gray
fog {color Gray80 40}
```

frequency

TYPE
NORMAL_PATTERN_MODIFIER

PURPOSE
Adjusts the spacing between waves or ripples in textures.

SYNTAX
`texture { frequency` *amount [TEXTURE_ITEM...]* `}`

DESCRIPTION
The `frequency` keyword lets you specify the amount of space between features when the texture normal perturbations `waves` or `ripples` are used. This keyword has no effect except when `waves` or `ripples` are used. The default value is `frequency` 1.0. If no scaling is used, this creates waves or ripples about one unit apart. Larger frequency values generate waves closer together and smaller values generate more widely spaced features.

SEE ALSO
NORMAL_PATTERN, `phase`, `ripples`, `texture`, `waves`

EXAMPLE
```
// FREQUENC.POV
#include "examp.inc"

object {
  box{UnitBox translate <-1 0 1>}
```

```
  texture {
    waves 0.2
    color Cyan phong 0.7 scale <.04 .04 .04>
    frequency 1.0  // default value
  }
}

object {
  box{UnitBox translate <1 0 1>}
  texture {
    waves 0.2
    color Cyan phong 0.7 scale <.04 .04 .04>
    frequency 2.0      // twice the frequency
                       // half the wavelength
  }
}
```

gif

TYPE
MAP_FILE_TYPE or *HT_FIELD_TYPE*

PURPOSE
Specifies a GIF file in an image map, bump map, material map, or Height-Field.

SYNTAX
gif *"FILESPEC"*

DESCRIPTION
POV-Ray uses files made of arrays of pixels for patterns in image maps, bump maps, and material maps as well as Height-Field shapes. The gif keyword specifies that a Graphic Interchange Format (GIF) file is to be used.

You specify a file type using the gif keyword followed by the file specification in quotes. If the file is not found in the current directory, library paths specified with the +L command-line switch are also searched. For complete details see the items listed below.

SEE ALSO
bump_map, dump, height_field, iff, image_map, material_map, pot, tga

EXAMPLE

See examples for `height_field,` `bump_map,` or `material_map.`

gradient

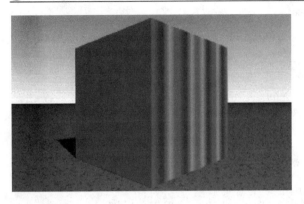

TYPE

COLOR_PATTERN

PURPOSE

Specifies a gradient color pattern in a texture.

SYNTAX

```
texture {
  gradient <orientation> COLOR_MAP
  [COLOR_PATTERN_MODIFIER...] [TEXTURE_ITEM...]
}
```

DESCRIPTION

The `gradient` keyword specifies a color pattern that generates parallel layers of color that blend into each other in a direction specified by an orientation vector. The *<orientation>* vector after the keyword points in the direction that the layers blend. For example, a value of `gradient <1 0 0>` blends layers along the *x* axis with layers in the *y-z* plane. The gradient pattern repeats the color map colors from 0.0 to 1.0 and then starts over at 0.0. The marble color pattern is similar except it blends from 0.0 to 1.0 back to 0.0 repeatedly.

You can use the turbulence and octaves keywords to stir up the pattern. Use a color_map statement with this pattern because a default color map is not provided. Color patterns can be translated, rotated, or scaled. Only one color pattern may be specified in each texture statement.

SEE ALSO

color_map, *COLOR_PATTERN*, marble, octaves, texture, turbulence

EXAMPLE

```
// GRADIENT.POV
#include "examp.inc"

object {
  box {UnitBox}
  texture {
   gradient <1 0 0> //colors blend along x axis
   color_map {
     [0.0 0.3 color Cyan    color Yellow]
     [0.3 0.6 color Yellow  color Magenta]
     [0.6 1.0 color Magenta color Cyan]
   }
  scale <0.5 0.5 0.5> ambient 0.3
  }
  rotate <0 -45 0> translate <0 0 1>
}
```

granite

TYPE
COLOR_PATTERN

PURPOSE
Specifies a granite color pattern in a texture.

SYNTAX
```
texture { granite [COLOR_PATTERN_MODIFIER...]
    [TEXTURE_ITEM...] }
```

DESCRIPTION
The `granite` keyword specifies a color pattern that uses a noise function to simulate the look of real granite.

You can use the `turbulence` and `octaves` keywords to stir up the pattern. A default color map is provided but normally you would add a `color_map` of your own. Color patterns may be translated, rotated, or scaled. Only one color pattern may be specified in each `texture` statement.

SEE ALSO
`color_map`, *COLOR_PATTERN*, `marble`, `octaves`, `texture`, `turbulence`

EXAMPLE
```
// GRANITE.POV
#include "examp.inc"
object {
  sphere { <0 0 0> 1 }
  texture {
    granite
    color_map {
      [0.0 0.8  color red 0.9 green 0.9 blue 0.9
                color red 0.7 green 0.5 blue 0.5]
      [0.8 1    color red 0.7 green 0.5 blue 0.5
                color red 0.2 green 0.2 blue 0.3]
    }
  }
}
```

green

TYPE
COLOR_COMPONENT

PURPOSE
Specifies the green component of a color.

SYNTAX
green *green_amount*

DESCRIPTION
All colors in POV-Ray consist of red, blue, green, and alpha components. By using various combinations of red, blue, and green, nearly any color can be specified. The green keyword is used to specify the amount of green color. The alpha part of a color specification describes the degree of transparency a given color has.

The float value after the keyword can range from 0.0 (no green) to 1.0 (full intensity green). If no value is given for a component then the default is 0.

SEE ALSO
alpha, blue, color, red

EXAMPLE
```
// GREEN.POV
#include "examp.inc"
```

```
object {
  sphere { <0 0 0> 1 }
  texture {
    checker
      color green 1.0        // This check is pure green.
      color blue 0.5 green 0.8   // This one is bluish green
    scale <0.5 0.5 0.5>
  }
}
```

height_field

TYPE
SHAPE

PURPOSE
Specifies a Height-Field shape in an object. An image file is used to define the
height of each point on the upper surface, creating terrain effects.

SYNTAX
`height_field` { *HT_FIELD_IDENTIFIER [HT_FIELD_MODIFIER...]*} |
`height_field` { *HT_FIELD_TYPE "FILESPEC"*
    [HT_FIELD_MODIFIER...] }

HT_FIELD_TYPE =
    `gif` | `pot` | `tga`

HT_FIELD_MODIFIER =
    SHAPE_MODIFIER | `water_level` *amount*

DESCRIPTION
The `height_field` keyword specifies a shape that uses an image file to define
the height of its top surface. The shape usually looks like mountains growing
out of a box shape. The shape fits entirely within a built-in bounding box whose
corners are <0 0 0> and <1 1 1>. This size makes it especially easy to use with
image map or material map color patterns and textures. The rows and columns
of pixels in the file correspond to the x and z axes respectively. The value of the

pixel determines the *y* coordinate of the shape at that (*x,z*) location. Two triangles are generated for each pixel. This mesh of triangles defines the shape.

When you use a GIF type file, the pixel index determines the height at that location. This is an 8-bit value. When a POT continuous potential file is used, 16 bits of resolution are available for the height. Similarly a TGA Targa file may be used to create 16 bits of height resolution. With TGA files, the red component of the pixel supplies the high-order 8 bits, the green component supplies the low-order 8 bits, and the blue component is discarded. Note that DUMP and IFF files are not supported. Regardless of file type or size in pixels, POV-Ray automatically scales the shape to fit within the 1-unit box, which can be translated, rotated, or scaled, as needed.

To use the `water_level` keyword, you follow it by a value from 0.0 to 256.0. All heights lower than this value are clipped away. The default value is 0.

Currently POV-Ray does not implement all of the calculations necessary to use Height-Field shapes in CSG intersection or CSG difference shapes or with `clipped_by` statements.

SEE ALSO

box, `clipped_by`, gif, `image_map`, object, pot, *SHAPE*, tga, `water_level`

EXAMPLE

```
// HFIELD.POV
#include "examp.inc"

object {
  height_field {
    gif "plasma2.gif"
//  gif "bumpmap_.gif" //Try these files too
//  gif "fract003.gif"
  }
  texture {color Green phong 0.3}
  translate <-.5 -.5 -.5>
  scale <3 0.4 3>
  rotate <-20 -40 0>
}
```

iff

TYPE
MAP_FILE_TYPE

PURPOSE
Specifies an IFF file in an image map, bump map, or material map.

SYNTAX
i f f *"FILESPEC"*

DESCRIPTION
POV-Ray uses files made of arrays of pixels for patterns in image maps, bump maps, and material maps. The i f f keyword specifies that an Amiga IFF file is to be used.

You specify a file type using the i f f keyword followed by the file specification in quotes. If the file is not found in the current directory, library paths specified with the +L command line are also searched. For complete details see the maps listed below. Note that Height-Field shapes cannot use i f f files.

SEE ALSO
bump_map, dump, gif, image_map, material_map, tga

EXAMPLE
See the example under image_map.

image_map

TYPE
COLOR_PATTERN

PURPOSE
Specifies a map file for a color pattern in a texture.

SYNTAX
```
texture {
    image_map {
```
MAP_PREFIX...] MAP_FILE_TYPE "FILESPEC"
[IMAGE_MAP_MODIFIER...]
```
    }
```
[TEXTURE_ITEM...]
```
}
```

MAP_PREFIX =
> *map_type* | *<orientation_vector>*

MAP_FILE_TYPE =
> `iff` | `gif` | `dump` | `tga`

IMAGE_MAP_MODIFIER =
> `once` | `interpolate` *type* | `map_type` *type* |
> `alpha all` *alpha_amount* | `alpha` *index alpha_amount*

DESCRIPTION
Use an `image_map` keyword to specify a color pattern that projects an image file onto an object. The file is an image of pixels in IFF, GIF, TGA, or DUMP format.

A float value may be given at the start of the statement to specify the *map_type* but this usage is outdated. Use the `map_type` keyword instead.

By default, the file will be mapped onto a square area of the *x,y* plane from 0,0 to 1,1. The `texture` statement may use the `translate`, `rotate`, or `scale` keywords to adjust the position of the map. You can also use an optional *<orientation_vector>* to change the orientation. One component of the vector must be positive; it specifies which of the three positive axes is used

for the width of the map. Another component of the vector must be negative; it specifies which of the three positive axes is used for the height. Note that the positive axis is always used. The sign only specifies a plus for width and a minus for height. The remaining component must be zero. For example, <0 1 -1> means that the file is mapped with the width along the positive *y* axis because the *y* component is positive. The height is along the positive *z* axis because the *z* component is negative.

You must specify a file type using `iff`, `gif`, `tga`, or `dump` keywords followed by the file specification in quotes. If the file is not found in the current directory, library paths specified with the +L command-line switch are also searched. You can follow the file specification with a number of options.

Because the supported image types do not allow for an alpha transparency value in the palette, you can use the `alpha` keyword to add transparency to any or all colors in the image. When you use `alpha all` *alpha_amount*, all colors will have the given amount of transparency. Values from 0.0 (no transparency) to 1.0 (fully transparent) may be used. Note that the red, green, and blue components of a color remain the same even when alpha is added. Thus the light passing through is filtered by the pixel color. Black pixels transmit no light regardless of the alpha value applied.

Individual colors may have various alpha components added by using the form `alpha` *index alpha_amount* for each transparent color. The *index* value is the index into the file's palette. Values range from 0 to 255. You may need a paint program or another utility to determine the proper value.

If the `image_map` is too small to cover the entire object, it is repeated over and over like tiles. The `once` keyword turns this feature off so that the image appears only once. Any area not covered by the image is rendered clear unless another texture layer is provided underneath.

A smoother look can be obtained by adding the `interpolate` keyword. The value after the keyword may be either 0 for no interpolation, 2 for bilinear interpolation, or 4 for normalized distribution.

An image map is a two-dimensional feature that must be applied to a three-dimensional object. The `map_type` keyword can be used to define how the map is wrapped around the object. The default is 0 for planar mapping. Use 1 for spherical, 2 for cylindrical, and 5 for torus. Types 3 and 4 are under development. (See `map_type` for further details.)

Unlike other color pattern types, the `turbulence` and `octaves` keywords do not apply to image maps. A `color_map` is not used with `image_map` because the color comes from the file. Color patterns may be

translated, rotated, or scaled. Only one color pattern may be specified in each `texture` statement.

SEE ALSO

all, alpha, *COLOR_PATTERN*, interpolate, map_type, once, texture

EXAMPLE

```
// IMAGEMAP.POV
#include "examp.inc"

object {
  sphere { <0 0 0> 1}
  texture {
    image_map{
      gif "bumpmap_.gif"
      map_type 0       // planar
      interpolate 4    // normalized distribution
    }
    translate <-0.5 -0.5 0> // center image
  }
}
```

include

TYPE
LANGUAGE_DIRECTIVE

PURPOSE

Causes the POV-Ray language parser to copy another file into the input stream.

SYNTAX

`#include` *"FILESPEC"*

DESCRIPTION

The input file may contain one or more `#include` directives that reference other text files containing POV-Ray statements. It is standard practice to give these files the extension .INC. POV-Ray has a number of standard include files, such as SHAPES.INC and TEXTURES.INC, that contain `#declare` directives for commonly used shapes and textures. POV-Ray begins parsing your input file at the first line and continues processing it line-by-line to the end. You can put an `#include` directive anywhere in the file between tokens.

POV-Ray remembers where it is in the current file and begins processing text from the FILE.INC file as if its contents had been copied into the main file at that point. When POV-Ray has finished processing the include file, it picks up where it paused and processes the remainder of the earlier file. You may nest `#include` directives ten levels deep. There is no restriction on the number of un-nested include files you can use.

SEE ALSO

+I, +L switches, `declare`

EXAMPLE

```
// INCLUDE.POV
#include "examp.inc"

// File "stones.inc" contains #declare for
// the texture Stone12

#include "stones.inc"

object {
  sphere { <0 0 0> 1 }
  texture { Stone12 scale <0.6 0.6 0.6>}
}
```

interpolate

TYPE

BUMP_MAP_MODIFIER or *IMAGE_MAP_MODIFIER* or
MATERIAL_MAP_MODIFIER

PURPOSE

Smoothes the pixels in a bump map, image map, or material map.

SYNTAX

`interpolate` *value*

DESCRIPTION

When bump maps, image maps, or material maps are viewed extremely close
up, individual pixels can appear chunky. Adding the `interpolate` keyword
can give a smoother look. The value after the keyword may be either 0 for no
interpolation, 2 for bilinear interpolation, or 4 for normalized distribution.
The bilinear method produces smoother results but is slower than normalized
distribution.

SEE ALSO

`bump_map`, `image_map`, `material_map`

EXAMPLE

```
// INTERPOL.POV
#include "examp.inc" camera{location <0 0 -5>}
```

```
object {
  box {UnitBox}
  texture {
    image_map{ gif "rough.gif"
      interpolate 0   // none
    }
    ambient 0.3
    scale <2 2 2> translate <-1 -1 0>
  }
  translate <-1 0 0>
}

object {
  box {UnitBox}
  texture {
    image_map{gif "rough.gif"
      interpolate 4   // normalized distribution
    }
    ambient 0.3
    scale <2 2 2> translate <-1 -1 0>
  }
  translate <1 0 0>
}
```

intersection

TYPE
SHAPE

PURPOSE
Creates a constructive solid geometry shape that is the intersection of other shapes.

SYNTAX

intersection { *INTERSECTION_IDENTIFIER [CSG_MODIFIER...] }* |
intersection { *SHAPE... [CSG_MODIFIER...]* |

CSG_MODIFIER =
    TRANSFORMATION | inverse

DESCRIPTION

The intersection keyword is used to define an intersection constructive solid geometry (CSG) shape: a shape made from two or more shapes. The intersection shape consists of all points that are inside all of the component shapes.

The intersection shape requires component shapes that have a well-defined inside and outside. Thus triangle, smooth triangle, and bicubic patch shapes cannot be used, and Height-Field shapes do not always work well with intersection.

The CSG difference is another kind of CSG intersection shape that allows you to cut away parts of a master shape. See the difference keyword for details.

Like all CSG shapes, intersection can only operate on other shapes; it cannot operate on objects. It cannot use texture or quick-render color specifications as a shape modifier. Only translate, rotate, scale, or inverse keywords may be used.

SEE ALSO

CSG_SHAPE, clipped_by, difference, inverse, object, *SHAPE*

EXAMPLE

```
// INTERSEC.POV
#include "examp.inc"

// Compare with union, clipped_by and
//  difference examples.

object {
  intersection {       // Start with sphere keep
    sphere {<0 0 0> 1} // only parts inside box.
    box {<-0.8 -0.8 -0.8> <0.8 0.8 0.8>}
  }
  texture { color White phong 1}
  rotate <0 50 0>
}
```

inverse

TYPE
SHAPE_MODIFIER

PURPOSE
Reverses the definition of inside and outside for a shape when used as part of a CSG shape.

SYNTAX
`inverse`

DESCRIPTION
The `inverse` keyword reverses the "inside" and "outside" of a shape. While it is often helpful to think of POV-Ray shapes as solid and we speak of constructive solid geometry (CSG), in fact all POV-Ray shapes are hollow surfaces. All shapes that divide space into two or more volumes have an inside and outside defined.

The inside/outside distinction is only important when using a shape in an `intersection`, `difference`, or `clipped_by` statement. The definitions of `intersection`, `difference`, and `clipped_by`, refer to the inside or outside of the shapes involved. Often, in order to get the desired effect from these CSG operations, you need to reverse the inside/outside status. When applying `clipped_by` to an object, for example, the definition says that all parts of the object "inside" the clipping shape are retained and all parts "outside" the clipping shape are discarded. If you want to keep the discarded part and discard the rest, you must reverse what is considered inside or outside by applying the inverse keyword to the clipping shape.

When a shape is not part of a CSG shape, the inside or outside status is insignificant. For example, a single sphere rendered with or without the inverse keyword will look exactly the same. Also note that to place the camera inside a shape you do not need to use inverse to hollow it out.

The inverse keyword has no effect on triangle, smooth triangle, bicubic patch, or Height-Field shapes.

SEE ALSO

clipped_by, composite, difference, intersection, object, *SHAPE*

EXAMPLE

```
// INVERSE.POV
#include "examp.inc"

// Note that the inverse on the box shape makes this
// identical to the difference example.
//
// Compare with union, intersection, inverse and
// clipped_by examples.  Keep parts inside box and
// not inside sphere.

object {
  intersection {
    box {<-0.8 -0.8 -0.8> <0.8 0.8 0.8>}
    sphere {<0 0 0> 1 inverse}
  }
  texture { color White phong 1}
  rotate <0 50 0>
}
```

ior

TYPE
FINISH_PARAMETER

PURPOSE
Specifies the index of refraction, the bending of light when it passes through a surface, for a transparent object. The `ior` value controls the amount a ray is bent.

SYNTAX
`texture { ior` *index_of_refraction [TEXTURE_ITEM...]* `}`

DESCRIPTION
When passing through a transparent surface between two substances of different density (such as air and glass), if a light ray strikes the surface at an angle, it is bent, or "refracted." The amount of bending depends on the density of the substances and the angle at which the ray of light hits the surface between them. Physicists assign an "index of refraction" value to substances of various densities to describe how much they refract light.

The `ior` keyword specifies the index of refraction in a texture. The `refraction` keyword specifies the amount of refracted light while the `ior` keyword specifies the amount the refracted light is bent. The default `ior` amount is 1.0, which means no bending. The default refraction is 0.0, which means no refraction. The standard POV-Ray include file IOR.INC contains index of refraction values for various substances. Note that this keyword has no

effect when the refraction value is 0.0 or if there is no alpha specified in the color to make it transparent.

SEE ALSO

alpha, refraction, texture

EXAMPLE

```
// IOR.POV
#include "examp.inc"
camera{location <0 0.2 -5> look_at<0 0 0>}

#declare Lens=  // build a lens shape
  intersection {
    quadric {Ellipsoid translate <0 0  0.6>}
    quadric {Ellipsoid translate <0 0 -0.6>}
    scale <1 1 0.2>
  }

object { // add a better background
  box{UnitBox scale <8 1 0.1>}
  texture {
    checker color Red color White
    scale <0.2 0.2 1>
  }
  translate <0 -1 2>
}

object {
  intersection {Lens translate <-2 0 0> }
  texture {color White alpha 0.9 phong 0.8
  refraction 1  ior 1.0 //default
  }
}

object {
  intersection {Lens translate <0 0 0> }
  texture {color White alpha 0.9 phong 0.8
  refraction 1  ior 1.33 // water
  }
}

object {
  intersection {Lens translate <2 0 0> }
  texture {color White alpha 0.9 phong 0.8
  refraction 1  ior 1.5  // glass
  }
}
```

leopard

TYPE
COLOR_PATTERN

PURPOSE
Specifies a leopard-spot color pattern in a texture.

SYNTAX
`texture { leopard` *[COLOR_PATTERN_MODIFIER...]*
   [TEXTURE_ITEM...] `}`

DESCRIPTION
The `leopard` color pattern creates a regular alternating array of spots that resemble leopard skin when appropriately colored. The `leopard` color pattern creates regularly spaced, distinct spots, and the `spotted` color pattern creates irregular, blended spots. The features are almost two units apart, so you should use small scaling values when applying this pattern to small shapes.

Mathematically the pattern is generated by the formula:

$$value = \left[\frac{\sin(x) + \sin(y) + \sin(z)}{3} \right]^2$$

where *x, y* and *z* are the 3D coordinates of the point on the surface of the object.

The `turbulence` and `octaves` keywords may be used to stir up the pattern. A default color map is provided, but normally you would add a color_map of your own. Color patterns may be translated, rotated, or scaled. Only one color pattern may be specified in each texture statement.

SEE ALSO

color_map, *COLOR_PATTERN*, octaves, texture, turbulence

EXAMPLE

```
// LEOPARD.POV
#include "examp.inc"

object {
  sphere {<0 0 0> 1}
  texture {
    leopard
    color_map {
      [0.0 0.3 color Yellow color Yellow]
      [0.3 0.8 color Yellow color Black]
      [0.8 1.0 color Black color Black]
    }
    scale <0.12 0.12 0.12>
  }
}
```

light_source

TYPE
SHAPE

PURPOSE

Specifies a source of diffuse light.

SYNTAX

```
light_source { LIGHT_SRC_IDENTIFIER
    [LIGHT_SRC_MODIFIER...] } |
light_source { <LOCATION> COLOR
    [LIGHT_SRC_MODIFIER...] }
```

LIGHT_SRC_MODIFIER =
    spotlight | point_at *<location>* |
    falloff *degrees* | radius *degrees* | tightness *value* |
    TRANSFORMATION | *COLOR*

DESCRIPTION

The light_source shape isn't really a shape at all. It is the way you specify a point light source in POV-Ray. It is implemented as a shape so that it can be part of a union or composite statement and therefore is easy to position along with other shapes.

The *<location>* vector gives the location of the point source. It must be followed by a color keyword and color specification that is the color of light that is emitted. For less intense light you should use darker colors or shades of gray.

If a light source shape is within the field of view of the camera, it will not be visible. To make a visible light you should combine it with another shape by using union or composite statements. If the light source is inside the other shape, the light may not be able to get out. See the no_shadow keyword on how to correct this problem.

A light source shape may be translated, rotated, and scaled. Note that because it is an infinitely small invisible point, the scaling only effects its position away from the origin.

Light normally diffuses outward equally in all directions from the source. However, the spotlight keyword can be used to create a cone of light that is bright in the center and falls off to darkness in a soft fringe effect at the edge. Although the cone of light fades to soft edges, objects illuminated by spotlights still cast hard shadows.

The point_at keyword tells the spotlight to point at a particular 3D coordinate. A line from the location of the spotlight to the point_at coordinate forms the center line of the cone of light. The falloff, radius, and tightness keywords control the way that light tapers off at the edges of the cone. These four keywords apply only when you use the spotlight keyword. (See the reference entry for spotlight for complete details.)

SEE ALSO

color, diffuse, falloff, no_shadow, object, point_at, radius, spotlight, tightness

EXAMPLE

```
/// Try these three examples separately.
// LIGHT1.POV
#include "examp.inc"

// EXAMPLE 1
// Note EXAMP.INC already contains
// object { light_source { <30 50 -50> color White } }
// now add another Orange source off to the left

object { light_source { <-30 30 -20> color Orange} }

// Something to light up
object {
  sphere {<0 0 0> 1}
  texture {color White specular 1 roughness 0.01}
}
/////////////////////////////
// LIGHT2.POV
#include "examp.inc"

// EXAMPLE 2
// Place a light source within the field of view.
// Light radiates from it but it remains invisible.
object {
  light_source { <0 0 0> color Orange}
  translate <-8 4 10>
}

// Something to light up
object {
  sphere {<1 0 0> 1}
  texture {color White specular 1 roughness 0.01}
}
//////////////////////////
// LIGHT3.POV
#include "examp.inc"
```

```
// EXAMPLE 3
// Create a union of sphere and light source
object {
  union {
    light_source { <0 0 0> color Orange}
    sphere {<0 0 0> 0.2}
  }
  no_shadow  // Make sure light can exit sphere
  texture {color Orange ambient 1 diffuse 0}
  translate <-8 4 10>
}
// Something to light up
object {
  sphere {<1 0 0> 1}
  texture {color White specular 1 roughness 0.01}
}
```

location

TYPE
CAMERA_ITEM

PURPOSE
Defines the camera location.

SYNTAX
camera { location *<vector>* *[CAMERA_ITEM...]* }

DESCRIPTION
The location keyword specifies a vector defining the location of the camera and thus the coordinate location from which the image is viewed. If a location

is not given, the default is location <0 0 0>. You can also use the trans-late, rotate, and scale keywords to modify the camera location. (For a complete discussion of the POV-Ray camera, see the camera keyword.)

SEE ALSO
camera

EXAMPLE

```
// LOCATION.POV
#include "examp.inc"

camera {
  location <0 4 -2> // try different values
  look_at <0 0 0>
}

object {
  sphere {<0 0 0> 1}
  texture {color SummerSky phong 1}
}
```

look_at

TYPE
CAMERA_ITEM

PURPOSE
Pans and tilts the camera to look at a specific point.

SYNTAX

```
camera { [CAMERA_ITEM...] look_at <vector>}
```

DESCRIPTION

Use the `look_at` keyword to pan and tilt the camera at a specific point.

The `location`, `direction`, `up`, and `right` vectors completely define the camera. Theoretically, that is all that is needed. However, it is very difficult to hand calculate the vectors for anything other than an orientation along an axis. The `up`, `right`, and `direction` vectors must be perpendicular to each other in order to avoid distortion. Typically, you would define a camera with the `direction`, `up`, and `right` vectors on an axis and then use `rotate` or `look_at` statements to turn the camera to the desired direction.

The `translate` and `rotate` keywords can be used to move the camera and point it, but this can still be difficult because rotations are always relative to the coordinate axis.

The `look_at` keyword can be used to point the camera more easily. You should specify the camera `location`, `up`, `right`, and `direction` keywords and vectors first. Then use `look_at` to define the 3D coordinates of the point you want to look at. POV-Ray pans the camera left or right until the view window lines up with the "look at" point. Then the camera tilts up or down until it is pointed directly at the proper point.

The `sky` keyword is used to define the way the camera is panned when a "look at" rotation is performed. During such rotations, the camera is first rotated so that the up vector matches the sky vector. The default value is `sky <0 1 0>`, so the camera generally is in this orientation. The `sky` vector then becomes the axis of rotation for the panning. The tilting part of a "look at" rotation is also done in line with the `sky` vector. If the "look at" point lies directly along the sky axis then it cannot pan left or right to line up with it and a blank image results. The `sky` keyword only effects the way subsequent `look_at` operations work. It has no other effect.

SEE ALSO

```
camera
```

EXAMPLE

```
// LOOKAT.POV
#include "examp.inc"
```

393

```
camera {
  location <0 0 -3>
  look_at <-1 0 0> // try different values
}
object {
  sphere {<0 0 0> 1}
  texture {color YellowGreen phong 1}
}
```

map_type

TYPE

BUMP_MAP_MODIFIER or *IMAGE_MAP_MODIFIER* or
    MATERIAL_MAP_MODIFIER

PURPOSE

Specifies a 2D to 3D map type in bump maps, image maps, and material maps.

SYNTAX

map_type *type*

DESCRIPTION

A bump map, image map, or material map is a two-dimensional feature that you apply to a three-dimensional object. The `map_type` keyword may be used to define how the map is wrapped around the object. The default for planar mapping is 0.

Planar mapping (type 0) projects the image flat onto the *x-y* plane from the -*z* to *z* direction. It covers the area of the *x,y* plane from (0,0) to (1,1) and passes straight through an object as if each pixel were a rod. The center of the image lies at (0.5, 0.5). The image can be translated, rotated, or scaled into any position from there.

Spherical mapping (type 1) assumes that a sphere is sitting at the origin. It stretches the image top to bottom to the poles at the +*y* and -*y* axis. The left edge of the image begins at the +*x* axis and wraps 360 degrees counterclockwise (completely around the sphere) when viewed from above—a -*y* rotation. The center of the image ends up with the -*x* axis sticking out.

Similarly, a cylindrical map (type 2) assumes that a cylinder sits at the origin along the *y* axis. The image is again wrapped from the +*x* axis 360 degrees counterclockwise. However, the image fits in a band between *x,z* planes at *y*=0 and *y*=1.

Finally toroidal mapping (type 5) presumes that a torus sits in the *x,z* plane with the *y* axis going through the hole. Like spherical mapping it wraps from +*x* counterclockwise back to +*x* with the center of the image at the -*x* axis. The top and bottom edges wrap around and meet each other inside the hole at the *x,z* plane. Toroidal mapping also assumes that the distance to the center of the ring cross-section is the *x* value of the map orientation vector. This allows you to fine tune the map for tori of various size.

Types 3 and 4 are under development.

The example below illustrates planar and spherical types. See the files MAPPER.POV & MAPR2.POV in the \POVRAY\SAMPLES\LEVEL1 directory for more examples.

SEE ALSO

```
bump_map, image_map, material_map
```

EXAMPLE

```
// MAPTYPE.POV
#include "examp.inc" camera {location <0 0 -4>}

// See MAPPER.POV & MAPPR2.POV for more map_type
// examples.
object {
  sphere {<0 0 0> 1}
  texture {
    image_map{gif "bumpmap_.gif"
      map_type 0 // planar
    }
    translate <-0.5 -0.5 0>
```

```
  }
  translate <-1 0 0>
}

object {
  sphere {<0 0 0> 1}
  texture {
    image_map{gif "bumpmap_.gif"
      map_type 1 // spherical
    }
  }
  translate <1 0 0>
}
```

marble

TYPE
COLOR_PATTERN

PURPOSE
Specifies a marble color pattern in a texture.

SYNTAX
`texture { marble` *[COLOR_PATTERN_MODIFIER...]*
    [TEXTURE_ITEM...] `}`

DESCRIPTION
The `marble` keyword generates a layered color pattern, similar to the `gradient` pattern, to simulate the look of real marble. The `gradient` pattern

repeats the color map colors from 0.0 to 1.0 and then starts over at 0.0. However, `marble` blends from 0.0 to 1.0 and back to 0.0 repeatedly.

You can use the `turbulence` and `octaves` keywords to stir up the pattern. A default color map is provided but normally you would add a `color_map` of your own. Color patterns may be translated, rotated, or scaled. Only one color pattern may be specified in each `texture` statement.

SEE ALSO

`color_map`, *COLOR_PATTERN*, `gradient`, `octaves`, `texture`, `turbulence`

EXAMPLE

```
// MARBLE.POV
#include "examp.inc"

object {
  sphere { <0 0 0> 1 }
  texture {
    marble turbulence 0.5
    color_map {
      [0.0 0.9  color red 0.9 green 0.9 blue 0.9
                color red 0.7 green 0.5 blue 0.5]
      [0.9 1    color red 0.7 green 0.5 blue 0.5
                color red 0.2 green 0.2 blue 0.3]
    }
    scale <0.5 0.5 0.5>
  }
}
```

material_map

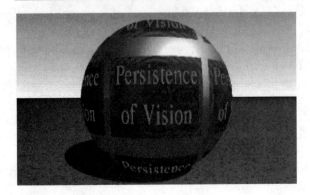

TYPE
SPECIAL_TEXTURE

PURPOSE
Specifies a map file for a pattern made up of multiple textures.

SYNTAX
```
texture {
 material_map {
    [MAP_PREFIX...] MAP_FILE_TYPE "FILESPEC"
    TEXTURE...
    [MATERIAL_MAP_MODIFIER...]
 }
}
```

MAP_PREFIX =
   map_type | *<orientation_vector>*

MAP_FILE_TYPE =
   `iff` | `gif` | `dump` | `tga`

MATERIAL_MAP_MODIFIER =
   `once` | `interpolate` *type* | `map_type` *type*

DESCRIPTION
A `material_map` statement in a texture uses an image file to define which of several textures will be projected onto an object. The file is an image of pixels in IFF, GIF, TGA, or DUMP format.

A float value may be given at the start of the statement to specify the *map_type* but this usage is outdated. Use the `map_type` keyword instead.

By default, the file will be mapped onto a square area of the *x,y* plane from 0,0 to 1,1. The `texture` statement may contain the `translate`, `rotate`, or `scale` keywords to adjust the position of the map.

You can use an *<orientation_vector>* to change the orientation. One component of the vector must be positive; it specifies which of the three positive axes is used for the width of the map. Another component of the vector must be negative; it specifies which of the three positive axes is used for the height. Note that the positive axis is always used. The sign only specifies a plus for

398

width and a minus for height. The remaining component must be zero. For example, <0 1 -1> means that the file is mapped with the width along the positive y axis because the y component is positive. The height is along the positive z axis because the z component is negative.

You must specify a file type using iff, gif, tga, or dump keywords followed by the file specification in quotes. If the file is not found in the current directory, library paths specified with the +L command-line switch are also searched.

After you give the file specification, you can add a number of options.

If the map is too small to cover the entire object, then it is repeated over and over like tiles. The once keyword turns this feature off so that the image only appears once. Any area not covered by the image is rendered clear unless another texture layer is provided underneath.

The interpolate keyword may be used with material maps, but it does not blend the colors. Instead it blends the indexes into the list of textures. This usually serves no useful purpose and may make the image look worse.

A material map is a two-dimensional feature that you apply to a three-dimensional object. The map_type keyword may be used to define how the map is wrapped around the object. The default for planar mapping is 0. Use 1 for spherical, 2 for cylindrical, and 5 for torus. Types 3 and 4 are under development. (See the map_type for details.)

Finally, you must specify a number of textures to be projected onto the shape. This list of textures is used like a "texture palette" rather than the usual color palette. For mapped file types, the index of the pixel is used as an index into the list of textures you supply. For unmapped files, the red component is used as an index. If the index is greater than the number of textures in your list, the index is taken modulo N where N is the number of textures in your list. If particular index values are not used in an image, it may be necessary to supply dummy textures. It may be necessary to use a paint program or other utility to examine the map file's palette to determine how to arrange the texture list.

A material map is called a "special texture" because no color patterns, normal perturbations, or finish modifiers have any effect on it. Translation, rotation, and scaling are the only texture items that you can apply. For example, the ambient keyword below has no effect, but the scale keyword does:

```
texture { material_map {....} ambient 0.5 scale <2 2 2>}
```

To actually apply the ambient keyword, you would have to place it inside each of the textures in the material map.

CREATIONS

SEE ALSO

interpolate, map_type, once, texture

EXAMPLE

```
// MATERIAL.POV
#include "examp.inc"

object {
  sphere { <0 0 0> 1}
  texture {
    material_map{<1 -1 0>
      gif "povmap.gif"
      texture {DMFWood4}
      texture {Chrome_Metal}
      texture {Luminous color NeonPink}
      texture {Jade}
    }
    translate <-0.5 -0.5 0> // center image
  }
}
```

max_trace_level

TYPE
LANGUAGE_DIRECTIVE

PURPOSE
Specifies how many nested levels deep reflected and transparent rays are traced.

SYNTAX

`#max_trace_level` *value*

DESCRIPTION

POV-Ray is capable of creating such spectacular photo-realistic effects because it traces not only rays from objects to the camera but also shadow rays, reflected rays, and transmitted rays in transparent textures. In a scene with many reflective or transparent surfaces the number of rays recursively traced can be enormous. See Chapter 1 for a discussion of these types of rays. The `#max_trace_level` directive lets you set the number of nested levels deep that POV-Ray traces. The default value is 5. Higher values produce more realistic tracings but this will slow things considerably. High trace levels can also cause a machine lockup from running out of memory during recursive function calls.

Note that setting this value affects all objects, regardless of where you put the directive. You cannot specify one value for some objects and another value for other objects. When multiple directives are given, only the last one counts.

SEE ALSO

`alpha`, `reflection`

EXAMPLE

```
// MAXTRACE.POV
#include "examp.inc"

// Four nested transparent spheres
// Try levels from 2 through 9

#max_trace_level 5 // default

#declare Ball=
 object {
   sphere {<0 0 0> 1}
   texture {color White alpha 0.8}
 }

object {Ball}
object {Ball scale <0.75 0.75 0.75>}
object {Ball scale <0.5  0.5  0.5>}
object {Ball scale <0.25 0.25 0.25>}
```

metallic

TYPE
FINISH_PARAMETER

PURPOSE
Causes a specular or Phong highlight to take on the color of the object's surface, giving objects a metallic look.

SYNTAX
`texture { metallic [TEXTURE_ITEM...] }`

DESCRIPTION
Normally, a specular or Phong highlight is the color of the light from the light source. By adding the `metallic` keyword you tell POV-Ray to filter the highlight color with the color of the texture. This causes the shape to look more metallic. The `metallic` keyword has no effect unless the `specular` or `phong` keywords are used with it.

SEE ALSO
FINISH_PARAMETER, `light_source`, `roughness`, `specular`, `phong`, `phong_size`

EXAMPLE
```
// METALLIC.POV
#include "examp.inc" camera {location <0 0 -4>}

object {
```

```
  sphere {<0 0 0> 1}
  texture {
    color Gold phong 1
// no metallic here
  }
  translate <-1 0 0>
}

object {
  sphere {<0 0 0> 1}
  texture {
    color Gold phong 1
    metallic
    }
  translate <1 0 0>
}
```

NORMAL_PATTERN

TYPE
TEXTURE_ITEM

PURPOSE
Specifies the pattern of a surface normal perturbation in a texture. Such patterns artificially modify the surface so that lighting, reflections, refractions, and highlights look as though the surface were bumped or embossed.

SYNTAX
texture {
   NORMAL_PATTERN [NORMAL_PATTERN_MODIFIER...]
   [TEXTURE_ITEM...]
}

NORMAL_PATTERN =
   bumps *amount* | dents *amount* | ripples *amount* |
   waves *amount* | wrinkles *amount* |
   bump_map {
      [MAP_PREFIX...] MAP_FILE_TYPE "FILESPEC"
      [BUMP_MAP_MODIFIER...]
   }

NORMAL_PATTERN_MODIFIER =

phase *amount* | frequency *amount*

DESCRIPTION

Textures consist of three basic parameters: color patterns, normal patterns, and finish parameters. Every point on a surface has a *surface normal vector* associated with it. Sometimes called a *surface normal*, or just *normal* for short, this vector is perpendicular to the surface at that point. Figure 7-4 illustrates some shapes and the surface normal vectors at various points. Every point on every surface has a surface normal vector.

Surface normals are important in ray tracing because reflection, refraction, Phong, specular, and diffuse lighting are affected by the angle between a ray of light and the surface normal at the point where the ray hits the surface. These reflection and lighting effects are critical to the way we perceive an image and an object's shape based on these visual clues.

Generally, when you look at the surface of a pool of water, you cannot see ripples on the surface unless the light reflecting off of the ripples makes them

Figure 7-4   Some Examples of Surface Normals

perceptible. The distorted reflections, highlights, and refractions tell you that the surface is not perfectly smooth.

It would be extremely difficult to create a bumpy or dented or rippled surface using the primitive shapes supported by POV-Ray or other ray tracers. It is much easier to simulate these features, however, by artificially modifying (perturbing) the surface normal vector in the proper pattern. Ray tracers use a surface normal perturbation pattern ("normal pattern" for short) to achieve such effects. When rays interact with such a modified surface, the effects that depend on the surface normal (highlights, reflection, etc.) make the surface appear bumpy even though the shape of the surface has not actually changed.

POV-Ray defines five surface normal perturbation patterns: `bumps`, `dents`, `ripples`, `waves`, and `wrinkles`. You can also use an image file as a `bump_map` to define normal patterns. Rather than mapping the colors onto the object as with an image map, a `bump_map` uses the pixels to define how the surface normal is perturbed.

The `frequency` and `phase` keywords modify the spacing and position of the features in a `ripples` or `waves` normal pattern.

Normal patterns may be translated, rotated, or scaled. Only one normal pattern may be specified in each `texture` statement.

(For complete details see each of the keywords listed below.)

SEE ALSO
`bumps`, `bump_map`, *COLOR_PATTERN*, `dents`, *FINISH_PARAMETER*, `frequency`, `phase`, `ripples`, `texture`, `waves`, `wrinkles`

EXAMPLE
(See examples for the keywords listed above.)

no_shadow

TYPE
OBJECT_MODIFIER

PURPOSE
Causes an object to cast no shadow.

SYNTAX
`object {` *SHAPE* `no_shadow` *[OBJECT_MODIFIER...]* `}`

DESCRIPTION
Unless an object has a fully transparent texture it will normally cast a shadow. Shadows block diffuse light from light sources and leave ambient light (or diffuse light from other sources) as the only illumination. Adding the `no_shadow` keyword to an object makes POV-Ray ignore the object when testing for blocked diffuse light.

You need this feature for at least two scenarios. The most common use is with light source shapes. If a light source shape is within the field of view of the camera, it will not be visible. To make a light visible, you should union it with a companion shape. If the light source shape is inside its companion shape, the light may not be able to get out. The companion shape effectively puts everything in shadow. To prevent the light from being trapped inside, you must add the `no_shadow` keyword to the object that contains the union of the light source and the companion shape.

Note: The `no_shadow` keyword does *not* mean that the light from the source will pass through any object. It means that light will pass through the companion shape only. The example below is meant to illustrate the `no_shadow` effect only. See LIGHT2.POV and LIGHT3.POV in the reference entry for `light_source` for examples of the `no_shadow` keyword with light sources.

The other time you can use the `no_shadow` keyword is when simulating beams of light. You might use a ruby red cylinder to simulate a laser beam, for example. Yet the beam should not cast a shadow on other surfaces. Adding `no_shadow` to the cylinder will fix this.

The `no_shadow` keyword can only be applied to objects; it cannot be used in shapes or composites.

SEE ALSO

`ambient`, `diffuse`, `light_source`, `object`

EXAMPLE

```
// NOSHADOW.POV
#include "examp.inc"

// This sphere casts a shadow on the ground
// and on the sphere behind it.
object {
  sphere {<1.25 0 0> 1}
  texture {color White}
}
// This sphere does not cast a shadow but
// shadows can be cast upon it.
object {
  sphere {<0 0 2.25> 1}
  texture {color White}
  no_shadow
}
```

object

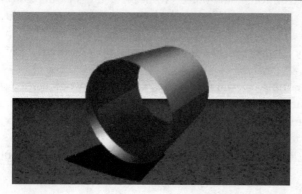

TYPE
SCENE_ITEM

PURPOSE
Specifies the shape, texture, bounding, and clipping shapes of an object.

SYNTAX
object { *OBJECT_IDENTIFIER [OBJECT_MODIFIER...]* } |
object { *SHAPE [OBJECT_MODIFIER...]* }

OBJECT_MODIFIER =
    SHAPE_MODIFIER | no_shadow |
    CLIPPED_BY | *BOUNDED_BY*

DESCRIPTION
The object statement puts together a shape with a texture, quick-render color, bounding shapes, and clipping shapes. You can specify only one shape per object but that shape can be a CSG shape made of other shapes. An object statement may contain translate, rotate, scale, or inverse keywords—as with a shape. You can also attach bounded_by or clipped_by statements. And the no_shadow keyword can be used. (For details on all of these options see their respective reference entries.)

    The example below uses most of the modifiers available for object statements. Note that the scale <0.6 0.6 0.6> applies to the shape, texture, and clipping shape, but not to the bounding shape because the `bounded_by` statement comes after the `scale` vector. The two `rotate` vectors apply to the entire object and all of its parts.

SEE ALSO

`bounded_by`, `clipped_by`, `color`, `inverse`, `no_shadow`, `rotate`, `scale`, *SHAPE*, `texture`, `translate`

EXAMPLE

```
// OBJECT.POV
#include "examp.inc"

object {
  quadric {Cylinder_X}       // shape
  texture {Chrome_Metal}     // texture
  color Red                  // quick-render color
  clipped_by {box{UnitBox}}  // clip
  scale <0.6 0.6 0.6>        // transformation
  bounded_by
    {sphere{<0 0 0> 1}}      // bound
  rotate <  0 -60 0>         // more transformations
  rotate <-20   0 0>
}
```

octaves

TYPE
COLOR_PATTERN_MODIFIER

PURPOSE

Controls the jaggedness of the turbulence applied to a pattern.

SYNTAX

```
texture {
   COLOR_PATTERN turbulence amount octaves number
   [TEXTURE_ITEM...]
}
```

DESCRIPTION

When POV-Ray computes turbulence to apply to a pattern it "stirs" the pattern in broad amounts and then "stirs" it again in successively smaller amounts with each step using details that are half as large as the previous step. Use the octaves keyword to specify how many of the successively finer calculations should be used in various noise functions. Low values give very smooth wavy turbulence while higher values give a more jagged look. The default value for octaves is 6. Higher values take longer to compute and lower values give faster results. The extra detail created by high octave settings may be unnoticible and thus unnecessary on small or distant objects.

The octaves keyword has no effect unless you include turbulence. Note, however, that the agate pattern has built-in turbulence, so octaves affects it despite the lack of a turbulence keyword. Neither the turbulence nor octaves keywords affects image maps, tiles, or material maps.

SEE ALSO

COLOR_PATTERN, texture, turbulence

EXAMPLE

```
// OCTAVES.POV
#include "examp.inc"  camera{location <0 0 -5>}

#default   // set up a default texture
 {texture{
   White_Marble rotate <0 0 90>
   turbulence 0.5 ambient 0.25
  }
 }

// Try different octaves values
object {sphere { <-2 0 0> 1 }
```

```
    texture {octaves 2}   // gentle turbulence
}

object {sphere { <0 0 0> 1 }
  texture {octaves 4}   // more jagged
}

object {sphere { <2 0 0> 1 }
  texture {octaves 6} //default very jagged
}
```

once

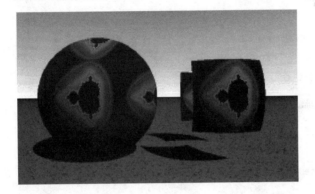

TYPE
IMAGE_MAP_MODIFIER or *BUMP_MAP_MODIFIER* or
MATERIAL_MAP_MODIFIER

PURPOSE
Suppresses repetition of image, bump, or material maps.

SYNTAX
```
image_map {
    [MAP_PREFIX...] MAP_FILE_TYPE "FILESPEC"
    once
    [IMAGE_MAP_MODIFIER...]
}
```
(or similarly for `bump_map` or `material_map`)

DESCRIPTION

By default, an image, bump, or material map that is too small to cover the
entire object is tiled or repeated over and over. The `once` keyword turns this
feature off so that the map only appears once. Any area not covered by the map
in an image map or material map is rendered clear unless another texture layer
is provided underneath.

SEE ALSO

`bump_map`, `image_map`, `material_map`

EXAMPLE

```
// ONCE.POV
#include "examp.inc"  camera{location <0 0 -4>}

object {
  sphere {<0 0 0> 1}
  texture {
    image_map{gif "bumpmap_.gif"
// not once but repeated over and over
    }
    translate <-0.5 -0.5 0>
  }
  translate <-1 0 0>
}


// Un-comment blue texture layer underneath to
// fill in missing areas.
object {
  sphere {<0 0 0> 1}
// texture {color blue 0.7}
  texture {
    image_map{gif "bumpmap_.gif"
      once
    }
    translate <-0.5 -0.5 0>
  }
  translate <1 0 0>
}
```

412

onion

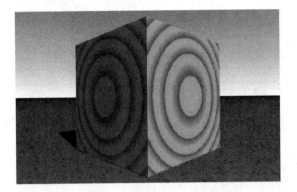

TYPE
COLOR_PATTERN

PURPOSE
Specifies a color pattern in a texture consisting of concentric spheres that resemble a sliced onion.

SYNTAX
`texture {` `onion` *[COLOR_PATTERN_MODIFIER...]*
[TEXTURE_ITEM...] `}`

DESCRIPTION
The `onion` keyword specifies a color pattern made of concentric spheres like the layers of an onion. The layers are 1 unit apart, so you should use small scaling values when applying this pattern to small shapes.

Mathematically, the pattern is generated by the formula

$$value = fract(\sqrt{x^2 + y^2 + z^2})$$

where *x*, *y*, and *z* are the 3D coordinates of the point on the surface of the object.

You can use the `turbulence` and `octaves` keywords to stir up the pattern. A default color map is provided, but normally you would add a color_map of your own. Color patterns may be translated, rotated, or scaled. Only one color pattern may be specified in each texture statement.

SEE ALSO

color_map, *COLOR_PATTERN*, octaves, texture, turbulence

EXAMPLE

```
// ONION.POV
#include "examp.inc"  camera{location<0 0 -4>}

object {
  box {UnitBox}
  texture {
    onion
    color_map {
      [0.0 0.5 color Gray60 color White]
      [0.5 0.7 color White color White]
      [0.7 1.0 color White color White blue 0.8]
    }
    scale <0.15 0.15 0.15>
    ambient 0.3
  }
  rotate <0 45 0>
}
```

phase

TYPE
NORMAL_PATTERN_MODIFIER

PURPOSE

Adjusts the phase of waves or ripples in textures. By changing the phase by small amounts for successive frames of an animation, the waves or ripples appear to move.

SYNTAX

```
texture { phase amount [TEXTURE_ITEM...] }
```

DESCRIPTION

The phase keyword lets you specify the phase of the wavy features when the texture normal patterns waves or ripples are used. This feature is useful when creating animation sequences; if you change the phase of the waves by small amounts on each frame, the waves will appear to move. This keyword has no effect except when waves or ripples are used. The default value is 0.0.

SEE ALSO

frequency, *NORMAL_PATTERN,* ripples, texture, waves

EXAMPLE

```
// PHASE.POV
#include "examp.inc"

object {
  box{UnitBox translate <-1 0 1>}
  texture {
    waves 0.2    frequency 2
    color Cyan phong 0.7 scale <.04 .04 .04>
    phase 0.0 // default
  }
}

object {
  box{UnitBox translate <1 0 1>}
  texture {
    waves 0.2    frequency 2
    color Cyan phong 0.7 scale <.04 .04 .04>
    phase 0.5 // 180 degrees out of phase
  }
}
```

phong

TYPE
FINISH_PARAMETER

PURPOSE
Specifies the amount of Phong highlighting on a surface.

SYNTAX
`texture { phong` *amount [TEXTURE_ITEM...]* `}`

DESCRIPTION
A Phong highlight simulates the bright spot seen on a surface when a light source reflects off it. It is a result of the diffuse light hitting micro facets over a broad area of the surface. This light reflects directly at the viewer and creates a highlight. The `phong` keyword specifies the brightness of the highlight. Typical values range from the default of 0.0 (no phong) to 1.0 (very bright). The highlight will be the color of the light source unless the `metallic` keyword is present. The `metallic` keyword causes the Phong highlight to be filtered by the surface color.

The size of the highlight is controlled by the `phong_size` keyword. The formula is

$$intensity = amount^* \cos (theta)^{size}$$

where *theta* is the angle between the viewing ray and the direction to the light source.

Another type of highlight method is available by using the `specular` and `roughness` keywords. Specular highlights generally give more realistic results than Phong in cases where a light source is behind an object and the highlight is near an edge.

SEE ALSO

diffuse, *FINISH_PARAMETER*, metallic, light_source, phong_size, roughness, specular

EXAMPLE

```
// PHONG.POV
#include "examp.inc"  camera{location <0 0 -5>}

// Three different phong values
object {sphere { <-2 0 0> 1 }
  texture {color Yellow phong 0} // default
}

object {sphere { <0 0 0> 1 }
  texture {color Yellow phong 0.5} // medium
}

object {sphere { <2 0 0> 1 }
  texture {color Yellow phong 1.0} // bright
}
```

phong_size

TYPE
FINISH_PARAMETER

417

PURPOSE

Specifies the size of a Phong highlight on a surface.

SYNTAX

```
texture { phong_size amount [TEXTURE_ITEM...] }
```

DESCRIPTION

A Phong highlight simulates the bright spot seen on a surface when a light source reflects off it. It is a result of the diffuse light hitting micro facets over a broad area of the surface. This light reflects directly at the viewer and creates a highlight. The `phong_size` keyword specifies the inverse of the size of the highlight. Typical values range from 1.0 (very large) to 100.0 (very small). The default value is 40.0.

The `phong_size` keyword only has effect when a `phong` keyword is used. It does not affect specular highlights (see `roughness`).

SEE ALSO

`diffuse`, *FINISH_PARAMETER*, `metallic`, `light_source`, `phong`, `roughness`, `specular`

EXAMPLE

```
// PHONGSIZ.POV
#include "examp.inc"  camera{location <0 0 -5>}

// Three different phong sizes
object {sphere { <-2 0 0> 1 }
  texture {
    color Cyan phong 1
    phong_size 10  // large
  }
}

object {sphere { <0 0 0> 1 }
  texture {
    color Cyan phong 1
    phong_size 40  // default
  }
}

object {sphere { <2 0 0> 1 }
  texture {
    color Cyan phong 1
```

```
    phong_size 80  // small
  }
}
```

plane

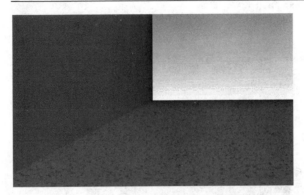

TYPE
SHAPE

PURPOSE
Specifies an infinite plane shape in an object.

SYNTAX
plane { *PLANE_IDENTIFIER [SHAPE_MODIFIER...]* } |
plane { *<normal> DISPLACEMENT [SHAPE_MODIFIER...]* }

DESCRIPTION
The plane statement specifies an infinite plane as a shape. The *<normal>* vector specifies the direction of the surface normal, a vector perpendicular to the plane's surface. The *displacement* value is the number of units that the plane is displaced away from the origin in the direction of the normal. A plane shape is infinitely large in two dimensions and infinitely thin in the third dimension. By definition, the normal vector points toward the outside and away from the inside for purposes of using planes in constructive solid geometry (CSG).

The plane statement can be used in CSG shapes, in clipped_by statements and can be scaled, rotated, and translated.

SEE ALSO

object, *SHAPE*

EXAMPLE

```
// PLANE.POV
#include "examp.inc"

object {
// Surface normal points in x direction.
// Plane moved -2 units in x direction.
  plane { <1 0 0> -2 }
  texture {color White ambient 0.2}
}
```

point_at

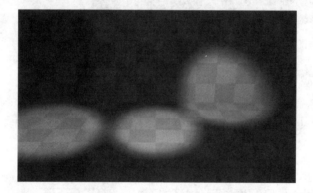

TYPE

LIGHT_SRC_MODIFIER

PURPOSE

Directs the diffuse light of a spotlight toward a given point.

SYNTAX

```
light_source {
<location> COLOR
[LIGHT_SRC_MODIFIER...]
   spotlight point_at <location>
}
```

DESCRIPTION

The point_at keyword is used to aim a spotlight. The *<location>* vector specifies the *x, y, z* location to which the spotlight points. The default value is point_at <0 0 1>. The point_at keyword has no effect unless you use the spotlight keyword. (For complete details see light_source.)

SEE ALSO

light_source, spotlight

EXAMPLE

```
// POINTAT.POV
#include "spotback.inc"

// These three spotlights all originate at
// the same point but point at different
// locations.

object {
  light_source {
    <0 6 -2> color White
    spotlight radius 8 falloff 15 tightness 1
    point_at <-4 -1 2>
  }
}

object {
  light_source {
    <0 6 -2> color White
    spotlight radius 8 falloff 15 tightness 1
    point_at <0 -1 2>
  }
}

object {
  light_source {
    <0 6 -2> color White
    spotlight radius 8 falloff 15 tightness 1
    point_at <3 0 4>
  }
}
```

poly

TYPE
SHAPE

PURPOSE
Defines a second- through seventh-order polynomial shape.

SYNTAX
poly { *POLY_IDENTIFIER [POLY_MODIFIER...]* } |
poly { *order < term1 term2 term3... term_m > [POLY_MODIFIER...]* }
    (total of "m" terms where m=(order+1)*(order+2)*(order+3)/6)

POLY_MODIFIER =
    SHAPE_MODIFIER | sturm

DESCRIPTION
A poly statement defines a shape based on a polynomial equation in *x, y,* and
z. The *order* specifies the order of the equation. Values from 2 through 7 are
allowed. The order of the equation is the highest order of its terms. For example, a fourth-order polynomial can have terms like x^4 or x^2y^2 but no term may
contain more than 4 powers of *x, y,* and *z* totaled. Therefore a term like x^3z^3 is
sixth order, not third. You must specify a coefficient for each possible term. The
number of coefficients is

422

$$(n+1)*(n+2)*(n+3)/6$$

for an nth-order equation.

Table 7-8 gives details on what power of x, y and z goes with each coefficient for polynomials of order 2 through 7. For example, the ten terms in column 2 tell you that a second-order polynomial is an equation of the form:

$$A_1 x^2 + A_2 xy + A_3 xz + A_4 x + A_5 y^2 + A_6 yz + A_7 y + A_8 z^2 + A_9 z + A_{10} = 0$$

Therefore the POV-Ray statement would be: `poly {2` *term1 term2...term10}* where *term1* through *term20* would contain the values A_1 through A_{20}.

Points where the equation is less than 0 are defined as inside the shape.

The `cubic` statement and `quartic` statements are alternate ways to specify third- and fourth-order polynomials. They are treated the same internally. A `quadric` statement can be used to specify second-order polynomials and is much faster and more accurate.

You can use a `poly` statement in CSG shapes, and poly shapes can be scaled, rotated, and translated. Because the calculations for polynomials need to be highly accurate, sometimes they will not render correctly. If this happens you may specify the `sturm` keyword to use POV-Ray's more accurate (but slower) Sturmian sequence root solver. Note that the Sturmian solver is automatically used for fifth-order and higher polynomials.

POV-Ray's standard include files have file SHAPESQ.INC, which contains many interesting `quartic` and `poly` examples.

SEE ALSO

`cubic`, `object`, `quartic`, *SHAPE*, `sturm`

EXAMPLE

```
// POLY.POV
#include "examp.inc"

// Try varying the y*y*y value from 3 down
// to 0.0 in small steps.
object {
  poly { 3
//        x*x            + y*y*y + y*y       + z*z   -1 =0
    <0 0 0 1 0 0 0 0 0 0  0.45 0  1  0 0 0 0 1 0 -1>
    sturm
  }
  translate <0 1 1>
  texture {color GreenYellow phong 1}
}
```

Table 7-8 Coefficients and Terms for Polynomials of Order 2 through 7

	2nd	3rd	4th	5th	6th	7th
A_1	x^2	x^3	x^4	x^5	x^6	x^7
A_2	xy	x^2y	x^3y	x^4y	x^5y	x^6y
A_3	xz	x^2z	x^3z	x^4z	x^5z	x^5z
A_4	x	x^2	x^3	x^4	x^5	x^5
A_5	y^2	xy^2	x^2y^2	x^3y^2	x^4y^2	x^5y^2
A_6	yz	xyz	x^2yz	x^3yz	x^4yz	x^5yz
A_7	y	xy	x^2y	x^3y	x^4y	x^5y
A_8	z^2	xz^2	x^2z^2	x^3z^2	x^4z^2	x^5z^2
A_9	z	xz	x^2z	x^3z	x^4z	x^5z
A_{10}	1	x	x^2	x^3	x^4	x^{55}
A_{11}		y^3	xy^3	x^2y^3	x^3y^3	x^4y^3
A_{12}		y^2z	xy^2z	x^2y^2z	x^3y^2z	x^4y^2z
A_{13}		y^2	xy^2	x^2y^2	x^3y^2	x^4y^2
A_{14}		yz^2	xyz^2	x^2yz^2	x^3yz^2	x^4yz
A_{15}		yz	xyz	x^2yz	x^3yz	x^4yz
A_{16}		y	xy	x^2y	x^3y	x^4y
A_{17}		z^3	xz^3	x^2z^3	x^3z^3	x^4z^3
A_{18}		z^2	xz^2	x^2z^2	x^3z^2	x^4z^2
A_{19}		z	xz	x^2z	x^3z	x^4z
A_{20}		1	x	x^2	x^3	x^4
A_{21}			y^4	xy^4	x^2y^4	x^3y^4
A_{22}			y^3z	xy^3z	x^2y^3z	x^3y^3z
A_{23}			y^3	xy^3	x^2y^3	x^3y^3
A_{24}			y^2z^2	xy^2z^2	x^2y^22	$x^3y^2z^2$
A_{25}			y^2z	$xy2z$	x^2y^2z	x^3y^2z
A_{26}			y^2	xy^2	x^2y^2	x^3y^2
A_{27}			yz^3	xyz^3	x^2yz^3	x^3yz^3
A_{28}			yz^2	xyz^2	x^2yz^2	x^3yz^2
A_{29}			yz	xyz	x^2yz	x^3yz
A_{30}			y	xy	x^2y	x^3y
A_{31}			z^4	xz^4	x^2z^4	x^3z^4
A_{32}			z^3	xz^3	x^2z^3	x^3z^3
A_{33}			z^2	xz^2	x^2z^2	x^3z^2
A_{34}			z	xz	x^2z	x^3z
A_{35}			1	x	x^2	x^3
A_{36}				y^5	xy^5	x^2y^5
A_{37}				y^4z	xy^4z	x^2y^4
A_{38}				y^4	xy^4	x^2y^4
A_{39}				y^3z^2	xy^3z^2	$x^2y^3z^2$
A_{40}				y^3z	xy^3z	x^2y^3z

	5th	6th	7th
A_{41}	y^3	xy^3	x^2y^3
A_{42}	y^2z^3	xy^2z^3	$x^2y^2z^3$
A_{43}	y^2z^2	xy^2z^2	$x^2y^2z^2$
A_{44}	y^2z	xy^2z	x^2y^2z
A_{45}	y^2	xy^2	x^2y^2
A_{46}	yz^4	xyz^4	x^2yz^4
A_{47}	yz^3	xyz^3	x^2yz^3
A_{48}	yz^2	xyz^2	x^2yz^2
A_{49}	yz	xyz	x^2yz
A_{50}	y	xy	x^2y
A_{51}	z^5	xz^5	x^2z^5
A_{52}	z^4	xz^4	x^2z^4
A_{53}	z^3	xz^3	x^2z^3
A_{54}	z^2	xz^2	x^2z^2
A_{55}	z	xz	x^2z
A_{56}	1	x	x^2
A_{57}		y^6	xy^6
A_{58}		y^5z	xy^5z
A_{59}		y^5	xy^5
A_{60}		y^4z^2	xy^4z2
A_{61}		y^4z	xy^4z
A_{62}		y^4	xy^4
A_{63}		y^3z^3	xy^3z^3
A_{64}		y^3z^2	xy^3z^2
A_{65}		$y3z$	xy^3z
A_{66}		$y3$	xy^3
A_{67}		y^2z^4	xy^2z^4
A_{68}		y^2z^3	xy^2z^3
A_{69}		y^2z^2	xy^2z^2
A_{70}		y^2z	xy^2z
A_{71}		y^2	xy^2
A_{72}		yz^5	xyz^5
A_{73}		yz^4	xyz^4
A_{74}		yz^3	xyz^3
A_{75}		yz^2	xyz^2
A_{76}		yz	xyz
A_{77}		y	xy
A_{78}		z^6	xz^6
A_{79}		z^5	xz^5
A_{80}		z^4	xz^4

	6th	7th
A_{81}	z^3	xz^3
A_{82}	z^2	xz^2
A_{83}	z	xz
A_{84}	1	x
A_{85}		y^7
A_{86}		y^6z
A_{87}		y^6
A_{88}		y^5z^2
A_{89}		y^5z
A_{90}		y^5
A_{91}		y^4z^3
A_{92}		y^4z^2
A_{93}		y^4z
A_{94}		y^4
A_{95}		y^3z^4
A_{96}		y^3z^3
A_{97}		y^3z^2
A_{98}		y^3z
A_{99}		y^3
A_{100}		y^2z^5
A_{101}		y^2z^4
A_{102}		y^2z^3
A_{103}		y^2z^2
A_{104}		y^2z
A_{105}		$y2$
A_{106}		yz^6
A_{107}		yz^5
A_{108}		yz^4
A_{109}		yz^3
A_{110}		yz^2
A_{111}		yz
A_{112}		y
A_{113}		z^7
A_{114}		z^6
A_{115}		z^5
A_{116}		z^4
A_{117}		z^3
A_{118}		z^2
A_{119}		z
A_{120}		1

pot

TYPE
HT_FIELD_TYPE

PURPOSE
Specifies a Fractint continuous POT file type in a Height-Field. This allows you to create fractal-based terrain.

SYNTAX
```
height_field {
  pot "FILESPEC"
    [water_level value] [SHAPE_MODIFIER...]
}
```

DESCRIPTION
POV-Ray uses files made of arrays of pixels to specify the upper surface in a Height-Field shape. The `pot` keyword specifies that a Fractint continuous potential file be used. Fractint is a popular fractal-generation program. For more details about Fractint, see *The Waite Group's Fractal Creations* (Waite Group Press, 1991). Unlike GIF, TGA, or DUMP file types, POT files cannot be used in image, bump, or material maps.

You specify a file type using the `pot` keyword followed by the file specification in quotes. If the file is not found in the current directory, library paths specified with the +L command-line switch are also searched. For complete details, see the items listed below.

SEE ALSO
`bump_map, dump, gif, height_field, iff, image_map, material_map, tga`

EXAMPLE
See the example for `height_field`.

quadric

TYPE
SHAPE

PURPOSE
Specifies a shape defined by a second order polynomial equation.

SYNTAX
quadric { *QUADRIC_IDENTIFIER [SHAPE_MODIFIER...]*} |
quadric {
<square_terms> <mixed_terms> <single_terms> constant
    [SHAPE_MODIFIER...]
}

DESCRIPTION
The quadric statement specifies a second-order polynomial shape. (Take care not to confuse a "quadric" with a "quartic" shape, which is a fourth-order polynomial shape.) A quadric statement renders faster and more accurately than a poly { 2 .... } shape. The ten floating-point values, which are specified by three vectors and a separate float, define the coefficients of the equation.

Given quadric{<A B C> <D E F> <G H I> J}, the equation is

$$Ax^2 + By^2 + Cz^2 + Dxy + Exz + Fyz + Gx + Hy + Iz + J = 0$$

All points where the equation is less than 0 are defined as inside the shape.

Many familiar shapes such as ellipsoid, paraboloid, hyperboloids, cones, and cylinders, can be specified using quadric. A sphere is also a quadric equation, but you should use `sphere` statements only where uneven scaling is not needed because while `sphere` renders faster it cannot be unevenly scaled. POV-Ray's SHAPES.INC file contains many interesting `quadric` examples.

You can use the `quadric` statement in CSG shapes and `clipped_by` and `bounded_by` statements. Quadric shapes can be scaled, rotated, and translated.

SEE ALSO

`object`, `poly`, `sphere`, *SHAPE*

EXAMPLE

```
// QUADRIC.POV
#include "examp.inc"

// y - x*x + z*z = 0
object {
  quadric {
    <-1  0  1>  < 0  0  0> < 0  1  0> 0
  }
  texture {color Cyan phong 1}
  translate <0 0 2>
}
```

quartic

TYPE
SHAPE

PURPOSE
Defines a fourth-order polynomial shape.

SYNTAX
```
quartic{ QUARTIC_IDENTIFIER [POLY_MODIFIER...]} |
quartic { POLY_4_IDENTIFIER [POLY_MODIFIER...]} |
quartic { < term1 term2 term3 term4... term_35 >
    [POLY_MODIFIER...]}
```

DESCRIPTION
A `quartic` statement is actually an alternate way to specify a fourth-order polynomial shape. The `poly { 4 <`*term1 term2... term35*`>}` statement creates the exact same representation internally in POV-Ray and produces the same results. (Take care not to confuse a "quartic" shape with a "quadric" shape, which is a second-order polynomial shape.) A quartic surface is defined by the equation

$$A_1x^4 + A_2x^3y + A_3x^3z + A_4x^3 + A_5x^2y^2 + A_6x^2yz + A_7x^2y + A_8x^2z^2 + A_9x^2z + A_{10}x^2 +$$
$$A_{11}xy^3 + A_{12}xy^2z + A_{13}xy^2 + A_{14}xyz^2 + A_{15}xyz + A_{16}xy + A_{17}xz^3 + A_{18}xz^2 + A_{19}xz$$
$$+ A_{20}x + A_{21}y^4 + A_{22}y^3z + A_{23}y^3 + A_{24}y^2z^2 + A_{25}y^2z + A_{26}y^2 + A_{27}yz^3 + A_{28}yz^2 +$$
$$A_{29}yz + A_{30}y + A_{31}z^4 + A_{32}z^3 + A_{33}z^2 + A_{34}z + A_{35}$$

where A_1 through A_{35} are specified by *term1* through *term 35*, respectively. All points where the equation is less than 0 are defined as inside the shape.

Quartic shapes can be used in CSG shapes and quartics can be scaled, rotated, and translated. Because the calculations for quartics need to be highly accurate, sometimes they will not trace correctly. If this happens, you can specify the `sturm` keyword to use POV-Ray's more accurate (but slower) Sturmian sequence root solver.

POV-Ray's SHAPESQ.INC file contains many interesting `quartic` and `poly` examples.

SEE ALSO
`object`, `poly`, *SHAPE*, `sturm`

EXAMPLE
```
// QUARTIC.POV
#include "examp.inc"
```

```
// Mathematicians call a "donut" shape a TORUS.
// If "r" is the minor radius of a torus and "R" is
// the major radius then its equation is
//   "xxxx+xxyy+xxzz-2(rr+RR)xx+yyyy+yyzz+
//   2(rr-RR)yy+zzzz-2(rr+RR)zz+(rr-RR)(rr-RR)=0"
// This torus uses r=1 and R=4.

object {
  quartic {
 //xxxx        2xxyy    2xxzz   -2(rr+RR)xx
     <1  0   0   0   2   0   0   2   0  -34
      0   0   0   0   0   0   0   0   0   0

 //yyyy      2yyzz    2(rr-RR)yy
       1   0   0   2   0    30      0   0   0   0

 //zzzz    -2(rr+RR)zz      (rr-RR)(rr-RR)
      1   0    -34         0  225>
}
  texture {color NeonPink phong 1}
  rotate <-45 0 0>  translate <0 2.5 8>
}
```

radius

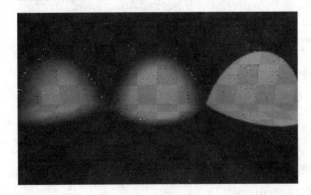

TYPE
LIGHT_SRC_MODIFIER

PURPOSE
Sets the size of the bright spot in the center of a spotlight.

SYNTAX

```
light_source {
  <location> COLOR
  spotlight radius degrees
  [LIGHT_SRC_MODIFIER...]
}
```

DESCRIPTION

Normally light diffuses outward equally in all directions from the source. However, the spotlight keyword can be used to create a cone of light that is bright in the center and falls off to darkness in a soft fringe effect at the edge. The falloff, radius, and tightness keywords control the way that light tapers off at the edges of the cone. These three keywords apply only when the spotlight keyword is used.

The radius keyword specifies the size of the "hot spot" at the center of the cone of light. The "hot spot" is a brighter cone of light inside the spotlight cone and has the same center line. See Figure 7-7 later, under the entry for spotlight. The radius value specifies the angle, in degrees, between the edge of this bright, inner cone and the center line. This value should be in the range from 0 to 180 degrees. The light inside the inner cone is of uniform intensity. The light between the inner and outer cones tapers off to zero. See Figure 7-9 later, for a graph showing the effect of various radius values.

(See spotlight and light_source for further details.)

SEE ALSO

falloff, light_source, spotlight, tightness

EXAMPLE

```
// RADIUS.POV
#include "spotback.inc"

// Three different radius values
object {
  light_source {
    <-5 4 0> color White
    spotlight point_at <-5 -1 5>
    tightness 1
    falloff 20 radius 0  // tiny hot spot
  }
}

object {
```

```
light_source {
  <0 4 0> color White
  spotlight point_at <0 -1 5>
  tightness 1
  falloff 20 radius 10 // medium hot spot
  }
}

object {
  light_source {
    <5 4 0> color White
    spotlight point_at <5 -1 5>
    tightness 1
    falloff 20 radius 19 // nearly full size
    }
}
```

red

TYPE
COLOR_COMPONENT

PURPOSE
Specifies the red component of a color.

SYNTAX
red *red_amount*

DESCRIPTION
All colors in POV-Ray consist of red, blue, green, and alpha components. Using various combinations of red, blue, and green, you can specify nearly any

431

color. The alpha part of a color specification describes the degree of transparency a given color has.

The float value after the keyword can range from 0.0 (no red) to 1.0 (full intensity red). If no value is given for a component, the default is 0.

SEE ALSO

alpha, blue, color, green

EXAMPLE

```
// RED.POV
#include "examp.inc"

object {
  sphere { <0 0 0> 1 }
  texture {
    checker
      color red 1.0            // This check is pure red.
      color red 0.8 blue 0.7  // This one is redish blue.
    scale <0.5 0.5 0.5>
  }
}
```

reflection

TYPE
FINISH_PARAMETER

PURPOSE
Controls the amount of reflection from a surface in a texture.

SYNTAX

```
texture { reflection amount [TEXTURE_ITEM...] }
```

DESCRIPTION

One of the main advantages of ray tracing over other rendering methods is its ability to accurately represent reflections in surfaces. The `reflection` keyword is used to specify the amount of reflected light. Values range from the default 0.0 (no reflection) to 1.0 (fully reflected mirror surface). Adding reflection to an object causes additional rays to be traced that slows down the rendering. The `#max_trace_level` directive controls the level of nesting of rays and thus affects how many reflections are computed.

Note that POV-Ray traces rays backwards from the camera to an object and then, if it is a reflective object, it traces on to other objects or light sources. It does not trace light the way it travels naturally: from light sources to objects to the camera. Thus when light from a light source strikes a reflective surface, even a fully reflective mirror, it does not continue on as diffuse light. This means you can see objects in a POV-Ray reflective surface but you cannot illuminate objects from reflected light. Such reflected illumination can be simulated by a technique called *radiosity*, and it is many times more difficult to compute. POV-Ray does not support radiosity.

SEE ALSO

`ambient`, `diffuse`, *FINISH_PARAMETER*, `light_source`, `texture`

EXAMPLE

```
// REFLECT.POV
#include "examp.inc"
camera{location <0 0.75 -5> look_at<0 0 0>}

// Three different reflection values
object {sphere { <-2 0 0> 1 }
  texture {
    color White reflection 0.0    // default none
  }
}

// Note that ambient + diffuse + reflection
// should usually total 1.0 or less.
object {sphere { <0 0 0> 1 }
  texture {
    color White reflection 0.3  // some reflection
```

```
        diffuse 0.4 ambient 0.1
    }
}

object {sphere { <2 0 0> 1 }
  texture {
    color White reflection 1.0  // full reflection
    diffuse 0.0 ambient 0.0
  }
}
```

refraction

TYPE
FINISH_PARAMETER

PURPOSE
Specifies the amount of refracted light for a transparent object. Refraction is the bending of light as it passes through a surface.

SYNTAX
`texture { refraction` *amount [TEXTURE_ITEM...]* `}`

DESCRIPTION
When a ray of light passes through a transparent surface between two substances of different density (such as air and glass), if it strikes the surface at an angle, the ray is bent. This bending is called "refraction." The amount of bending depends on the density of the substances and the angle at which the ray of

light hits the surface between them. Physicists assign a value called the "index of refraction" to substances to describe how much they refract light.

The `refraction` keyword specifies the amount of refracted light while the `ior` keyword specifies the amount the refracted light is bent. The default ior amount is 1.0 (no bending). The default refraction is 0.0 (also no refraction). In this instance, light passes through without bending. A refraction value of 1.0 turns refraction on. Although values from 0.0 through 1.0 are possible, such values are known to produce an unrealistic darkening of the object. The behavior of POV-Ray when values are between 0.0 and 1.0 will likely be changed in future versions of POV-Ray.

The default ior value is 1.0 which is no bending. Therefore unless an ior amount is given, refraction will have no visible effect. The `refraction` keyword also has no effect if there is no alpha specified in the color.

SEE ALSO

`alpha, refraction, texture`

EXAMPLE

```
// REFRACT.POV
#include "examp.inc"
camera{location <0 0.2 -5> look_at<0 0 0>}

#declare Lens=  // build a lens shape
  intersection {
    quadric {Ellipsoid translate <0 0  0.6>}
    quadric {Ellipsoid translate <0 0 -0.6>}
    scale <1 1 0.2>
  }

object { // add a better background
  box{UnitBox scale <8 1 0.1>}
  texture {
    checker color Red color White
    scale <0.2 0.2 1>
  }
  translate <0 -1 2>
}

object {
  intersection {Lens translate <-2 0 0> }
  texture {color White alpha 0.9 phong 0.8
  ior 1.33  refraction 0   //default
  }
```

```
}

object {
  intersection {Lens translate <0 0 0> }
  texture {color White alpha 0.9 phong 0.8
  ior 1.33  refraction 0.8   // 80% let through
  }
}

object {
  intersection {Lens translate <2 0 0> }
  texture {color White alpha 0.9 phong 0.8
  ior 1.33  refraction 1.0   // full amount
  }
}
```

right

TYPE
CAMERA_ITEM

PURPOSE
Specifies the horizontal direction and width of the camera's view window and specifies left- or right-handedness of the POV-Ray coordinate system.

SYNTAX
`camera { right <vector> [CAMERA_ITEM...] }`

DESCRIPTION

The `right` keyword defines the horizontal direction and width of the view window of the camera. The default value is `right <1.33 0 0>`. With a default value of `up <0 1 0>`, this gives an aspect ratio (width-to-height ratio) of about 4:3, typical of a landscape-oriented computer screen.

You should specify `up` and `right` values in the ratio you want the overall image to have, independent of pixel size or video mode. If you intend the image to fill such a 4:3 ratio screen, you should use values for the `right` and `up` vectors which are in a 4:3 ratio regardless of the pixel size or shape. For example, VGA 640x480 mode, MCGA 320x200 mode, EGA 640x350 mode, and Hercules monochrome 720x350 mode are all designed to fill a 4:3 aspect ratio screen when displayed on a properly adjusted monitor. Images intended for these modes should all use the same values for `up` and `right`. This helps to preserve scene compatibility across hardware platforms.

If square pixels are used, such as VGA 640x480, 800x600, or 1024x768, then the +W and +H command-line values should also have the same ratio as the `right` and `up` vectors, respectively. For nonsquare pixels, however, the compensation should be made in the +W and +H values and not in the `right` and `up` lengths.

In Figure 7-5a, we see an image that was rendered with switches +W640 +H480 and with vectors `right <1.33 0 0>`, `up <0 1 0>`. It is intended to be viewed on a VGA 640x480 mode. Everything works properly in this image. Suppose you decide you want a square image. Figure 7-5b shows the same `right` and `up` values but rendered with +W480 +H480. Although the overall image is square, there is distortion because the `right` and `up` settings are for a 4:3 aspect ratio. Figure 7-5c was rendered with +W640 +H480 and with vectors `right <1 0 0>`, `up <0 1 0>`, which is also incorrect because the aspect ratio was square but the number of pixels was not. Finally Figure 7-5d was rendered with +W480 +H480 and with vectors `right <1 0 0>`, `up <0 1 0>`. It correctly produced a square image.

The `right` vector's length defines the width of the view window but the vector does not always point to the right side of the window. The absolute value of the `right` vector does point to the right. The sign of the `right` vector determines the handedness of the coordinate system. A positive vector means a left-handed system is used. A negative vector means right-handed coordinates are used. See *VECTOR* for more on left- and right-handed coordinate systems.

(a) Correct with +W640 +H480
up<0 1 0>, right<1.33 0 0>

(b) Wrong with +W480 +H480
up<0 1 0>, right<1.33 0 0>

(c) Wrong with +W640 +H480
up<0 1 0>, right<1 0 0>

(d) Correct with +W480 +H480
up<0 1 0>, right<1 0 0>

Figure 7-5 Adjusting the Image Aspect Ratio

SEE ALSO

+H, +W, camera, direction, location, look_at, sky, up, *VECTOR*

EXAMPLE

```
// RIGHT10.POV
#include "examp.inc"
```

```
// Render at +W640 +H480 then try +W480 +H480
// Then change to right <1.33 0 0> end render each again.

camera {
  location <0 0 -3>
  up    <0 1 0>
  right <1 0 0>
}

object {
  sphere {<0 0 0> 1}
  texture {color Yellow}
}
```

ripples

TYPE
NORMAL_PATTERN

PURPOSE
Specifies a normal pattern consisting of sets of concentric rings that resemble ripples in water.

SYNTAX
`texture { ripples` *amount [TEXTURE_ITEM...] }*

RAY TRACING

DESCRIPTION

The `ripples` keyword specifies a surface normal perturbation pattern that modifies the surface normal to look like ripples on water. (See *NORMAL_PAT-TERN* for details on surface normals.) The ripples radiate from ten locations. These locations are randomly placed within 1 unit of the origin. The required float value after the keyword specifies an apparent depth of the ripples. Values from 0.0 (no ripples) to 1.0 (deep ripples) are typical. Each ripple is about 1 or 2 units wide so for small objects a scale modifier is often used to alter the size.

The `waves` keyword is an alternative to `ripples` which more closely resembles ocean waves.

The `frequency` keyword controls the space between `ripples` and `phase` can be varied to make the ripples seem to move in an animation sequence.

Note that the use of a normal pattern to perturb the surface normal does not actually change the shape of the object. It artificially modifies the surface normal so that lighting, reflections, refractions, and highlights look as though the surface were bumped. Only one normal pattern may be used in each `texture` statement.

SEE ALSO

NORMAL_PATTERN, `texture`

EXAMPLE

```
// RIPPLES.POV
#include "examp.inc"

object {
  box {UnitBox}
  texture
   {color Cyan phong 1
    ripples 0.4
    scale <0.1 0.1 0.1>
   }
}
```

rotate

TYPE
TRANSFORMATION

PURPOSE
Rotates an object, shape, or texture.

SYNTAX
`rotate` *<x_degrees y_degrees z_degrees>*

DESCRIPTION
The `rotate` keyword specifies the number of degrees to rotate an item about the *x, y,* and *z* coordinate axes. Rotations always occur about the scene's axis, not about an object's center (unless it lies on an axis). Therefore, an object some distance away from the origin would not be rotated in place but would rotate and also "orbit" about the axis of rotation. To avoid this, you should first rotate the object into the proper orientation while it is at the origin and then use `translate` to move it into place.

The values specified in the vector are the number of degrees to rotate about the *x, y* ,or *z* axes. In general, at least one and preferably two of the values should be 0. The rotations are performed around the *x* axis first, then *y*, then *z*. The axis rotations may produce unexpected results because such three-part rotations are difficult to visualize. When in doubt about the order of rotations, simply use separate `rotation` specifications for each axis.

When using POV-Ray's default left-handed coordinate system, use the following method to determine proper rotations: With your left hand, curl your fingers and extend your thumb. Turn so that your thumb points in the direction of a positive axis. This makes your fingers curl in the positive rotation direction. Similarly, when the thumb is pointed in the direction of a negative axis, the fingers curl in the negative rotation direction. You can change the system's handedness. (See the `right` keyword and *VECTOR* section for details.)

All transformations (translate, rotate, or scale) can be applied to shapes, objects, composites, textures, and the camera.

SEE ALSO

`camera`, `object`, `scale`, *SHAPE,* `texture`, `translate`, *VECTOR*

EXAMPLE

```
// ROTATE.POV
#include "examp.inc" camera{location<0 0 -5>}

object {
  box {UnitBox}
  texture {color YellowGreen}
  rotate <0 0 0>          // no rotation
  translate <-1.3 0 0>
}

object {
  box {UnitBox}
  texture {color NeonPink}
  rotate <0 45 0>         // 45 degrees y axis
  translate <1.3 0 0>
}
```

roughness

TYPE
FINISH_PARAMETER

PURPOSE
Specifies the size of a specular highlight on a surface.

SYNTAX
`texture { roughness` *amount [TEXTURE_ITEM...]* `}`

DESCRIPTION
A specular highlight simulates the bright spot seen on a surface when a light source reflects off it. It is a result of the diffuse light hitting micro facets over a broad area of the surface. This light reflects directly at the viewer and creates a highlight. The `roughness` keyword specifies the size of the highlight. A larger `roughness` value simulates more and larger micro facets which causes a larger highlight to appear. Typical values range from 1.0 (very rough, large highlight) to 0.001 (very smooth, small highlight). The default values is 0.05.

The formula used is

$$intensity = amount^* \cos(theta)^{\frac{1}{roughness}}$$

where *H* is a vector halfway between the viewing ray and the surface normal and *theta* is the angle between the *H* vector and the direction to the light source.

The `roughness` keyword only has effect when a `specular` keyword is used. It does not affect Phong highlights (see `phong_size`).

SEE ALSO
`diffuse`, *FINISH_PARAMETER*, `metallic`, `light_source`, `phong`, `phong_size`, `specular`

EXAMPLE
```
// ROUGHNES.POV
#include "examp.inc" camera{location<0 0 -5>}

// Three different roughness values
object {sphere { <-2 0 0> 1 }
```

```
    texture {
      color Cyan specular 0.7
      roughness 0.01  // smooth, small highlight
    }
  }

object {sphere { <0 0 0> 1 }
    texture {
      color Cyan specular 0.7
      roughness 0.05   // default
    }
  }

object {sphere { <2 0 0> 1 }
    texture {
      color Cyan specular 0.7
      roughness 0.10   // rough, large highlight
    }
  }
```

scale

TYPE
TRANSFORMATION

PURPOSE
Scales the size of an object, shape, or texture.

SYNTAX
scale <*x_amount y_amount z_amount*>

DESCRIPTION

The `scale` keyword specifies the amount to scale an item in the *x*, *y*, and *z* directions. Scaling always occurs about the scene's axis, not about the object's center (unless it lies on an axis). Therefore, an object some distance away from the origin not only changes size, but it moves closer or farther from the origin in the direction of the scaling. To avoid this, you should first scale the object to the proper size while it is at the origin and then use `translate` to move it into place.

The values specified in the vector are the multiplier of size in the *x*, *y*, or *z* axis. For example, <2 2 2> doubles the size in all directions, while <0.5 0.5 0.5> scales to one-half the previous size. Note that none of the three values may be 0. The sphere shape only allows scaling by the same amount in all directions. All other shapes (except CSG shapes containing a sphere) may be scaled by uneven amounts in one, two, or three directions. For example, to scale an item twice its previous size in the *x* direction, you would use <2 1 1>.

All transformations (translate, rotate, or scale) can be applied to shapes, objects, composites, and textures.

SEE ALSO

`object`, `rotate`, *SHAPE*, `texture`, `translate`, *VECTOR*

EXAMPLE

```
// SCALE.POV
#include "examp.inc" camera{location<0 0 -5>}

object {
  box {UnitBox}
  texture {color YellowGreen}
  scale <1 1 1>  // no scaling
  translate <-1.3 0 0>
}

object {
  box {UnitBox}
  texture {color NeonPink}
  scale <0.2 0.5 2>  // uneven scaling
  translate <1.3 0 0>
}
```

SHAPE

PURPOSE
Defines the shape of an object.

SYNTAX
SHAPE =
      BICUBIC_PATCH | BLOB | BOX | CUBIC |
      DIFFERENCE | HEIGHT_FIELD | INTERSECTION |
      LIGHT_SOURCE | PLANE | POLY | QUADRIC |
      QUARTIC | SMOOTH_TRIANGLE | SPHERE |
      TRIANGLE | UNION

CSG_SHAPE =
      INTERSECTION | DIFFERENCE | UNION

DESCRIPTION
A shape is the part of an `object` statement that defines the object's shape. Although shape identifiers can be declared and shapes can be combined and manipulated, shapes do not exist in a scene unless they are contained in an `object` statement.

Although the syntax for most shapes allows for `texture` statements and quick-render `color` specifications, shapes generally do not use these modifiers unless they are part of a CSG shape and have different textures for different parts. Such modifiers are typically attached to the objects outside the shape but inside the object. CSG shapes cannot have textures or quick-render colors as modifiers.

You can declare all types of shapes as identifiers. When you invoke a shape identifier it must be enclosed in a statement of the same type. For example, Disk_Y is an intersection shape declared in SHAPES.INC.

```
object {Disk_Y}  // ERROR!  Disk_Y is an intersection, not an object
intersection {Disk_Y}  // ERROR!  Must be in an object statement
object {intersection{Disk_Y}}  // This is correct
object {intersection{Cylinder_Y}}  // ERROR! Cylinder_Y is a quadric
object {quadric{Cylinder_Y}}  // This is correct
```

SEE ALSO
All shape types listed in syntax above and *CSG_SHAPE,* `color`, `object`, `texture`

EXAMPLE
See the examples in each shape type.

sky

TYPE
CAMERA_ITEM

PURPOSE
Defines the axis for panning and tilting the camera with `look_at`.

SYNTAX
`camera {` *[CAMERA_ITEM...]* `sky` *<vector>* `look_at` *<point>}*

DESCRIPTION
Use the `sky` keyword to define the axis of rotation of the camera when the `look_at` keyword aims the camera. The default value is `sky <0 1 0>`, which means that a `look_at` rotation will pan the camera around the *y* axis and then tilt towards the desired location.

The `location`, `direction`, `up`, and `right` vectors completely define the camera. Theoretically, that is all that is needed. However, it is very difficult to hand calculate the vectors for anything other than an orientation along an axis. The up, right, and direction vectors must be perpendicular to each other in order to avoid distortion.

You can use the look_at keyword to point the camera more easily. Specify the camera location, up, right, and direction keywords and vectors first. Then use look_at to define the 3D coordinates of the point you want to look at. POV-Ray pans the camera left or right until the view window lines up with the "look at" point. The camera then tilts up or down until it is pointed directly at the proper point.

When look_at aims it, the camera is first rotated so that the Up vector matches the sky vector. The default value is sky <0 1 0>, which is the same as the default value of the up keyword. This means that in most cases the camera is already in this orientation. The sky vector then becomes the axis of rotation for the panning. The tilting part of a "look at" rotation is also done in line with the sky vector. If the "look at" point lies directly along the sky axis, it cannot pan left or right to line up with it, and a blank image results. The sky keyword only affects the way subsequent look_at operations work. It has no other effect.

SEE ALSO

camera, direction, location, look_at, right, rotate, up, *VECTOR*

EXAMPLE

```
// SKY.POV
#include "examp.inc"

camera {
  location <0 0 -3>
  sky <1 1 0>      // the default is sky <0 1 0>
                   // this sky is 45 deg. angle
  look_at <0 0 0>
}

// Something to look at
object {
  sphere {<0 0 0> 1}
  texture {color NeonBlue}
}
```

smooth_triangle

TYPE
SHAPE

PURPOSE
Specifies a triangle shape with modified surface normal vectors. A `smooth_triangle` shape uses modified surface normals to make groups of triangles blend together in a way that hides the sharp edges between individual triangles.

SYNTAX
`smooth_triangle` { *SM_TRIANGLE_IDENTIFIER*
    [SHAPE_MODIFIER...] } |
`smooth_triangle` {
    <vertex_1> <normal_1>   <vertex_2> <normal_2>   <vertex_3> <normal_3>
    [SHAPE_MODIFIER...]
}

DESCRIPTION
The `smooth_triangle` statement defines a shape that is a finite plane surface with three vertices and three straight edges. Although totally flat, a smooth triangle generally appears to be a curved surface because the surface normals of the shape are modified to give it a curved appearance. A `smooth_triangle` shape uses modified surface normals to make groups of triangles blend together in a way that hides the sharp edges between individual triangles. (See *NORMAL_PATTERN* for details on surface normals.)

449

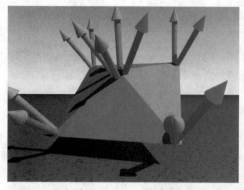
(a) Pyramid of Nonsmoothed Triangles

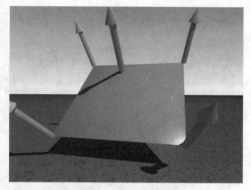
(b) Pyramid of Smoothed Triangles

Figure 7-6 Surface Normals of Smoothed and Nonsmoothed Triangles

As with `triangle` statements, you supply three vectors that are the 3D coordinates of the three vertices. Each vertex is followed by a vector that defines the direction of the surface normal at the corresponding vertex. Proper specification of these surface normals gives the shape a curved appearance. When groups of smoothed triangles with common vertices are assembled and their surface normals are properly aligned, it gives the appearance of a perfectly smooth continuous surface. (See Figure 7-6b.)

A smooth triangle shape can be translated, rotated, or scaled. Because it is an open finite shape it has no inside or outside defined. Therefore it cannot be used for constructive solid geometry (CSG) in intersection or difference shapes, nor can it be used in `clipped_by` or `bounded_by` statements. It may be included in a `union` shape.

Usually large numbers of smooth triangles are created by external utilities such as CAD programs or other 3D modelers. These programs define shapes that POV-Ray cannot generate on its own. Other utilities are then used to compute the modified surface normal vectors to create the desired effect of a smooth surface. The example below was generated by laying out four triangles by hand and using a utility program called RAW2POV to compute the normals. It is the same shape used in the `triangle` example.

SEE ALSO
CSG_SHAPE, `object`, `triangle`, *SHAPE*

450

EXAMPLE

```
// SMOOTHTR.POV
#include "examp.inc"

// This is the same set of triangles which
// create a pyramid in the triangle example
// except these have been smoothed.
object {
  union {
    smooth_triangle {
      <-1.0000 0.0000 -1.0000> <0.2357 -0.9428 0.2357>
      <-1.0000 0.0000 1.0000>  <0.2357 -0.9428 -0.2357>
      <0.0000 0.5000 0.0000>   <0.0000 -1.0000 0.0000> }
    smooth_triangle {
      <1.0000 0.0000 -1.0000>  <-0.2357 -0.9428 0.2357>
      <-1.0000 0.0000 -1.0000> <0.2357 -0.9428 0.2357>
      <0.0000 0.5000 0.0000>   <0.0000 -1.0000 0.0000> }
    smooth_triangle {
      <-1.0000 0.0000 1.0000>  <0.2357 -0.9428 -0.2357>
      <1.0000 0.0000 1.0000>   <-0.2357 -0.9428 -0.2357>
      <0.0000 0.5000 0.0000>   <0.0000 -1.0000 0.0000> }
    smooth_triangle {
      <1.0000 0.0000 1.0000>   <-0.2357 -0.9428 -0.2357>
      <1.0000 0.0000 -1.0000>  <-0.2357 -0.9428 0.2357>
      <0.0000 0.5000 0.0000>   <0.0000 -1.0000 0.0000> }
  }
  texture {color White phong 1}
  rotate <-40 15 0>
}
```

specular

 CREATIONS

RAY TRACING

TYPE
FINISH_PARAMETER

PURPOSE
Specifies the amount of specular highlighting on a surface.

SYNTAX
`texture {` `specular` *amount* *[TEXTURE_ITEM...]* `}`

DESCRIPTION
A specular highlight simulates the bright spot seen on a surface when a light source reflects off it. It is a result of the diffuse light hitting micro facets over a broad area of the surface. This light reflects directly at the viewer and creates a highlight. The `specular` keyword specifies the brightness of the highlight. Typical values range from the default of 0.0 (no highlight) to 1.0 (very bright highlight). The highlight will be the color of the light source unless the `metallic` keyword is present. The `metallic` keyword causes the highlight to be filtered by the surface color.

The size of the highlight is controlled by the `roughness` keyword. The formula is

$$intensity = amount * \cos(theta)^{\frac{1}{roughness}}$$

where *H* is a vector halfway between the viewing ray and the surface normal and *theta* is the angle between the *H* vector and the direction to the light source.

Another type of highlight method is available by using the `phong` and `phong_size` keywords. Specular highlights generally give more realistic results than Phong in cases where a light source is behind an object and the highlight is near an edge.

SEE ALSO
`diffuse`, *FINISH_PARAMETER*, `metallic`, `light_source`, `phong`, `phong_size`, `roughness`

452

EXAMPLE

```
// SPECULAR.POV
#include "examp.inc"  camera{location <0 0 -5>}

// Three different specular values
object {sphere { <-2 0 0> 1 }
  texture {color Yellow specular 0} // default
}

object {sphere { <0 0 0> 1 }
  texture {color Yellow specular 0.5} // medium
}

object {sphere { <2 0 0> 1 }
  texture {color Yellow specular 1.0} // bright
}
```

sphere

TYPE
SHAPE

PURPOSE
Specifies a sphere shape in an object.

SYNTAX
sphere { *SPHERE_IDENTIFIER [SHAPE_MODIFIER...]* } |
sphere { *<center> radius [SHAPE_MODIFIER...]* }

DESCRIPTION

The sphere statement specifies a sphere shape. You specify a vector that is the 3D coordinates of the center, followed by a float value for the radius. A sphere at location A, B, C with radius R is defined by the equation:

$$(x-A)^2 + (y-B)^2 + (z-C)^2 - R^2 = 0$$

Points where the equation is less than 0 are defined as inside the shape.

Although the equation of a sphere can also be specified by a quartic statement or a poly { 2 .... } statement, a sphere statement renders much faster.

One important restriction is that a sphere statement or any statement containing a sphere statement must be scaled equally in all directions. If uneven scaling is required, you should use a quartic statement instead. POV-Ray's standard Include file SHAPES.INC contains a quartic identifier "Ellipsoid" that can be used as a scalable spherical shape.

You can use the sphere statement in CSG shapes, in clipped_by and bounded_by statements, and they can be scaled uniformly or rotated and translated.

SEE ALSO

object, poly, quadric, *SHAPE*

EXAMPLE

```
// SPHERE.POV
#include "examp.inc" camera{location <0 0 -4>}

object {
  sphere {<0 0 0> 1}
  texture {color SummerSky phong 1}
  scale <0.8 0.8 0.8> // can only scale evenly
  translate <-1 0 0>
}

object {
  quadric {Ellipsoid}
  texture {color YellowGreen phong 1}
  scale <0.4 1.5 1> // can scale unevenly
  translate <1 0 0>
}
```

spotlight

TYPE
LIGHT_SRC_MODIFIER

PURPOSE
Specifies that light from a source be constrained to a cone with soft shadowed edges.

SYNTAX
```
light_source {
 <location> COLOR
 spotlight
 [LIGHT_SRC_MODIFIER...]
}
```

DESCRIPTION
Normally light diffuses outward equally in all directions from the source. However, you can use the `spotlight` keyword to create a cone of light that is bright in the center and falls off to darkness in a soft fringe effect at the edge. Although the cone of light fades to soft edges, objects illuminated by spotlights still cast hard shadows.

The `point_at` keyword tells the spotlight to point at a particular 3D coordinate. A line from the location of the spotlight to the `point_at` coordinate forms the center line of the cone of light. The `falloff`, `radius`, and `tightness` keywords control the way that light tapers off at the edges of the cone. These four keywords apply only when the `spotlight` keyword is used.

455

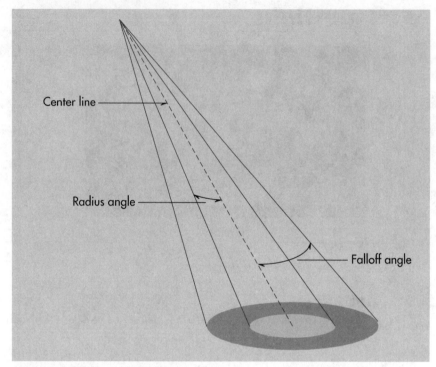

Figure 7-7 Radius and Falloff Angles in a Spotlight

The falloff keyword specifies the overall size of the cone of light. This is the point where the light falls off to zero intensity. The float value you specify is the angle, in degrees, between the edge of the cone and center line. See Figure 7-7. The radius keyword specifies the size of the "hot spot" at the center of the cone of light. The "hot spot" is a brighter cone of light inside the spotlight cone and has the same center line. The radius value specifies the angle, in degrees, between the edge of this bright inner cone and the center line. The light inside the inner cone is of uniform intensity. The light between the inner and outer cones tapers off to zero.

For example, with radius 10 and falloff 20, the light from the center line out to 10 degrees is full intensity. From 10 to 20 degrees from the center line the light falls off to zero intensity. At 20 degrees or greater there is no light. See the examples under the radius and falloff keywords. Note that if the radius and falloff values are close or equal the light intensity drops rapidly and the spotlight has a sharp edge. The default values for both `radius` and `falloff` are 70.

Use the `tightness` keyword to specify an additional exponential softening of the edges. See Figure 7-8. The intensity of light at an angle from the center line is given by

$$intensity = cos(angle)^{\,tightness}$$

With a value of `tightness` 1, the effect is unnoticeable. Higher values produce a softer edge. Typical values range from 1 to 100, with the default of 10.

The scene examples under each of the spotlight-related keywords illustrate the effects of their usage. The example that follows shows how colored spotlights can be combined for an interesting effect.

SEE ALSO

`color, diffuse, falloff, light_source, no_shadow, object, point_at, radius, tightness`

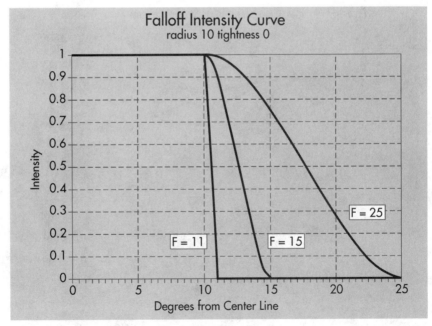

Figure 7-8 How `falloff` Affects Spotlight Intensity

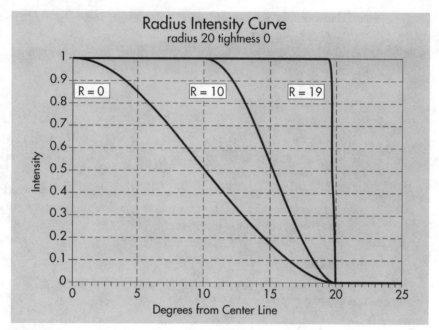

Figure 7-9 How radius Affects Spotlight Intensity

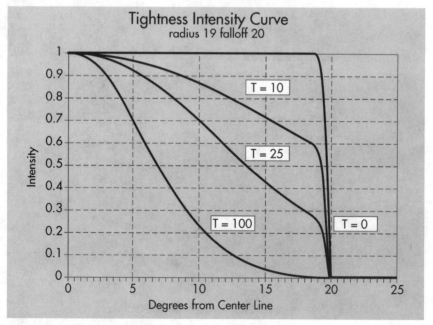

Figure 7-10 How tightness Affects Spotlight Intensity

EXAMPLE

```
// SPOTLIGH.POV
#include "spotback.inc"

// Three different colored spotlights
object {
  light_source {
    <-5 6 -2> color Red
    spotlight point_at <-1 -1 2>
    radius 8 falloff 25 tightness 1
  }
}

object {
  light_source {
    <0 6 -2> color Green
    spotlight point_at <0 -1 1>
    radius 8 falloff 25 tightness 1
  }
}

object {
  light_source {
    <5 6 -2> color Blue
    spotlight point_at <1 -1 2>
    radius 8 falloff 25 tightness 1
  }
}

// object to illuminate
object {
 sphere {<0 0 1> 1}
 texture {color White}
}
```

spotted

TYPE
COLOR_PATTERN

PURPOSE
Specifies a spotted color pattern in a texture.

SYNTAX
`texture { spotted` *[COLOR_PATTERN_MODIFIER...]*
　　　[TEXTURE_ITEM...] `}`

DESCRIPTION
The `spotted` keyword specifies a color pattern of irregular blended spots. The features are almost 2 units apart, so you should use small scaling values when applying to small shapes. The `leopard` color pattern creates regularly spaced, distinct spots, and `spotted` creates irregular, blended spots.

　　You can use the `turbulence` and `octaves` keywords to stir up the pattern. A default color map is provided, but normally you would add a `color_map` of your own. Color patterns may be translated, rotated, or scaled. Only one color pattern may be specified in each `texture` statement.

SEE ALSO
`color_map`, *COLOR_PATTERN*, `octaves`, `texture`, `turbulence`

EXAMPLE

```
// SPOTTED.POV
#include "examp.inc"

object {
  sphere {<0 0 0> 1}
  texture {
    spotted
    color_map {
      [0.0 0.5 color Yellow color Yellow]
      [0.5 0.9 color Yellow color Black]
      [0.9 1.0 color Black color Black]
    }
    scale <0.2 0.2 0.2>
  }
}
```

sturm

TYPE

POLY_MODIFIER

PURPOSE

Causes the slower, yet more accurate, Sturmian sequence root solver to be used in blob, poly, cubic, or quartic shapes.

SYNTAX

```
blob { BLOB_BODY sturm [SHAPE_MODIFIER...]} |
cubic { CUBIC_BODY sturm [SHAPE_MODIFIER...]} |
poly { POLY_BODY sturm [SHAPE_MODIFIER...]} |
quartic { QUARTIC_BODY sturm [SHAPE_MODIFIER...]}
```

DESCRIPTION

You can add the sturm keyword to blob, cubic, poly, or quartic shapes to specify use of the slower, yet more accurate, Sturmian sequence root solver. These require highly accurate calculations. Adding the sturm keyword may clear up math errors in these shapes if they render improperly.

SEE ALSO

```
blob, cubic, poly, quartic
```

EXAMPLE

See examples of the supported shapes.

texture

TYPE

SHAPE_MODIFIER or *OBJECT_MODIFIER*

PURPOSE

Specifies the color pattern, normal pattern, and finish parameters of a shape or object.

SYNTAX

```
texture { TEXTURE_ITEM... }
```

TEXTURE_ITEM =
 COLOR_PATTERN | COLOR_PATTERN_MODIFIER |
 NORMAL_PATTERN | NORMAL_PATTERN_MODIFIER |
 FINISH_PARAMETER | SPECIAL_TEXTURE |
 TRANSFORMATION | TEXTURE_IDENTIFIER

COLOR_PATTERN =
```
agate | bozo | granite | leopard | marble |
onion | spotted | wood |
checker COLOR COLOR | gradient <vector> |
color [COLOR_COMPONENT...] |
image_map {
```

[MAP_PREFIX...] MAP_FILE_TYPE "FILESPEC"
        [IMAGE_MAP_MODIFIER...]
    }

COLOR_PATTERN_MODIFIER =
    turbulence *turb_amount* | octaves *octave_number* |
    color_map { [COLOR_MAP_ENTRY...] }

NORMAL_PATTERN =
    bumps *amount* | dents *amount* | ripples *amount* |
    waves *amount* | wrinkles *amount* |
    bump_map {
        [MAP_PREFIX...] MAP_FILE_TYPE "FILESPEC"
        [BUMP_MAP_MODIFIER...]
    }

NORMAL_PATTERN_MODIFIER =
    phase *amount* | frequency *amount*

FINISH_PARAMETER =
    crand_value | metallic | ambient *value* |
    diffuse *value* | specular *value* | roughness *value* |
    phong *value* | phong_size *size* | brilliance *value* |
    ior *index_of_refraction* | refraction *amount* |
    reflection *amount*

SPECIAL_TEXTURE =
    tiles { *TEXTURE...* tile2 *TEXTURE...* } |
    material_map {
        [MAP_PREFIX...] MAP_FILE_TYPE "FILESPEC"
        [MATERIAL_MAP_MODIFIER...]
    }

TRANSFORMATION =
    translate *<vector>* | rotate *<angles>* | scale *<amount>*

DESCRIPTION

The texture statement is a modifier for shapes and objects that specifies its
color pattern, normal perturbation, and finish properties. You can specify over

463

40 different statements, values, and keywords in a texture statement. Each is documented in its own section of this chapter. Each has a default value, which you may change using the #default language directive.

A texture statement may appear in object statements but not in composite statements. It may also be used inside any shape statement except constructive solid geometry (CSG) shapes intersection, difference, or union. Therefore, it is sometimes possible to have CSG shapes with different textures on different parts, but you cannot apply different textures if you have a CSG shape made of other CSG shapes.

A texture may be translated, rotated, and scaled independently of the shape or object. Transformations in a shape or object that are made *before* the texture statement will apply only to the shape or object but not to the texture. Transformations given in a shape or object *after* the texture statement cause both the texture and shape or object to be transformed.

The principles in the paragraph above do not apply inside the texture statement. Transformations given *inside* the texture statement apply only to the texture and do not affect the shape or object. Placing translate, rotate, or scale keywords before, after, or between color pattern keywords and normal pattern keywords does not change the way they work. You cannot independently transform parts of a texture. Any transformations inside the texture statement applies to the entire texture regardless of their position relative to other keywords.

Although the syntax for texture allows placing a texture identifier anywhere in the texture statement, you should only use it as the first item. This is because a texture identifier includes in it all of the default values, whether you specify them or not. Thus invoking a texture identifier overwrites all previous texture items in that statement.

If more than one texture statement appears in a shape or object, the textures are layered on top of each other. The last specified texture is the topmost layer. Layered textures only work if the top layers have some transparency in them from alpha components of the colors. Deeper layers can only be seen through the transparent areas and the color is filtered by the upper layers. You can declare layered textures by simply placing more than one texture statement after the = sign. Note that various combinations of layered textures will not work in tiles or material_map special textures.

SEE ALSO

composite, *SHAPE*, object, all keywords listed above in the syntax

464

EXAMPLE

```
// TEXTURE.POV
#include "examp.inc"  camera{location <0 0 -5>}

#declare MyTexture =
  texture {
    wood
      color_map {
        [0.0 0.7 color Tan   color Tan]
        [0.7 1.0 color Tan   color Brown]
      }
    phong 0.8 phong_size 50
    reflection 0.05
    dents 0.4
    turbulence 0.07 octaves 3
    scale <0.15 0.15 0.15>
  }

object {
  sphere { <0 0 0> 1 }
  translate <-2 0 0>  // translate before texture
  texture {MyTexture}
}

object {
  sphere { <0 0 0> 1 }
  texture {MyTexture} // no translate
}

object {
  sphere { <0 0 0> 1 }
  texture {MyTexture}
  translate <2 0 0>  // translate after texture
}
```

tga

TYPE
MAP_FILE_TYPE "FILESPEC" or *HT_FIELD_TYPE*

PURPOSE
Specifies a file type of TGA to use a Targa 24-bit format in an image map, bump map, material map, or Height-Field.

SYNTAX

tga *"FILESPEC"*

DESCRIPTION

POV-Ray uses files made of arrays of pixels for patterns in image maps, bump maps, and material maps as well as in Height-Field shapes. The tga keyword specifies that a 24-bit Targa (TGA) file is to be used.

You specify a file type using the tga keyword followed by the file specification in quotes. If the file is not found in the current directory, library paths specified with the +L command-line switch are also searched. For complete details see the items listed below.

SEE ALSO

bump_map, dump, gif, height_field, iff, image_map, material_map, pot

EXAMPLE

See the examples for height_field, image_map, bump_map, or material_map.

threshold

TYPE

BLOB_ITEM

PURPOSE

Specifies the threshold level in a blob shape, which determines the blob's boundaries and extent.

SYNTAX

`blob { threshold` *value [BLOB_ITEM...] [POLY_MODIFIER...]* `}`

DESCRIPTION

Use the `threshold` keyword to define the threshold value for a blob shape. Blobs are shapes made from spheres that flow and blend into each other smoothly to create a liquid effect. The individual components attract and repel each other and result in "blobby" organic-looking shapes.

Mathematically, each component of the blob represents a field density function that starts at the center of the component at the strength value given and tapers off to zero at the radius given. The density falls off according to the function

$$field\_strength = \left[1 - \left[\frac{r}{radius} \right]^2 \right]^2$$

where *r* is the distance from the center of the component and *radius* is the radius where the density falls off to zero.

At every point, the densities of all components of the blob are added together. Components in different blob shapes do not affect each other. The surface of the blob is defined by all points in space with accumulated densities equal to the `threshold` value. Points with greater density are inside the blob. Points with lower density are outside the blob.

SEE ALSO

`blob, component`

EXAMPLE

```
// THRESH.POV
#include "examp.inc"  camera{location <0 0 -5>}

// Three identical blobs with different thresholds
object {
  blob {
```

```
      component 1 1 <0 -0.5 0>
      component 1 1 <0  0.7 0>
      threshold 0.1  // Fat blobs
    }
    texture {color Yellow phong 1 }
    translate <-2 0 0>
}

object {
  blob {
    component 1 1 <0 -0.5 0>
    component 1 1 <0  0.7 0>
    threshold 0.4  // Medium blobs
  }
  texture {color Yellow phong 1 }
}

object {
  blob {
    component 1 1 <0 -0.5 0>
    component 1 1 <0  0.7 0>
    threshold 0.8  // Thin blobs
  }
  texture {color Yellow phong 1 }
  translate <2 0 0>
}
```

tightness

TYPE
LIGHT_SRC_MODIFIER

PURPOSE

Specifies how rapidly the light from a spotlight's soft shadowed edges diminishes.

SYNTAX

```
light_source {
 <location> COLOR
 spotlight tightness value
 [LIGHT_SRC_MODIFIER...]
}
```

DESCRIPTION

Normally light diffuses outward equally in all directions from the source. However, you can use the `spotlight` keyword to create a cone of light that is bright in the center and falls off to darkness in a soft fringe effect at the edge. Although the cone of light fades to soft edges, objects illuminated by spotlights still cast hard shadows.

The `falloff`, `radius`, and `tightness` keywords control the way that light tapers off at the edges of the cone. These three keywords apply only when the `spotlight` keyword is used.

The `falloff` keyword specifies the overall size of the cone of light. This is the point where the light falls off to zero intensity. The `radius` keyword specifies the size of the "hot spot" at the center of the cone of light. The `radius` value specifies the angle, in degrees, between the edge of this bright inner cone and the center line. The light inside the inner cone is of uniform intensity. The light between the inner and outer cones tapers off to zero. (See Figure 7-7.)

The `tightness` keyword is used to specify an additional exponential softening of the edges. (See Figure 7-10.) With a value of `tightness` 0 the effect is unnoticeable. Higher values produce a softer edge. Typical values range from 1 to 100; the default is 10. (See the reference entries for `light_source` and `spotlight` for further details.)

SEE ALSO

`falloff`, `light_source`, `radius`, `spotlight`

EXAMPLE

```
// TIGHTNES.POV
#include "spotback.inc"
```

```
// Three different tightness values
object {
  light_source {
    <-5 4 0> color White
    spotlight point_at <-5 -1 5>
    radius 19 falloff 20
    tightness 0  // wide angle
  }
}

object {
  light_source {
    <0 4 0> color White
    spotlight point_at <0 -1 5>
    radius 20 falloff 20
    tightness 25 // tighter angle
  }
}

object {
  light_source {
    <5 4 0> color White
    spotlight point_at <5 -1 5>
    radius 20 falloff 20
    tightness 100 // very tight
  }
}
```

tiles and tile2

TYPE
SPECIAL_TEXTURE

PURPOSE

Specifies a texture that consists of a checkered combination of two textures.

SYNTAX

```
texture { tile { TEXTURE... tile2 TEXTURE... } }
```

DESCRIPTION

Use the `tiles` and `tile2` keywords to create a checkered pattern similar to the `checker` keyword; however, the tiles are complete textures and not just solid colors. The pattern is made of cubes of alternating textures and is three dimensional. The cubes are 1 unit in all directions and are parallel to all three axes. You can use the `translate`, `rotate`, and `scale` keywords to modify the size and orientation of the pattern.

SEE ALSO

`checker, texture`

EXAMPLE

```
// TILES.POV
#include "examp.inc"

object {
  sphere { <0 0 0> 1}
  texture {
    tiles {
      texture {DMFWood4}
        tile2
      texture {Red_Marble}
    }
  scale <0.5 0.5 0.5>
  }
}
```

translate

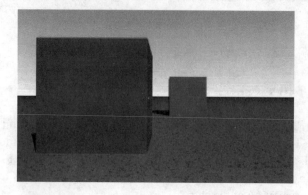

TYPE
TRANSFORMATION

PURPOSE
Moves a camera, object, shape, or texture.

SYNTAX
`translate` *<x_amount y_amount z_amount>*

DESCRIPTION
The `translate` keyword specifies the amount to move an item in the *x, y,* and *z* directions. It is not a movement to an absolute coordinate; the movement is relative to the item's previous location. All transformations (translate, rotate, or scale) can be applied to the camera, shapes, objects, composites, and textures.

SEE ALSO
`object, rotate,` *SHAPE,* `scale, texture`

EXAMPLE
```
// TRANSLATE.POV
#include "examp.inc"

object {
  box {UnitBox}
  texture {color NeonPink}
```

```
    translate <-1.3 0 2> // move back and left
}

object {
  box {UnitBox}
  texture {color GreenYellow}
  translate <1.3 0 10> // move way back & right
}
```

triangle

TYPE
SHAPE

PURPOSE
Specifies a triangle shape in an object.

SYNTAX
`triangle {` *TRIANGLE_IDENTIFIER [SHAPE_MODIFIER...]* `}` |
`triangle {` *<vertex_1> <vertex_2> <vertex_3> [SHAPE_MODIFIER...]* `}`

DESCRIPTION
The `triangle` statement defines a shape that is a finite plane surface with three vertices and three straight edges. You supply three vectors that are the 3D coordinates of the three vertices.

A triangle shape may be translated, rotated, or scaled. Because it is an open finite shape it has no defined inside or outside. Therefore it cannot be used for constructive solid geometry (CSG) in intersection or difference shapes nor can

it be used in `clipped_by` and `bounded_by` statements. It may be included in a `union` shape.

Usually, large numbers of triangles are created by external utilities to define shapes that POV-Ray cannot generate on its own. A `smooth_triangle` shape uses modified surface normals to make groups of triangles blend together in a way that hides the sharp edges between individual triangles. See `smooth_triangle` and Figure 7-6 for details.

SEE ALSO
CSG_SHAPE, `object`, `smooth_triangle`, *SHAPE*

EXAMPLE

```
// TRIANGLE.POV
#include "examp.inc"

// This is the same set of triangles that is shown
// smoothed in the smooth triangle example
object {
  union {
    triangle {<-1 0 -1> <-1 0  1> <0 0.5 0>}
    triangle {< 1 0 -1> <-1 0 -1> <0 0.5 0>}
    triangle {<-1 0  1> < 1 0  1> <0 0.5 0>}
    triangle {< 1 0  1> < 1 0 -1> <0 0.5 0>}
  }
  texture {color White phong 1}
  rotate <-40 15 0>
}
```

turbulence

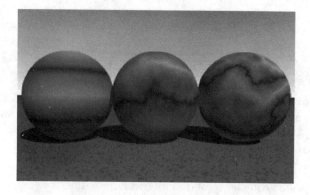

TYPE
COLOR_PATTERN_MODIFIER

PURPOSE
Mixes up a color pattern in a texture.

SYNTAX
```
texture {
   COLOR_PATTERN turbulence amount octaves number
   [TEXTURE_ITEM...]
}
```

DESCRIPTION
Use the `turbulence` keyword to specify how much a color pattern should be mixed up or swirled. Typical values range from the default of 0.0 (no turbulence) to 1.0 (very turbulent).

When POV-Ray computes turbulence to apply to a pattern it "stirs" the pattern in broad amounts, and then "stirs" it again in successively smaller amounts with each step using details that are half as large as the previous step. Use the `octaves` keyword to specify how many of the successively finer calculations should be used in various noise functions. Low values give very smooth wavy turbulence while higher values give a more jagged look. The default value for `octaves` is 6.

The `octaves` keyword has no effect unless `turbulence` is used. Note however that the `agate` pattern has built-in turbulence, so `octaves` does affect it despite the lack of `turbulence`. Neither `turbulence` nor `octaves` affect image maps, tiles, or material maps.

SEE ALSO
`texture, octaves`

EXAMPLE
```
// TURBULEN.POV
#include "examp.inc"  camera{location <0 0 -5>}

#default   // set up a default texture
 {texture{
   White_Marble rotate <0 0 90>
```

```
    ambient 0.25
  }
}

// Try different turbulence values
object {sphere { <-2 0 0> 1 }
  texture {turbulence 0.0} // default none
}

object {sphere { <0 0 0> 1 }
  texture {turbulence 0.5} // some turbulence
}

object {sphere { <2 0 0> 1 }
  texture {turbulence 1.0} // very turbulent
}
```

union

TYPE
SHAPE

PURPOSE
Creates a constructive solid geometry shape that is a combination of other shapes.

SYNTAX
union { *UNION_IDENTIFIER [CSG_MODIFIER...]* } |
union { *SHAPE... [CSG_MODIFIER...]* }

CSG_MODIFIER =
    TRANSFORMATION | `inverse`

DESCRIPTION

It is often convenient to group objects together so they may be translated, rotated, scaled, or textured as a single unit. The `union` statement defines a shape combining two or more shapes together as a unit in constructive solid geometry (CSG). Keywords `translate`, `rotate`, `scale`, or `inverse` may be used.

Like all CSG shapes, `union` can only operate on other shapes; it cannot operate on objects. (See `composite`.) It cannot use `texture` or quick-render `color` specifications as a shape modifier.

SEE ALSO

CSG_SHAPE, `composite,` `object,` *SHAPE*

EXAMPLE

```
// UNION.POV
#include "examp.inc"

// Compare with intersection, clipped_by and
//  difference examples.
//
// Combination of both box and sphere
object {
  union {
    sphere {<0 0 0> 1}
    box {<-0.8 -0.8 -0.8> <0.8 0.8 0.8>}
  }
  texture {color White phong 1}
  rotate <0 50 0>
}
```

up

TYPE

CAMERA_ITEM

PURPOSE

Specifies the vertical direction and height of the camera's view window.

SYNTAX

```
camera { up <vector> [CAMERA_ITEM...] }
```

DESCRIPTION

The `up` vector in a `camera` statement specifies the vertical direction and height of the camera's view window. Rays start at the camera's location and travel outward toward an imaginary rectangular viewing window. The view window is divided into rows and columns of points that will be the pixels of the completed image. The number of pixels is controlled by the +W and +H command-line switches.

The keywords `direction`, `up`, and `right` specify vectors that dictate the position of this view window relative to the camera's location.

The `direction` keyword defines the direction the camera is looking. The ray that is traced in the center of the image follows this vector. The default value is `direction <0 0 1>`. This means that the camera is looking in the positive z direction.

The `up` keyword defines which direction is "up" in the view window. The length of the up vector determines the height of the view window. The `up` default value is `<0 1 0>`. This means that the "up" direction of the image is in the positive y direction.

The `right` keyword defines the horizontal direction and width of the view window, but the vector does not always point to the right side of the window. The absolute value of the right vector does point to the right. The sign of the right vector determines the handedness of the coordinate system. A positive right vector means a left-handed system is in use. A negative vector means right-handed coordinates are used. (See *VECTOR* for more on left- and right-handed coordinate systems.)

(See the entry for the `right` keyword for a detailed discussion of the way the `right` and `up` vectors and +W and +H command-line switches control the aspect ratio [width-to-height ratio] of the image.)

(See the `camera` keyword for further details.)

SEE ALSO

+H, +W, `camera`, `direction`, `location`, `look_at`, `right`, `sky`, *VECTOR*

EXAMPLE

See the example under `right`.

use_color and use_index

TYPE
BUMP_MAP_MODIFIER

PURPOSE
Specifies whether the color value of a pixel or the pixel's index is used in a bump map.

SYNTAX
```
bump_map {
    [MAP_PREFIX...] MAP_FILE_TYPE "FILESPEC"
    use_color
    [BUMP_MAP_MODIFIER...]
}
```

```
bump_map {
    [MAP_PREFIX...] MAP_FILE_TYPE "FILESPEC"
    use_index
    [BUMP_MAP_MODIFIER...]
}
```

DESCRIPTION
Normally a bump map converts the color of the map pixel to grayscale and then uses the intensity of the pixel to determine the bump height at that point. The `use_index` keyword tells POV-Ray to use the pixel's index rather than the color of the pixel. On nonpalette-based file types that do not have index values, the `use_index` keyword is ignored. A `use_color` keyword can also be given to document that the color method is used.

SEE ALSO
`bump_map`

EXAMPLE
See the example under `bump_map`.

VECTOR

PURPOSE

Specifies a 3D coordinate, surface normal, rotation, scale, or other three float values.

SYNTAX

< *x_value y_value z_value* >

DESCRIPTION

Vector values are required in many places in the language. In a syntax specification, any lone, lowercase italic word between angle brackets such as *<location>* is calling for a *VECTOR* to be given. Technically, any ordered group of values is a vector but in POV-Ray's language we are most often referring to a three-component vector. Three-component vectors normally correspond to the *x, y, z* coordinate system.

POV-Ray uses a left-handed 3D coordinate system. Figure 7-11 illustrates left- and right-handed systems. To visualize this system, extend your left hand and point with your index finger. Extend your thumb upwards at a right angle to your finger. Point your other fingers to the right. In this position your index finger points in the positive *z* direction, your thumb points in the positive *y* direction, and your remaining fingers point in the positive *x* direction. A right-handed coordinate system would assign the same axis to the same fingers on your right hand.

The sign of the `right` vector in a `camera` statement determines the left- or right-handedness of the coordinate system. A positive value specifies a left-handed system; that is the default. A negative value specifies a right-handed system. See the example that follows.

Most vectors in POV-Ray specify a 3D location in the coordinate space. The three float values correspond to a unit distance along the *x, y,* and *z* axes, respectively. Some vectors specify how much to do something in the *x, y,* and *z* directions. For example, the `translate` keyword specifies the amount a shape or object should be moved relative to its previous position. Similarly, the `rotate` keyword specifies the amount of rotation about the *x, y,* or *z* axis. In a left-handed system you should point your thumb along an axis and curl all your fingers. Your fingers will point in the direction of positive rotation about that axis.

SEE ALSO

FLOAT, `right`, `rotate`, `scale`, `translate`

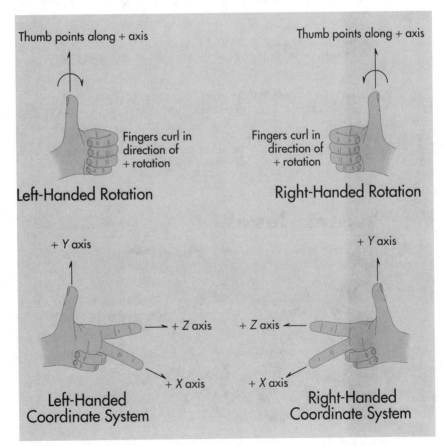

Figure 7-11　Left- and Right-Handed Coordinate System

EXAMPLE

```
// VECTORL.POV
#include "examp.inc"

// Changing handedness changes the x direction.
// Try switching the sign on the right vector
// and notice the location of the Cyan ball.
camera {
  location <0 1.2 -3>
  right <1.33 0 0>   // left-handed
//right <-1.33 0 0>  // right-handed
  look_at <0 0 1>
}

object {sphere{<0 0 0> 0.2} texture {color Cyan}
  translate <1 0 0> // move 1 unit in x direction
}

object {sphere{<0 0 0> 0.2} texture {color Green}
  translate <0 1 0> // move 1 unit in y direction
}

object {sphere{<0 0 0> 0.2} texture {color Yellow}
  translate <0 0 1> // move 1 unit in z direction
}

object {sphere{<0 0 0> 0.2} texture {color White}
  translate <0 0 0> // remain at origin
}
```

water_level

TYPE

HT_FIELD_MODIFIER

PURPOSE
Specifies a low cut-off level in a Height-Field shape.

SYNTAX
```
height_field {
    HT_FIELD_TYPE "FILESPEC"
    [water_level value] [SHAPE_MODIFIER...]
}
```

DESCRIPTION
Use the `water_level` keyword and a value from 0.0 to 256.0 and all heights lower than this value are clipped away. The default value is 0.

SEE ALSO
```
height_field
```

EXAMPLE
```
// WATERLEV.POV
#include "examp.inc"

object {
  height_field {
    gif "plasma2.gif"
//  gif "bumpmap_.gif" //Try these files too
//  gif "fract003.gif"
    water_level 128
  }
  texture {color Green phong 0.3}
  translate <-.5 -.5 -.5>
  scale <3 0.4 3>
  rotate <-20 -40 0>
}
```

waves

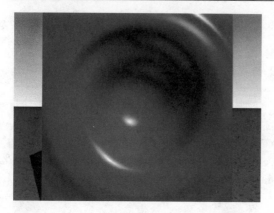

TYPE
NORMAL_PATTERN

PURPOSE
Makes a texture look wavy by applying a normal pattern to it. Specifies a set of concentric rings that resemble ocean waves.

SYNTAX
`texture { waves` *amount [TEXTURE_ITEM...]* `}`

DESCRIPTION
The `waves` keyword specifies a surface normal perturbation pattern that modifies the surface normal to look like the ocean. (See *NORMAL_PATTERN* for details on surface normals.) The waves radiate from ten locations, randomly placed within 1 unit of the origin. The required float value after the keyword specifies an apparent depth of the waves. Values from 0.0 (no waves) to 1.0 (deep waves) are typical. Each wave is about 1 or 2 units wide so for small objects a scale modifier is often used to alter the size.

The `ripples` keyword is an alternative to `waves` that more closely resembles small ripples in water.

The `frequency` keyword controls the space between waves and you can vary `phase` to make the waves seem to move when animated in a series of frames.

Note that the use of a normal pattern to perturb the surface normal does not actually change the shape of the object. It artificially modifies the surface normal so that lighting, reflections, refractions, and highlights look as though the surface were bumped. Only one normal pattern may be used in each `texture` statement.

SEE ALSO

`frequency`, *NORMAL_PATTERN*, `phase`, `ripples`, `texture`

EXAMPLE

```
// WAVES.POV
#include "examp.inc"

object {
  box {UnitBox}
  texture
   {color Cyan phong 1
    waves 0.4
    scale <0.1 0.1 0.1>
   }
}
```

wood

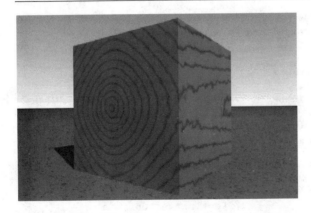

TYPE
COLOR_PATTERN

485

RAY TRACING

PURPOSE

Specifies a color pattern in a texture consisting of concentric cylinders that resembles wood grain.

SYNTAX

```
texture { wood [COLOR_PATTERN_MODIFIER...]
    [TEXTURE_ITEM...] }
```

DESCRIPTION

The `wood` keyword specifies a color pattern made of concentric cylinders along the z axis. When properly colored, this resembles the concentric growth rings in real wood. The rings are 1 unit apart so you should use small scaling values when applying `wood` to small shapes.

Use the `turbulence` and `octaves` keywords to stir up the pattern. A default color map is provided, but normally you would add a `color_map` of your own. Color patterns may be translated, rotated, or scaled. Only one color pattern may be specified in each `texture` statement.

SEE ALSO

`color_map`, `octaves`, `texture`, `turbulence`

EXAMPLE

```
// WOOD.POV
#include "examp.inc"   camera{location<0 0 -4>}

object {
  box {UnitBox}
  texture {
    wood
      color_map {
        [0.0 0.7 color Tan   color Tan]
        [0.7 1.0 color Tan   color Brown]
      }
    turbulence 0.05 octaves 3
    scale <0.12 0.12 0.12>
    rotate <0 5 0> // slight rotate helps grain
                   // look better on side
    ambient 0.3
  }
  rotate <0 35 0>
}
```

wrinkles

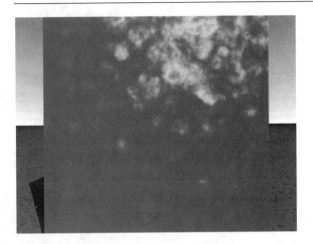

TYPE
NORMAL_PATTERN

PURPOSE
Makes a texture look like wrinkled cloth by applying a normal pattern to it.

SYNTAX
`texture { wrinkled` *amount [TEXTURE_ITEM...]* `}`

DESCRIPTION
The `wrinkles` keyword specifies a surface normal perturbation pattern that causes the surface normal to look like wrinkled cloth. (See *NORMAL_PATTERN* for details on surface normals.) The required float value after the keyword specifies an apparent depth of the wrinkles. Values from 0.0 (no wrinkles) to 1.0 (very wrinkled) are typical. Each wrinkle is about 1 or 2 units wide, so for small objects a scale modifier is often used.

Note that the use of a normal pattern to perturb the surface normal does not actually change the shape of the object. It artificially modifies the surface normal so that lighting, reflections, refractions, and highlights look as though the surface were bumped. Only one normal pattern may be used in each `texture` statement.

487

SEE ALSO

NORMAL_PATTERN, texture

EXAMPLE

```
// WRINKLES.POV
#include "examp.inc"

object {
  box {UnitBox}
  texture
   {color Cyan phong 0.8
    wrinkles 0.3
    scale <0.2 0.2 0.2>
   }
}
```

A

Standard Include Files

INTRODUCTION

Your POV-Ray input files can contain one or more #include directives that refer to other text files containing POV-Ray statements. It is standard practice to give these files the .INC extension. POV-Ray has a number of standard Include files that contain #declare directives defining commonly used shapes and textures. This appendix provides an annotated listing of these files and information on how to use them.

SETTING UP INCLUDE FILES

First, create a special directory for the standard Include files. You may also add Include files of your own in that directory, or you may wish to create another directory for your own customized files. The +L command-line switch for POV-Ray allows you to better manage your files by placing them in separate directories and specifying a path where they can be found. For example:

```
POVRAY MYDEFS.DEF +Lc:\povray\includes +Imyfile.pov
```

This causes POV-Ray to search the C:\POVRAY\INCLUDES directory if the file specified in an #include directive is not found on the current directory. (See +L switch in Chapter 7 for details.)

491

POV-Ray begins parsing your input file at the first line and continues processing it line-by-line to the end. You may put an `#include` directive anywhere in the file but the standard includes should be near the top of the file because they contain `#declare` directives that you will reference later. For example, many POV-Ray files begin with

```
#include "colors.inc"
#include "textures.inc"
#include "shapes.inc"
```

POV-Ray remembers where it is in the current file and begins processing text from these files as if their contents had been copied into your file at that point. When POV-Ray has finished processing the Include file, it picks up where it paused and processes the remainder of the earlier file.

USING INCLUDED IDENTIFIERS

Although Include files may contain any legal POV-Ray statements, most often they contain only `#declare` directives that specify identifiers for use later in your scene. The standard Include files are made entirely of such directives.

POV-Ray allows you to declare 23 different types of identifier. This helps you to modularize and parameterize your scene descriptions, and it makes them more readable. You might declare a complex object and then translate, rotate, or scale multiple copies of that object into different positions by simply invoking the identifier in several places.

You can declare floating-point values or vectors describing various parameters. By using these parameters you need only change the one declaration to change all of the places it is used. Identifiers may be used anywhere that the items they represent could be used, including in the declarations of other identifiers. (See the `#declare` directive in Chapter 7 for further details on declaring identifiers.)

A float identifier, or vector identifier, is invoked by simply using the identifier wherever a floating-point value or vector can be used. *Do not enclose* a vector identifier in angle brackets. For example:

```
#declare Radius = 2          // declare a float identifier
#declare Center = <1 5 3>    // declare a vector identifier
object {
  sphere { Center Radius }   // same as "sphere {<1 5 3> 2}"
}                            // Note vector identifier has no <>
```

492

You can place a color identifier after the color keyword, but every other type of identifier must be invoked by surrounding it with { } braces and placing the type before it. For example, if MyObject is an object identifier, it is invoked by object {MyObject}. The type of the identifier must match the keyword.

Although the syntax for invoking a color identifier, camera identifier, or texture identifier allows for other items appearing before the identifier, you should *not* do this: An identifier completely defines the entire item and invoking it will overwrite all previous specifications.

INCLUDE FILE LISTINGS

The files listed in Table A-1 are on disk in the \POVRAY\INCLUDE directory.

Below is a more detailed description of each and a complete listing for reference purposes. In some cases, the files have been reformatted from the disk versions but they contain the same information.

Table A-1	List of Standard Include Files
File	**Contents**
COLORS.INC	Colors and special float values for maps
SHAPES.INC	Fundamental shapes such as cones, cylinders, disks, and boxes scaled to fit inside a 2x2x2 box at origin
TEXTURES.INC	Sample textures of many kinds including woods, metals, and glass
SHAPESQ.INC	Quartic and other fancy polynomial shapes, including torus (donut) shapes
SHAPES2.INC	More basic shapes including Platonic solids
STONES.INC	Wide variety of marble and granite stone textures
IOR.INC	Index of refraction values for transparent textures
FOV.INC	Values for changing the camera field of view
SHAPES. OLD	Older version of SHAPES.INC, compatible with an earlier version of POV-Ray

COLORS.INC INCLUDE FILE

The COLORS.INC file contains a wide variety of standard colors. When you use these colors keep in mind that the final appearance of a surface depends upon the lighting used. By changing the position and number of light sources as well as ambient, diffuse, and brilliance setting, you can achieve a variety of looks for the same basic color.

The first colors listed are gray values ranging from 5 to 95 percent of full white. These are primarily for use in light sources. The intensity of light from a source depends upon the color used in the specification. A "White" or "Gray70" through "Gray90" provides bright light. Lower gray values provide less light.

At the end of COLORS.INC you will find a set of float identifiers for use with the `map_type` and `interpolate` keywords. See the reference entry for these keywords for details on their values.

Listing A-1 COLORS.INC Include File

```
// Persistence of Vision Raytracer
// Colors.inc
//
// Many pre defined colors for use in scene files.
// Also includes constants for Map Types and Interpolation Types
// for use with image_map, bump_map, and material_map

//
// These grays are useful for fine-tuning lighting color values
// and for other areas where subtle variations of grays are needed.
#declare Gray05 = color red 0.05 green 0.05 blue 0.05
#declare Gray10 = color red 0.10 green 0.10 blue 0.10
#declare Gray15 = color red 0.15 green 0.15 blue 0.15
#declare Gray20 = color red 0.20 green 0.20 blue 0.20
#declare Gray25 = color red 0.25 green 0.25 blue 0.25
#declare Gray30 = color red 0.30 green 0.30 blue 0.30
#declare Gray35 = color red 0.35 green 0.35 blue 0.35
#declare Gray40 = color red 0.40 green 0.40 blue 0.40
#declare Gray45 = color red 0.45 green 0.45 blue 0.45
#declare Gray50 = color red 0.50 green 0.50 blue 0.50
#declare Gray55 = color red 0.55 green 0.55 blue 0.55
#declare Gray60 = color red 0.60 green 0.60 blue 0.60
#declare Gray65 = color red 0.65 green 0.65 blue 0.65
#declare Gray70 = color red 0.70 green 0.70 blue 0.70
#declare Gray75 = color red 0.75 green 0.75 blue 0.75
```

```
#declare Gray80 = color red 0.80 green 0.80 blue 0.80
#declare Gray85 = color red 0.85 green 0.85 blue 0.85
#declare Gray90 = color red 0.90 green 0.90 blue 0.90
#declare Gray95 = color red 0.95 green 0.95 blue 0.95

#declare DimGray = color red 0.329412 green 0.329412 blue 0.329412
#declare DimGrey = color red 0.329412 green 0.329412 blue 0.329412
#declare Gray = color red 0.752941 green 0.752941 blue 0.752941
#declare Grey = color red 0.752941 green 0.752941 blue 0.752941
#declare LightGray = color red 0.658824 green 0.658824 blue 0.658824
#declare LightGrey = color red 0.658824 green 0.658824 blue 0.658824
#declare VLightGrey = color red 0.80 green 0.80 blue 0.80

#declare Clear = color red 1.0 green 1.0 blue 1.0 alpha 1.0
#declare White = color red 1.0 green 1.0 blue 1.0
#declare Red = color red 1.0
#declare Green = color green 1.0
#declare Blue = color blue 1.0
#declare Yellow = color red 1.0 green 1.0
#declare Cyan = color blue 1.0 green 1.0
#declare Magenta = color red 1.0 blue 1.0
#declare Black = color red 0.0 green 0.0 blue 0.0
#declare Aquamarine =
    color red 0.439216 green 0.858824 blue 0.576471
#declare BlueViolet = color red 0.62352 green 0.372549 blue 0.623529
#declare Brown = color red 0.647059 green 0.164706 blue 0.164706
#declare CadetBlue = color red 0.372549 green 0.623529 blue 0.623529
#declare Coral = color red 1.0 green 0.498039 blue 0.0
#declare CornflowerBlue =
    color red 0.258824 green 0.258824 blue 0.435294
#declare DarkGreen = color red 0.184314 green 0.309804 blue 0.184314
#declare DarkOliveGreen =
    color red 0.309804 green 0.309804 blue 0.184314
#declare DarkOrchid = color red 0.6 green 0.196078 blue 0.8
#declare DarkSlateBlue =
    color red 0.419608 green 0.137255 blue 0.556863
#declare DarkSlateGray =
    color red 0.184314 green 0.309804 blue 0.309804
#declare DarkSlateGrey =
    color red 0.184314 green 0.309804 blue 0.309804
#declare DarkTurquoise =
    color red 0.439216 green 0.576471 blue 0.858824
#declare Firebrick = color red 0.556863 green 0.137255 blue 0.137255
#declare ForestGreen =
    color red 0.137255 green 0.556863 blue 0.137255
#declare Gold = color red 0.8 green 0.498039 blue 0.196078
#declare Goldenrod = color red 0.858824 green 0.858824 blue 0.439216
#declare GreenYellow =
    color red 0.576471 green 0.858824 blue 0.439216
#declare IndianRed = color red 0.309804 green 0.184314 blue 0.184314
```

```
#declare Khaki = color red 0.623529 green 0.623529 blue 0.372549
#declare LightBlue = color red 0.74902 green 0.847059 blue 0.847059
#declare LightSteelBlue =
    color red 0.560784 green 0.560784 blue 0.737255
#declare LimeGreen = color red 0.196078 green 0.8 blue 0.196078
#declare Maroon = color red 0.556863 green 0.137255 blue 0.419608
#declare MediumAquamarine = color red 0.196078 green 0.8 blue 0.6
#declare MediumBlue = color red 0.196078 green 0.196078 blue 0.8
#declare MediumForestGreen =
    color red 0.419608 green 0.556863 blue 0.137255
#declare MediumGoldenrod =
    color red 0.917647 green 0.917647 blue 0.678431
#declare MediumOrchid =
    color red 0.576471 green 0.439216 blue 0.858824
#declare MediumSeaGreen =
    color red 0.258824 green 0.435294 blue 0.258824
#declare MediumSlateBlue = color red 0.498039 blue 1.0
#declare MediumSpringGreen = color red 0.498039 green 1.0
#declare MediumTurquoise =
    color red 0.439216 green 0.858824 blue 0.858824
#declare MediumVioletRed =
    color red 0.858824 green 0.439216 blue 0.576471
#declare MidnightBlue =
    color red 0.184314 green 0.184314 blue 0.309804
#declare Navy = color red 0.137255 green 0.137255 blue 0.556863
#declare NavyBlue = color red 0.137255 green 0.137255 blue 0.556863
#declare Orange = color red 1 green 0.5 blue 0.0
#declare OrangeRed = color red 1.0 blue 0.498039
#declare Orchid = color red 0.858824 green 0.439216 blue 0.858824
#declare PaleGreen = color red 0.560784 green 0.737255 blue 0.560784
#declare Pink = color red 0.737255 green 0.560784 blue 0.560784
#declare Plum = color red 0.917647 green 0.678431 blue 0.917647
#declare Salmon = color red 0.435294 green 0.258824 blue 0.258824
#declare SeaGreen = color red 0.137255 green 0.556863 blue 0.419608
#declare Sienna = color red 0.556863 green 0.419608 blue 0.137255
#declare SkyBlue = color red 0.196078 green 0.6 blue 0.8
#declare SlateBlue = color green 0.498039 blue 1.0
#declare SpringGreen = color green 1.0 blue 0.498039
#declare SteelBlue = color red 0.137255 green 0.419608 blue 0.556863
#declare Tan = color red 0.858824 green 0.576471 blue 0.439216
#declare Thistle = color red 0.847059 green 0.74902 blue 0.847059
#declare Turquoise = color red 0.678431 green 0.917647 blue 0.917647
#declare Violet = color red 0.309804 green 0.184314 blue 0.309804
#declare VioletRed = color red 0.8 green 0.196078 blue 0.6
#declare Wheat = color red 0.847059 green 0.847059 blue 0.74902
#declare YellowGreen = color red 0.6 green 0.8 blue 0.196078
#declare SummerSky = color red 0.22 green 0.69 blue 0.87
#declare RichBlue = color red 0.35 green 0.35 blue 0.67
#declare Brass =  color red 0.71 green 0.65 blue 0.26
#declare Copper = color red 0.72 green 0.45 blue 0.20
```

```
#declare Bronze = color red 0.55 green 0.47 blue 0.14
#declare Bronze2 = color red 0.65 green 0.49 blue 0.24
#declare Silver = color red 0.90 green 0.91 blue 0.98
#declare BrightGold = color red 0.85 green 0.85 blue 0.10
#declare OldGold =  color red 0.81 green 0.71 blue 0.23
#declare Feldspar = color red 0.82 green 0.57 blue 0.46
#declare Quartz = color red 0.85 green 0.85 blue 0.95
#declare Mica = color Black  // needed in textures.inc
#declare NeonPink = color red 1.00 green 0.43 blue 0.78
#declare DarkPurple = color red 0.53 green 0.12 blue 0.47
#declare NeonBlue = color red 0.30 green 0.30 blue 1.00
#declare CoolCopper = color red 0.85 green 0.53 blue 0.10
#declare MandarinOrange = color red 0.89 green 0.47 blue 0.20
#declare LightWood = color red 0.91 green 0.76 blue 0.65
#declare MediumWood = color red 0.65 green 0.50 blue 0.39
#declare DarkWood = color red 0.52 green 0.37 blue 0.26
#declare SpicyPink = color red 1.00 green 0.11 blue 0.68
#declare SemiSweetChoc = color red 0.42 green 0.26 blue 0.15
#declare BakersChoc = color red 0.36 green 0.20 blue 0.09
#declare Flesh = color red 0.96 green 0.80 blue 0.69
#declare NewTan = color red 0.92 green 0.78 blue 0.62
#declare NewMidnightBlue = color red 0.00 green 0.00 blue 0.61
#declare VeryDarkBrown = color red 0.35 green 0.16 blue 0.14
#declare DarkBrown = color red 0.36 green 0.25 blue 0.20
#declare DarkTan = color red 0.59 green 0.41 blue 0.31
#declare GreenCopper = color red 0.32 green 0.49 blue 0.46
#declare DkGreenCopper = color red 0.29 green 0.46 blue 0.43
#declare DustyRose = color red 0.52 green 0.39 blue 0.39
#declare HuntersGreen = color red 0.13 green 0.37 blue 0.31
#declare Scarlet = color red 0.55 green 0.09 blue 0.09


// Map types constants
// for use with image_map, bump_map, and material_map
//
// Format:
//   map_type Sphere_Map or map_type Torus_Map
//
#declare Plane_Map = 0
#declare Sphere_Map = 1
#declare Cylinder_Map = 2
#declare Torus_Map = 5


// Interpolation constants
// Use in image_map and bump_map in form:
//
// interpolate Bi or interpolate Norm
//
#declare Bi  = 2    // Bilinear interpolation is best
#declare Norm = 4    // Normalized distance is a bit faster
```

SHAPES.INC INCLUDE FILE

The SHAPES.INC file contains a set of fundamental shapes such as cones, cylinders, disks, and boxes. The Disk, Cone, UnitBox, and Ellipsoid shapes have been scaled to the same proportion as a sphere with a radius of 1 unit. This means that they will fit inside a 2x2x2-unit box at the origin. Typically, you use these shapes with a scale statement to obtain the proper size. For example, if you want a thin, flat disk 1 unit thick and 10 units in radius you would use

```
object {
  intersection {Disk_Y scale <10.0 0.5 10.0>}
}
```

The Disk_Y shape extends 1 unit in the positive y direction and 1 unit in the negative y direction, so it is initially 2 units thick. To make the final object 1 unit thick, you would make the y term of the scale vector 0.5. The Disk_Y shape is initially 1 unit in radius so the x and z terms of the scale vector are 10.0 in order to give the desired radius of 10.

Other shapes such as QCone and Cylinder are infinitely long on one axis but are scaled in proportion to the unit shapes along the other axes.

A file SHAPES.OLD is also provided. It is an earlier, slightly different version of SHAPES.INC. Use it only for scenes created before the final version of POV-Ray was released to the public.

Listing A-2 SHAPES.INC Include File

```
// Persistence Of Vision Raytracer
// Standard shapes include file.

/*
NOTE: Some of these shapes, in particular, the "Disk_?" group, have been
changed in such a way that they will not work correctly with some of the
old scene files. The file "shapes.old" is also included in this package
for exactly this purpose. The reason for this change was to provide a set
of shapes that would scale in a consistant fashion. We apologize for any
inconvenience that this may cause in the short term, but expect that
you'll quickly come to agree that this is easier to learn and to use.

The quadric Sphere has been duplicated under the preferred name of
Ellipsoid to differentiate it from the internal sphere primitive. Please
refer to Ellipsoid when you wish to use a quadric sphere.
```

```
Revised shapes.inc
All primitives scale the same as a sphere with radius=1.
 Changes:
   Disk_X (was X_Disk)
   Disk_Y (was Y_Disk)
   Disk_Z (was Z_Disk)
   QCone_X (was Cone_X)
   QCone_Y (was Cone_Y)
   QCone_Z (was Cone_Z)
 New:
   UnitBox
   Ellipsoid
   Cone_X (now unit shape intersection instead of infinite quadric)
   Cone_Y (now unit shape intersection instead of infinite quadric)
   Cone_Z (now unit shape intersection instead of infinite quadric)
 Moved: to shapes2.pov
   Square_X
   Square_Y
   Square_Z
   Pyramid
   Tetrahedron
*/

#declare Ellipsoid =
quadric {
   <1.0 1.0 1.0> <0.0 0.0 0.0> <0.0 0.0 0.0> -1.0
}

#declare Sphere =
quadric {
   <1.0 1.0 1.0> <0.0 0.0 0.0> <0.0 0.0 0.0> -1.0
}

#declare Cylinder_X =
quadric {
   <0.0 1.0 1.0> <0.0 0.0 0.0> <0.0 0.0 0.0> -1.0
}

#declare Cylinder_Y =
quadric {
   <1.0 0.0 1.0> <0.0 0.0 0.0> <0.0 0.0 0.0> -1.0
}

#declare Cylinder_Z =
quadric {
   <1.0 1.0 0.0> <0.0 0.0 0.0> <0.0 0.0 0.0> -1.0
}

// Infinite cones
```

```
#declare QCone_X =
quadric {
   <-1.0 1.0 1.0> <0.0 0.0 0.0> <0.0 0.0 0.0> 0.0
}


#declare QCone_Y =
quadric {
   <1.0 -1.0 1.0> <0.0 0.0 0.0> <0.0 0.0 0.0> 0.0
}


#declare QCone_Z =
quadric {
   <1.0 1.0 -1.0> <0.0 0.0 0.0> <0.0 0.0 0.0> 0.0
}


// Unit cones
//
// Use: intersection { Cone_X }
//
#declare Cone_X =
intersection {
   quadric { QCone_X translate <1 0 0> }
   box { <-1 -2 -2> <1 2 2> }
   scale <1 .5 .5>
}
#declare Cone_Y =
intersection {
   quadric { QCone_Y  translate <0 1 0>}
   box { <-2 -1 -2> <2 1 2> }
   scale <.5 1 .5>
}
#declare Cone_Z =
intersection {
   quadric { QCone_Z translate <0 0 1>}
   box { <-2 -2 -1> <2 2 1> }
   scale <.5 .5 1>
}


#declare Plane_YZ =
quadric {
   <0.0 0.0 0.0> <0.0 0.0 0.0> <1.0 0.0 0.0> 0.0
}


#declare Plane_XZ =
quadric {
   <0.0 0.0 0.0> <0.0 0.0 0.0> <0.0 1.0 0.0> 0.0
}


#declare Plane_XY =
quadric {
```

```
      <0.0 0.0 0.0> <0.0 0.0 0.0> <0.0 0.0 1.0> 0.0
}

/* y^2 + z^2 - x = 0 */
#declare Paraboloid_X =
quadric {
   <0.0 1.0  1.0> <0.0  0.0  0.0> <-1.0 0.0  0.0> 0.0
}

/* x^2 + z^2 - y = 0 */
#declare Paraboloid_Y =
quadric {
   <1.0  0.0  1.0> <0.0  0.0  0.0> <0.0 -1.0  0.0> 0.0
}

/* x^2 + y^2 - z = 0 */
#declare Paraboloid_Z =
quadric {
   <1.0  1.0  0.0> <0.0  0.0  0.0> <0.0  0.0 -1.0> 0.0
}

/* y - x^2 + z^2 = 0 */
#declare Hyperboloid =
quadric {
   <-1.0  0.0  1.0> < 0.0  0.0  0.0> < 0.0  1.0  0.0> 0.0
}

// Vertical hyperboloid, like this:          \  /
#declare Hyperboloid_Y =          //          ) (
quadric {                         //          /  \
   <1.0 -1.0  1.0> <0.0  0.0  0.0> <0.0  0.0  0.0> -1.0
}

// Cube using the procedural box primitive
#declare UnitBox = box { <-1.0 -1.0 -1.0> <1.0 1.0 1.0> }

// This primitive used to be an intersection of six planes.
// For speed, it's now an intersection of a box and nothing else.
#declare Cube = intersection { box { <-1 -1 -1> <1 1 1>} }

// The Disk primitives are "capped" cylinders of 2 unit length.
//
// Note: These three shapes have been changed for Version 1.0.
// They are now "unit" size, the same as a sphere with a radius
// of 1.
// They will now scale evenly in all directions.
// Old files may need to be modified to work with these shapes, but
// I think you'll find them to be more consistent with the rest
// of the POV-Ray primitives and easier for novices to understand.
```

```
#declare Disk_X =
intersection {          /* Capped cylinder, Length in x axis */
   quadric { Cylinder_X }
   plane { <1.0 0.0 0.0> -1 inverse  }
   plane { <1.0 0.0 0.0>  1  }
}

#declare Disk_Y =
intersection {          /* Capped cylinder, Length in y axis */
   quadric { Cylinder_Y }
   plane { <0.0 1.0 0.0> -1 inverse >
   plane { <0.0 1.0 0.0>  1 }
}

#declare Disk_Z =
intersection {          /* Capped cylinder, Length in z axis */
   quadric { Cylinder_Z }
   plane { <0.0 0.0 1.0> -1 inverse  }
   plane { <0.0 0.0 1.0>  1  }
}
```

TEXTURES.INC INCLUDE FILE

The TEXTURES.INC file contains a variety of sample textures including woods, metals, and glass. You may use these directly or create textures of your own using one or more of these as a basis.

Listing A-3 TEXTURES.INC Include File

```
// Persistence of Vision Raytracer
// Standard textures include file
// See textures.doc for info.

//************************************************************ //
//                    STONE TEXTURES                          //
//************************************************************ //

// A nice Jade. Color map works nicely with other textures, too.
#declare Jade =
 texture {
   marble
   turbulence 1.8
   color_map {
     [0.0 0.8  color red 0.1 green 0.6 blue 0.1
           color red 0.0 green 0.3 blue 0.0]
     [0.8 1    color red 0.1 green 0.6 blue 0.1
```

```
            color red 0.0 green 0.2 blue 0.0]
  }
 }

// Classic white marble with red veins. Overworked, like checkers.
#declare Red_Marble =
 texture {
   marble
   turbulence 1.0
   color_map {
     [0.0 0.8  color red 0.8 green 0.8 blue 0.6
          color red 0.8 green 0.4 blue 0.4]
     [0.8 1    color red 0.8 green 0.4 blue 0.4
          color red 0.8 green 0.2 blue 0.2]
   }
 }

// White marble with black veins.
#declare White_Marble =
 texture {
   marble
   turbulence 1.0
   color_map {
     [0.0 0.8  color red 0.9 green 0.9 blue 0.9
          color red 0.5 green 0.5 blue 0.5]
     [0.8 1    color red 0.5 green 0.5 blue 0.5
          color red 0.2 green 0.2 blue 0.2]
   }
 }

// Light blue and black marble with a thin red vein
// Try changing LBlue and Vein below to modify the marble.
#declare LBlue = color red 0.0 green 0.6 blue 0.6
#declare Vein  = color red 0.6 green 0.0 blue 0.0
#declare Blood_Marble =
 texture {
   marble
   turbulence 2.3
   color_map {
     [0.0 0.8  color Black  color LBlue]
     [0.8 0.9  color LBlue  color Vein]
     [0.9 1    color Vein   color Black]
   }
 }

// A grey blue agate--kind of purplish.
#declare Blue_Agate =
 texture {
   agate
   color_map {
```

```
       [0.0 0.5  color red 0.30 green 0.30 blue 0.50
             color red 0.30 green 0.30 blue 0.50]
       [0.5 0.55 color red 0.30 green 0.30 blue 0.50
             color red 0.20 green 0.20 blue 0.30]
       [0.55 0.6 color red 0.20 green 0.20 blue 0.30
             color red 0.25 green 0.25 blue 0.35]
       [0.6 0.7  color red 0.25 green 0.25 blue 0.35
             color red 0.15 green 0.15 blue 0.26]
       [0.7 0.8  color red 0.15 green 0.15 blue 0.26
             color red 0.10 green 0.10 blue 0.20]
       [0.8 0.9  color red 0.10 green 0.10 blue 0.20
             color red 0.30 green 0.30 blue 0.50]
       [0.9 1    color red 0.30 green 0.30 blue 0.50
             color red 0.10 green 0.10 blue 0.20]
    }
 }


// Deep blue agate--almost glows.
#declare Sapphire_Agate =
 texture {
   agate
   color_map {
     [0.0 0.3  color red 0.0 green 0.0 blue 0.9
           color red 0.0 green 0.0 blue 0.8]
     [0.3 1    color red 0.0 green 0.0 blue 0.8
           color red 0.0 green 0.0 blue 0.4]
   }
 }


// Brown and white agate--very pretty.
#declare Brown_Agate =
 texture {
   agate
   color_map {
     [0.0 0.5  color red 1.0 green 1.0 blue 1.0
           color red 0.9 green 0.7 blue 0.6]
     [0.5 0.6  color red 0.9 green 0.7 blue 0.6
           color red 0.9 green 0.7 blue 0.4]
     [0.6 1    color red 0.9 green 0.7 blue 0.4
           color red 0.7 green 0.4 blue 0.2]
   }
 }

#declare Pink_Granite =
 texture {
   granite
   turbulence 0
   color_map {
     [0.0  0.4   color Black color Black]
     [0.4  0.45  color Quartz color Quartz]
```

```
      [0.45 0.5   color Quartz color Gray]
      [0.5  0.55  color Gray color Feldspar]
      [0.55 0.8   color Feldspar color Feldspar]
      [0.8  1.0   color Feldspar color Orange]
    }
  }

// Gray-pink alabaster or marble. Layers are scaled for a unit
// object and relative to each other.
#declare PinkAlabaster =
// Underlying surface is very subtly mottled with bozo
  texture {
    ambient 0.25
    bozo
    turbulence 0.25
    color_map {
      [0.0 1.0  color red 0.9 green 0.75 blue 0.75
            color red 0.6 green 0.6 blue 0.6 ]
    }
    scale <.4 .4 .4>
  }

// Second layer texture has some alpha values, yet a fair amount
// of color. Veining is kept quite thin in color map and by
// the largish scale.
  texture {
    granite
    color_map {
      [0.0 0.9 color DustyRose alpha 1 color DustyRose alpha 0.5 ]
      [0.9 1.0 color DarkSlateGray     color DarkSlateGray ]
    }
    // I know this seems contradictory, but it seems to work!
    specular 1.0    roughness 0.001
    phong 0.25      phong_size 75
    brilliance 4
    scale <2 2 2>        // Twice as large as unit shape
  }


//********************************************************** //
//                    SKY TEXTURES                          //
//********************************************************** //

// Basic Blue Sky w/ clouds.
#declare Blue_Sky =
  texture {
    bozo
    turbulence 0.3
    color_map {
      [0.0 0.5  color red 0.25 green 0.25 blue 0.5
```

```
          color red 0.25 green 0.25 blue 0.5]
     [0.5 0.6  color red 0.25 green 0.25 blue 0.5
          color red 0.7 green 0.7 blue 0.7]
     [0.6 1    color red 0.7 green 0.7 blue 0.7
          color red 0.3 green 0.3 blue 0.3]
   }
  }


// Bright Blue Sky w/ very white clouds.
#declare Bright_Blue_Sky =
 texture {
   bozo
   turbulence 0.56
   color_map {
     [0.0 0.5  color red 0.5 green 0.5 blue 1.0
          color red 0.5 green 0.5 blue 1.0]
     [0.5 0.6  color red 0.5 green 0.5 blue 1.0
          color red 1.0 green 1.0 blue 1.0]
     [0.6 1    color red 1.0 green 1.0 blue 1.0
          color red 0.5 green 0.5 blue 0.5]
   }
 }


// Another sky.
#declare Blue_Sky2 =
 texture {
   agate
   color_map {
     [ 0 .3  color Blue color Blue ]
     [.3  1  color Blue color White   ]
   }
   scale <.75 .15 .75>
 }


// Small puffs of white clouds
#declare Blue_Sky3 =
 texture {
   granite
   turbulence 0.1
   color_map {
     [ 0 .3  color Blue color Blue ]
     [.3  1  color Blue color White   ]
   }
   scale <.75 .15 .75>
 }


// Red sky w/ yellow clouds--very surreal.
#declare Blood_Sky =
 texture {
   bozo
```

```
   turbulence 0.5
   color_map {
     [0.0 0.5  color red 0.9 green 0.7 blue 0.0
          color red 0.3 green 0.2 blue 0.0]
     [0.5 0.6  color red 0.6 green 0.025 blue 0.0
          color red 0.9 green 0.7 blue 0.0]
     [0.6 1    color red 0.6 green 0.025 blue 0.0
          color red 0.6 green 0.025 blue 0.0]
   }
 }


// Black sky with red and purple clouds.
// Try adding turbulence values from 0.1 - 5.0 ñ CdW
#declare Apocalypse =
 texture {
   bozo
   color_map {
     [0.0 0.4  color red 0.8 green 0.0 blue 0.0
          color red 0.4 green 0.0 blue 0.4]
     [0.4 0.6  color red 0.4 green 0.0 blue 0.4
          color red 0.0 green 0.0 blue 0.2]
     [0.6 1    color red 0.0 green 0.0 blue 0.2
          color red 0.0 green 0.0 blue 0.0]
   }
 }


// White clouds w/ transparent sky.
#declare Clouds =
 texture {
   bozo
   turbulence 0.0
   color_map {
     [0.0 0.1  color red 0.8 green 0.8 blue 0.8
          color red 0.8 green 0.8 blue 0.8]
     [0.1 0.5  color red 0.8 green 0.8 blue 0.8 alpha 0.0
          color red 1.0 green 1.0 blue 1.0 alpha 1.0 ]
     [0.5 1    color red 1.0 green 1.0 blue 1.0 alpha 1.0
          color red 1.0 green 1.0 blue 1.0 alpha 1.0]
   }
 }


//*************************************************************//
//                    WOODEN TEXTURES                        //
//*************************************************************//

// A light reddish wood.
#declare Cherry_Wood =
 texture {
   wood
   turbulence 0.3
```

```
    color_map {
      [0.0 0.8  color red 0.666 green 0.312 blue 0.2
            color red 0.666 green 0.312 blue 0.2]
      [0.8 1    color red 0.4 green 0.133 blue 0.066
            color red 0.2 green 0.065 blue 0.033]
    }
  }


// A light tan wood with greenish rings.
#declare Pine_Wood =
  texture {
    wood
    turbulence 0.2
    color_map {
      [0.0 0.8  color red 1.0 green 0.71875 blue 0.25
            color red 1.0 green 0.71875 blue 0.25]
      [0.8 1    color red 0.5 green 0.5 blue 0.066
            color red 0.4 green 0.4 blue 0.033]
    }
  }


// Dark wood with a greenish hue to it.
#declare Dark_Wood =
  texture {
    wood
    turbulence 0.2
    color_map {
      [0.0 0.8  color red 0.42857 green 0.23810 blue 0.04762
            color red 0.42857 green 0.23810 blue 0.04762]
      [0.8 1    color red 0.4 green 0.333 blue 0.066
            color red 0.2 green 0.033 blue 0.033]
    }
  }


// Light tan wood with brown rings.
#declare Tan_Wood =
  texture {
    wood
    turbulence 0.1
    color_map {
      [0.0 0.8  color red 0.888 green 0.600 blue 0.3
            color red 0.888 green 0.600 blue 0.3]
      [0.8 1    color red 0.6 green 0.4 blue 0.2
            color red 0.4 green 0.3 blue 0.2]
    }
  }


// A very pale wood with tan rings--kind of balsa-ish.
#declare White_Wood =
  texture {
```

```
    wood
    turbulence 0.6
    color_map {
      [0.0 0.8  color red 0.93 green 0.71 blue 0.532
           color red 0.98 green 0.81 blue 0.6]
      [0.8 1    color red 0.6 green 0.333 blue 0.266
           color red 0.7 green 0.6 blue 0.23]
    }
 }

// Brown wood--looks stained.
#declare Tom_Wood =
 texture {
   wood
   turbulence 0.31
   color_map {
     [0.0 0.8  color red 0.7 green 0.3 blue 0.0
          color red 0.7 green 0.3 blue 0.0]
     [0.8 1    color red 0.5 green 0.2 blue 0.0
          color red 0.4 green 0.1 blue 0.0]
   }
 }

// The scaling in these definitions is relative to a unit-sized
// object (radius 1). Note that woods are functionally
// equivalent to a log lying along the z axis. For best
// results, think like a woodcutter trying to extract the
// nicest board out of that log. A little tilt along the
// x axis will give elliptical rings of grain like you'd expect
// to find on most boards. Experiment. (The first five came
// from DODEC2.POV in the POV-Ray Scenefile Library.)
#declare DMFWood1 =
 texture {
   wood
   turbulence 0.04
   octaves 3
   scale <0.05 .05 1>
   color_map {
     [0.00 0.10  color red 0.60 green 0.30 blue 0.18
          color red 0.60 green 0.30 blue 0.18]
     [0.10 0.90  color red 0.60 green 0.30 blue 0.18
          color red 0.30 green 0.15 blue 0.09]
     [0.90 1.0   color red 0.30 green 0.15 blue 0.09
          color red 0.30 green 0.15 blue 0.09]
   }
 }

#declare DMFWood2 =
 texture {
   wood
```

```
      turbulence 0.03
      octaves 4
      scale <0.05 .05 1>
      color_map {
        [0.00 0.10   color red 0.52 green 0.37 blue 0.26
                color red 0.52 green 0.37 blue 0.26]
        [0.10 0.90   color red 0.52 green 0.37 blue 0.26
                color red 0.42 green 0.26 blue 0.15]
        [0.90 1.0    color red 0.42 green 0.26 blue 0.15
                color red 0.42 green 0.26 blue 0.15]
      }
   }

#declare DMFWood3 =
 texture {
   wood
   turbulence 0.05
   octaves 2
   scale <0.05 .05 1>
   color_map {
      [0.00 0.10   color red 0.4 green 0.133 blue 0.066
              color red 0.4 green 0.133 blue 0.066]
      [0.10 0.90   color red 0.4 green 0.133 blue 0.066
              color red 0.2 green 0.065 blue 0.033]
      [0.90 1.0    color red 0.2 green 0.065 blue 0.033
              color red 0.2 green 0.065 blue 0.033]
   }
 }

#declare DMFWood4 =
 texture {
   wood
   turbulence 0.04
   octaves 3
   scale <0.05 .05 1>
   color_map {
      [0.00 0.10   color red 0.888 green 0.600 blue 0.3
              color red 0.888 green 0.600 blue 0.3]
      [0.10 0.90   color red 0.888 green 0.600 blue 0.3
              color red 0.6 green 0.4 blue 0.2]
      [0.90 1.0    color red 0.6 green 0.4 blue 0.2
              color red 0.6 green 0.4 blue 0.2]
   }
 }

#declare DMFWood5 =
 texture {
   wood
   turbulence 0.05
   octaves 6
```

```
    scale <0.075 .075 1>
    color_map {
      [0.00 0.10   color red 0.3 green 0.1 blue 0.05
            color red 0.3 green 0.1 blue 0.05]
      [0.10 0.90   color red 0.3 green 0.1 blue 0.05
            color red 0.25 green 0.07 blue 0.038]
      [0.90 1.0    color red 0.25 green 0.07 blue 0.038
            color red 0.25 green 0.07 blue 0.038]
    }
  }


// Is this really oak?  I dunno. Quite light, maybe more
// like spruce.
#declare DMFLightOak =
  texture {
    wood
    turbulence 0.05            // For best results,  keep this low!
    scale <0.2 0.2 1>          // Scaled or a unit object
    color_map {
      [0.00 0.10   color red 0.42 green 0.26 blue 0.15
            color red 0.42 green 0.26 blue 0.15]
      [0.10 0.90   color red 0.42 green 0.26 blue 0.15
            color red 0.52 green 0.37 blue 0.26]
      [0.90 1      color red 0.52 green 0.37 blue 0.26
            color red 0.52 green 0.37 blue 0.26]
    }
  }


// Looks like old desk oak if used correctly.
#declare DMFDarkOak =
  texture {
    wood
    turbulence 0.04            // For best results,  keep this low!
    octaves 3
    scale <0.2 0.2 1>          // Scaled or a unit object
    color_map {
      [0.00 0.10   color red 0.60 green 0.30 blue 0.18
            color red 0.60 green 0.30 blue 0.18]
      [0.10 0.90   color red 0.60 green 0.30 blue 0.18
            color red 0.30 green 0.15 blue 0.09]
      [0.90 1      color red 0.30 green 0.15 blue 0.09
            color red 0.30 green 0.15 blue 0.09]
    }
  }


// Doug Otwell woods
// Yellow pine, close grained
//
#declare Yellow_Pine =
  texture {
```

```
      wood
      turbulence 0.02
      color_map {
      [0.000 0.222 color red 0.808 green 0.671 blue 0.251 alpha 0.0
              color red 0.808 green 0.671 blue 0.251 alpha 0.0]
      [0.222 0.342 color red 0.808 green 0.671 blue 0.251 alpha 0.0
              color red 0.600 green 0.349 blue 0.043 alpha 0.0]
      [0.342 0.393 color red 0.600 green 0.349 blue 0.043 alpha 0.0
              color red 0.808 green 0.671 blue 0.251 alpha 0.0]
      [0.393 0.709 color red 0.808 green 0.671 blue 0.251 alpha 0.0
              color red 0.808 green 0.671 blue 0.251 alpha 0.0]
      [0.709 0.821 color red 0.808 green 0.671 blue 0.251 alpha 0.0
              color red 0.533 green 0.298 blue 0.027 alpha 0.0]
      [0.821 1     color red 0.533 green 0.298 blue 0.027 alpha 0.0
              color red 0.808 green 0.671 blue 0.251 alpha 0.0]
      }
      scale <0.1 0.1 0.1>
      translate <10 0 0>
    }
// Yellow_Pine layer 2
  texture {
    wood
    turbulence 0.01
    color_map {
      [0.000 0.120 color red 1.000 green 1.000 blue 1.000 alpha 1.000
              color red 0.702 green 0.412 blue 0.118 alpha 0.608]
      [0.120 0.231 color red 0.702 green 0.412 blue 0.118 alpha 0.608
              color red 0.702 green 0.467 blue 0.118 alpha 0.608]
      [0.231 0.496 color red 0.702 green 0.467 blue 0.118 alpha 0.608
              color red 1.000 green 1.000 blue 1.000 alpha 1.000]
      [0.496 0.701 color red 1.000 green 1.000 blue 1.000 alpha 1.000
              color red 1.000 green 1.000 blue 1.000 alpha 1.000]
      [0.701 0.829 color red 1.000 green 1.000 blue 1.000 alpha 1.000
              color red 0.702 green 0.467 blue 0.118 alpha 0.608]
      [0.829 1     color red 0.702 green 0.467 blue 0.118 alpha 0.608
              color red 1.000 green 1.000 blue 1.000 alpha 1.000]
    }
    scale <0.5 0.5 0.5>
    translate <10 0 0>
  }

//
// Rosewood
//
#declare Rosewood =
  texture {
    bozo
    turbulence 0.04
    color_map {
      [0.000 0.256 color red 0.204 green 0.110 blue 0.078 alpha 0.0
```

```
                  color red 0.231 green 0.125 blue 0.090 alpha 0.0]
        [0.256 0.393 color red 0.231 green 0.125 blue 0.090 alpha 0.0
                  color red 0.247 green 0.133 blue 0.090 alpha 0.0]
        [0.393 0.581 color red 0.247 green 0.133 blue 0.090 alpha 0.0
                  color red 0.204 green 0.110 blue 0.075 alpha 0.0]
        [0.581 0.726 color red 0.204 green 0.110 blue 0.075 alpha 0.0
                  color red 0.259 green 0.122 blue 0.102 alpha 0.0]
        [0.726 0.983 color red 0.259 green 0.122 blue 0.102 alpha 0.0
                  color red 0.231 green 0.125 blue 0.086 alpha 0.0]
        [0.983 1    color red 0.231 green 0.125 blue 0.086 alpha 0.0
                  color red 0.204 green 0.110 blue 0.078 alpha 0.0]
      }
      scale <0.5 0.5 1>
      translate <10 0 0>
      ambient 0.5
      diffuse 0.8
  }
// Rosewood layer 2
 texture {
   wood
   turbulence 0.04
   color_map {
     [0.000 0.139 color red 0.545 green 0.349 blue 0.247 alpha 1.000
               color red 0.000 green 0.000 blue 0.000 alpha 0.004]
     [0.139 0.148 color red 0.000 green 0.000 blue 0.000 alpha 0.004
               color red 0.000 green 0.000 blue 0.000 alpha 0.004]
     [0.148 0.287 color red 0.000 green 0.000 blue 0.000 alpha 0.004
               color red 0.545 green 0.349 blue 0.247 alpha 1.000]
     [0.287 0.443 color red 0.545 green 0.349 blue 0.247 alpha 1.000
               color red 0.545 green 0.349 blue 0.247 alpha 1.000]
     [0.443 0.626 color red 0.545 green 0.349 blue 0.247 alpha 1.000
               color red 0.000 green 0.000 blue 0.000 alpha 0.004]
     [0.626 0.635 color red 0.000 green 0.000 blue 0.000 alpha 0.004
               color red 0.000 green 0.000 blue 0.000 alpha 0.004]
     [0.635 0.843 color red 0.000 green 0.000 blue 0.000 alpha 0.004
               color red 0.545 green 0.349 blue 0.247 alpha 1.000]
     [0.843 1    color red 0.545 green 0.349 blue 0.247 alpha 1.000
               color red 0.545 green 0.349 blue 0.247 alpha 1.000]
   }
   scale <0.5 0.5 1>
   translate <10 0 0>
   ambient 0.5
   diffuse 0.8
  }

//
// Sandalwood (makes a great burled maple, too)
//
#declare Sandalwood =
 texture {
```

```
    bozo
    turbulence 0.2
    color_map {
    [0.000 0.171 color red 0.725 green 0.659 blue 0.455 alpha 0.0
            color red 0.682 green 0.549 blue 0.420 alpha 0.0]
    [0.171 0.274 color red 0.682 green 0.549 blue 0.420 alpha 0.0
            color red 0.557 green 0.451 blue 0.322 alpha 0.0]
    [0.274 0.393 color red 0.557 green 0.451 blue 0.322 alpha 0.0
            color red 0.725 green 0.659 blue 0.455 alpha 0.0]
    [0.393 0.564 color red 0.725 green 0.659 blue 0.455 alpha 0.0
            color red 0.682 green 0.549 blue 0.420 alpha 0.0]
    [0.564 0.701 color red 0.682 green 0.549 blue 0.420 alpha 0.0
            color red 0.482 green 0.392 blue 0.278 alpha 0.0]
    [0.701 1     color red 0.482 green 0.392 blue 0.278 alpha 0.0
            color red 0.725 green 0.659 blue 0.455 alpha 0.0]
    }
    scale <0.2 0.2 1>
    scale <2 2 2>
  }
// Sandalwood layer 2
  texture {
    bozo
    turbulence 0.8
    color_map {
    [0.000 0.087 color red 0.682 green 0.604 blue 0.380 alpha 1.000
            color red 0.761 green 0.694 blue 0.600 alpha 0.020]
    [0.087 0.226 color red 0.761 green 0.694 blue 0.600 alpha 0.020
            color red 0.635 green 0.553 blue 0.325 alpha 1.000]
    [0.226 0.348 color red 0.635 green 0.553 blue 0.325 alpha 1.000
            color red 0.761 green 0.694 blue 0.600 alpha 0.020]
    [0.348 0.496 color red 0.761 green 0.694 blue 0.600 alpha 0.020
            color red 0.682 green 0.604 blue 0.380 alpha 1.000]
    [0.496 0.565 color red 0.682 green 0.604 blue 0.380 alpha 1.000
            color red 0.761 green 0.694 blue 0.600 alpha 0.020]
    [0.565 0.661 color red 0.761 green 0.694 blue 0.600 alpha 0.020
            color red 0.682 green 0.604 blue 0.380 alpha 1.000]
    [0.661 0.835 color red 0.682 green 0.604 blue 0.380 alpha 1.000
            color red 0.761 green 0.694 blue 0.600 alpha 0.020]
    [0.835 1     color red 0.761 green 0.694 blue 0.600 alpha 0.020
            color red 0.682 green 0.604 blue 0.380 alpha 1.000]
    }
    scale <0.2 0.2 2.0>
    scale <2 2 2>
  }


//*********************************************************** //
//                    SURFACE TEXTURES                       //
//*********************************************************** //
```

```
// Dull creates a large, soft highlight on the object's surface
#declare Dull = texture { specular 0.5 roughness 0.15   }

// Shiny creates a small, tight highlight on the object's surface
#declare Shiny = texture { specular 1.0 roughness 0.001 }

// Phong highlights are less "realistic" than specular, but useful
// for different effects.
// Dull creates a large, soft highlight on the object's surface
#declare Phong_Dull = texture { phong 0.5  phong_size 1 }

// Shiny creates a small, tight highlight on the object's surface
#declare Phong_Shiny = texture { phong 1.0  phong_size 200 }

// Very shiny with very tight highlights and a fair amount of
// reflection
#declare Glossy =
texture { specular 1.0 roughness 0.001 reflection 0.13}

#declare Phong_Glossy =
texture {phong 1 phong_size 300 reflection 0.13}

// Luminous for shadowless skies and light_sources.
#declare Luminous = texture { ambient 1.0  diffuse 0.0 }

// A perfectly mirrored texture with no highlights
#declare Mirror =
texture {
   ambient 0.0
   diffuse 0.0
   reflection 1.0
}

#declare Glass =
texture {
   Shiny
   color red 1.0 green 1.0 blue 1.0 alpha 0.7
   ambient 0.0
   diffuse 0.0
   reflection 0.1
   refraction 1.0
   ior 1.5
}

// Probably more of a "Plexiglas" than glass
#declare Glass2 =
texture {
   color red 1.0 green 1.0 blue 1.0 alpha 1.0
   ambient 0.0
   diffuse 0.0
```

515

```
      reflection 0.5
      refraction 0.85
      ior 1.5
      phong 0.3
      phong_size 60
   }


// An excellent lead crystal glass!
#declare Glass3 =
texture {
   color red 0.98 green 0.98 blue 0.98 alpha 0.9
   ambient 0.1
   diffuse 0.1
   specular 0.8
   reflection 0.1
   refraction 0.9
   ior 1.45
   roughness 0.001
   phong 1 phong_size 400
  }


#declare Green_Glass =
 texture {
   Glass3
   color red 0.8 green 1 blue 0.95 alpha 0.9
 }


//***************************************************************** //
//                       METAL TEXTURES                            //
//***************************************************************** //

// Good looking "metal" textures
// IMPORTANT: They REQUIRE that colors.inc be included
// BEFORE textures.inc!
#declare Chrome_Texture =
texture {
   ambient 0.3
   diffuse 0.7
   reflection 0.15
   brilliance 8.0
   specular 0.8
   roughness 0.1
   color LightGray
}

// You need to specify a color when Metal is used
#declare Metal =
texture {
   metallic
   ambient 0.2
```

```
    diffuse 0.7
    brilliance 6.0
    reflection 0.25
    phong 0.75
    phong_size 80
}

// A series of metallic textures using the Metal texture:
#declare Brass_Texture   = texture { Metal  color Brass      }
#declare Gold_Texture    = texture { Metal  color BrightGold }
#declare Bronze_Texture  = texture { Metal  color Bronze     }
#declare Copper_Texture  = texture { Metal  color Copper     }
#declare Silver_Texture  = texture { Metal  color Silver     }

// In the future, please refer to Chrome_Texture by this name.
// I'd like to scrap the old name someday. Ditto with other
// "_Texture" names!
#declare Chrome_Metal = texture { Chrome_Texture }
#declare Brass_Metal  = texture { Brass_Texture  }
#declare Gold_Metal   = texture { Gold_Texture   }
#declare Bronze_Metal = texture { Bronze_Texture }
#declare Copper_Metal = texture { Copper_Texture }
#declare Silver_Metal = texture { Metal  color Silver }

// Interesting texture--Give it a try.
// Sort of a "Black Hills Gold", black, white, and orange
// specks or splotches.
#declare Brass_Valley =
texture {
   granite
   metallic
   brilliance 6.0
   reflection 0.75
   phong 0.75
   color_map {
     [0.0 0.3 color Feldspar  color Feldspar]
     [0.3 0.6 color Mica      color Quartz]
     [0.6 1   color Feldspar  color Quartz]
   }
}

#declare Rusty_Iron =
texture {
   agate
   color_map {
     [0.0 0.5  color red 0.21 green 0.1 blue 0.1
          color red 0.25 green 0.25 blue 0.01]
     [0.5 0.6  color red 0.25 green 0.25 blue 0.01
          color red 0.3 green 0.1 blue 0.1]
     [0.6 1    color red 0.15 green 0.1 blue 0.1
```

```
                color red 0.15 green 0.1 blue 0.1]
      }
}


#declare Rust =
texture {
   spotted
   color_map {
      [0.0 0.4  color red 0.89 green 0.51 blue 0.28
                color red 0.70 green 0.13 blue 0.00]
      [0.4 0.5  color red 0.70 green 0.13 blue 0.00
                color red 0.69 green 0.41 blue 0.08]
      [0.5 0.6  color red 0.69 green 0.41 blue 0.08
                color red 0.49 green 0.31 blue 0.28]
      [0.6 1    color red 0.49 green 0.31 blue 0.28
                color red 0.89 green 0.51 blue 0.28]
   }
}


//*************************************************************** //
//                    SPECIAL EFFECTS                            //
//*************************************************************** //

// Red & white stripes--Looks best on a y axis Cylinder
// It "spirals" because it's gradient on two axis
#declare Candy_Cane =
texture {
   gradient < 1.0 1.0 0.0 >
   color_map {
      [0.00 0.25 color red 1.0 green 0.0 blue 0.0
                 color red 1.0 green 0.0 blue 0.0]
      [0.25 0.75 color red 1.0 green 1.0 blue 1.0
                 color red 1.0 green 1.0 blue 1.0]
      [0.75 1    color red 1.0 green 0.0 blue 0.0
                 color red 1.0 green 0.0 blue 0.0]
   }
}


// Orange and Clear stripes spiral around the texture
// to make an object look like it was "Peeled"
// Now, you too can be M.C. Escher
#declare Peel =
texture {
   gradient < 1.0 1.0 0.0 >
   color_map {
      [0.00 0.25  color Orange   color Orange]
      [0.25 0.75  color Clear    color Clear]
      [0.75 1.001 color Orange   color Orange]
   }
}
```

```
#declare Y_Gradient =
texture {
   gradient < 0.0 1.0 0.0 >
   color_map {
     [0.00 0.33 color red 1.0 green 0.0 blue 0.0
            color red 0.0 green 0.0 blue 1.0]
     [0.33 0.66 color red 0.0 green 0.0 blue 1.0
            color red 0.0 green 1.0 blue 0.0]
     [0.66 1    color red 0.0 green 1.0 blue 0.0
            color red 1.0 green 0.0 blue 0.0]
   }
}

#declare X_Gradient =
texture {
   gradient < 1.0 0.0 0.0 >
   color_map {
     [0.00 0.33 color red 1.0 green 0.0 blue 0.0
            color red 0.0 green 0.0 blue 1.0]
     [0.33 0.66 color red 0.0 green 0.0 blue 1.0
            color red 1.0 green 1.0 blue 1.0]
     [0.66 1    color red 1.0 green 1.0 blue 1.0
            color red 1.0 green 1.0 blue 1.0]
   }
}

// A good wavy water example.
// Requires a sub-plane, and may require scaling to fit your scene.
#declare Water =
texture {
   color Blue alpha 0.9
   ripples 0.75
   frequency 10.0
   reflection 0.3
   refraction 0.5
   ior 1.33
}

#declare Cork =
texture {
   granite
   color_map {
     [0.0 0.6   color red 0.93 green 0.71 blue 0.532
            color red 0.98 green 0.81 blue 0.60]
     [0.6 0.65  color red 0.50 green 0.30 blue 0.20
            color red 0.50 green 0.30 blue 0.20]
     [0.65 1.0  color red 0.80 green 0.53 blue 0.46
            color red 0.85 green 0.75 blue 0.35]
   }
   scale <0.25 0.25 0.25>      // Generally looks best scaled
```

519

```
      // longer on one axis
      specular 0.1 roughness 0.5 // Very dull
}
```

SHAPESQ.INC INCLUDE FILE

The SHAPESQ.INC file contains a variety of quartic and high-order polynomial shapes. The most useful shape in this file is a torus. "Torus" is the mathematical name for a donut shape. The majority of these are of interest only to mathematicians but a creative ray trace enthusiast should be able to come up with practical uses for them.

Listing A-4 SHAPESQ.INC Include File

```
// Persistence of Vision Raytracer
// Standard include file.

// Quartic shapes include file
//
// Several cubic and quartic shape definitions
// by Alexander Enzmann

/* In the following descriptions, multiplication of two terms is
   shown as the two terms next to each other (i.e. x y, rather than
   x*y. The expression c(n, m) is the binomial coefficient,
   n!/m!(n-m)!. */

/* Bicorn
   This curve looks like the top part of a paraboloid, bounded
   from below by another paraboloid. The basic equation is:
      y^2 - (x^2 + z^2) y^2 - (x^2 + z^2 + 2 y - 1)^2 = 0. */
#declare Bicorn =
quartic {
   < 1.0   0.0   0.0   0.0 1.0   0.0   4.0   2.0   0.0 -2.0
     0.0   0.0   0.0   0.0 0.0   0.0   0.0   0.0   0.0 0.0
     0.0   0.0   0.0   1.0 0.0   3.0   0.0   4.0   0.0 -4.0
     1.0   0.0  -2.0   0.0 1.0 >
}

/* Crossed Trough
   This is a surface with four pieces that sweep up from the x-z
   plane. The equation is: y = x^2 z^2. */
#declare Crossed_Trough =
quartic {
   < 0.0   0.0   0.0   0.0 0.0   0.0   0.0   4.0   0.0 0.0
```

```
     0.0    0.0    0.0     0.0   0.0    0.0    0.0    0.0    0.0  0.0
     0.0    0.0    0.0     0.0   0.0    0.0    0.0    0.0    0.0 -1.0
     0.0    0.0    0.0     0.0   0.0 >
}

/* a drop coming out of water? This is a curve formed by using
   the equation  y = 1/2 x^2 (x + 1) as the radius of a cylinder
   having the x-axis as its central axis. The final form of the
   equation is:
      y^2 + z^2 = 0.5 (x^3 + x^2) */
#declare Cubic_Cylinder =
quartic {
   < 0.0    0.0    0.0    -0.5  0.0    0.0    0.0    0.0    0.0 -0.5
     0.0    0.0    0.0     0.0  0.0    0.0    0.0    0.0    0.0  0.0
     0.0    0.0    0.0     0.0  0.0    1.0    0.0    0.0    0.0  0.0
     0.0    0.0    1.0     0.0  0.0 >
}

/* a cubic saddle. The equation is: z = x^3 - y^3. */
#declare Cubic_Saddle_1 =
quartic {
   < 0.0    0.0    0.0     1.0   0.0    0.0    0.0    0.0    0.0  0.0
     0.0    0.0    0.0     0.0   0.0    0.0    0.0    0.0    0.0  0.0
     0.0    0.0   -1.0     0.0   0.0    0.0    0.0    0.0    0.0  0.0
     0.0    0.0    0.0    -1.0   0.0 >
}

/* Variant of a devil's curve in 3-space. This figure has a top
   and bottom part that are very similar to a hyperboloid of one
   sheet, however the central region is pinched in the middle
   leaving two teardrop shaped holes. The equation is:
      x^4 + 2 x^2 z^2 - 0.36 x^2 - y^4 + 0.25 y^2 + z^4 = 0. */
#declare Devils_Curve =
quartic {
   <-1.0    0.0    0.0     0.0  0.0    0.0    0.0   -2.0    0.0  0.36
     0.0    0.0    0.0     0.0  0.0    0.0    0.0    0.0    0.0  0.0
     1.0    0.0    0.0     0.0  0.0   -0.25   0.0    0.0    0.0  0.0
    -1.0    0.0    0.0     0.0  0.0 >
}

/* Folium
   This is a folium rotated about the x-axis. The formula is:
      2 x^2 - 3 x y^2 - 3 x z^2 + y^2 + z^2 = 0. */
#declare Folium =
quartic {
   < 0.0    0.0    0.0     0.0  0.0    0.0    0.0    0.0    0.0  2.0
     0.0    0.0   -3.0     0.0  0.0    0.0    0.0   -3.0    0.0  0.0
     0.0    0.0    0.0     0.0  0.0    1.0    0.0    0.0    0.0  0.0
     0.0    0.0    1.0     0.0  0.0 >
}
```

521

```
/* Glob--sort of like basic teardrop shape. The equation is:
   y^2 + z^2 = 0.5 x^5 + 0.5 x^4. */
#declare Glob_5 =
poly { 5
  <-0.5   0.0   0.0  -0.5   0.0   0.0   0.0   0.0   0.0  0.0
   0.0   0.0   0.0   0.0   0.0   0.0   0.0   0.0   0.0  0.0
   0.0   0.0   0.0   0.0   0.0   0.0   0.0   0.0   0.0  0.0
   0.0   0.0   0.0   0.0   0.0   0.0   0.0   0.0   0.0  0.0
   0.0   0.0   0.0   0.0   1.0   0.0   0.0   0.0   0.0  0.0
   0.0   0.0   0.0   1.0   0.0   0.0 >
}
```

```
/* Variant of a lemniscate--the two lobes are much more
     teardrop-like. */
#declare Twin_Glob =
poly { 6
  < 4.0   0.0   0.0   0.0   0.0   0.0   0.0   0.0   0.0 -4.0
   0.0   0.0   0.0   0.0   0.0   0.0   0.0   0.0   0.0  0.0
   0.0   0.0   0.0   0.0   0.0   0.0   0.0   0.0   0.0  0.0
   0.0   0.0   0.0   0.0   0.0   0.0   0.0   0.0   0.0  0.0
   0.0   0.0   0.0   0.0   0.0   0.0   0.0   0.0   0.0  0.0
   0.0   0.0   0.0   0.0   0.0   0.0   0.0   0.0   0.0  0.0
   0.0   0.0   0.0   0.0   0.0   0.0   0.0   0.0   0.0  0.0
   1.0   0.0   0.0   0.0   0.0   0.0   0.0   0.0   0.0  0.0
   0.0   1.0   0.0   0.0 >
}
```

```
/*  Approximation to the helix z = arctan(y/x).
```

The helix can be approximated with an algebraic equation (kept to the range of a quartic) with the following steps:

$$\tan(z) = y/x \quad \Rightarrow \quad \sin(z)/\cos(z) = y/x \quad \Rightarrow$$

(1) $x \sin(z) - y \cos(z) = 0$

Using the taylor expansions for sin, cos about $z = 0$,

$$\sin(z) = z - z^3/3! + z^5/5! - \ldots$$
$$\cos(z) = 1 - z^2/2! + z^6/6! - \ldots$$

Throwing out the high-order terms, the expression (1) can be written as:

$$x (z - z^3/6) - y (1 + z^2/2) = 0, \text{ or}$$

(2) $-1/6 \, x \, z^3 + x \, z + 1/2 \, y \, z^2 - y = 0$

This helix (2) turns 90 degrees in the range $0 \le z \le \sqrt{2}/2$.

```
   By using scale <2 2 2>, the helix defined below turns 90 degrees
   in the range 0 <= z <= sqrt(2) = 1.4042.
*/
#declare Helix =
object {
   intersection {
      quadric { Cylinder_Z
         scale <2.0 2.0 2.0>
         texture { color Clear }
      }
      plane { <0.0 0.0 1.0> 1.4142 texture { color Clear } }
      plane { <0.0 0.0 -1.0> 0.0 texture { color Clear } }
      quartic {
         < 0.0 0.0   0.0    0.0 0.0   0.0   0.0     0.0   0.0 0.0
           0.0   0.0   0.0    0.0 0.0   0.0  -0.1666 0.0   1.0 0.0
           0.0   0.0   0.0    0.0 0.0   0.0   0.0     0.5   0.0 -1.0
           0.0   0.0   0.0    0.0 0.0 >
      }
   }
}


/* This is an alternate Helix, using clipped_by instead of csg
   intersection. */
#declare Helix_1 =
object {
   quartic {
      < 0.0    0.0   0.0    0.0 0.0   0.0   0.0     0.0   0.0 0.0
        0.0    0.0   0.0    0.0 0.0   0.0  -0.1666 0.0   1.0 0.0
        0.0    0.0   0.0    0.0 0.0   0.0   0.0     0.5   0.0 -1.0
        0.0    0.0   0.0    0.0 0.0 >
   }
   clipped_by {
      quadric { Cylinder_Z scale <2.0 2.0 2.0> }
      plane { <0.0 0.0 1.0> 1.4142 }
      plane { <0.0 0.0 -1.0> 0.0 }
   }
   bounded_by {
      intersection {
         quadric { Cylinder_Z scale <2.0 2.0 2.0> }
         plane { <0.0 0.0 1.0> 1.4142 }
         plane { <0.0 0.0 -1.0> 0.0 }
      }
   }
}

/* Hyperbolic Torus having major radius sqrt(40), minor radius
   sqrt(12). This figure is generated by sweeping a circle along
   the arms of a hyperbola. The equation is:
```

$$x^4 + 2 x^2 y^2 - 2 x^2 z^2 - 104 x^2 + y^4 - 2 y^2 z^2 +$$

523

```
    56 y^2 + z^4 + 104 z^2 + 784 = 0.

  See the description for the torus below. */
#declare Hyperbolic_Torus_40_12 =
quartic {
  < 1.0   0.0   0.0    0.0    2.0   0.0   0.0  -2.0   0.0 -104.0
    0.0   0.0   0.0    0.0    0.0   0.0   0.0   0.0   0.0   0.0
    1.0   0.0   0.0   -2.0    0.0  56.0   0.0   0.0   0.0   0.0
    1.0   0.0 104.0    0.0  784.0 >
}
```

```
/* Lemniscate of Gerono
  This figure looks like two teardrops with their pointed ends con-
nected.
  It is formed by rotating the Lemniscate of Gerono about the x-axis.
  The formula is:
     x^4 - x^2 + y^2 + z^2 = 0. */
#declare Lemniscate =
quartic {
  < 1.0   0.0   0.0   0.0   0.0   0.0   0.0   0.0   0.0 -1.0
    0.0   0.0   0.0   0.0   0.0   0.0   0.0   0.0   0.0  0.0
    0.0   0.0   0.0   0.0   0.0   1.0   0.0   0.0   0.0  0.0
    0.0   0.0   1.0   0.0   0.0 >
}
```

```
/* This is a figure with a bumpy sheet on one side and something
   that looks like a paraboloid (but with an internal bubble). The
   formula is:
     (x^2 + y^2 + a c x)^2 - (x^2 + y^2)(c - a x)^2.

   -99*x^4 +40*x^3 -98*x^2*y^2 -98*x^2*z^2 +99*x^2+40*x*y^2
   +40*x*z^2 +y^4 +2*y^2*z^2 -y^2+z^4-z^2

*/
#declare Quartic_Loop_1 =
quartic {
  <99.0    0.0   0.0 -40.0  98.0   0.0   0.0  98.0   0.0 -99.0
    0.0    0.0 -40.0   0.0   0.0   0.0   0.0 -40.0   0.0   0.0
   -1.0    0.0   0.0  -2.0   0.0   1.0   0.0   0.0   0.0   0.0
   -1.0    0.0   1.0   0.0   0.0 >
}
```

```
/* Monkey Saddle
  This surface has three parts that sweep up and three down. This
  gives a saddle that has a place for two legs and a tail... The
  equation is:

     z = c (x^3 - 3 x y^2).
```

The value c gives a vertical scale to the surface--the smaller
the value of c, the flatter the surface will be (near the origin). */
#declare Monkey_Saddle =
quartic {
```
< 0.0   0.0   0.0   1.0 0.0   0.0   0.0   0.0   0.0 0.0
  0.0   0.0  -3.0   0.0 0.0   0.0   0.0   0.0   0.0 0.0
  0.0   0.0   0.0   0.0 0.0   0.0   0.0   0.0   0.0 0.0
  0.0   0.0   0.0  -1.0 0.0 >
```
}

/* Parabolic Torus having major radius sqrt(40), minor radius sqrt(12).
   This figure is generated by sweeping a circle along the arms of a
   parabola. The equation is:

   x^4 + 2 x^2 y^2 - 2 x^2 z - 104 x^2 + y^4 - 2 y^2 z +
   56 y^2 + z^2 + 104 z + 784 = 0.

   See the description for the torus below. */
#declare Parabolic_Torus_40_12 =
quartic {
```
< 1.0   0.0   0.0   0.0    2.0   0.0   0.0   0.0  -2.0 -104.0
  0.0   0.0   0.0   0.0    0.0   0.0   0.0   0.0   0.0   0.0
  1.0   0.0   0.0   0.0   -2.0  56.0   0.0   0.0   0.0   0.0
  0.0   0.0   1.0 104.0  784.0 >
```
}

/* Piriform
   This figure looks like a hersheys kiss. It is formed by sweeping
   a Piriform about the x-axis. A basic form of the equation is:
      (x^4 - x^3) + y^2 + z^2 = 0.
*/
#declare Piriform =
quartic {
```
< 4.0   0.0   0.0  -4.0 0.0   0.0   0.0   0.0   0.0 0.0
  0.0   0.0   0.0   0.0 0.0   0.0   0.0   0.0   0.0 0.0
  0.0   0.0   0.0   0.0 0.0   1.0   0.0   0.0   0.0 0.0
  0.0   0.0   1.0   0.0 0.0 >
```
}

/* n-Roll Mill
   This curve in the plane looks like several hyperbolas with their
   bumps arranged about the origin. The general formula is:

   x^n - c(n,2) x^(n-2) y^2 + c(n,4) x^(n-4) y^4 - ... = a

   When rendering in 3-Space, the resulting figure looks like a
   cylinder with indented sides.
*/

/* Quartic parabola - a 4th degree polynomial (has two bumps at the

bottom) that has been swept around the z axis. The equation is:
0.1 x^4 - x^2 - y^2 - z^2 + 0.9 = 0. */

```
#declare Quartic_Paraboloid =
quartic {
  < 0.1  0.0   0.0  0.0   0.0   0.0   0.0   0.0   0.0 -1.0
    0.0  0.0   0.0  0.0   0.0   0.0   0.0   0.0   0.0  0.0
    0.0  0.0   0.0  0.0   0.0  0.0   0.0   0.0   0.0 -1.0
    0.0  0.0  -1.0  0.0   0.9 >
}
```

```
/* Quartic Cylinder - a Space Needle?  */
#declare Quartic_Cylinder =
quartic {
  < 0.0  0.0   0.0  0.0   1.0   0.0   0.0   0.0   0.0   0.01
    0.0  0.0   0.0  0.0   0.0   0.0   0.0   0.0   0.0  0.0
    0.0  0.0   0.0  1.0   0.0  0.0   0.0   0.0   0.0  0.0
    0.0  0.0   0.01 0.0  -0.01 >
}
```

```
/* Steiners quartic surface */
#declare Steiner_Surface =
quartic {
  < 0.0  0.0   0.0  0.0  1.0   0.0   0.0   1.0   0.0  0.0
    0.0  0.0   0.0  0.0  1.0   0.0   0.0   0.0   0.0  0.0
    0.0  0.0   0.0  1.0  0.0   0.0   0.0   0.0   0.0  0.0
    0.0  0.0   0.0  0.0  0.0 >
}
```

```
/* Torus having major radius sqrt(40), minor radius sqrt(12) */
#declare Torus_40_12 =
quartic {
  < 1.0   0.0   0.0   0.0    2.0   0.0   0.0   2.0   0.0 -104.0
    0.0   0.0   0.0   0.0    0.0   0.0   0.0   0.0   0.0   0.0
    1.0   0.0   0.0   2.0    0.0  56.0   0.0   0.0   0.0   0.0
    1.0   0.0 -104.0  0.0  784.0 >
}
```

```
/* Witch of Agnesi */
#declare Witch_Hat =
quartic {
  < 0.0  0.0   0.0   0.0   0.0   0.0   1.0   0.0   0.0   0.0
    0.0  0.0   0.0   0.0   0.0   0.0   0.0   0.0   0.0   0.0
    0.0  0.0   0.0   0.0   0.0   0.0   0.0   1.0   0.0   0.04
    0.0  0.0   0.0   0.0   0.04 >
}
```

```
/* very rough approximation to the sin-wave surface
   z = sin(2 pi x y).
   In order to get an approximation good to 7 decimals at a distance
   of 1 from the origin would require a polynomial of degree around
```

```
   60. This would require around 200k coefficients. For best
   results, scale by something like <1 1 0.2>. */
#declare Sinsurf =
poly { 6
   < 0.0    0.0    0.0     0.0  0.0    0.0    0.0    0.0   0.0  0.0
   -1116.226 0.0   0.0     0.0  0.0    0.0    0.0    0.0   0.0  0.0
    0.0    0.0    0.0      0.0  0.0    0.0    0.0    0.0   0.0  0.0
    0.0    0.0    0.0      0.0  0.0    0.0    0.0    0.0   0.0  0.0
    0.0    0.0    0.0      0.0  0.0    0.0    0.0    0.0   0.0 18.8496
    0.0    0.0    0.0      0.0  0.0    0.0    0.0    0.0   0.0  0.0
    0.0    0.0    0.0      0.0  0.0    0.0    0.0    0.0   0.0  0.0
    0.0    0.0    0.0      0.0  0.0    0.0    0.0    0.0   0.0  0.0
    0.0    0.0   -1.0      0.0 >
}

/* Empty quartic equation. Ready to be filled with numbers...
   quartic
    {< 0.0    0.0    0.0    0.0    0.0    0.0    0.0    0.0    0.0    0.0
       0.0    0.0    0.0    0.0    0.0    0.0    0.0    0.0    0.0    0.0
       0.0    0.0    0.0    0.0    0.0    0.0    0.0    0.0    0.0    0.0
       0.0    0.0    0.0    0.0    0.0 >
    }
*/
```

SHAPES2.INC INCLUDE FILE

The SHAPES2.INC file is a supplement to the regular SHAPES.INC shapes. It contains a variety of shapes made of plane surfaces including standard Platonic solids such as pyramids, tetrahedrons, and icosahedrons. These shapes were formerly part of SHAPES.INC but were separated because they are infrequently used.

Listing A-5 SHAPESQ.INC Include File

```
// Persistence Of Vision Raytracer
// Standard shapes include file #2.
//
/* Contents:
      Tetrahedron, Octahedron, Dodecahedron, Icosahedron
      Rhomboid, Hexagon, HalfCone_Y, Pyramid, Pyramid2
      Square_X, Square_Y, Square_Z
*/

// Shapes by Tom Price [75300,620]:
#declare Tetrahedron = intersection {
```

```
  plane { <0.0 -1.0 0.0> 1.0 }
  plane { <0.0 0.0 -1.0> 1.0 rotate <19.47 0.0 0.0> }
  plane { <0.0 0.0 -1.0> 1.0 rotate <19.47 -120.0 0.0> }
  plane { <0.0 0.0 -1.0> 1.0 rotate <19.47 120.0 0.0> }
}

#declare Octahedron = intersection {
  plane { <0.0 0.0 1.0> 1.0 rotate <35.26438968275 0.0 0.0> }
  plane { <0.0 0.0 1.0> 1.0 rotate <-35.26438968275 0.0 0.0> }
  plane { <0.0 0.0 -1.0> 1.0 rotate <35.26438968275 0.0 0.0> }
  plane { <0.0 0.0 -1.0> 1.0 rotate <-35.26438968275 0.0 0.0> }

  plane { <1.0 0.0 0.0> 1.0 rotate <0.0 0.0 -35.26438968275> }
  plane { <1.0 0.0 0.0> 1.0 rotate <0.0 0.0 35.26438968275> }
  plane { <-1.0 0.0 0.0> 1.0 rotate <0.0 0.0 -35.26438968275> }
  plane { <-1.0 0.0 0.0> 1.0 rotate <0.0 0.0 35.26438968275> }
}

#declare Dodecahedron = intersection {
  plane { <0.0 0.0 -1.0>  1.0 rotate <-26.56505117708 0.0 0.0> }
  plane { <0.0 0.0 -1.0>  1.0 rotate <-26.56505117708 -72.0 0.0> }
  plane { <0.0 0.0 -1.0>  1.0 rotate <-26.56505117708 -144.0 0.0> }
  plane { <0.0 0.0 -1.0>  1.0 rotate <-26.56505117708 -216.0 0.0> }
  plane { <0.0 0.0 -1.0>  1.0 rotate <-26.56505117708 -288.0 0.0> }

  plane { <0.0 0.0 -1.0>  1.0 rotate <26.56505117708 -36.0 0.0> }
  plane { <0.0 0.0 -1.0>  1.0 rotate <26.56505117708 -108.0 0.0> }
  plane { <0.0 0.0 -1.0>  1.0 rotate <26.56505117708 -180.0 0.0> }
  plane { <0.0 0.0 -1.0>  1.0 rotate <26.56505117708 -252.0 0.0> }
  plane { <0.0 0.0 -1.0>  1.0 rotate <26.56505117708 -324.0 0.0> }

  plane { <0.0 1.0 0.0> 1.0 }
  plane { <0.0 -1.0 0.0> 1.0 }
}

#declare Icosahedron = intersection {

  plane { <0.0 0.0 -1.0> 1.0 rotate <52.6625 0.0 0.0> }
  plane { <0.0 0.0 -1.0> 1.0 rotate <52.6625 -72.0 0.0> }
  plane { <0.0 0.0 -1.0> 1.0 rotate <52.6625 -144.0 0.0> }
  plane { <0.0 0.0 -1.0> 1.0 rotate <52.6625 -216.0 0.0> }
  plane { <0.0 0.0 -1.0> 1.0 rotate <52.6625 -288.0 0.0> }

  plane { <0.0 0.0 -1.0> 1.0 rotate <10.8125 0.0 0.0> }
  plane { <0.0 0.0 -1.0> 1.0 rotate <10.8125 -72.0 0.0> }
  plane { <0.0 0.0 -1.0> 1.0 rotate <10.8125 -144.0 0.0> }
  plane { <0.0 0.0 -1.0> 1.0 rotate <10.8125 -216.0 0.0> }
  plane { <0.0 0.0 -1.0> 1.0 rotate <10.8125 -288.0 0.0> }

  plane { <0.0 0.0 -1.0> 1.0 rotate <-52.6625 -36.0 0.0> }
```

```
plane { <0.0 0.0 -1.0> 1.0 rotate <-52.6625 -108.0 0.0> }
plane { <0.0 0.0 -1.0> 1.0 rotate <-52.6625 -180.0 0.0> }
plane { <0.0 0.0 -1.0> 1.0 rotate <-52.6625 -252.0 0.0> }
plane { <0.0 0.0 -1.0> 1.0 rotate <-52.6625 -324.0 0.0> }

plane { <0.0 0.0 -1.0> 1.0 rotate <-10.8125 -36.0 0.0> }
plane { <0.0 0.0 -1.0> 1.0 rotate <-10.8125 -108.0 0.0> }
plane { <0.0 0.0 -1.0> 1.0 rotate <-10.8125 -180.0 0.0> }
plane { <0.0 0.0 -1.0> 1.0 rotate <-10.8125 -252.0 0.0> }
plane { <0.0 0.0 -1.0> 1.0 rotate <-10.8125 -324.0 0.0> }
}

// Shapes by others

// Convenient  finite cone primitive, pointing up in the Y axis
// Cone_Y, X & Z in SHAPES.INC should be used instead of this shape
#declare HalfCone_Y = intersection {
 quadric { // QCone_Y
   <1.0 -1.0 1.0>
   <0.0 0.0 0.0>
   <0.0 0.0 0.0>
    0.0
 }
 plane { <0 1 0 >  0 }
 plane { <0 1 0 > -2 inverse }
 translate <0 1 0>
 scale <0.5 1 0.5>
}

/* Hexagonal Solid, axis along x */
#declare  Hexagon = intersection {
 plane { <0.0 0.0 1.0> 1.0  }  /* Rotate 90 in z axis to stand up */
 plane { <0.0 0.0 1.0> 1.0 rotate <60.0 0.0 0.0> }
 plane { <0.0 0.0 1.0> 1.0 rotate <120.0 0.0 0.0> }
 plane { <0.0 0.0 1.0> 1.0 rotate <180.0 0.0 0.0> }
 plane { <0.0 0.0 1.0> 1.0 rotate <240.0 0.0 0.0> }
 plane { <0.0 0.0 1.0> 1.0 rotate <300.0 0.0 0.0> }
 plane { <1.0 0.0 0.0> 1.0 }
 plane { <1.0 0.0 0.0> -1.0 inverse }
}

/* Three Dimensional 4-Sided Diamond */
#declare Rhomboid = intersection {
 plane { <-1.0  0.0  0.0>  1.0 rotate <0.0 0.0 -30.0> }
 plane { < 1.0  0.0  0.0>  1.0 rotate <0.0 0.0 -30.0> }
 plane { < 0.0  0.0  1.0>  1.0 }
 plane { < 0.0  0.0 -1.0>  1.0 }
 plane { < 0.0  1.0  0.0>  1.0 }
 plane { < 0.0 -1.0  0.0>  1.0 }
}
```

```
// Classic four-sided pyramids.
// The first can't be used correctly in CSG, the second can.
#declare Pyramid = intersection {
 union { // This isn't true CSG, it's just used for convenience
  triangle { <-1 0 -1> <+1 0 -1> <0 1 0>  }
  triangle { <+1 0 -1> <+1 0 +1> <0 1 0>  }
  triangle { <-1 0 +1> <+1 0 +1> <0 1 0>  }
  triangle { <-1 0 +1> <-1 0 -1> <0 1 0>  }
 }
 scale <1 2 1>
 translate <0 -1 0>
}
#declare Pyramid2 = intersection {
 plane { <1 0 0> 1  rotate <0 0 40> }
 plane { <-1 0 0> 1 rotate <0 0 -40>}
 plane { <0 0 1> 1  rotate <-40 0 0> }
 plane { <0 0 -1> 1 rotate <40 0 0> }
 plane { <0 -1 0> 0 }
 translate <0 -1 0>
}

// These next three are finite planes.
#declare Square_X = union {    /* Scale-able plane in x */
 triangle { < 0  1 -1> < 0 -1  1> < 0  1  1>  }
 triangle { < 0  1 -1> < 0 -1  1> < 0 -1 -1>  }
}

#declare Square_Y = union {    /* Scale-able plane in y */
 triangle { <-1 0 1>  < 1 0 -1>  <1 0 1>  }
 triangle { <-1 0  1>  < 1 0 -1>  <-1 0 -1>}
}

#declare Square_Z = union {    /* Scale-able plane in z */
 triangle { <-1 1 0.0> <1 -1 0.0> <-1 -1 0.0> }
 triangle { <-1 1 0.0> <1 -1 0.0> <1 1 0.0>    }
}
```

IOR.INC INCLUDE FILE

The IOR.INC file is a brief table of float identifiers, which contain the index of refraction (IOR) values for various types of substances. The index of refraction is a measurement of the density of a transparent substance. High-density objects refract (bend) light more than lower-density substances.

Here is an example that uses the IOR.INC file.

Listing A-6 Using the IOR.INC Include File

```
// IORINC.POV
#include "examp.inc"
#include "ior.inc"

camera{location <0 0.2 -5> look_at<0 0 0>}

#declare Lens=  // build a lens shape
 intersection {
    quadric {Ellipsoid translate <0 0  0.6>}
    quadric {Ellipsoid translate <0 0 -0.6>}
    scale <1 1 0.2>
 }

object { // add a better background
 box{UnitBox scale <8 1 0.1>}
 texture {
    checker color Red color White
    scale <0.2 0.2 1>
 }
 translate <0 -1 2>
}

object {
 intersection {Lens translate <-2 0 0> }
 texture {color White alpha 0.9 phong 0.8
 refraction 1  ior Air_Ior
 }
}

object {
 intersection {Lens translate <0 0 0> }
 texture {color White alpha 0.9 phong 0.8
 refraction 1  ior Flint_Glass_Ior
 }
}

object {
 intersection {Lens translate <2 0 0> }
 texture {color White alpha 0.9 phong 0.8
 refraction 1  ior Diamond_Ior
 }
}
```

Listing A-7 IOR.INC Include File

```
// Persistence of Vision Raytracer
//
// This file defines a few Index of Refractions for various
```

```
// materials for sodium light. Source: College Physics by
// Arthur L. Kimball, PhD. 4th Edition (1923)
// --------------------
#declare Flint_Glass_Ior = 1.71
#declare Crown_Glass_Ior = 1.51
#declare Diamond_Ior = 2.47
#declare Water_Ior = 1.33
#declare Air_Ior = 1.000292
```

FOV.INC INCLUDE FILE

The FOV.INC file is a brief table of float identifiers, which contain values to control the camera field of view angle using the direction vector. (See the Chapter 7 entries on `camera` and `direction` for more details.)

Here is an example that uses the FOV.INC file.

Listing A-8 Using the FOV.INC Include File

```
// FOV60.POV
#include "examp.inc"
#include "fov.inc"

// Something to look at.
object {
  sphere { <0 0 0> 1 }
  texture {color NeonPink phong 1}
}

// Camera with wide view
camera {
  location <0 0 -3.5>
  direction <0 0 FoV_60> // 60 degree field of view
}
```

Listing A-9 FOV.INC Include File

```
// Persistence of Vision Raytracer
//
// Direction Vectors for various Field of View angles.
// Use in camera in form:
//
//   direction <0 0 FoV_45>
//
// The formula used to calculate these is: FoV = 0.5 / tan(angle/2)
// You will also need to adjust the location vector if you change
// FoV and want to keep the same visual distance from your scene.

 #declare FoV_15 = 7.595981
```

```
#declare FoV_30 = 3.732166
#declare FoV_45 = 2.414293
#declare FoV_60 = 1.732113
#declare FoV_75 = 1.303277
#declare FoV_90 = 1.000046
#declare FoV_105 = 0.767370
#declare FoV_120 = 0.577391
#declare FoV_135 = 0.414254
#declare FoV_150 = 0.267991
#declare FoV_165 = 0.131696
```

STONES.INC INCLUDE FILE

Computer artist Mike Miller is recognized as one of the most skilled users of the POV-Ray program. His work consistently wins CompuServe's Go Graphics Forum's monthly Hall of Fame awards. Among his skills are the ability to create realistic stone textures. The STONES.INC file is a large collection of textures created by Miller.

Listing A-10 STONES.INC Include File

```
/*
            Persistence of Vision Raytracer
            Stone textures by Mike Miller  1992

Contains declared texture statements defining a variety of
stone granite & marble textures. Most use the granite texture.
Turbulence has no effect on granite, but turbulence is stated
before the color map for convenience of switching to marble, which
does need a turbulence to swirl the color. I tried to avoid using
a random dither, but I find it helps create a subtle grain & can
spark lost colors in the map. On multi-layered texture, try a
float of about 0.05 on the first texture.

Final Note: I would not "INCLUDE" this whole data file into a
            scene file if only one or two of these textures were
            being used...There are too many declares being used.


-----------------------------------
The textures Grnt0-Grnt29, Grnt0A-Grnt24A and Crack1-Crack4 are
"building blocks" that are used to create the final "usable"
textures, Stone1 - Stone24 (and other textures that *you* design,
of course!)

  INDEX:
  Grnt0  - Grnt29   color maps (generally) contain no alpha values
```

```
--------------------
        Grnt0  - Gray/Tan with Rose.
        Grnt1  - Creamy Whites with Yellow & Light Gray.
        Grnt2  - Deep Cream with Light Rose, Yellow, Orchid, & Tan.
        Grnt3  - Warm tans olive & light rose with cream.
        Grnt4  - Orchid, Sand & Mauve.
        Grnt5  - Medium Mauve Med.Rose & Deep Cream.
        Grnt6  - Med. Orchid, Olive & Dark Tan "mud pie".
        Grnt7  - Dark Orchid, Olive & Dark Putty.
        Grnt8  - Rose & Light Cream Yellows
        Grnt9  - Light Steely Grays
        Grnt10 - Gray Creams & Lavender Tans
        Grnt11 - Creams & Grays  Kahki
        Grnt12 - Tan Cream & Red Rose
        Grnt13 - Cream Rose Orange
        Grnt14 - Cream Rose & Light Moss w/Light Violet
        Grnt15 - Black with subtle chroma
        Grnt16 - White Cream & Peach
        Grnt17 - Bug Juice & Green
        Grnt18 - Rose & Creamy Yellow
        Grnt19 - Gray Marble with White feather Veins
        Grnt20 - White Marble with Gray feather Veins
        Grnt21 - Green Jade
        Grnt22 - Clear with White feather Veins (has some
        transparency)
        Grnt23 - Light Tan to Mauve
        Grnt24 - Light Grays
        Grnt25 - Moss Greens & Tan
        Grnt26 - Salmon with thin Green Veins
        Grnt27 - Dark Green & Browns
        Grnt28 - Red Swirl
        Grnt29 - White, Tan, w/ thin Red Veins

    Grnt0A - Grnt24A  color maps containing alpha
--------------------
        Grnt0a  - Translucent Grnt0
        Grnt1a  - Translucent Grnt1
        Grnt2a  - Translucent Grnt2
        Grnt3a  - Translucent Grnt3
        Grnt4a  - Translucent Grnt4
        Grnt5a  - Translucent Grnt5
        Grnt6a  - Translucent Grnt6
        Grnt7a  - Translucent Grnt7
        Grnt8a  - Aqua Tints
        Grnt9a  - Alpha Creams With Cracks
        Grnt10a - Alpha Cream Rose & light yellow
        Grnt11a - Alpha Light Grays
        Grnt12a - Alpha Creams & Tans
        Grnt13a - Alpha Creams & Grays
        Grnt14a - Cream Rose & light moss
```

```
        Grnt15a - Alpha Sand & Light Orange
        Grnt16a - Cream Rose & Light moss (again?)
        Grnt17a - ???
        Grnt18a - ???
        Grnt19a - Gray Marble with White feather Veins with Alpha
        Grnt20a - White Feather Veins
        Grnt21a - Thin White Feather Veins
        Grnt22a - ???
        Grnt23a - Transparent Green Moss
        Grnt24a - ???


    Crack1 - Crack4    clear with a thin opaque band for Cracks
    ------------------
        Crack1 - Crack & Red Overtint
        Crack2 - Translucent Dark Cracks
        Crack3 - Overtint Green w/ Black Cracks
        Crack4 - Overtint w/ White Crack


    OTHERS
    Stone1 - Stone24   complete texture statements - edit to your
             scene & lighting situations.
    ------------------
        Stone1 - Deep Rose & Green Marble with large White Swirls
        Stone2 - Light Greenish Tan Marble with Agate style veining
        Stone3 - Rose & Yellow Marble with fog white veining
        Stone4 - Tan Marble with Rose patches
        Stone5 - White Cream Marble with Pink veining
        Stone6 - Rose & Yellow Cream Marble
        Stone7 - Light Coffee Marble with darker patches
        Stone8 - Gray Granite with white patches
        Stone9 - White & Light Blue Marble with light violets
        Stone10- Dark Brown & Tan swirl Granite with gray undertones
        Stone11- Rose & White Marble with dark tan swirl
        Stone12- White & Pinkish Tan Marble
        Stone13- Medium Gray Blue Marble
        Stone14- Tan & Olive Marble with gray white veins
        Stone15- Deep Gray Marble with white veining
        Stone16- Peach & Yellow Marble with white veining
        Stone17- White Marble with gray veining
        Stone18- Green Jade with white veining
        Stone19- Peach Granite with white patches & green trim
        Stone20- Brown & Olive Marble with white veining
        Stone21- Red Marble with gray & white veining
        Stone22- Dark Tan Marble with gray & white veining
        Stone23- Peach & Cream Marble with orange veining
        Stone24- Green & Tan Moss Marble


    -----------------------------------
*/
```

```
//---- Gray  Tan with Rose
#declare Grnt0 = texture {
 granite
 turbulence 0.4
 color_map {
 [0.000 0.153 color red 0.729 green 0.502 blue 0.451 alpha 0.0
        color red 0.769 green 0.686 blue 0.592 alpha 0.0]
 [0.153 0.398 color red 0.769 green 0.686 blue 0.592 alpha 0.0
        color red 0.843 green 0.753 blue 0.718 alpha 0.0]
 [0.398 0.559 color red 0.843 green 0.753 blue 0.718 alpha 0.0
        color red 0.780 green 0.667 blue 0.561 alpha 0.0]
 [0.559 0.729 color red 0.780 green 0.667 blue 0.561 alpha 0.0
        color red 0.741 green 0.659 blue 0.576 alpha 0.0]
 [0.729 1.001 color red 0.741 green 0.659 blue 0.576 alpha 0.0
        color red 0.729 green 0.502 blue 0.451 alpha 0.0]
 }
}


//--- Creamy Whites with yellow & light gray
#declare Grnt1 = texture {
 granite
 turbulence 0.6
 color_map {
 [0.000 0.212 color red 0.898 green 0.898 blue 0.851 alpha 0.0
        color red 0.969 green 0.980 blue 0.875 alpha 0.0]
 [0.212 0.424 color red 0.969 green 0.980 blue 0.875 alpha 0.0
        color red 0.859 green 0.859 blue 0.859 alpha 0.0]
 [0.424 0.627 color red 0.859 green 0.859 blue 0.859 alpha 0.0
        color red 0.992 green 0.922 blue 0.659 alpha 0.0]
 [0.627 0.881 color red 0.992 green 0.922 blue 0.659 alpha 0.0
        color red 0.937 green 0.965 blue 0.902 alpha 0.0]
 [0.881 1.001 color red 0.937 green 0.965 blue 0.902 alpha 0.0
        color red 0.898 green 0.898 blue 0.851 alpha 0.0]
 }
}


//---- Deep Cream with light rose, yellow orchid & tan
#declare Grnt2 = texture {
 granite
 turbulence 0.5
 color_map {
 [0.000 0.178 color red 0.863 green 0.757 blue 0.596 alpha 0.0
        color red 0.925 green 0.792 blue 0.714 alpha 0.0]
 [0.178 0.356 color red 0.925 green 0.792 blue 0.714 alpha 0.0
        color red 0.871 green 0.702 blue 0.659 alpha 0.0]
 [0.356 0.525 color red 0.871 green 0.702 blue 0.659 alpha 0.0
        color red 0.992 green 0.922 blue 0.659 alpha 0.0]
 [0.525 0.729 color red 0.992 green 0.922 blue 0.659 alpha 0.0
        color red 0.902 green 0.812 blue 0.714 alpha 0.0]
 [0.729 1.001 color red 0.902 green 0.812 blue 0.714 alpha 0.0
```

```
          color red 0.863 green 0.757 blue 0.596 alpha 0.0]
  }
}


//---- Warm tans olive & light rose with cream
#declare Grnt3 = texture {
  granite
  turbulence 0.5
  color_map {
  [0.000 0.178 color red 0.831 green 0.631 blue 0.569 alpha 0.0
           color red 0.925 green 0.831 blue 0.714 alpha 0.0]
  [0.178 0.356 color red 0.925 green 0.831 blue 0.714 alpha 0.0
           color red 0.871 green 0.702 blue 0.659 alpha 0.0]
  [0.356 0.525 color red 0.871 green 0.702 blue 0.659 alpha 0.0
           color red 0.831 green 0.631 blue 0.569 alpha 0.0]
  [0.525 0.729 color red 0.831 green 0.631 blue 0.569 alpha 0.0
           color red 0.937 green 0.882 blue 0.820 alpha 0.0]
  [0.729 1.001 color red 0.937 green 0.882 blue 0.820 alpha 0.0
           color red 0.831 green 0.631 blue 0.569 alpha 0.0]
  }
}


//---- Orchid sand & mauve
#declare Grnt4 = texture {
  granite
  turbulence 0.5
  color_map {
  [0.000 0.178 color red 0.804 green 0.569 blue 0.494 alpha 0.0
           color red 0.816 green 0.725 blue 0.537 alpha 0.0]
  [0.178 0.356 color red 0.816 green 0.725 blue 0.537 alpha 0.0
           color red 0.820 green 0.580 blue 0.522 alpha 0.0]
  [0.356 0.525 color red 0.820 green 0.580 blue 0.522 alpha 0.0
           color red 0.882 green 0.725 blue 0.537 alpha 0.0]
  [0.525 0.729 color red 0.882 green 0.725 blue 0.537 alpha 0.0
           color red 0.855 green 0.729 blue 0.584 alpha 0.0]
  [0.729 1.001 color red 0.855 green 0.729 blue 0.584 alpha 0.0
           color red 0.804 green 0.569 blue 0.494 alpha 0.0]
  }
}


//---- Medium Mauve Med.Rose & deep cream
#declare Grnt5 = texture {
  granite
  turbulence 0.5
  color_map {
  [0.000 0.178 color red 0.804 green 0.569 blue 0.494 alpha 0.0
           color red 0.855 green 0.729 blue 0.584 alpha 0.0]
  [0.178 0.356 color red 0.855 green 0.729 blue 0.584 alpha 0.0
           color red 0.667 green 0.502 blue 0.478 alpha 0.0]
  [0.356 0.525 color red 0.667 green 0.502 blue 0.478 alpha 0.0
```

```
              color red 0.859 green 0.624 blue 0.545 alpha 0.0]
    [0.525 0.729 color red 0.859 green 0.624 blue 0.545 alpha 0.0
              color red 0.855 green 0.729 blue 0.584 alpha 0.0]
    [0.729 1.001 color red 0.855 green 0.729 blue 0.584 alpha 0.0
              color red 0.804 green 0.569 blue 0.494 alpha 0.0]
    }
}


//----- Med. Orchid Olive & Dark Tan "mud pie"
#declare Grnt6 = texture {
  granite
  turbulence 0.5
  color_map {
  [0.000 0.153 color red 0.545 green 0.380 blue 0.345 alpha 0.0
              color red 0.588 green 0.475 blue 0.333 alpha 0.0]
  [0.153 0.398 color red 0.588 green 0.475 blue 0.333 alpha 0.0
              color red 0.675 green 0.478 blue 0.404 alpha 0.0]
  [0.398 0.559 color red 0.675 green 0.478 blue 0.404 alpha 0.0
              color red 0.757 green 0.635 blue 0.522 alpha 0.0]
  [0.559 0.729 color red 0.757 green 0.635 blue 0.522 alpha 0.0
              color red 0.659 green 0.549 blue 0.443 alpha 0.0]
  [0.729 1.001 color red 0.659 green 0.549 blue 0.443 alpha 0.0
              color red 0.545 green 0.380 blue 0.345 alpha 0.0]
  }
}


//---- Dark Orchid Olive & Dark Putty
#declare Grnt7 = texture {
  granite
  turbulence 0.5
  color_map {
  [0.000 0.153 color red 0.439 green 0.310 blue 0.282 alpha 0.0
              color red 0.463 green 0.369 blue 0.259 alpha 0.0]
  [0.153 0.398 color red 0.463 green 0.369 blue 0.259 alpha 0.0
              color red 0.541 green 0.369 blue 0.298 alpha 0.0]
  [0.398 0.559 color red 0.541 green 0.369 blue 0.298 alpha 0.0
              color red 0.573 green 0.424 blue 0.286 alpha 0.0]
  [0.559 0.729 color red 0.573 green 0.424 blue 0.286 alpha 0.0
              color red 0.494 green 0.396 blue 0.306 alpha 0.0]
  [0.729 1.001 color red 0.494 green 0.396 blue 0.306 alpha 0.0
              color red 0.439 green 0.310 blue 0.282 alpha 0.0]
  }
}


//----- Rose & Light cream Yellows
#declare Grnt8 = texture {
  granite
  turbulence 0.6
  color_map {
  [0.000 0.179 color red 0.843 green 0.655 blue 0.655 alpha 0.0
```

```
             color red 0.886 green 0.769 blue 0.627 alpha 0.0]
 [0.179 0.368 color red 0.886 green 0.769 blue 0.627 alpha 0.0
             color red 0.906 green 0.820 blue 0.714 alpha 0.0]
 [0.368 0.538 color red 0.906 green 0.820 blue 0.714 alpha 0.0
             color red 0.851 green 0.671 blue 0.671 alpha 0.0]
 [0.538 0.846 color red 0.851 green 0.671 blue 0.671 alpha 0.0
             color red 0.890 green 0.792 blue 0.675 alpha 0.0]
 [0.846 0.983 color red 0.890 green 0.792 blue 0.675 alpha 0.0
             color red 0.827 green 0.612 blue 0.612 alpha 0.0]
 [0.983 1.001 color red 0.827 green 0.612 blue 0.612 alpha 0.0
             color red 0.843 green 0.655 blue 0.655 alpha 0.0]
 }
}


//----- Light Steely Grays
#declare Grnt9 = texture {
 granite
 turbulence 0.6
 color_map {
 [0.000 0.154 color red 0.894 green 0.886 blue 0.886 alpha 0.0
             color red 0.745 green 0.745 blue 0.753 alpha 0.0]
 [0.154 0.308 color red 0.745 green 0.745 blue 0.753 alpha 0.0
             color red 0.902 green 0.902 blue 0.859 alpha 0.0]
 [0.308 0.444 color red 0.902 green 0.902 blue 0.859 alpha 0.0
             color red 0.729 green 0.706 blue 0.694 alpha 0.0]
 [0.444 0.615 color red 0.729 green 0.706 blue 0.694 alpha 0.0
             color red 0.588 green 0.592 blue 0.635 alpha 0.0]
 [0.615 0.803 color red 0.588 green 0.592 blue 0.635 alpha 0.0
             color red 0.608 green 0.616 blue 0.659 alpha 0.0]
 [0.803 1.001 color red 0.608 green 0.616 blue 0.659 alpha 0.0
             color red 0.894 green 0.886 blue 0.886 alpha 0.0]
 }
}


//----- Gray Creams & lavender tans
#declare Grnt10 = texture {
 granite
 turbulence 0.6
 color_map {
 [0.000 0.154 color red 0.890 green 0.690 blue 0.690 alpha 0.0
             color red 0.996 green 0.835 blue 0.737 alpha 0.0]
 [0.154 0.308 color red 0.996 green 0.835 blue 0.737 alpha 0.0
             color red 0.745 green 0.635 blue 0.651 alpha 0.004]
 [0.308 0.444 color red 0.745 green 0.635 blue 0.651 alpha 0.004
             color red 0.733 green 0.596 blue 0.557 alpha 0.004]
 [0.444 0.615 color red 0.733 green 0.596 blue 0.557 alpha 0.004
             color red 0.996 green 0.835 blue 0.737 alpha 0.0]
 [0.615 0.803 color red 0.996 green 0.835 blue 0.737 alpha 0.0
             color red 0.765 green 0.616 blue 0.659 alpha 0.0]
 [0.803 1.001 color red 0.765 green 0.616 blue 0.659 alpha 0.0
```

```
              color red 0.890 green 0.690 blue 0.690 alpha 0.0]
  }
}


//----- Creams & Grays Kakhi
#declare Grnt11 = texture {
  granite
  turbulence 0.6
  color_map {
  [0.000 0.154 color red 0.800 green 0.651 blue 0.557 alpha 0.0
          color red 0.996 green 0.835 blue 0.737 alpha 0.0]
  [0.154 0.308 color red 0.996 green 0.835 blue 0.737 alpha 0.0
          color red 0.800 green 0.651 blue 0.557 alpha 0.0]
  [0.308 0.444 color red 0.800 green 0.651 blue 0.557 alpha 0.0
          color red 0.694 green 0.624 blue 0.604 alpha 0.004]
  [0.444 0.615 color red 0.694 green 0.624 blue 0.604 alpha 0.004
          color red 0.800 green 0.651 blue 0.557 alpha 0.0]
  [0.615 0.812 color red 0.800 green 0.651 blue 0.557 alpha 0.0
          color red 0.725 green 0.655 blue 0.651 alpha 0.0]
  [0.812 1.001 color red 0.725 green 0.655 blue 0.651 alpha 0.0
          color red 0.800 green 0.651 blue 0.557 alpha 0.0]
  }
}


//----- Tan Cream & Red Rose
#declare Grnt12 = texture {
  granite
  turbulence 0.6
  color_map {
  [0.000 0.154 color red 0.996 green 0.969 blue 0.800 alpha 0.0
          color red 0.996 green 0.682 blue 0.604 alpha 0.0]
  [0.154 0.308 color red 0.996 green 0.682 blue 0.604 alpha 0.0
          color red 0.906 green 0.820 blue 0.714 alpha 0.0]
  [0.308 0.444 color red 0.906 green 0.820 blue 0.714 alpha 0.0
          color red 0.816 green 0.631 blue 0.537 alpha 0.0]
  [0.444 0.615 color red 0.816 green 0.631 blue 0.537 alpha 0.0
          color red 0.890 green 0.792 blue 0.675 alpha 0.0]
  [0.615 0.812 color red 0.890 green 0.792 blue 0.675 alpha 0.0
          color red 0.973 green 0.627 blue 0.627 alpha 0.0]
  [0.812 1.001 color red 0.973 green 0.627 blue 0.627 alpha 0.0
          color red 0.996 green 0.969 blue 0.800 alpha 0.0]
  }
}


//----- Cream Rose orange
#declare Grnt13 = texture {
  granite
  turbulence 0.6
  color_map {
  [0.000 0.154 color red 0.996 green 0.824 blue 0.780 alpha 0.0
```

```
           color red 0.996 green 0.698 blue 0.624 alpha 0.0]
 [0.154 0.308 color red 0.996 green 0.698 blue 0.624 alpha 0.0
           color red 0.906 green 0.675 blue 0.553 alpha 0.0]
 [0.308 0.444 color red 0.906 green 0.675 blue 0.553 alpha 0.0
           color red 0.996 green 0.682 blue 0.604 alpha 0.0]
 [0.444 0.615 color red 0.996 green 0.682 blue 0.604 alpha 0.0
           color red 0.996 green 0.824 blue 0.780 alpha 0.0]
 [0.615 0.812 color red 0.996 green 0.824 blue 0.780 alpha 0.0
           color red 0.973 green 0.627 blue 0.627 alpha 0.0]
 [0.812 1.001 color red 0.973 green 0.627 blue 0.627 alpha 0.0
           color red 0.996 green 0.824 blue 0.780 alpha 0.0]
 }
}

//----- Cream Rose & light moss & light Violet
#declare Grnt14 = texture {
 granite
 turbulence 0.6
 color_map {
 [0.000 0.154 color red 0.690 green 0.612 blue 0.569 alpha 0.0
          color red 0.737 green 0.596 blue 0.522 alpha 0.0]
 [0.154 0.368 color red 0.737 green 0.596 blue 0.522 alpha 0.0
          color red 0.776 green 0.702 blue 0.624 alpha 0.0]
 [0.368 0.538 color red 0.776 green 0.702 blue 0.624 alpha 0.0
          color red 0.796 green 0.678 blue 0.643 alpha 0.0]
 [0.538 0.846 color red 0.796 green 0.678 blue 0.643 alpha 0.0
          color red 0.690 green 0.612 blue 0.569 alpha 0.0]
 [0.846 0.932 color red 0.690 green 0.612 blue 0.569 alpha 0.0
          color red 0.773 green 0.612 blue 0.569 alpha 0.0]
 [0.932 1.001 color red 0.773 green 0.612 blue 0.569 alpha 0.0
          color red 0.690 green 0.612 blue 0.569 alpha 0.0]
 }
}

//----- Black with subtle chroma
#declare Grnt15 = texture {
 granite
 turbulence 0.6
 color_map {
 [0.000 0.104 color red 0.161 green 0.133 blue 0.118 alpha 0.0
          color red 0.110 green 0.082 blue 0.071 alpha 0.0]
 [0.104 0.252 color red 0.110 green 0.082 blue 0.071 alpha 0.0
          color red 0.161 green 0.133 blue 0.118 alpha 0.0]
  [0.252 0.383 color red 0.161 green 0.133 blue 0.118 alpha 0.0
          color red 0.000 green 0.000 blue 0.000 alpha 0.0]
 [0.383 0.643 color red 0.000 green 0.000 blue 0.000 alpha 0.0
          color red 0.161 green 0.133 blue 0.118 alpha 0.0]
 [0.643 0.783 color red 0.161 green 0.133 blue 0.118 alpha 0.0
          color red 0.220 green 0.149 blue 0.137 alpha 0.0]
 [0.783 0.922 color red 0.220 green 0.149 blue 0.137 alpha 0.0
```

```
                color red 0.000 green 0.000 blue 0.000 alpha 0.0]
   [0.922 0.983 color red 0.000 green 0.000 blue 0.000 alpha 0.0
                color red 0.220 green 0.149 blue 0.137 alpha 0.0]
   [0.983 1.001 color red 0.220 green 0.149 blue 0.137 alpha 0.0
                color red 0.161 green 0.133 blue 0.118 alpha 0.0]
   }
 }


 //--- White Cream & Peach
 #declare Grnt16 = texture {
  granite
  turbulence 0.6
  color_map {
  [0.000 0.316 color red 0.910 green 0.788 blue 0.788 alpha 0.0
               color red 0.922 green 0.914 blue 0.871 alpha 0.0]
  [0.316 0.453 color red 0.922 green 0.914 blue 0.871 alpha 0.0
               color red 0.894 green 0.867 blue 0.780 alpha 0.0]
  [0.453 0.624 color red 0.894 green 0.867 blue 0.780 alpha 0.0
               color red 0.784 green 0.788 blue 0.788 alpha 0.0]
  [0.624 0.726 color red 0.784 green 0.788 blue 0.788 alpha 0.0
               color red 0.851 green 0.812 blue 0.741 alpha 0.0]
  [0.726 0.863 color red 0.851 green 0.812 blue 0.741 alpha 0.0
               color red 0.647 green 0.655 blue 0.655 alpha 0.0]
  [0.863 1.001 color red 0.647 green 0.655 blue 0.655 alpha 0.0
               color red 0.910 green 0.788 blue 0.788 alpha 0.0]
  }
 }


 //--- Bug Juice & Green
 #declare Grnt17 = texture {
  granite
  turbulence 0.6
  color_map {
  [0.000 0.303 color red 0.000 green 0.239 blue 0.000 alpha 0.0
               color red 0.333 green 0.294 blue 0.000 alpha 0.0]
  [0.303 0.588 color red 0.333 green 0.294 blue 0.000 alpha 0.0
               color red 0.000 green 0.239 blue 0.341 alpha 0.0]
  [0.588 0.790 color red 0.000 green 0.239 blue 0.341 alpha 0.0
               color red 0.000 green 0.020 blue 0.000 alpha 0.0]
  [0.790 1.001 color red 0.000 green 0.020 blue 0.000 alpha 0.0
               color red 0.000 green 0.239 blue 0.000 alpha 0.0]
  }
 }


 //------ Rose & cream yellow
 #declare Grnt18 = texture {
  granite
  turbulence 0.4
  color_map {
  [0.000 0.202 color red 1.000 green 0.718 blue 0.541 alpha 0.0
```

```
               color red 0.890 green 0.651 blue 0.612 alpha 0.0]
[0.202 0.298 color red 0.890 green 0.651 blue 0.612 alpha 0.0
               color red 1.000 green 0.820 blue 0.675 alpha 0.0]
[0.298 0.377 color red 1.000 green 0.820 blue 0.675 alpha 0.0
               color red 0.890 green 0.643 blue 0.612 alpha 0.0]
[0.377 0.465 color red 0.890 green 0.643 blue 0.612 alpha 0.0
               color red 0.937 green 0.729 blue 0.561 alpha 0.0]
[0.465 0.544 color red 0.937 green 0.729 blue 0.561 alpha 0.0
               color red 0.878 green 0.604 blue 0.565 alpha 0.0]
[0.544 0.640 color red 0.878 green 0.604 blue 0.565 alpha 0.0
               color red 0.984 green 0.780 blue 0.655 alpha 0.0]
[0.640 0.860 color red 0.984 green 0.780 blue 0.655 alpha 0.0
               color red 1.000 green 0.863 blue 0.635 alpha 0.0]
   [0.860 0.982        color red 1.000 green 0.863 blue 0.635 alpha 0.0
               color red 1.000 green 0.765 blue 0.620 alpha 0.0]
[0.982 1.001 color red 1.000 green 0.765 blue 0.620 alpha 0.0
               color red 1.000 green 0.718 blue 0.541 alpha 0.0]
 }
}


//----- Gray Marble with White feather Veins
#declare Grnt19 = texture {
 granite
 turbulence 0.0
 color_map {
 [0.0 0.3 color White color DimGray]
 [0.2 0.4 color DimGray color DimGray]
 [0.4 0.6 color DimGray color DimGray]
 [0.6 1.0 color DimGray color DimGray]
 }
 0.02
}


//----- White Marble with Gray feather Veins
#declare Grnt20 = texture {
 granite
 turbulence 0.0
 color_map {
 [0.0 0.3 color Mica color White]
 [0.2 0.4 color White color White]
 [0.4 0.6 color White color White]
 [0.6 1.0 color White color White]
 }
 0.02
}


//---- Declare Green Colors
#declare g1 = color red 0.26 green 0.41 blue 0.31
         //--Light Gray Green
#declare g2 = color red 0.27 green 0.34 blue 0.26
```

```
        //--Med Gray Green
#declare g3 = color red 0.13 green 0.29 blue 0.28 //ñ-Med Gray Aqua
#declare g4 = color red 0.03 green 0.18 blue 0.08 //ñ-Dark Green

//----- Green Jade
#declare Grnt21 = texture {
 granite
 turbulence 0.0
 color_map {
 [0.0 0.1 color White alpha 0.3 color SeaGreen alpha 0.4]
 [0.1 0.3 color SeaGreen alpha 0.4 color g2 alpha 0.7]
 [0.3 0.5 color g2 alpha 0.7 color DarkGreen alpha 0.7]
 [0.5 0.7 color DarkGreen alpha 0.7 color g4 alpha 0.7]
 [0.7 0.8 color g4 color alpha 0.7 DarkGreen alpha 0.7]
 [0.8 1.0 color DarkGreen alpha 0.7 color DarkGreen alpha 0.7]
 }
 0.02
}


//----- Clear with White feather Veins --- This one does
//            contain Alpha
#declare Grnt22 = texture {
 granite
 turbulence 0.0
 color_map {
 [0.0 0.07 color White color White]
 [0.07 0.2 color White color DimGray]
 [0.2 0.3 color DimGray color Clear]
 [0.3 0.7 color Clear color Clear]
 [0.7 1.0 color Clear color DimGray]
 }
 0.02
}


//----- Light Tan to Mauve
#declare Grnt23 = texture {
 marble
 turbulence 0.5
 color_map {
 [0.000 0.178 color red 0.831 green 0.631 blue 0.569 alpha 0.0
         color red 0.925 green 0.831 blue 0.714 alpha 0.0]
 [0.178 0.356 color red 0.925 green 0.831 blue 0.714 alpha 0.0
         color red 0.871 green 0.702 blue 0.659 alpha 0.0]
 [0.356 0.525 color red 0.871 green 0.702 blue 0.659 alpha 0.0
         color red 0.831 green 0.631 blue 0.569 alpha 0.0]
 [0.525 0.729 color red 0.831 green 0.631 blue 0.569 alpha 0.0
         color red 0.937 green 0.882 blue 0.820 alpha 0.0]
 [0.729 1.001 color red 0.937 green 0.882 blue 0.820 alpha 0.0
         color red 0.831 green 0.631 blue 0.569 alpha 0.0]
 }
```

544

```
}

//----- Light Grays
#declare Grnt24 = texture {
 marble
 turbulence 0.6
 color_map {
 [0.000 0.154 color red 0.894 green 0.886 blue 0.886 alpha 0.0
         color red 0.745 green 0.745 blue 0.753 alpha 0.0]
 [0.154 0.308 color red 0.745 green 0.745 blue 0.753 alpha 0.0
         color red 0.902 green 0.902 blue 0.859 alpha 0.0]
 [0.308 0.444 color red 0.902 green 0.902 blue 0.859 alpha 0.0
         color red 0.729 green 0.706 blue 0.694 alpha 0.0]
 [0.444 0.615 color red 0.729 green 0.706 blue 0.694 alpha 0.0
         color red 0.588 green 0.592 blue 0.635 alpha 0.0]
 [0.615 0.803 color red 0.588 green 0.592 blue 0.635 alpha 0.0
         color red 0.608 green 0.616 blue 0.659 alpha 0.0]
 [0.803 1.001 color red 0.608 green 0.616 blue 0.659 alpha 0.0
         color red 0.894 green 0.886 blue 0.886 alpha 0.0]
 }
}

//------ Moss Greens & Tan
#declare Grnt25 = texture {
 marble
 turbulence 0.7
 color_map {
 [0.000 0.168 color red 0.824 green 0.725 blue 0.584 alpha 0.0
         color red 0.514 green 0.584 blue 0.533 alpha 0.0]
 [0.168 0.301 color red 0.514 green 0.584 blue 0.533 alpha 0.0
         color red 0.298 green 0.376 blue 0.318 alpha 0.0]
 [0.301 0.398 color red 0.298 green 0.376 blue 0.318 alpha 0.0
         color red 0.263 green 0.337 blue 0.282 alpha 0.0]
 [0.398 0.558 color red 0.263 green 0.337 blue 0.282 alpha 0.0
         color red 0.431 green 0.506 blue 0.451 alpha 0.0]
 [0.558 0.655 color red 0.431 green 0.506 blue 0.451 alpha 0.0
         color red 0.529 green 0.631 blue 0.471 alpha 0.0]
 [0.655 0.735 color red 0.529 green 0.631 blue 0.471 alpha 0.0
         color red 0.333 green 0.376 blue 0.318 alpha 0.0]
 [0.735 0.823 color red 0.333 green 0.376 blue 0.318 alpha 0.0
         color red 0.298 green 0.376 blue 0.318 alpha 0.0]
 [0.823 0.876 color red 0.298 green 0.376 blue 0.318 alpha 0.0
         color red 0.416 green 0.376 blue 0.318 alpha 0.0]
 [0.876 0.929 color red 0.416 green 0.376 blue 0.318 alpha 0.0
         color red 0.416 green 0.376 blue 0.318 alpha 0.0]
 [0.929 1.001 color red 0.416 green 0.376 blue 0.318 alpha 0.0
         color red 0.824 green 0.725 blue 0.584 alpha 0.0]
 }
}
```

```
//----- Salmon with thin Green Veins
#declare Grnt26 = texture {
 granite
 color_map {
 [0.000 0.241 color red 0.973 green 0.973 blue 0.976 alpha 0.0
         color red 0.973 green 0.973 blue 0.976 alpha 0.0]
 [0.241 0.284 color red 0.973 green 0.973 blue 0.976 alpha 0.0
         color red 0.600 green 0.741 blue 0.608 alpha 0.0]
 [0.284 0.336 color red 0.600 green 0.741 blue 0.608 alpha 0.0
         color red 0.820 green 0.643 blue 0.537 alpha 0.0]
 [0.336 0.474 color red 0.820 green 0.643 blue 0.537 alpha 0.0
         color red 0.886 green 0.780 blue 0.714 alpha 0.0]
 [0.474 0.810 color red 0.886 green 0.780 blue 0.714 alpha 0.0
         color red 0.996 green 0.643 blue 0.537 alpha 0.0]
 [0.810 0.836 color red 0.996 green 0.643 blue 0.537 alpha 0.0
         color red 0.973 green 0.973 blue 0.976 alpha 0.0]
 [0.836 1.001 color red 0.973 green 0.973 blue 0.976 alpha 0.0
         color red 0.973 green 0.973 blue 0.976 alpha 0.0]
 }
 0.02
}


//--- Dark Green & Browns
#declare Grnt27 = texture {
 granite
 color_map {
 [0.000 0.043 color red 0.773 green 0.647 blue 0.569 alpha 0.0
         color red 0.431 green 0.322 blue 0.227 alpha 0.0]
 [0.043 0.113 color red 0.431 green 0.322 blue 0.227 alpha 0.0
         color red 0.278 green 0.282 blue 0.216 alpha 0.0]
 [0.113 0.304 color red 0.278 green 0.282 blue 0.216 alpha 0.0
         color red 0.278 green 0.282 blue 0.216 alpha 0.0]
 [0.304 0.426 color red 0.278 green 0.282 blue 0.216 alpha 0.0
         color red 0.459 green 0.341 blue 0.243 alpha 0.0]
 [0.426 0.843 color red 0.459 green 0.341 blue 0.243 alpha 0.0
         color red 0.459 green 0.341 blue 0.243 alpha 0.0]
 [0.843 0.878 color red 0.459 green 0.341 blue 0.243 alpha 0.0
         color red 0.459 green 0.341 blue 0.243 alpha 0.0]
 [0.878 0.983 color red 0.459 green 0.341 blue 0.243 alpha 0.0
         color red 0.278 green 0.282 blue 0.216 alpha 0.0]
 [0.983 1.001 color red 0.278 green 0.282 blue 0.216 alpha 0.0
         color red 0.773 green 0.647 blue 0.569 alpha 0.0]
 }
}


//---- Red Swirl
#declare Grnt28 = texture {
 marble
 turbulence 0.7
 color_map {
```

```
[0.000 0.155 color red 0.686 green 0.235 blue 0.282 alpha 0.0
        color red 0.686 green 0.235 blue 0.282 alpha 0.0]
[0.155 0.328 color red 0.686 green 0.235 blue 0.282 alpha 0.0
        color red 0.494 green 0.243 blue 0.294 alpha 0.0]
[0.328 0.474 color red 0.494 green 0.243 blue 0.294 alpha 0.0
        color red 0.769 green 0.329 blue 0.373 alpha 0.0]
[0.474 0.647 color red 0.769 green 0.329 blue 0.373 alpha 0.0
        color red 0.769 green 0.329 blue 0.373 alpha 0.0]
[0.647 0.810 color red 0.769 green 0.329 blue 0.373 alpha 0.0
        color red 0.686 green 0.235 blue 0.282 alpha 0.0]
[0.810 0.922 color red 0.686 green 0.235 blue 0.282 alpha 0.0
        color red 0.792 green 0.388 blue 0.427 alpha 0.0]
[0.922 1.001 color red 0.792 green 0.388 blue 0.427 alpha 0.0
        color red 0.686 green 0.235 blue 0.282 alpha 0.0]
 }
 0.03
}


//---- White Tan & thin Reds
#declare Grnt29 = texture {
 marble
 turbulence 0.5
 color_map {
[0.000 0.053 color red 0.784 green 0.627 blue 0.522 alpha 0.0
        color red 0.784 green 0.627 blue 0.624 alpha 0.0]
[0.053 0.263 color red 0.784 green 0.627 blue 0.624 alpha 0.0
        color red 0.824 green 0.557 blue 0.376 alpha 0.0]
[0.263 0.281 color red 0.824 green 0.557 blue 0.376 alpha 0.0
        color red 0.643 green 0.380 blue 0.376 alpha 0.0]
[0.281 0.325 color red 0.643 green 0.380 blue 0.376 alpha 0.0
        color red 0.839 green 0.722 blue 0.722 alpha 0.0]
[0.325 0.711 color red 0.839 green 0.722 blue 0.722 alpha 0.0
        color red 0.784 green 0.627 blue 0.522 alpha 0.0]
[0.711 0.798 color red 0.784 green 0.627 blue 0.522 alpha 0.0
        color red 0.769 green 0.380 blue 0.376 alpha 0.0]
[0.798 0.895 color red 0.769 green 0.380 blue 0.376 alpha 0.0
        color red 0.824 green 0.557 blue 0.376 alpha 0.0]
[0.895 0.982 color red 0.824 green 0.557 blue 0.376 alpha 0.0
        color red 0.784 green 0.627 blue 0.522 alpha 0.0]
[0.982 1.001 color red 0.784 green 0.627 blue 0.522 alpha 0.0
        color red 0.784 green 0.627 blue 0.522 alpha 0.0]
 }
}


//***************************************************************
//------ start of textures with alpha

//--- Translucent Grnt0
#declare Grnt0a = texture {
 granite
```

```
     turbulence 0.6
     color_map {
     [0.000 0.153 color red 0.729 green 0.502 blue 0.451 alpha 0.306
            color red 0.769 green 0.686 blue 0.592 alpha 0.792]
     [0.153 0.398 color red 0.769 green 0.686 blue 0.592 alpha 0.792
            color red 0.843 green 0.753 blue 0.718 alpha 0.396]
     [0.398 0.559 color red 0.843 green 0.753 blue 0.718 alpha 0.396
            color red 0.780 green 0.667 blue 0.561 alpha 0.976]
     [0.559 0.729 color red 0.780 green 0.667 blue 0.561 alpha 0.976
            color red 0.741 green 0.659 blue 0.576 alpha 0.820]
     [0.729 1.001 color red 0.741 green 0.659 blue 0.576 alpha 0.820
            color red 0.729 green 0.502 blue 0.451 alpha 0.306]
     }
     }


//--- Translucent Grnt1
#declare Grnt1a = texture {
     granite
     turbulence 0.6
     color_map {
     [0.000 0.212 color red 0.898 green 0.898 blue 0.851 alpha 0.306
            color red 0.969 green 0.980 blue 0.875 alpha 0.792]
     [0.212 0.424 color red 0.969 green 0.980 blue 0.875 alpha 0.792
            color red 0.859 green 0.859 blue 0.859 alpha 0.396]
     [0.424 0.627 color red 0.859 green 0.859 blue 0.859 alpha 0.396
            color red 0.992 green 0.922 blue 0.659 alpha 0.976]
     [0.627 0.881 color red 0.992 green 0.922 blue 0.659 alpha 0.976
            color red 0.937 green 0.965 blue 0.902 alpha 0.820]
     [0.881 1.001 color red 0.937 green 0.965 blue 0.902 alpha 0.820
            color red 0.898 green 0.898 blue 0.851 alpha 0.306]
     }
     }


//---Translucent Grnt2
#declare Grnt2a = texture {
     granite
     turbulence 0.6
     color_map {
     [0.000 0.144 color red 0.863 green 0.757 blue 0.596 alpha 0.596
            color red 0.925 green 0.792 blue 0.714 alpha 0.349]
     [0.144 0.288 color red 0.925 green 0.792 blue 0.714 alpha 0.349
            color red 0.871 green 0.702 blue 0.659 alpha 0.784]
     [0.288 0.644 color red 0.871 green 0.702 blue 0.659 alpha 0.784
            color red 0.992 green 0.922 blue 0.659 alpha 0.498]
     [0.644 0.983 color red 0.992 green 0.922 blue 0.659 alpha 0.498
            color red 0.902 green 0.812 blue 0.714 alpha 0.722]
     [0.983 1.001 color red 0.902 green 0.812 blue 0.714 alpha 0.722
            color red 0.863 green 0.757 blue 0.596 alpha 0.596]
     }
     }
```

548

```
//---Translucent Grnt3
#declare Grnt3a = texture {
 granite
 turbulence 0.6
 color_map {
 [0.000 0.153 color red 0.831 green 0.631 blue 0.569 alpha 0.447
         color red 0.925 green 0.831 blue 0.714 alpha 0.678]
 [0.153 0.297 color red 0.925 green 0.831 blue 0.714 alpha 0.678
         color red 0.871 green 0.702 blue 0.659 alpha 0.475]
 [0.297 0.441 color red 0.871 green 0.702 blue 0.659 alpha 0.475
         color red 0.831 green 0.631 blue 0.569 alpha 0.918]
 [0.441 0.763 olor red 0.831 green 0.631 blue 0.569 alpha 0.918
         color red 0.937 green 0.882 blue 0.820 alpha 0.655]
 [0.763 1.001 color red 0.937 green 0.882 blue 0.820 alpha 0.655
         color red 0.831 green 0.631 blue 0.569 alpha 0.447]
 }
}

//---Translucent Grnt4
#declare Grnt4a = texture {
 granite
 turbulence 0.6
 color_map {
 [0.000 0.144 color red 0.804 green 0.569 blue 0.494 alpha 0.569
         color red 0.816 green 0.725 blue 0.537 alpha 0.467]
 [0.144 0.449 color red 0.816 green 0.725 blue 0.537 alpha 0.467
         color red 0.820 green 0.580 blue 0.522 alpha 0.584]
 [0.449 0.568 color red 0.820 green 0.580 blue 0.522 alpha 0.584
         color red 0.882 green 0.725 blue 0.537 alpha 0.871]
 [0.568 0.754 color red 0.882 green 0.725 blue 0.537 alpha 0.871
         color red 0.855 green 0.729 blue 0.584 alpha 0.816]
 [0.754 1.001 color red 0.855 green 0.729 blue 0.584 alpha 0.816
         color red 0.804 green 0.569 blue 0.494 alpha 0.569]
 }
}

//---Translucent Grnt4
#declare Grnt5a = texture {
 granite
 turbulence 0.5
 color_map {
 [0.000 0.178 color red 0.804 green 0.569 blue 0.494 alpha 0.569
         color red 0.855 green 0.729 blue 0.584 alpha 0.467]
 [0.178 0.356 color red 0.855 green 0.729 blue 0.584 alpha 0.467
         color red 0.667 green 0.502 blue 0.478 alpha 0.584]
 [0.356 0.525 color red 0.667 green 0.502 blue 0.478 alpha 0.584
         color red 0.859 green 0.624 blue 0.545 alpha 0.871]
 [0.525 0.729 color red 0.859 green 0.624 blue 0.545 alpha 0.871
         color red 0.855 green 0.729 blue 0.584 alpha 0.816]
```

```
[0.729 1.001 color red 0.855 green 0.729 blue 0.584 alpha 0.816
        color red 0.804 green 0.569 blue 0.494 alpha 0.569]
  }
}


//---Translucent Grnt6
#declare Grnt6a = texture {
  granite
  turbulence 0.6
  color_map {
  [0.000 0.263 color red 0.545 green 0.380 blue 0.345 alpha 0.733
          color red 0.588 green 0.475 blue 0.333 alpha 0.741]
  [0.263 0.432 color red 0.588 green 0.475 blue 0.333 alpha 0.741
          color red 0.675 green 0.478 blue 0.404 alpha 0.545]
  [0.432 0.551 color red 0.675 green 0.478 blue 0.404 alpha 0.545
          color red 0.757 green 0.635 blue 0.522 alpha 0.384]
  [0.551 0.720 color red 0.757 green 0.635 blue 0.522 alpha 0.384
          color red 0.659 green 0.549 blue 0.443 alpha 0.675]
  [0.720 1.001 color red 0.659 green 0.549 blue 0.443 alpha 0.675
          color red 0.545 green 0.380 blue 0.345 alpha 0.733]
  }
}


//---Translucent Grnt7
#declare Grnt7a = texture {
  granite
  turbulence 0.6
  color_map {
  [0.000 0.119 color red 0.439 green 0.310 blue 0.282 alpha 0.631
          color red 0.463 green 0.369 blue 0.259 alpha 0.847]
  [0.119 0.322 color red 0.463 green 0.369 blue 0.259 alpha 0.847
          color red 0.541 green 0.369 blue 0.298 alpha 0.549]
  [0.322 0.449 color red 0.541 green 0.369 blue 0.298 alpha 0.549
          color red 0.573 green 0.424 blue 0.286 alpha 0.965]
  [0.449 0.729 color red 0.573 green 0.424 blue 0.286 alpha 0.965
          color red 0.494 green 0.396 blue 0.306 alpha 0.741]
  [0.729 1.001 color red 0.494 green 0.396 blue 0.306 alpha 0.741
          color red 0.439 green 0.310 blue 0.282 alpha 0.631]
  }
}


//---Aqua Tints
#declare Grnt8a = texture {
  granite
  turbulence 0.6
  color_map {
  [0.000 0.119 color red 0.310 green 0.384 blue 0.420 alpha 0.631
          color red 0.322 green 0.369 blue 0.416 alpha 0.847]
  [0.119 0.322 color red 0.322 green 0.369 blue 0.416 alpha 0.847
          color red 0.424 green 0.369 blue 0.420 alpha 0.549]
```

```
   [0.322 0.449 color red 0.424 green 0.369 blue 0.420 alpha 0.549
           color red 0.373 green 0.424 blue 0.518 alpha 0.965]
   [0.449 0.729 color red 0.373 green 0.424 blue 0.518 alpha 0.965
           color red 0.482 green 0.573 blue 0.533 alpha 0.741]
   [0.729 1.001 color red 0.482 green 0.573 blue 0.533 alpha 0.741
           color red 0.310 green 0.384 blue 0.420 alpha 0.631]
   }
 }


//---Alpha Creams With Cracks
#declare Grnt9a = texture {
 granite
 turbulence 0.6
 color_map {
   [0.000 0.216 color red 0.812 green 0.812 blue 0.812 alpha 0.835
           color red 0.745 green 0.843 blue 0.835 alpha 0.847]
   [0.216 0.241 color red 0.745 green 0.843 blue 0.835 alpha 0.847
           color red 0.404 green 0.337 blue 0.337 alpha 0.463]
   [0.241 0.267 color red 0.404 green 0.337 blue 0.337 alpha 0.463
           color red 0.773 green 0.729 blue 0.745 alpha 0.622]
   [0.267 0.759 color red 0.773 green 0.729 blue 0.745 alpha 0.622
           color red 0.914 green 0.843 blue 0.725 alpha 0.651]
   [0.759 0.784 color red 0.914 green 0.843 blue 0.725 alpha 0.651
           color red 0.153 green 0.133 blue 0.208 alpha 0.437]
   [0.784 0.810 color red 0.153 green 0.133 blue 0.208 alpha 0.437
           color red 0.812 green 0.812 blue 0.812 alpha 0.835]
   [0.810 1.001 color red 0.812 green 0.812 blue 0.812 alpha 0.835
           color red 0.812 green 0.812 blue 0.812 alpha 0.835]
   }
 }


//----- Alpha Cream Rose & light yellow
#declare Grnt10a = texture {
 granite
 turbulence 0.6
 color_map {
   [0.000 0.179 color red 0.843 green 0.655 blue 0.655 alpha 0.455
           color red 0.886 green 0.769 blue 0.627 alpha 0.608]
   [0.179 0.368 color red 0.886 green 0.769 blue 0.627 alpha 0.608
           color red 0.906 green 0.820 blue 0.714 alpha 0.392]
   [0.368 0.538 color red 0.906 green 0.820 blue 0.714 alpha 0.392
           color red 0.851 green 0.671 blue 0.671 alpha 0.659]
   [0.538 0.744 color red 0.851 green 0.671 blue 0.671 alpha 0.659
           color red 0.890 green 0.792 blue 0.675 alpha 0.392]
   [0.744 0.983 color red 0.890 green 0.792 blue 0.675 alpha 0.392
           color red 0.827 green 0.612 blue 0.612 alpha 0.706]
   [0.983 1.001 color red 0.827 green 0.612 blue 0.612 alpha 0.706
           color red 0.843 green 0.655 blue 0.655 alpha 0.455]
   }
 }
```

551

```
//----- Alpha Light Grays
#declare Grnt11a = texture {
 granite
 turbulence 0.6
 color_map {
 [0.000 0.154 color red 0.894 green 0.886 blue 0.886 alpha 0.659
         color red 0.745 green 0.745 blue 0.753 alpha 0.584]
 [0.154 0.308 color red 0.745 green 0.745 blue 0.753 alpha 0.584
         color red 0.902 green 0.902 blue 0.859 alpha 0.780]
 [0.308 0.444 color red 0.902 green 0.902 blue 0.859 alpha 0.780
         color red 0.729 green 0.706 blue 0.694 alpha 0.686]
  [0.444 0.615 color red 0.729 green 0.706 blue 0.694 alpha 0.686
         color red 0.588 green 0.592 blue 0.635 alpha 0.424]
 [0.615 0.803 color red 0.588 green 0.592 blue 0.635 alpha 0.424
         color red 0.608 green 0.616 blue 0.659 alpha 0.761]
 [0.803 1.001 color red 0.608 green 0.616 blue 0.659 alpha 0.761
         color red 0.894 green 0.886 blue 0.886 alpha 0.659]
 }
}


//----- Alpha Creams & Tans
#declare Grnt12a = texture {
 granite
 turbulence 0.6
 color_map {
 [0.000 0.154 color red 0.890 green 0.690 blue 0.690 alpha 0.659
         color red 0.996 green 0.835 blue 0.737 alpha 0.659]
 [0.154 0.308 color red 0.996 green 0.835 blue 0.737 alpha 0.659
         color red 0.745 green 0.635 blue 0.651 alpha 0.780]
 [0.308 0.444 color red 0.745 green 0.635 blue 0.651 alpha 0.780
         color red 0.733 green 0.596 blue 0.557 alpha 0.686]
 [0.444 0.615 color red 0.733 green 0.596 blue 0.557 alpha 0.686
         color red 0.996 green 0.835 blue 0.737 alpha 0.659]
 [0.615 0.803 color red 0.996 green 0.835 blue 0.737 alpha 0.659
         color red 0.765 green 0.616 blue 0.659 alpha 0.761]
  [0.803 1.001 color red 0.765 green 0.616 blue 0.659 alpha 0.761
         color red 0.890 green 0.690 blue 0.690 alpha 0.659]
 }
}


//----- Alpha Creams & Grays
#declare Grnt13a = texture {
 granite
 turbulence 0.6
 color_map {
 [0.000 0.154 color red 0.800 green 0.651 blue 0.557 alpha 0.0
         color red 0.996 green 0.835 blue 0.737 alpha 0.608]
 [0.154 0.308 color red 0.996 green 0.835 blue 0.737 alpha 0.608
         color red 0.800 green 0.651 blue 0.557 alpha 0.635]
 [0.308 0.444 color red 0.800 green 0.651 blue 0.557 alpha 0.635
         color red 0.694 green 0.624 blue 0.604 alpha 0.294]
```

```
    [0.444 0.615 color red 0.694 green 0.624 blue 0.604 alpha 0.294
           color red 0.800 green 0.651 blue 0.557 alpha 0.816]
    [0.615 0.812 color red 0.800 green 0.651 blue 0.557 alpha 0.816
           color red 0.725 green 0.655 blue 0.651 alpha 0.957]
    [0.812 1.001 color red 0.725 green 0.655 blue 0.651 alpha 0.957
           color red 0.800 green 0.651 blue 0.557 alpha 0.0]
    }
}


//----- Cream Rose & light moss
#declare Grnt14a = texture {
 granite
 turbulence 0.6
 color_map {
 [0.000 0.154 color red 0.996 green 0.969 blue 0.800 alpha 0.373
        color red 0.996 green 0.682 blue 0.604 alpha 0.412]
 [0.154 0.308 color red 0.996 green 0.682 blue 0.604 alpha 0.412
        color red 0.906 green 0.820 blue 0.714 alpha 0.616]
 [0.308 0.444 color red 0.906 green 0.820 blue 0.714 alpha 0.616
        color red 0.816 green 0.631 blue 0.537 alpha 0.443]
 [0.444 0.615 color red 0.816 green 0.631 blue 0.537 alpha 0.443
        color red 0.890 green 0.792 blue 0.675 alpha 0.745]
 [0.615 0.812 color red 0.890 green 0.792 blue 0.675 alpha 0.745
        color red 0.973 green 0.627 blue 0.627 alpha 0.600]
 [0.812 1.001 color red 0.973 green 0.627 blue 0.627 alpha 0.600
        color red 0.996 green 0.969 blue 0.800 alpha 0.373]
 }
}


//----- Alpha Sand & light Orange
#declare Grnt15a = texture {
 granite
 turbulence 0.6
 color_map {
 [0.000 0.154 color red 0.996 green 0.824 blue 0.780 alpha 0.412
        color red 0.996 green 0.698 blue 0.624 alpha 0.412]
 [0.154 0.308 color red 0.996 green 0.698 blue 0.624 alpha 0.412
        color red 0.906 green 0.675 blue 0.553 alpha 0.616]
 [0.308 0.444 color red 0.906 green 0.675 blue 0.553 alpha 0.616
        color red 0.996 green 0.682 blue 0.604 alpha 0.412]
 [0.444 0.615 color red 0.996 green 0.682 blue 0.604 alpha 0.412
        color red 0.996 green 0.824 blue 0.780 alpha 0.412]
 [0.615 0.812 color red 0.996 green 0.824 blue 0.780 alpha 0.412
        color red 0.973 green 0.627 blue 0.627 alpha 0.600]
 [0.812 1.001 color red 0.973 green 0.627 blue 0.627 alpha 0.600
        color red 0.996 green 0.824 blue 0.780 alpha 0.412]
 }
}


//----- Cream Rose & light moss
#declare Grnt16a = texture {
```

```
    granite
    turbulence 0.6
    color_map {
    [0.000 0.078 color red 0.769 green 0.722 blue 0.690 alpha 0.180
           color red 0.745 green 0.690 blue 0.655 alpha 1.000]
    [0.078 0.96   color red 0.745 green 0.690 blue 0.655 alpha 1.000
           color red 0.839 green 0.804 blue 0.780 alpha 1.000]
    [0.96 1.001   color red 0.839 green 0.804 blue 0.780 alpha 0.278
           color red 0.769 green 0.722 blue 0.690 alpha 0.180]
    }
    }


#declare Grnt17a = texture {
    granite
    turbulence 0.6
    color_map {
    [0.000 0.034 color red 0.027 green 0.012 blue 0.012 alpha 0.0
           color red 0.851 green 0.812 blue 0.741 alpha 0.235]
    [0.034 0.342 color red 0.851 green 0.812 blue 0.741 alpha 0.235
           color red 0.792 green 0.694 blue 0.690 alpha 0.839]
    [0.342 0.462 color red 0.792 green 0.694 blue 0.690 alpha 0.839
           color red 0.631 green 0.506 blue 0.471 alpha 0.608]
    [0.462 0.632 color red 0.631 green 0.506 blue 0.471 alpha 0.608
           color red 0.851 green 0.812 blue 0.741 alpha 0.922]
    [0.632 0.983 color red 0.851 green 0.812 blue 0.741 alpha 0.922
           color red 0.647 green 0.655 blue 0.655 alpha 0.282]
    [0.983 1.001 color red 0.647 green 0.655 blue 0.655 alpha 0.282
           color red 0.027 green 0.012 blue 0.012 alpha 0.0]
    }
    }


#declare Grnt18a = texture {
    granite
    turbulence 0.6
    color_map {
     [0.000 0.128color red 0.820 green 0.580 blue 0.580 alpha 0.0
           color red 0.851 green 0.812 blue 0.741 alpha 0.235]
    [0.128 0.282 color red 0.851 green 0.812 blue 0.741 alpha 0.235
           color red 0.792 green 0.694 blue 0.690 alpha 0.282]
    [0.282 0.393 color red 0.792 green 0.694 blue 0.690 alpha 0.282
           color red 0.647 green 0.655 blue 0.655 alpha 0.133]
    [0.393 0.590 color red 0.647 green 0.655 blue 0.655 alpha 0.133
           color red 0.851 green 0.812 blue 0.741 alpha 0.333]
    [0.590 0.983 color red 0.851 green 0.812 blue 0.741 alpha 0.333
           color red 0.647 green 0.655 blue 0.655 alpha 0.282]
    [0.983 1.001 color red 0.647 green 0.655 blue 0.655 alpha 0.282
           color red 0.820 green 0.580 blue 0.580 alpha 0.0]
    }
    }
```

```
//----- Gray Marble with White feather Veins with Alpha
#declare Grnt19a = texture {
 granite
 turbulence 0.0
 color_map {
 [0.0 0.3 color White alpha 0.0 color DimGray alpha 0.5]
 [0.2 0.4 color DimGray alpha 0.5 color DimGray alpha 0.8]
 [0.4 1.0 color DimGray alpha 0.8 color DimGray alpha 0.9]
 }
 0.02
}

//----- White Feature Veins
#declare Grnt20a = texture {
 granite
 turbulence 0.0
 color_map {
 [0.0 0.2 color White alpha 0.0 color White alpha 0.7]
 [0.2 0.3 color White alpha 0.7 color Clear]
 [0.3 1.0 color Clear color Clear]
 }
 0.02
}
//----- Thinner White Feature Veins
#declare Grnt21a = texture {
 granite
 turbulence 0.0
 color_map {
 [0.0 0.2 color White alpha 0.4 color White alpha 0.8]
 [0.2 0.3 color White alpha 0.8 color Clear]
 [0.3 1.0 color Clear color Clear]
 }
 0.02
}

#declare Grnt22a = texture {
 granite
 turbulence 0.5
 color_map {
 [0.000 0.175 color red 1.000 green 0.718 blue 0.541 alpha 0.890
         color red 0.843 green 0.678 blue 0.655 alpha 0.753]
 [0.175 0.228 color red 0.843 green 0.678 blue 0.655 alpha 0.753
         color red 0.906 green 0.831 blue 0.773 alpha 0.98]
 [0.228 0.386 color red 0.906 green 0.831 blue 0.773 alpha 0.698
         color red 0.992 green 0.718 blue 0.545 alpha 0.794]
 [0.386 0.412 color red 0.992 green 0.718 blue 0.545 alpha 0.794
         color red 0.333 green 0.188 blue 0.067 alpha 0.784]
 [0.412 0.439 color red 0.333 green 0.188 blue 0.067 alpha 0.784
         color red 0.925 green 0.557 blue 0.514 alpha 0.778]
 [0.439 0.684 color red 0.925 green 0.557 blue 0.514 alpha 0.678
         color red 0.984 green 0.780 blue 0.655 alpha 0.696]
```

```
    [0.684 0.781 color red 0.984 green 0.780 blue 0.655 alpha 0.696
            color red 0.965 green 0.847 blue 0.675 alpha 0.880]
    [0.781 0.982 color red 0.965 green 0.847 blue 0.675 alpha 0.880
            color red 1.000 green 0.718 blue 0.541 alpha 0.990]
    [0.982 1.001 color red 1.000 green 0.718 blue 0.541 alpha 0.890
            color red 1.000 green 0.718 blue 0.541 alpha 0.890]
  }
}


//----- Transparent Green Moss Colors
#declare Grnt23a = texture {
  granite
  color_map {
  [0.000 0.168 color red 0.824 green 0.725 blue 0.584 alpha 0.600
            color red 0.514 green 0.584 blue 0.533 alpha 0.600]
  [0.168 0.301 color red 0.514 green 0.584 blue 0.533 alpha 0.600
            color red 0.298 green 0.376 blue 0.318 alpha 0.600]
  [0.301 0.398 color red 0.298 green 0.376 blue 0.318 alpha 0.600
            color red 0.263 green 0.337 blue 0.282 alpha 0.700]
  [0.398 0.558 color red 0.263 green 0.337 blue 0.282 alpha 0.700
            color red 0.431 green 0.506 blue 0.451 alpha 0.600]
  [0.558 0.655 color red 0.431 green 0.506 blue 0.451 alpha 0.600
            color red 0.529 green 0.631 blue 0.471 alpha 0.500]
  [0.655 0.735 color red 0.529 green 0.631 blue 0.471 alpha 0.500
            color red 0.333 green 0.376 blue 0.318 alpha 0.700]
  [0.735 0.823 color red 0.333 green 0.376 blue 0.318 alpha 0.700
            color red 0.298 green 0.376 blue 0.318 alpha 0.600]
  [0.823 0.876 color red 0.298 green 0.376 blue 0.318 alpha 0.600
            color red 0.416 green 0.376 blue 0.318 alpha 0.500]
  [0.876 0.929 color red 0.416 green 0.376 blue 0.318 alpha 0.500
            color red 0.416 green 0.376 blue 0.318 alpha 0.600]
  [0.929 1.001 color red 0.416 green 0.376 blue 0.318 alpha 0.600
            color red 0.824 green 0.725 blue 0.584 alpha 0.700]
  }
}


#declare Grnt24a = texture {
  granite
  turbulence 0.5
  color_map {
  [0.000 0.053 color red 0.784 green 0.627 blue 0.522 alpha 0.500
            color red 0.784 green 0.627 blue 0.624 alpha 0.500]
  [0.053 0.263 color red 0.784 green 0.627 blue 0.624 alpha 0.500
            color red 0.824 green 0.557 blue 0.376 alpha 0.500]
  [0.263 0.281 color red 0.824 green 0.557 blue 0.376 alpha 0.500
            color red 0.643 green 0.380 blue 0.376 alpha 0.500]
  [0.281 0.325 color red 0.643 green 0.380 blue 0.376 alpha 0.500
            color red 0.839 green 0.722 blue 0.722 alpha 0.500]
  [0.325 0.711 color red 0.839 green 0.722 blue 0.722 alpha 0.500
            color red 0.784 green 0.627 blue 0.522 alpha 0.500]
  [0.711 0.798 color red 0.784 green 0.627 blue 0.522 alpha 0.500
```

```
              color red 0.769 green 0.380 blue 0.376 alpha 0.500]
  [0.798 0.895 color red 0.769 green 0.380 blue 0.376 alpha 0.500
              color red 0.824 green 0.557 blue 0.376 alpha 0.500]
  [0.895 0.982 color red 0.824 green 0.557 blue 0.376 alpha 0.500
              color red 0.784 green 0.627 blue 0.522 alpha 0.500]
  [0.982 1.001 color red 0.784 green 0.627 blue 0.522 alpha 0.500
              color red 0.784 green 0.627 blue 0.522 alpha 0.500]
 }
}


/*----------Crack & OverTint /Red----------*/
#declare Crack1 = texture {
 marble
 turbulence 0.85
 color_map {
 [0.0 0.04 color Black alpha 0.6 color Black alpha 1.0]
 [0.04 0.97 color Scarlet alpha 0.80 color DimGray alpha 0.90]
 [0.97 1.001 color Black alpha 0.9 color Black alpha 1.0]
 }
}


//---Alpha Dark Cracks
#declare Crack2 = texture {
 granite
 turbulence 0.8
 color_map {
 [0.0 0.5 color Clear color Clear]
 [0.5 0.54 color Clear color Black]
 [0.54 1.0 color Clear color Clear]
 }
}


//----- Overtint Green with Black Cracks
#declare Crack3 = texture {
 marble
 turbulence 0.85
 color_map {
 [0.0 0.04 color Black alpha 0.6 color Black alpha 1.0]
 [0.04 0.97 color DarkGreen alpha 0.80
        color DarkGreen alpha 0.90]
 [0.97 1.001 color Black alpha 0.9 color Black alpha 1.0]
 }
}


//----- Overtint with White Crack
#declare Crack4 = texture {
 marble
 turbulence 0.85
 color_map {
 [0.0 0.03 color White alpha 0.3 color White alpha 1.0]
 [0.03 0.97 color Black alpha 0.70 color DimGray alpha 0.90]
```

```
[0.97 1.001 color White alpha 0.9 color White alpha 1.0]
  }
}



//----------    complete texture { statements
//          Scaled to cover nicely over a 2 unit Cube

//-------- Deep Rose & Green Marble with large White Swirls
#declare Stone1 =
texture { Grnt7 scale <2 3 2> rotate <0 0 40> }
texture { Grnt0a scale <2 3 2> rotate <0 0 -30>
     phong 1.0 phong_size 90
}


//-------- Light Greenish Tan Marble with Agate style veining
#declare Stone2 =
texture { Grnt0 scale <2 3 2> rotate <0 0 40> }
texture { Grnt7a scale <1.3 2 1.3> rotate <0 0 -30> rotate <40 0 0>
     ambient 0.2 phong 1.0 phong_size 90 }


//-------- Rose & Yellow Marble with fog white veining
#declare Stone3 =
texture { Grnt5 scale <2 3 2> rotate <0 0 40> }
texture { Grnt0a scale <2 3 2> rotate <0 0 -30>
     phong 1.0 phong_size 90
}


//-------- Tan Marble with Rose patches
#declare Stone4 =
texture { Grnt6 scale <1.5 3 2> rotate <0 0 40> diffuse 0.5 }
texture { Grnt10a scale <1 3 2> rotate <0 0 -30>
     phong 1.0 phong_size 90
}


//-------- White Cream Marble with Pink veining
#declare Stone5 =
texture { Grnt12 scale <2 3 2> rotate <0 0 40> }
texture { Grnt17a scale <2 3 2> rotate <0 0 -30>  }
texture { Crack1 scale <1 2 1.4> rotate <10 0 -20> ambient 0.2
      phong 1.0 phong_size 90 }


//-------- Rose & Yellow Cream Marble
#declare Stone6 =
texture { Grnt18 scale <1.5 3 3> rotate <0 0 40> }
texture { Grnt19 scale <2 4 1.3> rotate <0 0 30>
     phong 1.0 phong_size 90 }
texture { Crack1 scale <1 2 1.4> rotate <10 0 -20> ambient 0.2
     phong 1.0 phong_size 90 }


//-------- Light Coffee Marble with darker patches
```

```
#declare Stone7 =
texture { color Salmon }
texture { Grnt6a scale <1 3 2> rotate <0 0 40> }
texture { Grnt9a scale <3.5 5 4> rotate <0 0 60>
       phong 1.0 phong_size 90 }


//------- Gray Granite with white patches
#declare Stone8 =
texture { color White ambient 0.4 0.06 diffuse 0.7 }
texture { Grnt0a scale <2 3 2> rotate <0 0 -30>    }
texture { Grnt9a scale <5 3 4> rotate <0 0 40>  ambient 0.2
       diffuse 0.5 phong 1.0 phong_size 90 }


//------- White & Light Blue Marble with light violets
#declare Stone9 =
texture { Grnt9 scale <1.2 2.4 1.2> rotate <0 0 -30>
       rotate <40 0 0> }
texture { Crack1 scale <1 2 1.4> rotate <10 0 -20> ambient 0.2
       phong 1.0 phong_size 90 }


//------- Dark Brown & Tan swirl Granite with gray undertones
#declare Stone10 =
texture { color Black }
texture { Grnt17a scale <3 6 2> rotate <0 0 50> }
texture { Grnt3a scale <1 2 1> rotate <0 0 -50>
       phong 1.0 phong_size 90 }


//------- Rose & White Marble with dark tan swirl
#declare Stone11 =
texture { color Black }
texture { Grnt15a scale <1.2 3 1.5> rotate <70 0 30> 0.03 }
texture { Grnt2a scale <3 3 4> rotate <0 0 40>   }
texture { Crack1 scale <1 2 1.4> rotate <10 0 -20>
       phong 1.0 phong_size 90 }


//------- White & Pinkish Tan Marble
#declare Stone12 =
texture { Grnt23 scale <1 5 1> rotate <0 0 50> ambient 0.2 0.03 }
texture { Grnt0a scale <1 3 2> rotate <0 0 -30>
     phong 1.0 phong_size 90
}


//------- Medium Gray Blue Marble
#declare Stone13 =
texture { Grnt24 scale <2 5 2> rotate <0 0 50> ambient 0.2 0.03 }
texture { Grnt8a scale <1 3 2> rotate <0 0 -30>
     phong 1.0 phong_size 90
}


//------- Tan & Olive Marble with gray white veins
#declare Stone14 =
```

```
texture { Grnt6 scale <2 3 2> rotate <0 0 -30> ambient 0.2
      diffuse 0.9 0.03 }
texture { Grnt19a scale <1 3 1> rotate <0 0 40>
      phong 1.0 phong_size 90 }

//------- Deep Gray Marble with white veining
#declare Stone15 =
texture { Grnt20 scale <1 2 2> rotate <0 0 -30> ambient 0.2
      diffuse 0.9 0.03 }
texture { Grnt8a scale <1 2 1> rotate <0 0 40>
      phong 1.0 phong_size 90 }

//------- Peach & Yellow Marble with white veining
#declare Stone16 =
texture { Grnt18 scale <1.3 2 2> rotate <0 0 -30> ambient 0.2
      diffuse 0.9 0.03 }
texture { Grnt19 scale <2 4 2> rotate <0 0 -30> ambient 0.2
      diffuse 0.9 0.03 }
texture { Grnt20a scale <1 2 1> rotate <0 0 40>
      phong 1.0 phong_size 90 }

//------- White Marble with gray veining
#declare Stone17 =
texture { Grnt20 scale <1 2 2> rotate <0 0 -30> ambient 0.2
      diffuse 0.9 0.03 }
//texture { Grnt8a scale <2.5 4.5 3.5> rotate <0 0 40>
//     phong 1.0 phong_size 90 }
texture { Crack3 scale <1 2 1.4> rotate <10 0 -20>
      phong 1.0 phong_size 90 }

//------- Green Jade with white veining
#declare Stone18 =
texture { color SeaGreen ambient 0.3 diffuse 0.6 0.03 }
texture { Grnt22 scale <1.5 0.7 0.5> rotate <0 0 40>  }
texture { Grnt20a scale <2.5 2 0.5> rotate <0 0 -50>  }
texture { Crack4 scale <0.7 1 1> rotate <10 0 -20>
      phong 1.0 phong_size 90 }

//------- Peach Granite with white patches & green trim
#declare Stone19 =
texture { Grnt26 scale <1 0.7 0.5> rotate <0 0 40>  }
texture { Grnt20a scale <2 3 1> rotate <10 0 -20>
      phong 1.0 phong_size 90 }

//------- Brown & Olive Marble with white veining
#declare Stone20 =
texture { Grnt27 scale <0.7 0.99 0.7> rotate <0 0 40>  }
texture { Grnt12a scale <1 1.3 2> rotate <0 0 40>  }
texture { Grnt20a scale <1.9 3 0.5> rotate <0 0 -50>  }
texture { Crack1 scale <1 0.6 1> rotate <10 0 -20>
      phong 1.0 phong_size 90 }
```

```
//------- Red Marble with gray & white veining
#declare Stone21 =
texture { Grnt28 scale <1.3 2.5 1.7> rotate <0 0 40>  }
texture { Grnt22 scale <1 2 2> rotate <0 0 40>  }
texture { Crack4 scale <1 0.6 1> rotate <10 0 -20>
       phong 1.0 phong_size 90 }

//------- Dark Tan Marble with gray & white veining
#declare Stone22 =
texture { color Feldspar  }
texture { Grnt8a scale <1 2 2> rotate <0 0 40>  }
texture { Grnt22 scale <2 4 1.5> rotate <0 0 -50>  }
texture { Crack4 scale <1 1 1> rotate <10 0 -40>
       phong 1.0 phong_size 90 }

//------- Peach & Cream Marble with orange veining
#declare Stone23 =
texture { Grnt29 scale <1 1 2> rotate <40 0 0> rotate <0 0 30> }
texture { Grnt24a scale <2 1 2> rotate <40 0 0> rotate <0 0 30> }
texture { Crack1 scale <1 2 1.5> rotate <0 0 40> }
texture { color Yellow alpha 0.9 phong 1.0 phong_size 90 }
 // tint to liking

//------- Green & Tan Moss Marble
#declare Stone24 =
texture { Grnt25 scale <1 1 2> rotate <0 0 50> rotate <20 0 30> }
texture { Grnt23a scale <2 1 2> rotate <40 0 0> rotate <0 0 -30> }
texture { color Gray alpha 0.8 phong 1.0 phong_size 90 }
 //   tint to liking
```

Index

Books have a substantial influence on the destruction of the forests of the Earth. For example, it takes 17 trees to produce one ton of paper. A first printing of 30,000 copies of a typical 480 page book consumes 108,000 pounds of paper which will require 918 trees!

Waite Group Press™ is against the clear-cutting of forests and supports reforestation of the Pacific Northwest of the United States and Canada, where most of this paper comes from. As a publisher with several hundred thousand books sold each year, we feel an obligation to give back to the planet. We will therefore support and contribute a percentage of our proceeds to organizations which seek to preserve the forests of planet Earth.

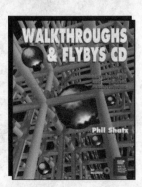

WALKTHROUGHS AND FLYBYS CD

Phil Shatz

Fly around buildings before they exist, tour the inner workings of imaginary machines, and play electronic music while watching the motion of atoms. Welcome to the world of animated PC demos, a new area of technology and design that relies on high-powered PCs, an assortment of graphics animation software, a Sound Blaster board, and some special tricks. The *Walkthroughs and Flybys CD* presents breathtaking computer animation and music including over 300 megabytes of Autodesk 3D Studio movies.

ISBN: 1-878739-40-9, 128 pages, 1-CD-ROM, $29.95, Available now

MAKING MOVIES ON YOUR PC
Dream Up, Design, and Direct 3-D Movies

David Mason and Alexander Enzmann

Flex your imagination and direct animated movies! You'll get everything you need in this book/disk package to create fantastic rotating television logos, MTV-style action clips, eye-boggling flybys and walkthroughs, or just about any movie effect you can dream up. The disks include the POLYRAY ray tracer for creating photorealistic images, and DTA, Dave's Targa Animator, the standard for converting ray traced images to FLI movies. You'll also get ready-to-run example movies and explanations. No need to draw precise locations of objects and shadows—the included programs make realistic animation a snap; programming skills aren't required.

ISBN: 1-878739-41-7, 200 pages, 2-5.25" disks, $34.95, Available now

MULTIMEDIA CREATIONS

Philip Shaddock

Jump into multimedia with **Multimedia Creations** and its powerful built-in GRASP program and utilities. Whether novice or professional, you'll get everything you need to create your own electronic brochures, interactive educational games, multimedia kiosks, digital real-time movies, and music videos. Hands-on step-by-step examples teach you animation, color-cycling, how to manipulate color palettes, synchronize sound effects and MIDI music to your presentations, and much more. The accompanying disks provide fully commented examples that you can run, modify, or incorporate into your own programs.

ISBN: 1-878739-26-3, 450 pages, 2-5.25" disks, $44.95, Available now

---

Send for our unique catalog for more information about these books, as well as our other outstanding titles, including:

Master C: *Let the PC Teach You C and Master C++, Let the PC Teach You Object-Oriented Programming*: Both book/disk software packages turn your computer into an infinitely patient C and C++ professor.

Workout C: Hundreds of C projects and exercises and a full-featured compiler make this an unbeatable training program and value.

OOP in Turbo C++ and OOP in Microsoft C++: Master teacher of the programming art, Robert Lafore, takes the prospective C++ programmer from the basics to the most complex concepts. It is also a comprehensive reference guide for all levels of programmer.

Image Lab: This unique book/disk set is a complete PC-based "digital darkroom" that covers virtually all areas of graphic processing and manipulation.

Artificial Life Playhouse: Turn your PC into an experimenter's lab to find out more about this new area of scientific exploration. Eight demo programs are included to allow you to experiment with "Wet-Life" concepts.

Flights of Fantasy: Programming 3-D Video Games in C++ Learn to use 3-D animation to make commercial quality video games. Plus it includes a complete flight simulator program and the full source code for the simulator.

FRACTALS FOR WINDOWS

Tim Wegner, Mark Peterson, Bert Tyler, Pieter Branderhorst

Create new fractals and control over 85 different fractal types with a zoom box, menus, and a mouse! Bundled with WINFRACT, a powerful Windows version of FRACTINT for DOS, this package is faster than lightning at computing mind-bending fractals. Novices and experienced programmers alike will love this rich resource of spectacular images that can be used with other Windows programs. Create fractal wallpaper for your desktop or copy them to the clipboard and paste them into other applications. The book includes 3-D glasses, world-class fractal recipes, and the source code for WINFRACT, as well as stunning color photos.

ISBN: 1-878739-25-5, 358 pages, 1-3.5" disk and 3-D glasses, $34.95 Available now

VIRTUAL REALITY PLAYHOUSE

Nicholas Lavroff

Jack-in to the world of virtual reality with this playful new book and disk package. Virtual reality is a new interactive technology which creates the convincing illusion that you are completely immersed in worlds existing only inside your computer. **Virtual Reality Playhouse** lets you enter those worlds and create your own personal digital dimension. Expand the parameters of your mind as you move rapidly from an introduction of virtual reality's basic concepts to visual explorations illustrating real-life applications. Put on the enclosed 3-D glasses and dive into any of the eight amazing VR simulations on the enclosed disk.

ISBN: 1-878739-19-0, 130 pages, 1-5.25" disk and 3-D glasses, $23.95 Available now

WAITE GROUP PRESS™

TO ORDER TOLL FREE CALL 1-800-368-9369

TELEPHONE 415-924-2575 • FAX 415-924-2576

OR SEND ORDER FORM TO: WAITE GROUP PRESS, 200 TAMAL PLAZA, CORTE MADERA, CA 94925

Qty.	Book	US/Can Price	Total
	Artificial Life Playhouse	$23.95/33.95	
	Flights of Fantasy	$34.95/48.95	
	Fractals for Windows	$34.95/48.95	
	Image Lab	$39.95/55.95	
	Making Movies on Your PC	$34.95/48.95	
	Master C ☐ 3.5" ☐ 5.25" disks	$44.95/62.95	
	Master C++ ☐ 3.5" ☐ 5.25" disks	$39.95/55.95	
	Multimedia Creations	$44.95/62.95	
	OOP in Microsoft C++	$29.95/41.95	
	OOP in Turbo C++	$29.95/41.95	
	Virtual Reality Playhouse	$23.95/33.95	
	Walkthroughs and Flybys CD	$29.95/41.95	
	Workout C	$39.95/55.95	

Calif. residents add 7.25% Sales Tax

Shipping

USPS ($5 first book/$1 each add'l)
UPS Two Day ($10/$2)
Canada ($10/$4)

TOTAL

Ship To

Name _____

Company _____

Address _____

City, State, Zip _____

Phone _____

ALL ORDERS MUST BE PREPAID

Payment Method

☐ Check Enclosed   ☐ VISA   ☐ MasterCard

Card#_____ Exp. Date _____

Signature _____

SATISFACTION GUARANTEED
OR YOUR MONEY BACK.

This is a legal agreement between you, the end user and purchaser, and The Waite Group®, Inc., and the authors of the programs contained in the disk. By opening the sealed disk package, you are agreeing to be bound by the terms of this Agreement. If you do not agree with the terms of this Agreement, promptly return the unopened disk package and the accompanying items (including the related book and other written material) to the place you obtained them for a refund.

SOFTWARE LICENSE

1. The Waite Group, Inc. grants you the right to use one copy of the enclosed software programs (the programs) on a single computer system (whether a single CPU, part of a licensed network, or a terminal connected to a single CPU). Each concurrent user of the program must have exclusive use of the related Waite Group, Inc. written materials.

2. Each of the programs, including the copyrights in each program, is owned by the respective author and the copyright in the entire work is owned by The Waite Group, Inc. and they are therefore protected under the copyright laws of the United States and other nations, under international treaties. You may make only one copy of the disk containing the programs exclusively for backup or archival purposes, or you may transfer the programs to one hard disk drive, using the original for backup or archival purposes. You may make no other copies of the programs, and you may make no copies of all or any part of the related Waite Group, Inc. written materials.

3. You may not rent or lease the programs, but you may transfer ownership of the programs and related written materials (including any and all updates and earlier versions) if you keep no copies of either, and if you make sure the transferee agrees to the terms of this license.

4. You may not decompile, reverse engineer, disassemble, copy, create a derivative work, or otherwise use the programs except as stated in this Agreement.

GOVERNING LAW

This Agreement is governed by the laws of the State of California.

LIMITED WARRANTY

The following warranties shall be effective for 90 days from the date of purchase: (i) The Waite Group, Inc. warrants the enclosed disk to be free of defects in materials and workmanship under normal use; and (ii) The Waite Group, Inc. warrants that the programs, unless modified by the purchaser, will substantially perform the functions described in the documentation provided by The Waite Group, Inc. when operated on the designated hardware and operating system. The Waite Group, Inc. does not warrant that the programs will meet purchaser's requirements or that operation of a program will be uninterrupted or error-free. The program warranty does not cover any program that has been altered or changed in any way by anyone other than The Waite Group, Inc. The Waite Group, Inc. is not responsible for problems caused by changes in the operating characteristics of computer hardware or computer operating systems that are made after the release of the programs, nor for problems in the interaction of the programs with each other or other software.

THESE WARRANTIES ARE EXCLUSIVE AND IN LIEU OF ALL OTHER WARRANTIES OF MERCHANTABILITY OR FITNESS FOR A PARTICULAR PURPOSE OR OF ANY OTHER WARRANTY, WHETHER EXPRESS OR IMPLIED.

EXCLUSIVE REMEDY

The Waite Group, Inc. will replace any defective disk without charge if the defective disk is returned to The Waite Group, Inc. within 90 days from date of purchase.

This is Purchaser's sole and exclusive remedy for any breach of warranty or claim for contract, tort, or damages.

LIMITATION OF LIABILITY

THE WAITE GROUP, INC. AND THE AUTHORS OF THE PROGRAMS SHALL NOT IN ANY CASE BE LIABLE FOR SPECIAL, INCIDENTAL, CONSEQUENTIAL, INDIRECT, OR OTHER SIMILAR DAMAGES ARISING FROM ANY BREACH OF THESE WARRANTIES EVEN IF THE WAITE GROUP, INC. OR ITS AGENT HAS BEEN ADVISED OF THE POSSIBILITY OF SUCH DAMAGES.

THE LIABILITY FOR DAMAGES OF THE WAITE GROUP, INC. AND THE AUTHORS OF THE PROGRAMS UNDER THIS AGREEMENT SHALL IN NO EVENT EXCEED THE PURCHASE PRICE PAID.

COMPLETE AGREEMENT

This Agreement constitutes the complete agreement between The Waite Group, Inc. and the authors of the programs, and you, the purchaser.

Some states do not allow the exclusion or limitation of implied warranties or liability for incidental or consequential damages, so the above exclusions or limitations may not apply to you. This limited warranty gives you specific legal rights; you may have others, which vary from state to state.

SATISFACTION REPORT CARD

Please fill out this card if you want to know of future updates to
Ray Tracing Creations, or to receive our catalog.

WAITE GROUP PRESS™

Company Name: _____

Division/Department: _____ **Mail Stop:** _____

Last Name: _____ **First Name:** _____ **Middle Initial:** _____

Street Address: _____

City: _____ **State:** _____ **Zip:** _____

Daytime telephone: (   ) _____

Date product was acquired: Month _____ **Day** _____ **Year** _____ **Your Occupation:** _____

Overall, how would you rate *Ray Tracing Creations*?

☐ Excellent   ☐ Very Good   ☐ Good
☐ Fair   ☐ Below Average   ☐ Poor

What did you like MOST about this book? _____
_____
_____

What did you like LEAST about this book? _____
_____
_____

How did you use this book (problem-solver, tutorial, reference...)?
_____

What is your level of computer expertise?
☐ New   ☐ Dabbler   ☐ Hacker
☐ Power User   ☐ Programmer   ☐ Experienced Professional

How did you find the pace of this book? _____

What computer languages are you familiar with? _____
_____

Please describe your computer hardware:

Computer _____ Hard disk _____
5.25" disk drives _____ 3.5" disk drives _____
Video card _____ Monitor _____
Printer _____ Peripherals _____
Sound Board _____ CD ROM _____

Where did you buy this book?

☐ Bookstore (name): _____
☐ Discount store (name): _____
☐ Computer store (name): _____
☐ Catalog (name): _____
☐ Direct from WGP   ☐ Other _____

What price did you pay for this book? _____

What influenced your purchase of this book?
☐ Recommendation   ☐ Advertisement
☐ Magazine review   ☐ Store display
☐ Mailing   ☐ Book's format
☐ Reputation of Waite Group Press   ☐ Other

How many computer books do you buy each year? _____

How many other Waite Group books do you own? _____

What is your favorite Waite Group book? _____
_____

Is there any program or subject you would like to see Waite Group Press cover in a similar approach? _____
_____

Additional comments? _____
_____
_____

☐ **Check here for a free Waite Group catalog**

Ray Tracing Creations

Waite Group Press, Inc.
Attention: *Ray Tracing Creations*
200 Tamal Plaza
Corte Madera, CA 94925

- **FOLD HERE** -